Re-Forming Gifted Education

Matching the Program to the Child

Karen B. Rogers, Ph.D.

Great Potential Press, Inc.
(formerly Gifted Psychology Press, Inc.)
P.O. Box 5057
Scottsdale, AZ 85261
www.giftedbooks.com

Re-Forming Gifted Education: Matching the Program to the Child

Cover Design: ATG Productions, Inc.
Interior Design/Layout: The 2ndShift

Published by **Great Potential Press, Inc.**
(formerly Gifted Psychology Press, Inc.)
P.O. Box 5057
Scottsdale, AZ 85261
www.giftedbooks.com

Printed and bound in the United States of America

05 04 03 02 01   6 5 4 3 2 1

Library of Congress Cataloging-in-Publication Data

Rogers, Karen A,
    Re-forming gifted education: matching the program to the child   p.cm
    Includes bibliographical references (p.) and index.
    ISBN 0-910707-46-4
        1. Gifted children-Education-United States. 2. Individualized instruction-United States. I. Title.
LC 3993.9 .R69 2002
371.95'0973__dc21   2002050183

ISBN: 0-910707-46-4

Dedication

For my three children, Jeanne, Jennifer, and Bill;
my grandsons, Ian, Colin, Jacob, and Carson;
and all those grandchildren yet to come,
may this book help you maneuver
the slopes of school.

Acknowledgements

This book would not have been written if it were not for James Webb and his persistent requests for me to "write a book." My thanks go first to him and to Janet Gore for their patient, persevering, diplomatic queries about what I had written, which helped to make what I want to say clearer to everyone who might read this book. Jen Ault Rosso provided excellent copy editing and helped ensure that there was consistency and clarity in the organization of the book throughout. I also wish to say thank you to the other members of Great Potential Press for helping me with myriad details.

My appreciation also goes to my husband, Bill, for his willingness to be neglected and ignored at times when I was on a writing roll. He is the easiest husband I know and definitely "low maintenance!"

I must also say thank you to the many parents of gifted children who allowed me to assess their children and who educated me about how to make an educational plan. We learned by experience, and I hope this book shows that our learning paid off.

Lastly, although I have dedicated the book to them, I must acknowledge my own three children, who did not experience the full benefits of an educational plan while they were in school, but who received a fine education in the public school system nonetheless. If I had known then what I know now, their education would have been very different.

–KBR

Table of Contents

Chapter 7: Program Provisions (Grouping) within the School 205

Chapter 6

Chapter 7

Preface

This book is written for all of those parents and teachers who have had even the slightest suspicion somewhere during a child's development that he or she could be gifted or talented. Perhaps the child spoke early, was quick to notice details, sat up and walked earlier than your friends' children, or seemed to understand things beyond his age. Perhaps he showed a remarkable ability to create imaginative stories, or could do complex puzzles, or draw recognizable pictures very early. Perhaps the high ability, special gift, or talent didn't show up until the child was much older. If you are a parent or a teacher of a child like this, this book is written for you. Likewise, if you, as an adult, believe you were advanced in your development as a child, this book may help you understand some of your own experiences in school growing up.

As a parent of a bright child, you have probably experienced some degree of frustration with schools—public or private. It is my belief, after more than 25 years of consulting with schools, that most public schools are not doing even a minimally adequate job of managing the education of gifted and talented learners.

In some cases, the inadequacy or neglect is due to teachers and administrators who hold an erroneous belief that all children are alike in their capacity to learn and produce, or a belief that all children learn at the same rate. In other cases, the deficiency stems from a deliberate attempt to level the playing field of education and thus limit what brighter youngsters can learn in the classroom. This represents an incorrect interpretation of the democratic ideal of "equal education for all."

Perhaps most pervasive is the belief that gifted children are simply able to make it on their own educationally without special accommodations, except perhaps for some brief weekly experience at school.

Most often, these beliefs are due to educators' lack of training and limited knowledge about the specific characteristics and needs of gifted learners. That is, they simply do not know enough about gifted children to know how to provide education and challenges that are appropriate and adequate for the many different kinds of gifted children.

Throughout most of the 20th century, parents delegated the education of their children to "the professionals," thinking that the school "experts" knew what was best for their children. Sometime in the 1980s, that trust began to wane. Parents who were frustrated with inflexible educational systems began to choose alternatives to the neighborhood public school. Increasingly, parents are now choosing alternatives that range from various types of private schools to charter schools to homeschooling. Some parents have become so frustrated with lack of services for gifted children in their local public schools that they have sued school districts to get assistance through the court system (Karnes & Marquardt, 1999).

While the courts can be helpful in those states that mandate gifted educational services, there is little case law or legislative law to support parents if they reside in a state without a legislative mandate that specifically addresses needs of gifted children. And although a lawsuit may become necessary if a child's educational needs are consistently and deliberately ignored or neglected by the schools, it is, of course, preferable to use other interventions such as mediation and due process based on sound educational planning before taking the issue to court.

This book is to be used for such sound educational planning. It is a guidebook for parents and educators to assist schools in providing appropriate education experiences for all gifted and talented children, regardless of the child's talent area, age, ethnic origin, or economic level. The ideas and suggestions listed should also hold true for those gifted children who may have a learning or physical disability—"twice exceptional" children. This guidebook will also address some tough questions about what we might reasonably call potential giftedness—that is, high ability that is not yet apparent.

The primary purpose of this book is to provide a series of blueprints to help children with high ability succeed in the K-12 school systems of our country, which are currently designed and structured for average and slower learners, and which are often stifling environments for rapid or advanced learners. The information in this book will help children who are advanced learners survive the system and come out with a strong foundation of knowledge and skills to sustain them in their adult years. Appropriate education will help these advanced learners be self-confident, prepared, and ready to make contributions to society and the world. Can one book do all of this? I hope so. You, the parents and teachers, will be the judge of that.

This book is based on two main sources of knowledge: (1) the vast body of research—spanning 100 years—in the field of gifted education that can inform parents and educators about what *does* and what *doesn't* work for these bright children, and (2) my one-on-one experiences with more than 150 high ability children for whom I have developed and monitored personalized educational plans over the past 15 years.

Educational planning and advising of gifted children is definitely a challenge. It is a long-term and time-intensive activity. It requires continuing advocacy, often with little support from others. But the goal of producing well-educated, self-confident, productive, life-long learners certainly makes the effort worthwhile, and it is my belief that the effort is unquestionably necessary if gifted children are to discover, enjoy, and reach their potential.

Educational planning for gifted youngsters is more than just planning. It is somewhat like high-level negotiation in the business world. In simplest terms, it is matching the child's needs to the school's ability to meet those needs. But such planning is often far from simple. It involves finding out first what the child needs. It includes researching the best ways to meet the child's needs. It entails collecting evidence. And it requires advocacy, diplomacy, and persuasion.

Developing and implementing an educational plan for any exceptional child can be difficult. But parents of gifted children can be very effective at it without hiring a college professor or a gifted child advocate or a professional educational planner like myself to do it. Any interested parent or conscientious teacher—or better yet, a team of parents and teachers together—can do it.

Successful educational planning for bright children requires positive collaboration between the parents (who, incidentally, *do* generally know their child better than anyone else!) and the teachers in the school that the parents select for their child. The goal is to achieve ongoing collaboration between parents and educators. Selection of the school and its specific services is the first step, as well as a key aspect of educational planning. A parent cannot just enroll a gifted child in the nearest neighborhood school and trust that the school will know what to do with a bright, educationally advanced youngster. Few classroom teachers have any in-depth training in what to do in the classroom for such youngsters, and school administrators lack such training also. Schools that have gifted education specialists on their staffs are increasingly rare in these days of tight budgets. If your child's school has such a specialist, you are fortunate, but even a gifted specialist will need—and want—additional input from you, and he or she can be an important ally in your advocacy and persuasion to accomplish the educational exceptions your child may need.

Educational planning for gifted children is complex because of the wide range of abilities and specific talents. Because these children often have both high academic potential and special areas of ability and particular areas of talent, there must be a conscious, systematic selection of services and strategies. These services and strategies should be agreed to by both parents and school personnel and should be written down to ensure follow-through and accountability. Within the resources that both parties can bring to bear, neither party should settle for less than the most appropriate experiences to meet the educational needs and to develop the recognizable talent of the high potential child.

This book will provide many examples to show how this process of planning can begin and how it should be continued throughout the child's school career. The process may be difficult at first but will become easier as time goes on and the plan begins to work. Such a plan is surely worth the effort. Gifted children who are appropriately stimulated and challenged are more likely to stay motivated to learn throughout their entire lives.

–KBR

Foreword

I want to share with you how much I respect Dr. Karen Rogers and her work, but first I must tell you that this book is a **"must read"** for everyone who works with the gifted. ***Re-Forming Gifted Education*** is a treasure chest of essential information about how to appropriately serve gifted children. The book should be entitled, *Everything You Ever Wanted to Know about Gifted Education.* It is the most comprehensive guide to educational planning for the gifted ever published. Every school should own a copy of this important book. If you are a parent, please purchase an extra copy as a gift to the school, so that educational decision-makers will have it available to help all the other gifted children who follow yours. Your parent group needs a copy as well.

In addition to parents of the gifted, every task force involved in planning provisions for the gifted, every parent advocacy committee, every library, every gifted education coordinator, every counselor, every educational planner, every administrator concerned with this population, and every teacher who deals with gifted children in the classroom should have this comprehensive guide to educational programming for gifted children. The key points, quizzes, and thoughtful activities will make this book ideal for in-service training for classroom teachers, as well as for college and university courses.

My favorite part of the book is the section, "When They Say…, What Will You Say?" Advocates have never had such a concise, powerful tool for addressing the typical arguments against provisions for gifted students.

The book contains a wealth of information on how to construct an educational plan for advanced learners, how to determine which provisions fit which types of children, all the possible options for meeting their needs, and how to evaluate the success of various provisions. It is an excellent, up-to-date resource guide that contains lists of talent searches; Saturday and summer programs; state residential and private schools; state Departments of Education gifted programs; magazines for children; social action and service projects for children; inspiring biographies and autobiographies for gifted children; recommended reading; competitions and contests; communication websites for children; potential resources for homeschooling curriculum; and much more. In addition, Karen has developed several forms to aid educational planning, including: *Parent Inventory for Finding Potential*; *Teacher Inventory of Learning Strengths*; *How Do You Like to Learn?*; and the *Rogers' Interest Inventory*—all instruments which are useful for her *Yearly Educational Planner*.

The best and most unique feature of this book is what Karen is famous for—every recommendation in the book is research-based. Karen Rogers is one of the most respected researchers in the field of gifted education, and in this book she has translated research so that it is accessible to parents and teachers, and to anyone, even those without a research background. Every provision discussed includes a section summarizing "What the Research Says." Karen has performed numerous meta-analyses on various interventions for gifted children and has studied extensively their relative merits. In an extremely clear and concise manner, she summarizes all of the relevant studies on acceleration, ability grouping, self-contained classes, curriculum compacting, cluster grouping, multi-age grouping, etc.

I had planned to start this Foreword with an anecdote about Karen, but I was so impressed by the book that I needed to share with you my reaction to it before I told you about the author. I have always admired Karen's work and have quoted her often. During the school reform movement, Karen was the major champion of gifted education, taking on the powerful Zeitgeist of anti-ability grouping and anti-gifted sentiment with solid documentation from a large body of research of the positive effects of ability grouping and special programs for the gifted. When others in the field capitulated to the pressure to become more "egalitarian," Karen stood firm in her commitment to the needs of gifted and highly gifted children. This book reflects that commitment.

One day we received a call from Karen on the answering machine at the Gifted Development Center inquiring about the possibility of doing a post-doctoral internship at the Center. I was speechless (a rarity for me)! The call couldn't be from **THE** Karen Rogers. There must be someone else with the same name. We looked up the area code, and, sure enough, the call came from Minnesota. I couldn't imagine what I might have to offer Karen. A few months later, when we were both invited to present in Vancouver, Washington, I asked her why she wanted to come to the Gifted Development Center. She said that she had decided to do her post-doc with me after she heard me speak at Jim Webb's SENG Conference in Chicago. (Thanks, Jim!) She wanted to learn how to administer the *Stanford-Binet Intelligence Scale (Form L-M)* and engage in research on our substantial population of exceptionally gifted children. I was overjoyed. During her five-month post-doc, I came to admire Karen ten times more.

In addition to her brilliant contributions, Karen has a sunny temperament and loves everyone. It was with great pleasure that I accepted the invitation to write this Foreword for a colleague and friend whose work has made such a difference in the lives of gifted children. Until I read it, I had no idea what a goldmine of resources she had brought together in this book. I know you will enjoy it and will refer to it many times.

Linda Kreger Silverman, Ph.D., Director
Gifted Development Center
Denver, Colorado

1

Who Needs an Educational Plan, and Who Makes It?

A Conversation

Parent: Dr. Rogers, my four-year-old daughter, Luisa, is gift-ed. Should I start her in school early?

KBR: Perhaps. Tell me, how do you know she is gifted?

Parent: Well, she began sounding out words at two and was reading first grade books at two and a half. She uses adult words like "appreciate" all the time, and she has already memorized all the states and capitals using a kid's computer program!

KBR: When is her birthday?

Parent: September 28th, so she'll miss the cut-off date for kindergarten this year.

KBR: Tell me about her friends. Who are they and what are they like?

Parent: Her best friend lives here in the neighborhood and is already in school. She gets along some of the time with other kids her age, but not all of the time. She gets upset when they are mean to each other or don't play fairly.

KBR: Have you talked to your neighborhood school about the possibility of having her enter kindergarten early?

Parent: They say they don't have a policy for early entrance. They won't let her do it, even if she is gifted and already reading. What should we do?

This kind of conversation has occurred for me many times during the past five years. Unfortunately, my experience shows that unless parents have detailed and objective information, such as psychological testing information or other data about their child, and unless parents can be quite specific about what they want the public or private school to provide, there will be little support from the school for the child's developmentally advanced academic needs until the child is five or six years old and ready to enroll in kindergarten at the "right" time. By this time, the child will be so far advanced in her reading skills that she will not be able to advance any farther in reading for another several years in school. Instead, her time will be spent being "socialized" with the other five-year-olds in her class.

For many bright, eager, and gifted children, kindergarten is a frustrating time. These children come to school excited to learn difficult things but are instead told to spend their time just playing nicely with the other children. They are often told to stop asking so many questions, or to stop answering so many questions "so that other children can have a chance." Since other children often do not share the gifted (more developmentally advanced) child's same sense of humor, fairness, creativity, or even interests, the gifted child feels very much out of place, as if no one understands him. He may go off to play alone and then may be seen as "lacking social skills."

Parents of these precocious children are often told, "All mothers (or fathers) think their child is gifted," or "No children can be identified as truly gifted until we test and 'identify' them in third (or *fourth* or *fifth*) grade." When parents express concern to the teacher or school principal about the too-easy curriculum, they may be given examples of other areas such as behaviors that are "problems" for their child and that their child is "not *that* much different" from the others. It is important for parents to know that both statements are false. If a gifted child is behaving in unusual ways, the so-called "problem" behaviors often disappear when the curriculum is appropriately matched to the child's ability. And gifted children *are* different from other children—often strikingly so and in very fundamental ways.

Sometimes the professional educators (teachers or administrators) make their arguments on a more abstract level in a way that does not even acknowledge individual learning differences of children. For example, parents might be told, "Our educational philosophy here at XYZ School is to help children learn social skills, because these are far more important than knowing facts and information," or "We believe that *all* of our children are gifted, and we believe we adequately meet the educational needs of all children in our school." If parents complain more than once, school personnel may label them as "difficult," "unreasonable," or "pushy" parents, making future parent input, collaboration, or negotiation even more difficult.

And, unfortunately, professional educators seldom have training in the learning differences of gifted children or methods for providing the rigorous and stimulating curriculum they need. So it is up to the parent to communicate with the school.

How do parents decide whether their bright child needs a personal education plan? Is having an advanced vocabulary or an intense interest or a playful imagination enough to require a personalized educational plan? Perhaps, but not always. A more reliable indicator is this: if a child demonstrates certain traits that are comparatively rare, then a special education plan should be considered. Your child may need an education plan if she is exhibiting a specific strength (such as music performance, high level of vocabulary usage, advanced mathematical understanding, etc.) considerably earlier than would be expected for her age—in other words, you don't see your child's class- or agemates doing these things, although children who are considerably older *are* doing these tasks.

Of course, there may be instances when your child's playmates are also exceptionally advanced, and so you can't tell if your child's behavior or performance is "comparatively rare" or "normal." In this case, your family pediatrician or a child psychologist may be a good professional to consult. Just as the doctor knows what is "normal" for physical development, he or she will also know whether your child's cognitive development is "normal" or "advanced."

Some examples of advanced cognitive development are: learning to read before it is taught in school; learning to add and subtract before most children learn to count; showing unusual dexterity in fine motor activities such as building complicated structures with blocks or other building tools; showing extraordinary spatial ability by putting complex puzzles together at a very young age; or asking "serious" existential questions about death, God, etc.

Chapter 2 provides greater detail about the kinds of abilities, gifts, and talents to look for. But for now, some words to keep in mind are:

- *comparatively rare.*
- *considerably earlier.*
- *significantly more advanced.*

If the child is gifted, one or more of these phrases will apply, no matter where the gift or talent lies.

It is also important to note that a gifted child need not be gifted "across the board" or in all areas. A child may be very advanced in reading or mathematics but may be average in some other areas.

Why an Educational Plan?

A well thought out written educational plan helps parents and teachers ensure that a gifted child (with advanced development in one or more areas) will receive consistent curriculum and school instruction that is geared to his academic ability and potential, rather than instruction directed to abilities and potentials of students who learn more slowly. Without an appropriate educational plan, gifted children often lose their excitement for learning because they must wait—sometimes for many years—so that others can learn what the children with advanced development already know. This is not appropriate education. Gifted children have the right to be given schoolwork that is motivating and challenging. Asking them to "slow down while others catch up" is not fair to them. Future Olympic swimmers aren't asked to sit idly on the side and wait while other swimmers practice the basic strokes. Yet too often, bright children are required to passively wait for others to finish the lesson before they are allowed to go on.

This book recommends that the parent present the school with a well thought out individualized educational plan. Such a plan is not likely to be adopted unless it is presented formally to school personnel several months before the child is to enter school or a new grade level. Why? Because schools typically need time to consider and accept evidence provided by the parent or guardian that the child may indeed be "different." Schools also need time to resolve administrative issues such as teacher selection and scheduling.

An educational plan tailored to the child's needs is particularly important during several critical periods in a child's schooling. These periods are approximately six months to a year before the child is to enter each new grade level—such as 1) kindergarten/primary grades, 2) intermediate grades, 3) middle school or junior high school, 4) high school, and 5) college. These junctures are important because the gifted child has generally already "used up" the learning opportunities available in her current grade level environment and is ready to make a transition earlier than expected into the next grade level.

The primary school years (K-3) are often a very difficult period for bright children. Why? Because prior to schooling, parents or other caregivers have been the child's chief source for learning and often have nurtured the child's knowledge and skills regardless of age or maturity. The child has been given freedom to explore, to be curious, and to learn things when he wants to, rather than when a particular school curriculum says it is time. The parent or guardian has listened to the child's questions and sought ways to find the answers. Upon entry into kindergarten or first grade, however, the child loses this one-to-one personalized learning; he must now go along with the needs and schedule of the larger group, as prescribed by a teacher who is dealing with an entire class. It is a shocking change for a bright child who no doubt liked his previous way of learning much better.

Being in a class with agemates usually means that bright children are required to slow down and "re-learn" what they already know. They must be patient with others who haven't yet acquired certain skills, and they must tolerate agemates who may tease them for knowing so many things, having different interests, or being so "different." Sometimes young children will even purposefully "forget" how to read so that they can be more like their age peers.

Unfortunately, being extra smart doesn't always mean being extra well-behaved, tolerant, patient, or considerate of others. It is difficult for a quick mind to "slow down." Thus, a bright child may begin to misbehave, stop paying attention, or say she dislikes school when the work is too easy or repetitive. She may say careless or insensitive things to other children who are struggling to learn. From her perspective, this is not being rude, but simply trying to get her own needs met. If she has finished her own work, she is eager to move on to new and different activities, and may sometimes misbehave, bother other children, or in other ways "act out" due to frustration with having nothing very interesting to do.

Although these misbehaviors actually result from a lack of educational fit, sometimes a label, such as Attention Deficit Disorder (ADD), Attention Deficit Disorder with Hyperactivity (ADHD), or Behaviorally Disturbed (BD), is incorrectly assigned to gifted children, which can then cause an ongoing negative cycle of mislabeling, mismanagement, and misunderstanding due to the misdiagnosis (Webb, 2001). If you think your child has possibly been mislabeled, look for a psychologist who is experienced and trained in characteristics of gifted individuals to test your child in any of these areas.

When parents of bright children go to their local schools to ask for testing, they are frequently told that special testing for gifted children is not available because school psychologists are too busy testing children at the other end of the intellectual curve—children with serious learning problems. Parents may be told, "Stop pushing your child; just allow him to be a child," or "Your child is no different from a lot of other children at this grade level." Regrettably, schools often simply don't believe that parents could accurately recognize a gifted child or that such children have special academic or other learning needs. Even more regrettably, schools seem to know very little about gifted children, and worse, they seldom know what to do with a gifted child if they do acknowledge that a child could be one.

Is this view of public school response to childrens' advanced development too harsh? I think not. Current literature in the field documents an alarming lack of teacher and administrator training. University preparation courses rarely focus on the unique characteristics and special needs of gifted children. Such training is likewise missing at both the pre-service (teacher training) and in-service (on the job) levels for teachers and administrators at all grade levels. Not surprisingly, however, the research consistently shows that the most effective teachers of gifted children are those who have received extensive training (Gallagher & Gallagher, 1994; Gross, 1991; Hansen & Feldhusen, 1994; Heath, 1997; Tomlinson, Callahan, Moon, Tomchin, Landrum & Imbeau, et al., 1995).

If it were possible to train all teachers, there might not be a need for parents to assist with a plan for their child's education. But with all of the factors troubling public education today, such improvements in teacher training seem years away. As matters now stand, parents of gifted children must often come to the school with a clear-cut educational plan and with the expectation and hope that the school will work with them to carry it out. Unless your school has an outstanding gifted education specialist with time to meet and consult with parents and teachers, it is unlikely that the schools will suggest a uniquely individualized educational plan. So, if a plan is going to be implemented, *you* must be the one to initiate it, to collect the data, and to design the initial plan. This isn't all bad; after all, you are the one who knows your child best.

Is a Formal Plan Necessary?

Parents of young children seldom think much about whether an infant is gifted. Somewhere along the way, though, usually through comparison with other children of the same age, parents notice several behaviors that seem different, and they may begin to suspect that their child is unusually bright or gifted. As parents who care, they wonder what to do. Which school system is best? Should their child enter school early? Do schools allow this? Should their child be grade-skipped? Will they need to ask their child's teacher to enrich the child's reading? Should they look for a private tutor to help their child expand her understanding and love of science beyond what the school can offer?

At this point in their thinking, parents often backtrack a little and ask, "Well, just how much potential *does* my child have? Do I really need a specific plan if my child is gifted? Or it is best not to draw special attention to my child at school and just provide enrichment at home?"

My answer to parents is this: If you have a gifted child, then a formal plan is necessary. Remember, if a child is exceptional, that child needs exceptions to the ordinary program.

What Is Reasonable to Ask Schools to Do?

It has been estimated that a fully developed gifted and talented program costs about 27% more than what regular education costs (Gallagher, 1965). This is largely due to the need for a specially trained resource teacher, special materials, and perhaps some occasional off-site learning opportunities. These additional costs cannot be covered by a simple readjustment of the regular school budget; to do so will reduce what can be offered to the rest of the school population. It is a fact that some of the services specified in the child's education plan may cost the district some additional money. However, many, or most, of the interventions and accommodations described in this book will require only a minor change of schedule and will require no extra funds. Even if the educational plan goes no further than modifying a school's attitude or selecting the most appropriate teacher to work with a child, that change will be one very important step toward meeting one child's needs.

What parents must do first when coming to the school with a plan is to try to determine how willing the school is to go beyond the ordinary programs that already exist. The next step is to negotiate with the school to get an agreement—and a commitment—as to just what the school will do. Further, the school should agree that when resources or personnel cannot be found to carry out something in the plan, the school will alert the parents to seek alternative means of providing this service or educational option.

It may be that parents will need to go somewhere other than a traditional public school. There are many choices. They may choose out-of-school learning opportunities, a private school, a charter school, a magnet school, homeschooling, or they may find a more cooperative public school. It is important for parents to know as soon as possible what the school is willing to do and to get the school's agreement that it will notify the parents if something changes. Too often, parents make requests and wait patiently all year for a plan to be carried out, only to find a year later that nothing was ever done.

What Kind of Teacher Is Best for a Gifted Child?

Many of the leading thinkers and researchers in gifted education have compiled lists of traits that are important for an effective teacher of gifted children. The traits most frequently mentioned in the research are listed below in the order of their importance.

High degree of intelligence. Parents should look for a teacher who uses language well, has an extensive vocabulary, and seems to think quickly. The teacher should be excited about learning and want to share that love of learning with students. Why is this important? It is often the case that a high potential child will find few, if any, other students with similar abilities and intense interests in her classroom unless the school has consciously planned for this, such as through some form of ability or achievement grouping. The gifted child's teacher may be the only person in her classroom who is capable of operating on the same intellectual level as the child. It is important for the teacher to recognize and be sensitive to that.

This does not imply that the teacher must be intellectually gifted; however, the child does need to be with someone who can observe, understand, and appreciate how he thinks and learns. Parents should avoid a teacher who seems interested only in doing the minimum amount of work with the curriculum, such as a teacher who uses a single basal text without supplying additional enriching information from other sources. Likewise, parents should avoid a teacher who only shows interest in teaching one content area, such as teaching reading but ignoring other subjects.

High degree of intellectual honesty. Parents should avoid a teacher who can't admit that he or she doesn't know something or who feels it appropriate to belittle a bright child if the child doesn't know every single answer. Teachers who say, "You should know that; you're gifted!" should be avoided at all costs.

Expertise in a specific academic area. A good teacher for gifted students is someone who has studied one or more academic areas in depth, such as having 15-30 credit hours in science or history or a foreign language. Many elementary teachers have majored in "Elementary Education" and lack in-depth knowledge of any one academic area. Teachers with extensive knowledge of even one academic area are more likely to be excited about learning because they understand better how much more there is to learn about the subjects they are teaching. Such teachers can better understand just how far one can delve into a given subject area and can better convey a love of learning to the gifted child. Enthusiasm for learning from such a teacher will be communicated to bright children.

Parents should avoid a teacher who leaves the campus right after school, who focuses extensively on all of the latest popular television shows, or who seems to have few interests outside of school and family. Such teachers tend to create a dull or sterile learning environment for gifted children because they do not understand the child's craving to learn new things, to be non-traditional, and to become enthusiastic about learning a subject area in depth.

A genuine interest in and liking of gifted learners. Parents should avoid a teacher who says, "All students are gifted," or comments that he or she has "never seen a gifted child." Likewise, avoid a teacher who claims to let the child do it alone, because, "if she is gifted, she can figure it out for herself." This may foreshadow a subconscious desire to "prove" that the child is not gifted when the child does stumble.

A teacher who likes and wants to work with gifted children will not be threatened when the child disagrees or challenges him or her. A teacher who works well with gifted children welcomes different opinions and encourages the child to make his case using evidence so as to promote higher-level thinking skills. A teacher who likes gifted children will understand and accept the gifted child and his "quirks."

Recognition of the importance of intellectual development. Parents should avoid a teacher who talks primarily about wanting all students to like themselves and feel successful. This kind of teacher may do little to foster individual differences in ability or to ensure that substantial new and challenging learning takes place. Instead, seek out the teachers who value high intellectual standards and achievements, as well as social and emotional well-being. Remember, solid self-esteem does not come from being successful at easy tasks; it develops from the mastery of difficult ones.

Strong belief in individual differences and individualization. Parents should avoid the teacher who can only talk about his or her "class" or "reading group," who seldom or never mentions individual names, or who doesn't know each child personally by the time of the first parent/teacher conference. Research conducted on the MacArthur Fellows—nationally recognized, innovative thinkers and contributors to society—found that the common factor these gifted individuals described as influential in their school years was having at least one teacher who saw them as unique and directed them toward enhancing that uniqueness (Cox, 1983). A teacher who supports each child's uniqueness is important.

Highly developed teaching skill and knowledge of how to teach. Parents should probably avoid a first or second year teacher, no matter how enthusiastic the teacher is. Bright children can be easily perceived by a new young teacher as "threatening" when they question certain activities or methods. Experienced teachers are more likely to understand the reasons for such questions because they have encountered such students in the past, and more experienced teachers can supply answers for why they teach the way they do without getting flustered or defensive.

Self-directed in their own learning, with a love for new, advanced knowledge. During the past three decades, psychologists Albert Bandura and Dale Schunk have noted consistently that humans choose role models by watching and learning from someone they perceive to be similar to themself who seems to be successful (Bandura, 1977; Schunk, 1987). Thus, a bright child is most likely to look up to her teacher for how to become self-directed and to continue to advance her learning. A teacher who clearly loves to learn will be a positive role model for a gifted child.

Level-headed and emotionally stable. Dr. Linda Silverman's research at the Gifted Development Center on over 3,000 high potential children shows that gifted children are both self-aware and interpersonally sensitive (Silverman, 1993). These children can easily figure out how others feel about them and are hurt when they recognize that they are not liked or valued. Gifted children need teachers who understand their giftedness, including their sensitivities and emotions. They also need teachers who can handle their own negative emotions appropriately. Gifted children will not thrive with a teacher who lashes out in anger, uses sarcasm, or belittles or shames them or others in the class.

These eight traits above, which educators and researchers have found to be important for a teacher of gifted children to have, are useful in helping parents choose the best teacher for their child. But what traits do gifted children themselves think are important for their teachers to have? In William Heath's research (1997), the following teacher characteristics are listed by gifted children as most important for a "good" teacher:

- *Being patient.*
- *Having a sense of humor.*
- *Moving quickly through learning material.*

- *Treating each person as an individual.*
- *Allowing others' opinions to be heard.*
- *Consistently giving "accurate" feedback.*

It is interesting to note that four of the six teacher-behavior characteristics listed by gifted children are personality traits, whereas only two reflect how these children wish to be taught. It is also interesting to note that accelerated pacing and specific, detailed comments about how well they have done on their assignments are extremely important to these gifted children. Simply writing "Great Paper" or placing a smiley face sticker or an "A+ Excellent" on their work does not suffice. A child who has taken great care forming each number on a page of math problems in addition to turning the assignment in very quickly and getting all of the problems correct will not be satisfied with just a sticker. Such a child wants acknowledgement of his additional effort. The student who has written a carefully developed set of arguments centered on a unique idea or perspective needs someone to challenge what he has written and will be suspicious about whether the paper was even read if it is returned with simply "Excellent" as the only teacher comment. These children, already intrinsically motivated and self-critical, want and need specific, detailed feedback that will help them improve and grow.

Summary

Gifted children deserve the best possible learning situations; unfortunately, few schools are ready, eager, or prepared to offer this to them. Parents must be ready to design an individualized educational plan for their child that uses research, and to present data to the school to support the services requested. Their plan should outline specific of stimulating learning opportunities the gifted student should receive at school.

Many options in the educational plan can enhance your child's school curriculum, and these options will be discussed in depth in later chapters. But for now, begin thinking about whether an educational plan is necessary for your gifted child and in what areas your child might need more enrichment. You know your child best, and if you want your gifted child to have a successful school education, you will almost certainly need to advocate for him. One of the best approaches to advocacy is to create a collaborative education plan with the school for your gifted child that will allow him to get the best possible stimulation, curriculum enhancement, and intellectual growth possible at school.

Key Points

- Gifted kindergarten children who are advanced readers often must wait two years in school before they can progress further in reading.

- Kindergarten is frustrating for many gifted children who may have advanced abilities and interests different from other children.

- The first step in making an educational plan work is to find the "right" teacher for the gifted child.

- Educators frequently lack training in characteristics and needs of gifted children.

- Schools often practice an educational philosophy that plays down individual differences in their belief that they should treat all children the same.

- Parents should determine through psychoeducational testing whether their child is developmentally advanced, and in what areas.

- Parents typically know their child best and are thus the logical ones to draw up the plan they would like the school to follow.

- A written educational plan can help to ensure that a gifted child will receive curriculum and instruction geared to the child's level, rather than geared to an average child of the same age.

- You will know if modification of an educational plan is necessary based on your child's performance and behavior in school. If your child seems bored or irritated with school, is acting out in class, doesn't like his agemates, or other signs, and there is no family crisis or other obvious reason for these behaviors, then you will need to actively advocate for the appropriate learning your child deserves.

- An educational plan should be presented to the school six or seven months in advance of when it will be used.

- Sometimes gifted children are mislabeled or misdiagnosed as ADD, ADHD, etc. Gifted children should be tested by a psychologist who has special training in giftedness.

- The best teachers of gifted children are those with specific training in gifted education and who have certain characteristics.

2

What Kind of Gifted Child Do You Have?

When someone says, "My child is gifted," what does it mean? Does it mean the child is really good at a particular subject such as math? Does the child have an unusually large vocabulary? Does the child show great talent for the piano at an unexpectedly early age? Or has the child consistently walked, talked, solved problems, and learned to do things more quickly or earlier than other children the same age? Any or all of these could be indications that a child is gifted. It is also possible that a child displays none of these behaviors and is still gifted.

Before we look further at who the gifted are and what kind of gifted child you have, take this quiz to see how much you already know about who the gifted are. Each example has been simplified to illustrate a different kind of giftedness or a different set of strengths. Keep in mind that most gifted children will show behaviors and characteristics that fit into more than one of these case descriptions.

A Quiz: Who Is Gifted?

Which of the five children described below are potentially gifted or talented? Some of these case examples will seem pretty obvious, while others may seem more difficult. After reading the description of each child's behaviors, decide whether you think that child is gifted.

ROB, aka "The Brain."
Rob may or may not be good-

Rob

looking. He may or may not be good at sports,
and he may or may not act like a nerd. Likewise,
he may or may not be the first to raise his hand when the teacher
asks questions in a discussion, but one thing teachers have noticed
about Rob—he seems to be very deep and very curious. Rob
would be voted "most intellectual" by his peers. Everything about
Rob perks up when a teacher suggests a new point of view.

Rob has behaviors in the classroom that are both endear-
ing and aggravating. He sometimes appears very slow and delib-
erate, especially when quick answers are being sought to low
level questions. He often seems to make too much out of a simple
question. He runs on his own timelines, which means there are
times when he is out of sorts because he has to put a project down
and turn to the next subject. His behaviors are usually very sys-
tematic and logical, which can make him very uncomfortable
with a teacher's attempts at creativity. He is not a willing risk-
taker and wants structure when long-term assignments are given.
When questions are asked in class, Rob can be annoying when he
so frequently re-words the question before answering.

It is very hard to find enough extra assignments to keep
Rob challenged in subjects such as mathematics and science;
usually the class is being taught the basic facts of that content
area. He generally soaks up information as quickly as it can be
put before him. On almost every aptitude and achievement test,
Rob scores in the higher ranges and will usually have topnotch
grades. Yet he may actually be a serious underachiever—at
least compared to his potential—because he is not being offered
enough content or enough complexity. Rob could spend any-
where from three to six years without learning a single new idea
or concept in the classroom. The only characteristic that may
keep Rob from complete disillusionment with school may be his
own perseverance and patience—waiting for the day when
school will be both challenging and fun.

IS ROB GIFTED?   *Yes*   *No*

MARIA, aka "The Specialist." Maria is a constant hand-raiser when social studies class is in session. She knows every answer to the teacher's questions in that class. She has read every children's book and a great many adult books on the Civil War in particular. No matter what the topic in social studies, she finds some way to relate it to something she has just read about the Civil War. She probably knows more about that period of history than her teachers do. In discussions, Maria gets so excited that she often forgets to let other children have a chance to answer. She usually forgets to raise her hand and simply blurts out answers. It is very important to her to make sure the teacher and her peers know what she knows.

Unfortunately, Maria does not have the same love or skill for math. Her test scores are consistently below grade level, and she displays no interest in working hard to bring up her scores in that area. More than one of her teachers suspects that if there were a way to relate basic math facts to events in the Civil War, Maria would learn math easily.

Maria was not selected for the gifted program in her school, despite the fact that many of that program's planned enrichment activities involved social studies. Her classroom teacher would not let her be considered because of her poor performance in math. She was, of course, highly disappointed. Probably the major reason Maria will continue to go along with the system in years to come is her natural love of learning and the support she receives for her talent area at home and from the occasional teacher at school who values the very specialized gift she possesses. We only hope that those teachers don't occur too many years apart as Maria progresses through school.

IS MARIA GIFTED?   *Yes   No*

JAMAL, aka "The Creative Spirit." Jamal is flamboyant in his dress, really into the "grunge" scene currently, but a real charge to be around. His excitement when he thinks of an idea is contagious, as is his sense of humor. His school performance is spotty, to say the least. In classes where the teacher recognizes and respects his fine, original mind, he outdoes himself in the quality and quantity of his work. But in classes where "no exceptions are made," where assignments are rigid and deadlines are enforced, Jamal refuses to produce and thus gets failing grades. This happens in every subject area in high school. He failed Rhetoric, but aced Creative Writing class. Geometry was easy, but Math Analysis resulted in another low grade. One can almost predict in which classes Jamal will do poorly by which teacher he is assigned. If he and his teacher clash, or if negotiations on assignments and opportunities to produce something unique are not available, if the work is too routine or repetitive, then Jamal refuses to put forth the effort needed to succeed. As a result, his general skill levels are poor, and there is some question about whether he will be able to get into college at all.

Unlike Maria, Jamal has no specialized talent area at present, and for him to be able to fully realize the potential of his high degree of originality, he must become an "expert" in some area. (That is what some researchers, such as David Feldman and David Perkins, have suggested.) Without that, his creativity will probably never be fully utilized.

There is no doubt that Jamal will be happy in adulthood; he has the natural flexibility to rearrange events to his own liking and comfort. However, it will be a severe loss to society if Jamal's creativity is not channeled into finding solutions and reformulating problems we have been grappling with for years—cures for cancer, prevention of ecological destruction, replenishing the ozone layer, or providing food for underdeveloped nations.

IS JAMAL GIFTED?   Yes   No

Nicole

NICOLE, aka "The Social Leader." Nicole has the uncommon knack of getting along with almost everyone. She seems to genuinely like everyone she meets, and those feelings are almost instantly mutual. She is unusually perceptive in understanding other people's feelings and concerns; at times, she has almost painful experiences when her empathy overwhelms her. Her parents tell of a time she cried and cried after seeing a documentary about children starving in Ethiopia. She kept asking, "How can I help them? What can I do?" She was six years old at the time.

In elementary school, Nicole got along well with teachers because she was so dependable. When teachers wanted group projects done for parents' night, they knew that putting Nicole in charge of the project would result in a high quality, visually pleasing project that every parent would perceive as a successful classroom experience. Nicole, of course, put loads of extra time into completing the project, time she seemed to genuinely enjoy despite the fact that others in her group were not doing their part.

In her high school, Nicole is well known for her wide participation in competitions, sports, fund raising efforts, cheerleading, Student Council, and yearbook. She looks for new experiences and often gravitates to a leadership role within an organization. In the classroom, her ideas are respected by her classmates.

There are problems for Nicole in school, however. In her enthusiasm for new experiences, it is easy for her to spread herself too thinly. Extracurricular activities often take up more time than her schoolwork. So far, she has been able to get along on her finely attuned intuitive sense, but as her course work becomes more difficult and as she gets closer to college, she may find that she has not acquired enough content or skill to let her get by on so little time for study and reflection. She runs a large risk of becoming one of the "college dropout" statistics. Nicole may help to keep her school life running smoothly, but college life down the road may not be so smooth for her unless her teachers can impress her with the importance of academic learning.

IS NICOLE GIFTED? **Yes** **No**

Thao

THAO, aka "Artiste Extraordinaire." Thao has always "marched to a different drummer." Life for him has been filled with perfecting a wonderful ability for playing the violin. This has meant getting up at 5 a.m. to practice for a couple of hours before getting ready for school, rushing to private music lessons after school is over, and practicing for a few more hours in the evening before going to bed. Thao's classroom teachers know how much time he spends practicing, and they call this "unhealthy" and "not normal." Thao's parents have constantly heard teachers say to them in conferences, "If Thao would put into his school work what he puts into music, he would be a straight A student!"

There is no question that Thao is very bright academically. There are flashes of brilliance in class when there are competitions, especially with tasks such as telling if two things are alike in appearance or in meaning. Thao has an amazing eye for details.

Socially, Thao gets along pretty well. He has one or two close friends (who are usually involved in some kind of artistic endeavor), but beyond that, he does not seem concerned about acquiring a large group of acquaintances. His favorite topic of conversation is music or something related to music. Most of the other kids find this either boring or just don't understand why he finds music so interesting.

Thao is a committed individual. To outsiders, he appears almost obsessive about his talent area. Long ago, Thao decided to further his talent and to become best at it, even if it meant being less than perfect in other areas. His performance in academic subjects is sporadic. He does projects and assignments only when he can find time that doesn't interfere with his violin.

Schools are committed to educating every child, and teachers have assumed that every child wants to learn everything there is to learn. When a child shows little or no motivation for academic learning, teachers usually conclude that something is wrong either with the home or the child. It can be difficult for a nurturing teacher to meet up with a child like Thao because this child has made unpopular decisions. We could argue that we should just let Thao be, but democratically, we cannot. Thao needs a thorough grounding in all aspects of education that our culture emphasizes. As E. D. Hirsch argues so persuasively in his book, Cultural Literacy, *the schools must provide Thao with this literacy. As things now stand, Thao will not get such a broad education.*

IS THAO GIFTED?   *Yes*   *No*

How Can Such Different Children Be Considered Gifted?

If you answered yes to each of the above five case study profiles, then you earned 100% on our quiz and are ready to move onto the next chapter in this book! But wait just a moment. Let's see where these case studies came from. Remember, this book is based on research.

The five personalities you met, with all their strengths and weaknesses, were drawn from a comprehensive review of research that I conducted several years ago (Rogers, 1986). More recent research reported since that time has not notably changed these profiles. My review encompassed 182 studies in which gifted individuals were compared with the general population based on objective, quantitative data that was collected and analyzed statistically.

I sorted the studies into separate clusters according to how the children had actually been identified as gifted, and each cluster produced a profile type. For example, if an IQ test was used in a study to distinguish the gifted students from the general population, then those studies were compiled into a cluster, which created the representative case study of Rob, "The Brain." The United States Office of Education (USOE) previously designated this category or domain of giftedness as the "Intellectual Ability" domain (Marland, 1972, U.S. OERI, 1994).

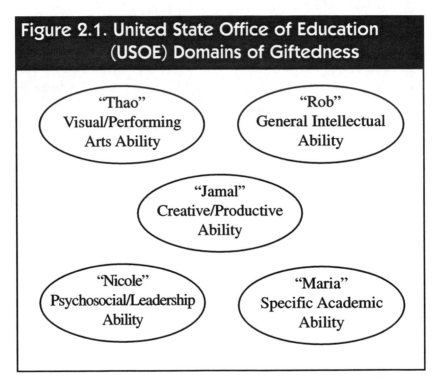

Figure 2.1. United State Office of Education (USOE) Domains of Giftedness

"Thao"
Visual/Performing
Arts Ability

"Rob"
General Intellectual
Ability

"Jamal"
Creative/Productive
Ability

"Nicole"
Psychosocial/Leadership
Ability

"Maria"
Specific Academic
Ability

If tests of achievement in specific subject areas were used to separate two groups of academic achievers, such as talented math students (working two or more grade levels ahead) versus regular math students (working at grade level), then the compiled studies were sorted and placed under the profile of Maria, "The Specialist." This domain is recognized in the USOE definitions of giftedness and talent as the "Specific Academic Ability" domain. (Later in this chapter we will distinguish between "gift" and "talent.")

Performance on tests of creative thinking, that is, separating those students with high scores in creativity from those with low scores, provided the basis for the many studies that, when compiled, were placed with Jamal's profile, which was titled, "The Creative Spirit." According to the USOE definition of giftedness, Jamal is gifted in the "Creativity" domain. Creativity tests include things like written and visual measures of how many ideas or solutions an individual can think of, how original and detailed these ideas are, and how many different perspectives the individual uses when coming up with an idea or solution.

For the psychosocial or "Leadership" domain of giftedness, according to USOE labels, you read about Nicole. To be identified as gifted or talented in this category requires recognition from peers and adults. Most of the studies which looked at this form of giftedness used teacher, counselor, or coach nominations, along with observations of how the student behaved when working with others or when taking on projects or tasks with groups or organizations. Thus far, researchers have not discovered a valid and reliable written test for identifying giftedness in leadership or the psychosocial domain. Identification, at this point in time, is fairly subjective for this domain.

Finally, you read about Thao, "Artiste Extraordinaire," who represented the large domain of talent, labeled by the USOE as the Visual and Performing Arts. Thao was a musician in our case study profile, but could just as easily have been a dancer, actor, creative writer, artist, or graphic designer. Being recognized as gifted or talented in this area is done primarily through observations of the individual's performance or product by specialists in that artistic field. There are no valid or reliable objective tests of giftedness in the arts areas. Seeing (or hearing) is believing.

One last domain of giftedness and talent has been omitted in the previous discussions of domains of ability—the area of physical coordination and athletic skill. There is no question that this area is an important ability domain, but it has been eliminated from USOE definitions of high ability domains primarily because society and communities already support the development of gifts and talents in this area. Because athletes and athletic events serve to entertain the public, the public gladly pays for the development of these gifts. With gifted education funding currently averaging only one cent of every $100 spent by the United States Government on education, it is clear that our society does not value education of some of its brightest students as much as it values athletic teams and social events. Because the purpose of this book is to help gifted children, this book will focus on the other "official" domains of ability and save the discussion of athletic gifts for another publication.

Descriptions thus far have only hinted at another truism of giftedness and talent—gifts and talents come to individuals across both sexes, all races and ethnic groups, all religious groups, and all socioeconomic levels. Children with high potential come in all shapes and sizes. We cannot know children are gifted just by looking at their faces. We have to describe the child's behaviors and characteristics in order to determine whether giftedness or talent is there. Furthermore, *which* gifts and talents are there and *how many* can sometimes be hard to discern. It is rare that we find a pure "Rob" or a pure "Jamal." Most gifted children demonstrate a mixture of traits from two or more areas or domains of giftedness.

Five Domains of Giftedness and Talent

You may have enjoyed taking the quiz, but now it is important to look at what those 182 research studies really showed about the significantly different characteristics and behaviors of children with potential gifts and talents. Table 2.1 lists and identifies actual behaviors or traits found for each of the five gifted profiles.

My synthesis of research (Rogers, 1986), updated in 1998, looked at each of the five domains used by the USOE: (1) intellectual ability, (2) specific academic ability, (3) creative/productive ability, (4) psychosocial/leadership ability, and (5) visual and performing arts abilities. Within each domain, certain characteristics or behaviors were found to be present significantly more often in individuals who were gifted in the domain than would be present in the general population. The following table lists the characteristics that were commonly found in each domain.

Table 2.1. Research-Based Behaviors of Five Major Domain Profiles

 **Intellectual Ability Domain aka "The Brain"**	*a. Contemplation/Reflection Time:* In solving a problem, a larger than expected proportion of the time is spent thinking "around" the problem rather than directly solving it. The thinker muses over what type of problem it is, other experiences with such problems, what solutions worked before, and whether they would work this time BEFORE actually starting the problem (not procrastination, but at times it may be hard to tell the two apart!). *b. Thinking in Analogies:* Making connections between what is currently being learned and previous learning in the same or different arenas. Often, an observer cannot easily understand how the connections were made, so the child may be seen as unrealistic. *c. Love of Learning:* A genuine love for intellectualizing, conceptual discussions, and school in general. Willingness to do whatever extra credit is available or to pursue any lead a teacher or mentor gives to learning something new. A craving for content that is new and different ALL THE TIME. *d. Concentration and Memory:* A remarkable ability to focus on what the task is regardless of what else is going on in a setting (concentration), and a rapid, extraordinary ability to retain new information in long-term memory with little obvious effort.

Table 2.1. Research-Based Behaviors of Five Major Domain Profiles *(continued)*

(continued)  **Intellectual Ability Domain**	*e. Problem Finding:* Ability to focus on what the "real" or important crux of a situation is, to understand how to sort relevant from irrelevant information in finding the real problem. *f. Accelerated Cognitive Development:* Tendency to reach the final stage of Piaget's theory of cognitive development—formal operations or abstract thinking and logic—considerably earlier than the general population. The higher the IQ, the faster the acceleration.
 **Specific Academic Ability Domain aka "The Specialist"**	*a. Intense, Focused Interest and Skill Set:* Tendency to "eat, drink, and sleep" a subject until all that can be learned about it is learned; interests are rarely broad and wide-ranging. *b. Intense, Focused Motivation to Learn:* See the characteristics listed in (a). *c. Self-Criticism:* Tendency to feel less good about self than children of similar ages in the general population; mistrust of own ability perhaps as a result of uneven set of skills. *d. Need to Achieve:* Intense drive to master a domain of knowledge and be recognized as "the expert." *e. Concentration and Memory:* Remarkable ability to focus on a task (in high interest/skill area), and rapid, extraordinary ability to retain new information in that area with little obvious effort. *f. Love of Learning:* A genuine love for intellectualizing and conceptual discussions about specific area of high interest and skill. A craving for content in that area.

Table 2.1. Research-Based Behaviors of Five Major Domain Profiles *(continued)*

Creative-Productive Thinking Domain aka "The Creative Spirit"

a. Flexibility: Ability to look at information from many different perspectives or directions; likewise, ability to come up with solutions from a variety of different angles.

b. Individual Structuring: Need to shape the environment around self, including desks and chairs in a classroom, assignments, and tasks at home and school; lots of negotiating about "how" things will be done.

c. Risk-Taking: Consistent urge to try something new, regardless of cognitive, emotional, or physical risks that might be incurred.

d. Tolerance for Ambiguity: Comfortable in "messy" situations, disorganized environments, and with tasks that are poorly structured or seemingly impossible to solve.

e. Self-Concept: Significantly more positive self-concept than the general population, with an unending supply of confidence that they can produce at will.

f. Inner Locus of Control: Tendency to attribute success and failure to own effort and abilities.

Leadership and Psychosocial Domain aka "The Social Leader"

a. Backwards Planning: Ability to sequentially break down a complex task into its parts by backwards planning—starting at ultimate goal, then working backwards to present.

b. Scanning: Ability to look holistically at complex information and "pick out" similarities or differences with little effort. Relatively independent and unaffected by situational and social pressures or others' attitudes.

c. Need to Achieve: Intense drive to master a domain of knowledge and be recognized as "the expert."

Table 2.1. Research-Based Behaviors of Five Major Domain Profiles *(continued)*

(continued)  **Leadership and Psychosocial Domain aka "The Social Leader"**	**d. Social Cognition:** Intuitive knowledge of how one should behave and treat others, from a very early age; not necessarily connected all the time to actual behavior. **e. Emotional Stability:** Tendency to be calm, even-tempered, and accepting of others' foibles with little tendency toward anxiety or nervousness. **f. Perspective-Taking:** Ability to understand someone else's ideas (ideological PT), someone's feelings or moods (affective PT), or to orient self in space (visual/perceptive PT).
 **Visual and Performing Arts Domain aka "The Artiste Extraordinaire"**	**a. Intense, Focused Interest and Skill Set:** Tendency to "eat, drink, and sleep" an art form until all that can be learned about it is learned. Interests are rarely broad or wide-ranging. **b. Intense, Focused Motivation to Learn:** See the above characteristics listed in (a). **c. Self-Criticism:** Tendency to feel that if they don't work hard, their ability may disappear; very self-evaluative of own products or performances. **d. Intense Concentration in Art Form:** Ability to stay focused on arts task, and to practice skills despite complex surrounding environment. **e. Cognitive Verbal, Visual Matching:** Ability to quickly and accurately match figural or symbol pairs (visual), words or syllables (verbal), or words and meanings (cognitive).

If you study this table carefully, you can probably figure out that you, the parent, are the key to finding and understanding your child's gifts and talents, especially if you are beginning the child's educational plan at an early age. Once the child is in elementary school, teachers may get to know your child fairly well, but you are the best first judge of the characteristics and behaviors listed in the tables above.

The *Parent Inventory for Finding Potential* (PIP)

To help parents identify their child as gifted or talented, a variety of nomination forms have been developed over the years. Most of them ask for biographical information (evidence of a child's earlier-than-expected interest, ability, or skill) and some of them ask parents to rate how frequently they have observed specific behaviors and characteristics that might be indications of giftedness.

None of the existing published forms, however, has used the research-based characteristics discussed earlier in this chapter. To overcome this inadequacy, I developed the *Parent Inventory for Finding Potential* (PIP), which allows you to assess your child's strengths. A copy of the PIP questionnaire is included in the supplementary materials at the end of this book (Appendix A). Use the PIP to rate how often you observe the behaviors listed in the inventory. Follow the directions at the end of the PIP to compute your child's average score for each domain scale. If you find that your child's scores are higher than an average of 3 ("regularly") on one or more of the scales, it will be important to use this score information as the starting point in the educational planning process.

You may wish to stop reading further in this book until you have answered the questions on the PIP in Appendix A. When you have your child's scores in front of you, you will be ready for the next section of this chapter—documenting your child's specific gifts and talents.

Not All Gifts Become Talents

Thus far in the chapter, the terms "gifted" and "talented" have been used almost interchangeably. Professor Françoys Gagné of Montreal, Canada, has suggested that such thinking is inaccurate and misleading (1985). He makes a distinction between gifts and talents, which serves as a fine base for this book about educational planning. He suggests that "gifts" or "giftedness" refers to the *innate ability* or *capacity in some domain of ability*, whether it is intellectual, perceptual, physical, creative, or social. It is something a child is born with. Every child is born with *some* ability or capacity—what we could call a strength—a *gifted* child is born with a *comparatively greater degree* of this ability or potential.

This potential giftedness may be very general. For example, if a child is born with great general intellectual potential, he could figure out *any* kind of logical solution, whether it were in a philosophical problem on paper or in some other real world problem. Another child's intellectual potential, equally as great, might be channeled into a very narrow or *specific* domain, such as mathematical reasoning or practical problem-solving ability. Likewise, the potential, whether general or specific, may not all lie in one domain. Perhaps a child is a great critical thinker (general intellectual) and also has a specific ability to organize a research project being carried out by a small group of children (psychosocial specific). Or perhaps she is very imaginative and creative in language and writing (creativity specific) and has an extraordinary ability to reason mathematically (intellectual specific).

Figure 2.2 illustrates Gagné's view of giftedness and talent. Readers who want to know more about Gagné's ideas will find his publications listed in the reference section.

Figure 2.2. Gagné Diagram

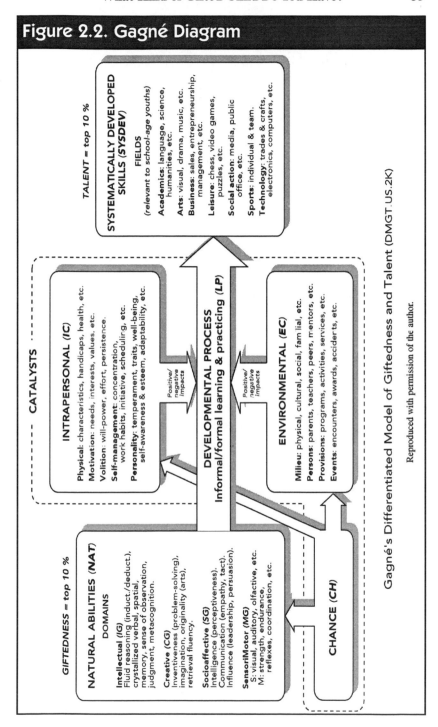

Gagné's Differentiated Model of Giftedness and Talent (DMGT. US.2K)

Reproduced with permission of the author.

On the right side of this model, Gagné defines "talents" as *extraordinary performance in a field of human endeavor.* Hence, according to Gagné, the child who is reading at sixth grade level in kindergarten is *talented* in reading, and the musician who can play Tschaikovsky's first violin concerto at age 10 is *talented* in music. Table 2.2 gives examples to show how gifts (i.e., potential) and talents (i.e., performance) are expressed for the five different U.S. Office of Education domains.

Although this all may seem unnecessarily theoretical, there is a purpose behind these explanations. A second glance at Gagné's Diagram shows where the child—and the child's family—fits in. In the center, between gifts and talents, are the catalysts—that is, the various important aspects of the child's environment, both external and internal. Some of these catalysts, such as physical characteristics or chance factors, are ones that a family usually cannot influence. However, the majority of these catalysts can be influenced either directly or indirectly by the child's family. A child's potential can either be developed or obstructed by these catalysts. If it is obstructed, then the child will remain gifted but will be what we call an underachiever (that is, not talented). If, however, the internal and external components of the catalyst enhance and help to develop the child's potential, the child will become talented and will demonstrate his potential through performance.

This model makes apparent two important aspects:

1. *It is possible to be gifted but not talented.* If something has not happened in the catalyst, the child will not be talented. For example, the child has a disability or has lost interest in doing something well, or friends made fun of him so he gave up trying, or his family disapproved of his gift, or the school didn't help to develop his potential. One classic example of this underachievement might be William Sidis, now deceased, who graduated from Harvard at age 15 but then spent the next 30 years of his life living alone, collecting different bus tokens from around the world.

He had great potential, but the demands placed on him by family and the media, as well as his own personal needs to shun publicity and seek solitude, led to his potential not being fully developed.

2. *It is not possible to be talented without being gifted.* That is, if a child is performing at very high levels, there had to be potential to start with. No matter how hard a person works, or how much exposure and enrichment a family provides, or how much a school works to help develop potential, if high potential isn't there to begin with, it can't be developed. In other words, there is no such thing as an overachiever. No one can do more than they have the capacity to do. If someone is working at higher levels than we thought they were capable of, then we were wrong in our assessment of potential—that's all! An example of this is Walt Disney, who received failing grades in high school art classes for not having "any ideas" (potential), but went on to amass a fortune for his cartoon characters (talent). The gift was there all along for Disney to be able to demonstrate his creative talent through such memorable characters as Mickey Mouse and Donald Duck. It had to be nurtured and developed.

Table 2.2. Characteristics and Behaviors of Gifts and Talents

Gifts (Potential) Examples	Talents (Performance) Evidence
Intellectual Giftedness Capacity to reason at high levels, think abstractly	**Intellectual Talent** Uses problem-solving abilities at higher levels than anyone else
Specific Academic Ability Capacity to function at extraordinary levels in a specific academic area, such as math or writing	**Specific Academic Talent** Performs well beyond expected age or grade levels in a specific academic area at all stages of life
Creative Ability Capacity to think divergently either in general or in very specific areas, such as personal decisions, problem solving, art, etc.	**Creative-Productive Talent** Produces unique, original solutions in a field, such as math, filmmaking, writing, software development, art, advertising, etc.
Psychosocial Ability Potential to become a leader and to understand others	**Leadership Talent** Takes on projects, runs organizations effectively and successfully
Visual and Performing Arts Ability Potential to become musician, artist, writer, actor, designer, or dancer, but hasn't yet developed the skills	**Visual and Performing Arts Talent** Produces or performs at proficient levels in a specific art form and is recognized for this proficiency

Is Your Child's Strength a Gift or a Talent?

Earlier, you were introduced to the process of identifying or recognizing gifts and talents in two ways: (1) you looked at research that showed significant differences in abilities, characteristics and behaviors for each of five domains of ability; and (2) you completed the PIP on your child. Although this book is primarily about educational planning, the topic of identification is both important and necessary. One of the first questions the school will ask you when you come to them with your idea for an educational plan is, "How do you know your child is gifted?" It will be important for you to show school personnel in a systematic way how you have come to that conclusion. And later, you will need to help them understand which educational options are most appropriate to help your type of gifted child develop her gifts into talents.

To do this, you need some sort of assessment that accurately describes the gifts and talents of your child. Although an IQ score or a cognitive abilities test score provides objective information for the intellectual domain, these tests are not as helpful for identifying someone with creative gifts or talents, nor do they identify leadership or abilities outside of academic areas. A more suitable assessment for giftedness and talent should include a variety of both *objective* (quantifiably measured) information and *subjective* (personally observed) information. Table 2.3 shows examples of both objective and subjective instruments that are helpful in the assessment of gifts and talents in each of the five domains.

Some of the objective measures may not be familiar to you at this time, and not every school or professional psychologist necessarily uses or is familiar with all of these measures. They are included simply to provide a reasonably thorough list of instruments that may be used. When you start the assessment process for your child, discuss with the testing professional what tests will be used; you may even ask whether you can recommend those that you feel will be most relevant for your child.

In Table 2.3, asterisks appear on those measures that are generally preferred for their accuracy, reliability, or comprehensiveness. Keep in mind that one *objective* and one *subjective* measure in each domain category of gift/talent will probably suffice. Furthermore, usually you only need to consider domains in which the PIP indicates that your child has a "strength."

Table 2.3. Objective and Subjective Measures of Gifts and Talents

Domain	Gifted Objective Measures	Gifted Subjective Measures	Talent Objective Measures	Talent Subjective Measures
Intellectual	• Stanford-Binet (LM), WISC-III, Woodcock Johnson* • Group mental ability tests (e.g., Otis-Lennon, CogAT, Hennon-Nelson, Ravens Progressive Matrices, Matrix Analogies Test)* • SAT or ACT tests taken at earlier age*	• Renzulli Scales* • Whitmore or Rimm Underachievement Scales • Cultural Characteristics Scales • Parent nomination • Teacher nomination • Renzulli Scales* • Purdue* Scales (PARS) in English, Science, Math, Social Studies, Foreign Language	• Intellectual competitions, such as Academic Decathlon, Destination Imagination, Knowledge Bowl, Future Problem Solving, Math Olympiad • Writing or speech competitions • Problem-solving and critical thinking tests (e.g. Ross, Cornell)*	• Journal • Diary • Writing samples (poetry, stories) • Biographical inventory • Self nomination • Peer nomination • Parent nomination • Teacher nomination • Personal Interview

*Generally preferred for their accuracy, reliability, or comprehensiveness.

Table 2.3. Objective and Subjective Measures of Gifts and Talents *(continued)*

Domain	Gifted Objective Measures	Gifted Subjective Measures	Talent Objective Measures	Talent Subjective Measures
Specific Academic	• Individual achievement tests, e.g., Wechsler Individual Achievement Test, Kaufman Tests of Educational Achievement, Woodcock Johnson Achievement Tests* • Out-of-level (2+ grades ahead) standardized achievement tests (subtest scores), e.g., SATs, ITBS, SRA, MATs* • Curriculum-based assessments	• Teacher nomination • Peer nomination • Parent nomination	• High scores on out-of-level standardized achievement tests* • High grades in an academic area • Successful work in advanced coursework in one or more academic areas	• Student products, science project, short story, etc.) • Self nomination • Biographical inventory • Teacher nomination • Peer nomination • Parent nomination • Interview

*Generally preferred for their accuracy, reliability, or comprehensiveness.

Table 2.3. Objective and Subjective Measures of Gifts and Talents (*continued*)

Domain	Gifted Objective Measures	Gifted Subjective Measures	Talent Objective Measures	Talent Subjective Measures
Specific Academic (*continued*)	• Developing Cognitive Abilities Test* (DCAT) • EXPLORE Test*			
Creativity	• Torrance Tests of Creative Thinking* • Guilford Creative Perception Inventory* • Meeker Structure of Intellect (SOI) Test* • Rimm GIFT and GIFFI tests	• Renzulli Scales* • Wallach & Kogan Scales* • Self nomination • Peer nomination • Teacher nomination • Parent nomination • Biographical inventory	• Creative product checklist • High score on student product or performance* • Auditions or exhibitions using juried panel of "expert" evaluators	• Student products • Self nomination • Biographical inventory • Teacher nomination • Parent nomination

*Generally preferred for their accuracy, reliability, or comprehensiveness.

Table 2.3. Objective and Subjective Measures of Gifts and Talents *(continued)*

Domain	Gifted Objective Measures	Gifted Subjective Measures	Talent Objective Measures	Talent Subjective Measures
Psychosocial Leadership	• Psychological Inventories that indicate emotional stability, self-awareness • Social Maturity Scales*	• Renzulli Scales* • Self nomination • Peer nomination • Teacher nomination • Journal • Diary • Interview • Parent nomination	• Ratings of performance in leadership, administrative role	• Success levels of project or task outcomes • Interview • Observation • Biographical inventory • Self nomination • Peer nomination • Coach/Advisor nomination • Journal • Diary

*Generally preferred for their accuracy, reliability, or comprehensiveness.

Table 2.3. Objective and Subjective Measures of Gifts and Talents *(continued)*

Domain	Gifted Objective Measures	Gifted Subjective Measures	Talent Objective Measures	Talent Subjective Measures
Visual and Performing Arts	• Horn Art Aptitude Test* • Seashore Test of Musical Ability* • Meier Art Judgment Test*	• Renzulli Scales* • Self nomination • Peer nomination • Interview • Diary • Teacher nomination • Parent nomination	• High score on check-list of student product or performance • Auditions or Exhibitions using juried panel of "expert in the field" evaluators	• Journal • Diary • Student products or performances • Self nomination • Biographical inventory • Sketchbook, composition notebook, journal, choreography plan, play notes • Artist/teacher nominations

*Generally preferred for their accuracy, reliability, or comprehensiveness.

Here is how you will use this list of tests. Looking at Table 2.3, let's say your child shows specific academic ability strengths in reading and social studies on the PIP. You want to know if these strengths are a gift or a talent, and you also want to know in which area the gift or talent lies. To find potential gifts in academic areas, you decide to ask a school professional to give your child the *Wechsler Individual Achievement Test (WIAT)*, an objective measure which compares her age-equivalent and grade-equivalent functioning in math, reading, spelling, writing, listening, and speaking. You will also ask your child's current teacher to complete the *Purdue Academic Rating Scales*, a subjective measure, but one which will provide additional observations that will help round out the picture.

The results from the *WIAT* will not only help you confirm that your child has a gift in a particular academic area, but also will help you decide if your child's academic potential is being demonstrated in actual performance (i.e., talent). To add to this, you might ask the school's gifted resource person to administer the regular achievement test (an objective measure) used by the district, but to do "advanced level testing," that is, to give your child a version of the achievement test that is designed for three grade levels above your child's current grade. For example, they would administer the sixth grade version of the test to your third grade child. You and your child should also select some examples of your child's work (a subjective measure) that show a high level of performance. With these four measures of gifts and talents (two objective and two subjective), you and school officials should be able to decide whether or not your child has an academic gift (and in what general area, e.g., language or mathematics) that needs to be developed, and whether your child has one or more academic talents in specific subject areas that should be enhanced and extended.

In another example, let us say your child's PIP shows intellectual domain strengths, and you wish to know if these are gifts or talents. In this case, using Table 2.3, you would request an individual intelligence test as your objective measure of potential. The *Wechsler Intelligence Scale for Children* is the most widely accepted test at present, but it has its limits. For instance, if your child is highly or profoundly gifted, a true score cannot be accurately obtained using this test because of a "ceiling effect." That is, even if your child gets all of the items correct, his score can only go as high as the test norms allow— usually a score of 150 or so. In such cases, an additional measure with a higher ceiling will be needed, such as the *Stanford-Binet Intelligence Scale, Form L-M*. This test is, in many ways, outdated but can estimate IQ scores up into the 200s. Thus, you may end up having to use two separate individual intelligence tests for your child. Schools often are reluctant to do such extra testing, and you may find that you will need to pay to have this testing done privately. You might be reluctant since the cost may be several hundred dollars. However, thorough professional interpretation of the test results is important. If you compare this cost to other frequent expenses for children, like orthodontic braces, this testing will cost approximately one-tenth as much, yet will have an effect on your child's future self-esteem and personal development that is every bit as important.

For a subjective measure of intellectual potential, you might choose an instrument titled the *Renzulli Scales for Rating the Behavioral Characteristics of Superior Students*. These scales are particularly useful for helping teachers and parents estimate learning, motivation, creativity, leadership, planning, communication expression, and communication precision.

Next we need to look at your child's talents. Talent in intellectual areas is best seen in competitive performance, such as that found in national programs like Knowledge Bowl, National Geography Bee, Spelling Bee, Future Problem Solving or Destination Imagination. If your child has engaged in any of these programs and has been a strong competitor or winner, you have an objective indication of intellectual talent. For a subjective view of talent, you and your child should select examples of his writing or problem solving. You could also complete a biographical inventory that lists extraordinary achievements at various times in the child's life. It is a bit harder to identify intellectual talent in young children, of course, because they have not yet had time to show what they can do with their minds. Just do the best you can to collect data, realizing that you will probably do better with measuring intellectual potential than intellectual talent.

If the table of measures seems confusing or overwhelming to you, you may want to do some further reading. You do not need to become an expert on testing for gifted children, but you should become an informed consumer. Cookson and Halberstam (1998) have written a very understandable book on tests, *A Parent's Guide to Standardized Tests in School: How to Improve Your Child's Chances for Success*. If you want to know more about assessment, this would be a good book to read. If you have access to the Internet, many of the major test publishers of standardized tests used in schools have websites that describe their tests. Three helpful resources are (1) CTB/McGraw-Hill (publishers of *Comprehensive Test of Basic Skills*, www.ctb.com), (2) Harcourt Brace (publishers of the *Otis-Lennon*, *Stanford Achievement* and *Metropolitan Achievement Tests*, www.hbem.com), and (3) Houghton Mifflin/ Riverside (publisher of *Iowa Tests of Basic Skills* and the *Cognitive Abilities Test*, www.hmco.com/hmco/riverside).

Summary

There are many different kinds of potential (or gifts), including abilities that are intellectual, academic, creative, social/managerial, and artistic. Likewise, there are many different forms in which children can show what they can do (their talents). When identifying the kinds of gift and/or talent a child might have, it is important to collect information about both potential and performance that is both *measurable* (through a test) and *observable* (through a checklist, work samples, etc.). All of this information will help identify the specific areas of cognitive functioning in which the child excels and where consequently the child has the greatest need for educational development.

Key Points

- There are at least six general domains in which gifts can be identified—1) general intellectual; 2) specific academic; 3) creativity; 4) psychosocial or leadership; 5) visual and performing arts; and 6) psychomotor.

- A gift is defined as extraordinary ability or potential in a domain. The gift itself can be focused on one part of that domain, or it can be more general for all aspects of that domain.

- A talent is extraordinary, and often creative, performance or achievement in a specialized field of human endeavor.

- There are many objective and subjective measures one can use to identify a child's gifts.

  A highly gifted child may show a "ceiling effect" on a test and may need to be tested with a measure that has a higher ceiling.

- There are various objective and subjective measures one can choose to identify and document a child's talents.

3

What Else Do You Need to Know about Your Gifted Child?

In the last chapter, you began to learn more about your child's gifts and/or talents. You used the PIP to find in which domains your child's strengths are, and you learned the difference between gifts (potential) and talents (performance), as well as appropriate ways to collect information about these gifts or talents—either objective (measured) or subjective (observed).

Parents probably will not get very far with schools unless they come in with more than a stated belief that their child is gifted or talented. The schools will need to know more of the specifics. Likewise, if parents are bringing a suggested educational plan to the school, it is important that every recommendation in that plan be supported by documented evidence. Remember, the more information—think of it as evidence—you can collect and present in a clear and convincing manner, the more likely you will be to get the school to agree to the suggested plan. At the same time, it does parents no good to collect and present extraneous, anecdotal information that has no direct connection to what they want their child to learn in school. For example, Billy, age six, is much more likely to be perceived as needing gifted services if his parents can provide evidence of his vocabulary (how many words he used at 12 months), oral expression (spoke in full sentences at 15 months), and reading ability (read "easy readers" at four years and chapter books at age five). His needs will be *less* likely to be recognized if his parents simply describe the creative games he makes up when wearing his Superman costume, how he loves to build with blocks, or how easily he remembers people's names in the neighborhood.

For this data collection process to work to your child's benefit, you will need to take the time—perhaps days, weeks, or even a few months—to gather the information on which to base the educational plan. You will need to gather information from all five areas below in order to fully support educational planning:

1. *Cognitive Functioning Information*—evidence of how quickly or how well a child learns.

2. *Learning Strength Information*—evidence of specific areas of high performance.

3. *Personality Characteristics Information*—evidence of specific behaviors and attitudes that enhance school success.

4. *Learning Preferences Information*—evidence of how the child prefers to acquire information and what learning formats are preferred.

5. *Personal Interests Information*—evidence of hobbies and favorite activities that indicate advanced development, areas of intense interest, and school success.

In addition, you will need to compile a comprehensive record of:

6. *Enrichment Activities*—a list of learning opportunities that the child has already engaged in, such as a trip to the Smoky Mountains, a trip to the local zoo, symphony concerts, visits to Grandma in another city, camping with Dad.

and also:

7. *Books Read*—a list of books read alone and at what approximate age to help avoid unnecessary overlap or duplication at school.

Cognitive Functioning Information

The first kind of information to be collected is about the *cognitive functioning* of the child. Cognitive functioning refers to how the child's mind works—how quickly or slowly she picks up information, how she thinks, how she goes about solving problems, how intelligent she is. This information should include both *objective* (using formal, systematic measures such as tests) and *subjective* (using informal measures, such as notes from observations) information to provide the clearest picture of functioning. If you believe your child's gifts lie in either the intellectual domain or in a specific academic ability domain, such as mathematical reasoning or reading comprehension, then it may be necessary to have a professional administer individual tests of ability and/or achievement.

Some objective measures can be administered to a group of students by a teacher or school counselor, but these are not considered as accurate as tests that are administered individually. Individual tests, such as the *Stanford-Binet (L-M)* and the *Wechsler Intelligence Scale for Children, 3rd Edition* (WISC-III), must be administered one-on-one by a certified examiner or psychologist. These tests generally take from 60-110 minutes to administer and will yield an IQ score as well as sub-scale scores from the different sub-test areas. Though outdated in some ways, the *Stanford-Binet* is preferred if you suspect that your child may be highly gifted or performing at the high end of the gifted range. If you do decide to get individual testing, try to find a psychologist who has some training in interpreting these tests for gifted individuals. If you are near a university with a department of psychology, staff members there should be able to make referrals.

Other individual tests of ability and achievement do not require a psychologist, but do require someone trained in test administration. It is rare that any individual test of either ability or achievement will typically be offered to gifted students by the school or district for whom you are collecting information, although it won't hurt to ask. More likely, you will probably need to pay for private testing in order to provide the district with this individualized information.

An IQ score in the range of 120-140 (97th to 98th percentile) on either of the two intelligence tests listed above suggests that your child needs consistent enrichment and modification of the curriculum in his areas of strength, in addition to a possible grade-skip of one year at the time when he is most out of sync with the regular curriculum. A score between 140-160 (99th percentile and above) on such tests suggests the need to consider two, or even three, years' grade-skipping over the course of grades K-12 (but not all at once), in addition to consistent enrichment in all academic areas of the curriculum. A score above 160 IQ suggests minimal years in the K-12 system with some radical forms of acceleration and differentiation, using a formal Individualized Education Plan (IEP).

If your child scores two or more levels above her current grade level on an individual achievement test, such as the *Wechsler Individual Achievement Test* (WIAT), the *Kaufman Tests of Educational Achievement* (KTEA), or the *Woodcock Johnson Achievement Tests* (W-J), this is also a sign that a possible grade-skip and consistent enrichment and differentiation will be a necessary part of the plan you prepare. It is important to note, however, that if your fifth-grade child scores at a ninth-grade, high school grade-equivalent level, this does not automatically mean she has learned everything she needs to know of ninth grade curriculum. What the grade-equivalent level tells you is that the child has the *capability* to do work at that level. Indeed, there will be gaps in some foundation skills that may require brief tutoring. For any of the tests mentioned above, it is important to use an outside professional as the examiner, in every case of objective data collection, in order to maintain the validity and reliability of your data collection process.

If the information to be collected is for a child with creative ability, the tests used for this can be administered by any professional educator who studies the test administration manuals and administers the tests according to protocol. The *Torrance Tests of Creative Thinking* (TTCT) is the most widely used measure of creative thinking and will tell you about the current level of creativity your child shows in both verbal and visual tasks. Since the test is very difficult to score, I recommend you pay the fee to have the test scored by the Torrance Center in Athens, Georgia.

If your child is talented in music, art, or creative writing, use work samples as evidence of the child's talent. If the child has been in a music competition, include notes from the judges. If the child writes poetry, an outside expert can be used to comment on the child's work. This "expert" can be a teacher who judges district poetry contest entries each year. If your child's talent seems to be in dance or theater, look for an expert with training in that area to comment on the child's performance. Scoring tools that use criteria for making ratings arc available and can help external evaluators or art specialists assess the products or performances you offer for their examination. Try to obtain a formal report of functioning in the talent area from an expert to add to the data collection portion of your educational plan. Later chapters list examples of what these external reports might contain or how they might be worded so that they will be taken seriously by the school.

Some subjective assessments of cognitive functioning collected by observation should also be included in your packet of evidence. These usually involve rating how often certain behaviors or characteristics associated with giftedness in the domain are observed by the child's current teacher and/or parent. The most widely used set of scales for teacher use covers 10 domains of ability and performance. It is called the *Scales for Rating Behavioral Characteristics of Superior Students* (Renzulli & Smith, 1977). You will want to order copies of the actual forms from the Creative Learning Press at the address provided in Appendix B. A list of the actual characteristics covered by these scales is shown in Table 3.1. However, it is not recommended that you use the abbreviated form in Table 3.1 to collect information since the abbreviated version does not provide either the rating scale or the specific details of the behaviors being observed. This abbreviated list is shown here only for your information and to show its breadth.

Table 3.1. Ability and Performance Areas Covered by *Renzulli and Smith Scales for Rating Behavioral Characteristics of Superior Students* (Renzulli & Smith, 1977)
Scale 1: Learning Strength
1. Has rich, extensive vocabulary 2. Has large storehouse of information 3. Shows quick mastery and recall 4. Needs to discover the "why" of things 5. Shows ease of higher order processing 6. Is a keen, alert observer 7. Reads widely in difficult materials 8. Reasons things out for self
Scale 2: Motivation
1. Is task oriented and persistent 2. Becomes bored with routine tasks 3. Has no need for external motivators 4. Is self-critical, perfectionistic 5. Is self-directed, independent 6. Demonstrates interest in topics beyond age level 7. Is self-assertive in beliefs 8. Is an organizer 9. Is an evaluator, concerned with ethics
Scale 3: Creativity
1. Is curious 2. Is fluent and flexible in responses 3. Is uninhibited in expressions of opinion 4. Demonstrates risk-taking

Table 3.1. Ability and Performance Areas Covered by *Renzulli and Smith Scales for Rating Behavioral Characteristics of Superior Students* (Renzulli & Smith, 1977) *(continued)*

Scale 3: Creativity *(continued)*

5. Is intellectually playful
6. Has a sense of humor
7. Is self-aware
8. Is appreciative of beauty
9. Is nonconforming
10. Is an evaluator, critical thinker

Scale 4: Leadership

1. Is responsible
2. Shows self-confidence
3. Is well liked
4. Is cooperative
5. Is verbally expressive
6. Shows flexibility
7. Is sociable
8. Dominates, directs
9. Is an active participant
10. Excels at games

Scale 5: Planning

1. Identifies resources needed for tasks
2. Easily relates steps of process to whole
3. Gauges time to accomplish task
4. Foresees consequences
5. Is an organizer
6. Accounts for details
7. Is a strategist
8. Finds alternative solutions
9. Identifies flaws easily
10. Uses sequences easily
11. Analyzes steps in a process

Table 3.1. Ability and Performance Areas Covered by *Renzulli and Smith Scales for Rating Behavioral Characteristics of Superior Students* (Renzulli & Smith, 1977) *(continued)*

Scale 5: Planning *(continued)*

12. Prioritizes
13. Recognizes limitations in resources
14. Provides specifics for a plan
15. Finds alternative methods

Scale 6: Communication Precision

1. Speaks, writes directly
2. Adjusts expression to suit audience
3. Revises, edits clearly
4. Explains clearly
5. Uses descriptive language
6. Expresses thoughts clearly
7. Expresses ideas in multiple forms
8. Describes effectively
9. Uses synonyms readily
10. Expresses ideas in alternative ways
11. Uses many related words/meanings

Scale 7: Communication Expression

1. Uses voice expressively
2. Conveys information nonverbally
3. Is an interesting story teller
4. Uses imaginative language

Scale 8: Dramatic

1. Participates in plays
2. Tells stories easily
3. Uses gestures, expressions
4. Is an adept role player
5. Readily "takes on" a character
6. Is poised

Table 3.1. Ability and Performance Areas Covered by *Renzulli and Smith Scales for Rating Behavioral Characteristics of Superior Students* (Renzulli & Smith, 1977) *(continued)*

Scale 8: Dramatic *(continued)*

7. Makes up plays
8. Is an attention getter
9. Evokes emotions in listeners
10. Is a good imitator

Scale 9: Musical

1. Has a sustained interest in music
2. Recognizes differences in musical elements
3. Shows good auditory memory
4. Loves musical activities
5. Plays instrument (or wants to)
6. Is sensitive to rhythm
7. Is sensitive to background sounds

Scale 10: Artistic

1. Loves art activities
2. Uses art elements readily
3. Makes unique art products
4. Shows concentration on art projects
5. Experiments with media
6. Chooses art in free time
7. Is a keen observer
8. Develops balanced, ordered products
9. Is self-critical
10. Has a high interest in others' art
11. Is elaborative, not imitative

Your plan will be more readily accepted by the school if the actual observation instrument has been completed by the child's current teacher or teachers. A "high" or "superior" strength on an instrument like this would show most items marked as "considerably" or "almost always" characteristics of the child. It will be useful for you, the parent, to complete a set of these rating scales as well, because many times, parents see very different learning and motivational behaviors than the teachers see at school. Ratings from a parent in addition to ratings from one or two teachers will more fully and accurately describe your child's level of cognitive functioning.

Another widely used and valuable source of subjective assessment of cognitive functioning level is the *Purdue Academic Rating Scales* (PARS). If your child has already been in school for a few years (grades four and beyond), this set of scales provides pertinent information about how the child performs in each academic core area (reading, mathematics, science, social studies). Again, you will want to ask a teacher who knows your child to complete these scales, and you might want to complete a set yourself. Addresses for ordering both the Renzulli and the PARS scales are found in Appendix B.

Learning Strengths Information

The second kind of information you will need to collect for your educational plan is *learning strengths information*. In some respects, you started collecting information about your child's learning strengths when you measured his cognitive functioning levels. Teacher rating scales, such as the Renzulli-Smith scales described in Table 3.1, will tell you something about learning strengths (and weaknesses), as will the PIP. But the actual achievement of a high potential child can best be obtained in two other ways.

One way is to have a professional educator administer the school's regular achievement test battery, but not for your child's current grade. Request a version of the test that is *two or more grade levels beyond the current grade* so that you can see exactly what your child has or has not achieved across each curriculum area. The reason for this is that if your child takes the current grade level test, he would score in the 99th percentile, which would be the "ceiling" of the test—that is, the highest he could possibly score. In other words, the test is limited and won't show how much farther he could have gone if he had the chance.

The *Iowa Tests of Basic Skills* (ITBS), the *Stanford Achievement Tests* (SAT), the *Metropolitan Achievement Tests* (MAT), the *Comprehensive Test of Basic Skills*, or the *California Achievement Tests* (CAT) are the standardized achievement test batteries used by most districts. Any of these will give approximately the same information. However, when recording your child's score, be sure to note the grade-level norms to which your child is being compared. A score of 75th percentile will not be a strong argument for grade advancement or curriculum differentiation unless the school realizes that it was on a test two to three grade levels more advanced than the student's current grade.

In order to understand achievement testing and test scores, it is helpful to understand some procedures and terms related to testing. Most schools test whole grade levels once a year using tests such as the *Stanford 9* or *Iowa Test of Basic Skills* or *California Achievement Test.*

The term "standardized" simply means that the tests were developed through pilot-testing in several parts of the country using a standard set of instructions in order to discover whether they were reliable and accurate, and whether they were valid—i.e., they seemed to measure what they were intended to measure. In the test development process, any test items or questions that show different patterns for any social class, ethnic group, or gender are removed. The data are then compiled into an overall database to provide a norm—usually the so-called "normal curve." Thus, when the final form of the test is given, a standard score is computed in a way that tells us how a child scores compared to the national average—that is, how far an individual child performs above or below the average of the national standard sample. However, when we say that a standard score is similar to an IQ score, we must explain that a group test score is never as accurate as an individual test score because group tests have fewer items—and thus are less comprehensive—and also because group tests are given in settings that are likely to have more distractions for the test-taker.

Another way to see a clear picture of your child's actual achievement is through the administration of an individual achievement test, such as the *Wechsler Individual Achievement Test* (WIAT), the *Kaufman Tests of Educational Achievement* (KTEA), or the achievement test battery of the *Woodcock-Johnson Test.* As discussed earlier in the cognitive functioning section, these tests will tell you how your child compares with others his age and at what grade level he has the capacity to function.

The tests mentioned above will report not only what the child does know, but also may show where there may be knowledge gaps are in the different academic areas. These individual tests typically use Standard Scores, somewhat similar to IQ scores, to report the results, making it relatively easy to compare a child's potential with his current development of that potential. Remember, it is important to have an "outside" evaluator administer these tests, such as a current teacher, a gifted education specialist in the local district, a local testing center, or another education professional.

For children farther along in school, from third or fourth grade on up, it is also important to measure how well the child has mastered school or district curriculum basic standards (sometimes called benchmarks or outcomes). This information may be given to parents at a parent/teacher conference, or a parent might request that an assessment along these lines be administered to help in preparing an educational plan. In Minnesota, for example, all children are assessed on mastery of reading, writing, and mathematics standards at grades three, five, and eight. Some states require students to pass or master basic standards before they can move to the next higher grade. Having a child take these assessments "early" might provide valuable information for the child's educational plan.

Among the 50 states, 24 currently have state-developed assessments similar to Minnesota's, and all but two of the remaining states require statewide testing using a commercial achievement test battery, such as those previously mentioned. South Dakota and Nebraska do not require such statewide assessments at present (Cookson & Halberstam, 1998). Check with your state department of education to learn what sort of comprehensive testing is done in public schools. In some states, students who attend private school, charter school, and home-schooled students are required to take the same statewide tests as public school students.

Personality Characteristics and Traits

The third family of information that your educational plan should include involves your child's personality characteristics and traits. The *Parent Inventory for Finding Potential* (PIP) asks questions about your child's learning strengths and personality characteristics that are relevant to learning. Your knowledge about your child's level of confidence, need for independence, persistence, sensitivity to others, and perceptiveness will be helpful in deciding how the child should be educated. For example, a child who is persistent and independent is likely to thrive when given a chance to do an independent study project. A child with little self-confidence or independence may not be a good candidate for grade advancement or for working individually.

Information gained from having a teacher fill out the *Teacher Inventory of Learning Strengths* (TILS) would complement the information gathered on the PIP form. Together, these forms will provide more complete information on personal characteristics that might suggest more or less success with certain options for gifted learners. For example, if both teacher and parent comment on a child's independence in action and persistence in his own interests, then using independent study as an option should be fully supported in the educational plan. If not, other options should be considered. The *Teacher Inventory of Learning Strengths* (TILS) can be found in Appendix A at the end of this book.

A measure of your child's attitudes toward learning will also be helpful information for understanding her characteristics and traits. What excites your child? What are her favorite subjects in school? What does she prefer to do on her own time? There are a variety of measures available commercially that will help you collect this information, but you may wish to adapt the *Interest and Attitudes* series of forms included in Appendix A. Either way, you can get fairly good readings of what motivates your child by looking at what she studies and what she likes about school and learning.

It is important to have your child complete these *Interests and Attitudes* forms at different times rather than at one sitting. Otherwise, the measures will not register her true feelings about each subject area. It is recommended that a break of two or three days occur between measures so that the questioning format is not frustrating. On the *Attitude toward School and Learning* section and the five *Interest and Attitudes* (IA) sections covering the different subject areas, you should compute your child's average score on each of the measures. An average score of 2.67 or higher across all items on a scale (see the scoring instructions at the end of each instrument) would indicate that your child has "motivation" in that subject area, and any average above 3.34 would suggest that your child is "highly motivated" in that subject area—important information to consider when making an educational plan.

Look at the example below of the *Science Interest and Attitudes* form completed by Jodi. When all of her checked answers were added up and divided by the total number of items on the IA, she scored a mean score of 3.58. We can then say that Jodi is "highly motivated" in science.

Table 3.2. Science Interest and Attitudes–Jodi

©2000 by Karen B. Rogers

Child ___Jodi___ Age __14__ Grade __8__ Gender __F__ Date_____

Please check the box that best describes your feelings about the statements below.

Behavior or Characteristic	Very True (1)	True (2)	Sometimes True (3)	Untrue (4)
1. Science is my favorite subject at school.	X			
2. My science teachers are usually the best teachers I have in school.		X		
3. It is important to work hard to be successful in science.	X			
4. I am very good in science.		X		
5. I plan to study science in high school and college.	X			
6. Learning new ideas in science is the most interesting part of class.	X			
7. Doing labs and experiments are the most interesting parts of class.		X		
8. I love to read about science.	X			
9. I try to learn more about science outside of school time.		X		
10. Science is easy for me.	X			
11. I try to do my best work in science and on science tasks.	X			

Table 3.2. Science Interest and Attitudes–Jodi *(continued)*

Behavior or Characteristic	Very True (1)	True (2)	Sometimes True (3)	Untrue (4)
12. I watch science programs on television outside of school.		X		
13. I enjoy visiting science museums and exhibits.	X			
14. I would like to be some sort of scientist someday.	X			
15. I wish I could take more than one science class each day.		X		
16. I could learn anything about science I wanted to if I worked hard enough.		X		
17. I wish most science periods could be longer.	X			

Scoring

Total Score 61 ÷ 17 = Average Score 3.58

10 scores of 4 = 40, plus 7 scores of 3 = 21, yields a Total Score of 61. Dividing the Total Score by 17 gives an average score of 3.58. Conclusion: Highly Motivated!!

Learning Preferences

It is also important to know your child's learning style preferences and personal interests. Renzulli and Smith (1978) developed a learning preference indicator, the *Learning Styles Inventory* (LSI), which allows students to examine how they prefer to learn. This inventory does have some difficulties, however. Because some items mention specific subject areas (and these subject areas may be favorites or distasteful to the child filling out the form), the results could reflect the child's like or dislike of a specific subject matter or a particular teacher's delivery rather than true learning preferences. Despite these flaws, the inventory, is still widely used for collecting information about how a gifted child prefers to learn. If you want to use this measure, it can be ordered from the Creative Learning Press at the address provided in Appendix B.

Another option for determining the learning preferences of your gifted child is to use the *How Do You Like to Learn?* questionnaire (Rogers, 2000) shown in Appendix A. This more general questionnaire allows children to tell what they like or don't like about group learning, individual learning, learning new information, and reviewing old information. Children respond to questions about whether they like receiving instruction by lecture, discussion, peer learning, drill and recitation, projects, independent study, self-instructional experiences, or games, competitions, and simulations. These last nine learning modalities are similar to the ones measured by the Renzulli and Smith *Learning Styles Inventory*.

Information about your child's learning preferences will help you decide if he should be placed in accelerative options or in ability-grouped situations, as well as how his instruction should be delivered. If your child rates all of the individual learning options on the questionnaire as a "preference" or "strong preference," then enrichments involving independent study and individual projects will probably be successful. If your child does not rate learning new information highly, then options for him should probably focus on accelerating the pace of his current learning, rather than adding new and different learning. A learning preferences inventory can provide direct information on both how instruction should be delivered and how instruction should be managed. It also provides insights into possible ways to modify and customize the child's learning opportunities and curriculum.

Your Child's Interests

The last set of information that will help you make an educational plan for your gifted child is information about your child's personal interests. When you read about the *Interest and Attitudes* questionnaires earlier in this chapter, you saw one method of collecting this information. About half of the items on these questionnaires simply ask whether a subject area is of general interest to your child (i.e., she looks forward to science days), and the other half deal with clear motivation in the subject area (i.e., behaviors that indicate interest, such as actually going to science museums or doing science projects at home). Questionnaires provide direct information to educational planners about whether your child's interests are wide-ranging or very narrow and focused. This information will help you determine what kinds of programs and enrichments would be most motivating for her. Knowledge about your child's interests makes it possible for teachers to be much more student-centered in their development of program options.

Your child's out-of-school interests can be measured by asking him a variety of questions about what he would like to do, what roles he would want to play, and what enrichment activities he would like to try outside of school. Renzulli (1977) has developed a tool called the *Interest-a-lyzer*, which is particularly suitable for children between the ages of six and twelve.

It focuses specifically on identifying a child's interests in the following areas: fine arts and crafts, performing arts, literature, science, mathematics, athletics, business, management, judicial areas, and history. It can be ordered from Creative Learning Press listed in Appendix B.

Another instrument, the *Rogers' Interest Inventory* (RII) shown in Appendix A, focuses on the kinds of programs and enrichment activities in which a gifted child might wish to participate. Many of these are activities you and your family can do outside of school, if you are not doing them already. Notice which activities your child wants to engage in most often; this will be a strong indicator of his out-of-school interests.

Now that you have assembled a collection of data on your child from all five families of information, how will all of this knowledge help you form the educational plan that you will need to present to your school? Using Rob "The Brain" and Maria "The Expert" from the previous chapter, you can see how the information about them—their cognitive functioning, learning strengths, learning preferences, and interests—can be documented. Look at Rob's *Data Collector* in Table 3.3, including the "Summary Comments" sections at the bottom of each column. Then look at Maria's *Data Collector* in Table 3.4, and fill in the "Summary Comments" for Maria based on the data in each of the four columns. In Chapter 8, you will practice completing the *Data Collector* for your own child to develop his educational plan. A copy of the *Data Collector* has been included for your use in Appendix A.

As you look at Table 3.3 and 3.4, please note that the following abbreviations have been used.

Abbreviations Key: GE = Grade equivalent; WISC = *Wechsler Intelligence Scale for Children*; CogAT = *Cognitive Abilities Test*; PIP = *Parent Inventory for Finding Potential*; IA = *Interests and Attitudes*; HDLL = *How Do You Like to Learn*; RIL = *Renzulli Interest-a-Lyzer*

Table 3.3. The Data Collector–Rob

©2000 by Karen B. Rogers

Child __Rob "The Brain"__ Age __9__ Gender __M__ Date _____

Cognitive Functioning	Learning Strengths	Learning Preferences	Interests
<u>Objective Measures</u> WISC-III @ age 7-1/2 Verbal IQ: 140 Performance IQ: 131 Full Scale IQ: 136 CogAT @ age 9 IQ equivalent: 132 WIAT @ age 7-1/2 Composite: 99th Percentile Reading Total: 99th Percentile Math Total: 99th Percentile Language Total: 98th Percentile Writing Total: 90th Percentile <u>Subjective Measures</u> Renzulli Scale @ age 9 "Learning": 30 (superior) "Creativity": 30 (high) "Communication Precision": 30 (superior) "Planning": 55 (superior)	<u>Parent Input</u> PIP @ age 7-1/2 Intellectual: 3.89 (gifted) Academic: 3.72 (gifted) Creative: 3.23 (strength) Social: 2.92 (strength) Arts: 1.75 (average) <u>Teacher Input</u> Renzulli Scale @ age 9 "Leadership": 30 (high) "Communication Expression": 14 (superior) "Artistic": 20 (average) "Musical": 20 (high) "Dramatic": 20 (average) TILS @ age 9 Academic: 3.76 (gifted) Personal: 3.25 (strength) Social: 3.01 (strength)	ITBS @ age 9 Total Battery: 98th% Reading Total: 99th% Math Total: 99th% Language Total: 97th% WIAT @ age 7-1/2 Composite: GE 6.5 Reading Composite: GE 8.0 Math Composite: GE 6.9 Language Composite: GE 7.2 Writing Composite: GE 4.0 IA @ 9-1/2 years Reading: highly motivated (3.88) Math: highly motivated (3.52) Science: highly motivated (3.42) Social Studies: highly motivated (3.77) Arts: motivated (2.73) HDLL @ 9-1/2 years Challenge: strong preference (4.52) Group Learning: neutral (3.01)	<u>In School</u> RIL@ age 9-1/2 Reading: high Language Arts: high Mathematics: high Science: high Technology: motivated Social Studies: high Arts: moderate School Attitude: Renzulli Scales @ 9 years "Motivation": 32 (superior) ASL @ 9-1/2 years 3.75- highly motivated <u>Outside of School</u> RII @ 9-1/2 years Building/Crafts: moderate Business: low Collections: low Fine Arts/Design: low Games, Competitions: high History: high Humor: moderate Law/Gov't/Religion: high

Table 3.3. The Data Collector–Rob *(continued)*

Cognitive Functioning	Learning Strengths	Learning Preferences	Interests
	Achievement	Individual Learning: strong preference (4.67)	Nature: moderate
	ITBS @ age 9	New Learning: strong preference (4.88)	Performing Arts: low
	Total Battery: 98th%	Old Learning: dislike (2.51)	Reading: high
	Reading Total: 99th%	Lecture: neutral (3.23)	Research: moderate
	Math Total: 99th%	Discussion: preference (4.16)	Science: moderate
	Language Total: 97th%	Peer Learning: neutral (3.19)	Sci Fi/Fantasy: high
	WIAT @ age 7-1/2	Drill and Recitation: neutral (2.67)	Service/Charity: low
	Composite: GE 6.5	Projects: preference (3.98)	Sports: low
	Reading Composite: GE 8.0	Independent Study: strong preference (4.70)	Technology: moderate
	Math Composite: GE 6.9	Self-Instruction: strong preference (4.42)	Writing: moderate
	Language Composite: GE 7.2	Games, Competitions: strong preference (4.49)	
	Writing Composite: GE 4.0		
Comments	**Comments**	**Comments**	**Comments**
Rob is functioning at 99 percentile of ability and can be considered gifted intellectually, both verbally and non-verbally.	Shows outstanding strengths in intellectual and academic domains; functioning at gifted level for both age and grade comparisons; capable of working several grade levels ahead except for writing.	Reading and social studies are strongest preferences, but highly motivated in all academic areas. Strong learning preferences for self-structured, challenging content acquisition with some interaction for competitions and discussion.	Highly motivated by academic pursuits in school; strong outside interests in reading, history, sci fi/fantasy, and social issues.

Summary Comments

Rob is functioning at the 99th percentile of ability and can be considered gifted intellectually, both verbally and non-verbally. He shows outstanding strengths in intellectual and academic domains; he is functioning at the gifted level for both age and grade comparisons; he is capable of working several grade levels ahead except in writing.

Reading and social studies are his strongest preferences, but he is highly motivated in all academic areas. He has strong learning preferences for self-structured, challenging content acquisition with some interaction through competitions and discussion.

Rob is highly motivated by academic pursuits in school; he has strong outside interests in reading, history, science fiction/fantasy, and social issues.

Table 3.4. The *Data Collector*–Maria

©2000 by Karen B. Rogers

Child *Maria* "*Specialist*" Age _11_ Gender _F_ Date _____

Cognitive Functioning	Learning Strengths	Learning Preferences	Interests
Objective Measures	Parent Input	*IA @ 11 years*	In School
Stanford-Binet @ age 4-1/2	*PIP @ age 11*	*Reading (3.52) highly motivated*	*RIL @ age 11*
IQ: 142	*Intellectual: 3.69 (gifted)*	*Math (2.12) –*	*Reading: high*
Otis Lennon @ age 9	*Academic: 3.87 (gifted)*	*Science (2.67) motivated*	*Language Arts: high*
Verbal IQ: 137	*Creative: 2.69 (strength)*	*Social Studies (3.91) highly motivated*	*Mathematics: –*
Quantitative IQ: 120	*Social: 2.32 (average)*	*Arts (3.0) motivated*	*Science: moderate*
Non-Verbal IQ: 127	*Arts: 2.49 (average)*	*HDLL @ 11 years*	*Technology: –*
WIAT @ age 11		*Challenge: prefer-ence (3.41)*	*Social Studies: high*
Composite: 96th%	Teacher Input	*Group Learning: neutral (3.29)*	*Arts: moderate*
Reading: 99th%	*Renzulli Scales @ age 9-1/2*	*Individual Learning: strong preference (4.72)*	*School Attitude:*
Math: 87th%	*"Leadership": 20 (average)*	*New Learning: strong preference (4.50)*	*Renzulli Scale @ age 9*
Language: 92nd%	*"Communication Expression": 8 (average)*	*Old Learning: neutral (3.01)*	*Motivation: 33 (superior)*
Writing: 95th%	*"Artistic": 22 (average)*	*Lecture: preference (4.16)*	*ASL @ 11 years 3:30- Motivated*
Subjective Measures	*"Musical": 14 (average)*	*Discussion: neutral (3.19)*	Outside of School
RS Scales @ age 11	*"Dramatic": 30 (superior)*	*Peer Learning: dislike (2.19)*	*R11 @ age 11*
Reading	*TILS @ age 11*	*Drill & Recitation: dislike (2.36)*	*Building/Crafts: low*
Math	*Academic: 3.43 (gifted)*	*Projects: preference (3.88)*	*Business: low*
Science	*Personal: 3.20 (strength)*		*Collections: moder-ate*
Social Studies	*Social: 2.51 (average)*		*Fine Arts/Design: moderate*
Renzulli Scales @ age 9			*Games, Competitions: moderate*
"Learning": 26 (high)			*History: high*
"Creativity": 27 (high)			*Humor: low*
"Communication Precision": 31 (superior)			
"Planning": 49 (superior)			

Table 3.4. The Data Collector–Maria *(continued)*

Cognitive Functioning	Learning Strengths	Learning Preferences	Interests
	Achievement MAT 7 @ age 9 Total Battery: 92nd% Reading Total: 98th% Math Total: 84th% Language Total: 90th% WIAT @ age 11 Composite: GE 7:0 Reading Comp: GE 8:5 Math Comp: GE 6:0 Language Comp: GE 7:9 Writing Comp: GE 7:2	independent Study: strong preference (4.61) Self-Instruction: strong preference (4.44) Games, Competitions: preference (4.01)	Outside of School Law/Gov't/Religion: high Nature: moderate Performing Arts: moderate Reading: high Research: high Science: moderate Sci Fi/Fantasy: moderate Service/Charity: high Sports: low Technology: low Writing: moderate
Comments	**Comments**	**Comments**	**Comments**

Abbreviations Key

GE = Grade equivalent; WISC = *Wechsler Intelligence Scale for Children*; CogAT = *Cognitive Abilities Test*; PIP = *Parent Inventory for Finding Potential*; IA = *Interests and Attitudes*; HDLL = *How Do You Like to Learn*; RIL = *Renzulli Interest-a-Lyzer*

Summary

In order to create an effective education plan, it is necessary to collect information from five "families' of information: (1) cognitive functioning; (2) learning strengths; (3) personality characteristics; (4) learning preferences; and (5) personal interests. Sources for this information are: school records, past and present teachers of the child, self-report by the child, parent input, and possibly a professional assessment specialist. A variety of forms are described in this chapter to help parents organize and document the information they collect on their child. Parents should also keep a list of enrichment activities and books read by the child. Collecting all the data will take time, patience, diplomacy, and energy. However, this is the important first step in the development of the education plan, and it sets the foundation and the rationale for all other decisions that will follow. It is important not to rush the data collecting process.

Key Points

- Both objective (test) and subjective (observation) sources of information are important for creating a picture of the gifted child's capabilities.

- The PIP (*Parent Inventory for Finding Potential*) helps collect information about the personality characteristics and personal behaviors of the child that might predict success in learning.

- The *Interest and Attitudes* forms in Appendix A will help you collect information about the in-school and out-of-school interests or passions of the child. This information is useful in designing motivating enrichments for the child in school.

- A learning preferences inventory, such as the *How Do You Like to Learn?* instrument, is useful in making recommendations to a child's teacher.

- It is critical to try to describe the whole child in order to develop the "best" plan.

- The more information the parents have about a child's potential, actual levels of performance, learning behaviors, and personal attitudes, the more relevant and effective will be the plan generated from the information.

4

What Kind of Education
Do You Want
for Your Gifted Child?

In the two previous chapters, you learned how to find and document your child's gifts and talents and how to collect information about the interests, attitudes, personality, and behaviors that will tell the school just who your child is and why you feel some out-of-the-ordinary options may be needed for her. In this chapter, you will begin to learn about what those educational options might be. The following quiz may help to expand your ideas of what is possible. Read each of the five case studies of gifted children below, and see if you can name the educational interventions or options that were made available to these students to better match the curriculum to their academic abilities.

Another Quiz

Chantal

Chantal was almost five years old when she entered kindergarten. From first grade on, she read independently apart from the class and completed the 1-8 basal reading series by grade four. She skipped fifth grade. In grades seven and eight, she was grouped with eight other bright students for enriched classes in typing, foreign language, and creative dramatics. In high school, she was placed in the "accelerated classes" for math, science, social studies, and English. She was allowed to work at her own pace in foreign language and was able to complete four years of high school Latin in two years, and three years of German in one year. During the spring semester of her senior year, she enrolled in two history classes at the local college in the afternoons for credit.

What Gifted Educational Options Were Used with Chantal?

————————————————　　　————————————————
————————————————　　　————————————————
————————————————　　　————————————————
————————————————　　　————————————————

Juan

Juan attended a school that allowed him to move at his own pace for every academic subject from grades one to seven. He skipped eighth grade. In high school, he was placed in honors classes for mathematics, science, and social studies. During the spring semester of his senior year, he enrolled in calculus at the local college, receiving one year's college credit for his work.

What Gifted Educational Options Were Used with Juan?

————————————————　　　————————————————
————————————————　　　————————————————
————————————————　　　————————————————
————————————————　　　————————————————

Ravi

Ravi was tested at age four, and she was found to be reading at the third-grade level with an accompanying high IQ. She was placed in first grade at age 4½ years. From grades one through five, she was grouped with other highly able students in her grade level for advanced instruction in reading and mathematics. In grade seven, she took the Scholastic Aptitude Test (normally given to high school students), achieved a high score, and was invited to participate in an accelerated mathematics program at the local college, where she received two years' high school credit for each year of program participation. In high school, she took advanced or accelerated classes in English, mathematics, science, and social studies. She was allowed to work at her own pace in German, receiving three years' credit in one year's time. In her senior year, she took the Advanced Placement (AP) courses offered at her school in English literature and calculus, scoring 5's on both AP exams. When Ravi entered college, she was given 10 credits of mathematics and six credits of English for her high AP test scores. She took additional placement tests at the university, receiving another 23 credits in foreign language and music theory.

What Gifted Educational Options Were Used with Ravi?

_____	_____
_____	_____
_____	_____
_____	_____

Colin

Colin entered school at the "appropriate" chronological age, even though he was already reading and thinking at advanced levels. In elementary school, he was grouped with other highly able students for enriched instruction in reading and math. In grades three through five, he was also removed from his regular class along with other bright students to participate in interdisciplinary enrichment units in the sciences and humanities. In middle school, he was placed in "advanced" sections of math, social studies, science, and English, and he continued with advanced sections in mathematics and English throughout high school as well. In some academic subjects, particularly social studies and

*science classes at the high school level, Colin was in heteroge-
neous classrooms, where he learned primarily through mixed-
ability cooperative groups. He and his fellow group members
would divide the work on a task they shared, such as answering
textbook questions or writing up a lab report. He took AP
courses and exams in American history and English literature,
and he received six credits, three for each course, in these subjects when he enrolled in college. In his senior year of high
school, Colin took a college course on rhetoric offered at his
school in the morning before classes began, and he received five
credits for it when he was admitted to college. He entered college with a total of 11 college credits.*

What Gifted Educational Options Were Used with Colin?

_____   _____
_____   _____
_____   _____
_____   _____

Jana

*Jana attended an "elementary
school of tomorrow" that was
intent on ensuring that every child could
learn. Jana had her own computer and her
own individualized learning plan (ILP) of activities to practice
in basic skills areas, such as mathematics, language, and reading. She was encouraged to schedule her time to work on her
ILP every day, although, as one of 60 students her "Master
Teacher" was responsible for, she was not regularly supervised
as to whether this was occurring. The teacher assumed that she
was self-directed and responsible enough to do this on her own.
Once every trimester, Jana signed up for general enrichment
units in reading, science, and social studies (three per day), as
did every other student in the school. These units often coordinated with other community facilities, such as museums, business experts, businesses, etc., to provide "real world" experiences for the students involved. Children were divided into*

mixed-ability learning teams in these units. No textbooks were used in any instruction, assignments were cooperatively completed and submitted, and no independent homework assignments were required of any student. Most of the instruction, whether computer-aided or in the "real world" enrichment experiences, focused on problem-solving strategies and developing research skills. Jana (and every other student in the school) was tested using an achievement test battery at the beginning and at the end of each of her three years in this new school.

What Gifted Educational Options Were Used with Jana?

_____	_____
_____	_____
_____	_____
_____	_____

Table 4.1. What Were the Options?
(Answers to the Quiz)

Chantal

- Early Entrance
- Subject Acceleration in Reading
- Grade-Skipping
- Ability Grouping for Enrichment
- Tracking
- Subject Acceleration in Foreign Languages
- Concurrent Enrollment

Juan

- Non-Graded Classes
- Grade-Skipping
- Ability Grouping for Enriched Classes (or Tracking)
- Concurrent Enrollment

Table 4.1. What Were the Options?
(Answers to the Quiz) *(continued)*

Ravi

- Early Entrance/Grade-Skipping
- Regrouping by Achievement Level for Specific Subject Instruction
- Subject Acceleration in Mathematics/SMPY Program
- Ability Grouping for Enriched Classes (or Tracking)
- Subject Acceleration in Foreign Language
- Advanced Placement
- Credit by Examination

Colin

- Regrouping by Achievement Level for Specific Subject Instruction
- Ability Grouping for Enrichment
- Ability Grouping for Enriched Classes (or Tracking)
- Regrouping by Achievement for Specific Subject Instruction
- Advanced Placement
- College-in-the-Schools
- (Note: Mixed-ability cooperative learning is not a gifted option)

Jana

- Individualized Learning Plan (flexible pacing)
- Enrichment in Problem Solving and Research
- (Note: General enrichment, lack of textbook use, and "real world problems" are not options specifically for gifted learners)

Understanding Educational Concepts and Language

The quiz showed that there are many possible educational options for gifted children. The five case studies also listed educational terms that you are likely to encounter, as well as a real mixture of instructional management strategies, instructional delivery strategies, and curriculum modifications. Sometimes all of these terms can be confusing. It will be helpful to define and clarify these options so that making the correct choices and decisions about the education of your gifted child will be easier.

First, it is important to distinguish between the terms *curriculum* and *instruction. Curriculum*, in general, is the *content that a teacher or school plans to teach*. Depending on how broadly or narrowly the term is defined, content is generally the "what" children will be expected to learn. The "what" could be facts and terms, concepts, principles, rules, generalizations, or even standards or outcomes that need to be mastered for state and national level competency tests or exams.

A well thought out curriculum will often have a "scope and sequence" so that teachers know specifically what to teach at each grade level and to what depth or degree they are to teach it. Many experts in the field of gifted education have argued that the general school curriculum does not contain enough breadth or depth of content for bright, eager learners who crave knowledge. As a result, many professionals in gifted education have attempted to develop examples of extensive and broad based "gifted" curricula. Some of the more successful of these curricula and programs will be described in later chapters.

If curriculum is "what" is being taught, the term *instruction* refers to *how the curriculum will be taught*. Components of instruction include: (a) management, (b) delivery, and (c) process modifications.

Managing the Curriculum

The first component of instruction is management, which refers to how children will be grouped (or not grouped) to receive their curriculum. One form of management is called *individualization*, which is further broken down into two separate techniques. Individualization could be *either:* (1) making individual decisions for a single child in how he will either proceed with or bypass the general school curriculum, *or* (2) allowing a group or class of students to move at their own pace through the general school curriculum. Table 4.2 in this chapter lists some of the strategies or techniques that would be examples of individualization.

Another form of instructional management is *grouping* by ability or achievement levels so that different curriculum at the appropriate level can be offered to each group. Grouping by grade level is an attempt to do this, though grade-level grouping makes the assumption that children of the same age are at approximately the same ability or achievement level. A variety of classroom grouping options, all utilizing different amounts of a child's school day, are illustrated in Table 4.2.

Still another form of instructional management is *acceleration*. This method either shortens the number of years a child spends learning the K-12 curriculum or allows a child to work ahead in curriculum that is above her current grade level. Acceleration is often used with gifted children because their rapid learning makes it imperative. There are many ways to offer acceleration to bright children, whether in a single subject, in several subjects, or in entire grades. The right hand column of Table 4.2 shows eight possible forms of acceleration that can be used in the education plan of a gifted or talented child.

Table 4.2. Types of Instructional Management Services for High Potential Children

Individualization	Grouping by Ability or Achievement	Acceleration
• Credit for Prior Learning	• Full-Time Ability Grouping (Tracking)	• Grade-Skipping
• Individual Educational (or Learning) Plan	• Regrouping by Achievement for Subject Instruction	• Early Entrance to School
• Talent Development	• Cluster Grouping	• Single Subject Acceleration
• One-on-One Mentoring or Tutoring	• Partial Day (or Send-Out) Grouping	• Grade Telescoping
• Independent Study	• Within-Class Performance Grouping	• Concurrent Enrollment
• Non-Graded/ Continuous Progress Classes	• Cooperative Grouping with Like-Ability Learners	• Advanced Placement/ International Baccalaureate
• Multigrade Classes	• Cross-Graded Classes	• Early Admission to College
• Compacting		• Credit by Examination

For a brief definition of each of the techniques listed above, see the glossary at the end of this chapter. Chapters 7 and 8 will describe each one in greater detail.

How Is Instruction Delivered?

Instructional delivery—the second component of curriculum—refers to the various strategies and techniques a teacher may use to bring the curriculum to the student. For example, the students in Miss Azar's class are about to begin a unit study of map reading. Miss Azar must decide how she will provide her students with the knowledge and skills she wants them to learn. Will she have them read a geography textbook and discuss what they learn about latitude and longitude? Or will she give them a worksheet with map-reading exercises and let them work out how to solve these exercises individually? Should she form them into three cooperative learning groups called the Nina, the Pinta, and the Santa Maria and have each group draw Christopher Columbus' route through the Caribbean using maps? Or should she come up with some other way of teaching map information to her students?

Renzulli (1975) identified nine instructional delivery modes. These methods, listed briefly below, are described more fully in Table 4.3.

1. *Discussion*–small group or whole class sharing ideas about some idea or concept all have learned in common.

2. *Drill and recitation*–teacher asking specific questions from materials students were responsible for learning.

3. *Projects*–small groups of students working together on a product that reflects their shared learning.

4. *Independent study*–students selecting a topic of interest and working on it individually.

5. *Lecture*–teacher orally sharing the knowledge and skills the students are to learn.

6. *Peer tutoring*–students who have already mastered the curriculum working one-on-one with students who still need to master it.

7. *Programmed instruction*–students working at their own pace through a set of materials that teach the knowledge and skills needed.

8. *Simulations*–students developing a scenario and then practice role-playing to learn knowledge and skills.

9. *Educational games*–competitive quizzes or contests testing whether the students have mastered the required knowledge and skills.

The literature in gifted education provides us with additional strategies or techniques for instruction.

1. *Individual projects*–students working on teacher-developed tasks on their own.

2. *Group projects*–students working in small groups on tasks that are teacher-developed.

3. *New content acquisition*–students learning new knowledge rather than reviewing what has already been learned.

4. *Competitions*–students participating in outside-of-school contests using the knowledge and skills they have learned.

5. *Discovery or problem-based learning*–students discovering on their own the knowledge and skills needed to solve a specific "problem."

6. *Inquiry*–teacher asking questions of students in order for them to discover the knowledge and skills they need.

7. *Group learning*–students learning needed knowledge and skills in small groups, often sharing this with other groups.

8. *Individual learning*–each student learning on his own.

9. *One-on-one tutoring*–an older student or adult working individually with a student to make up for what he does not know or to expand on what he does know.

10. *Learning contracts*–student and teacher formally agreeing on what the student will learn, by what date, and the conditions under which it will be learned.

An offshoot of instructional delivery is *process modification*, a term first introduced by June Maker (1983). This term refers to changing the processes by which a student will learn *or* changing the processes by which a teacher will teach. These modifications include:

1. *Accelerated pace*–teacher varying the amount of time a student is given to learn the knowledge and skills.

2. *Flexible project deadlines*–teacher allowing the student to determine how much time is needed to complete a learning task.

3. *Flexible tasks*–teacher allowing the student to design the task that will result in acquired knowledge and skills.

4. *Higher order thinking*–teacher using thinking processes such as analysis, synthesis, and evaluation to help students learn knowledge and skills.

5. *Open-endedness*–teacher designing questions and tasks that require students to think of many answers or solutions.

6. *Personal goal setting*–teacher helping student set own learning goals and benchmarks of learning progress.

7. *Proof and reasoning*–teacher requiring students to support their arguments and ideas with evidence from their learning materials.

Table 4.3. Instructional Delivery Methods that Teachers Can Use with Gifted Students

Instructional Delivery Method	Definition
Accelerated Pace	Students progress faster as the teacher speeds up rate of presentation of information in order to match the significantly faster learning rate of intellectually and academically gifted learners.
Competitions	Students participate in contests outside of school using the knowledge and skills they have learned.
Discovery Learning	Students find information and answers themselves through active, often hands-on inquiry-based or problem-based learning activities.
Discussion	Students reflect orally on learned information with whole class or small group of students. When questions include conceptualization/ generalization, this is particularly appropriate for gifted students.
Drill and Recitation	Students respond to teacher's one-right-answer questions on mastered materials in a whole class situation, an opportunity to repeat information for those who haven't mastered it yet.
Flexible Project Deadlines	Students negotiate for more or less time to complete a learning experience and its matching product or performance.
Flexible Tasks	Students (or teachers) change the requirements and parameters of a required product or performance.
Group Projects and Group Learning	Group of students work together on teacher-chosen or group-chosen topic, developing either a traditional or nontraditional product of the learning acquired; as a process modification, it requires that the tasks be designed so that bright students will perceive the group product as more valuable than how they think they could have done individually.

Table 4.3. Instructional Delivery Methods that Teachers Can Use with Gifted Students
(continued)

Instructional Delivery Method	Definition
Higher Order Thinking	Students are required to use higher order thinking (application, analysis, synthesis, evaluation, etc.) in their learning responses.
Independent Study	Students research teacher-chosen or self-chosen topic on their own, developing either a traditional or nontraditional product to demonstrate the learning acquired.
Individual Project	Students learn about teacher-chosen or self-chosen topic, which may or may not involve research on own, developing either a traditional or nontraditional product of the learning acquired.
Inquiry	Students respond to teacher-led questioning in order to learn new concepts or draw conclusions and generalizations about what has been learned.
Learning Contracts	Students negotiate individually with teacher about what and how much will be learned and when product will be due; often connected with an independent study or individual project.
Lecture	Students listen and take notes as the teacher presents information to be learned to either whole class or small group of students.
New Content	Students learn new knowledge rather than what is already learned.
One-on-One Tutoring	Students are assigned a special instructor or other content expert to develop their expertise in a specific subject. Most effective when used to enhance learning with gifted children, not to remediate what is missing.
Open-Endedness, Creative Thinking	Students are encouraged to brainstorm or think divergently in order to produce more than one idea, answer, or solution.

Table 4.3. Instructional Delivery Methods that Teachers Can Use with Gifted Students
(continued)

Instructional Delivery Method	Definition
Peer Tutoring	Students are paired with one or more other students to help other students who have not mastered a topic to learn it.
Personal Goal-Setting	Students identify their personal goals and learn how to prioritize their time and activities to reach those goals.
Problem-Based Learning	Students are provided with an unstructured problem/task and are expected to "discover" a method for solving/accomplishing it.
Programmed Instruction	Students proceed at own pace through a set of self-instructional materials, answering the embedded test questions as they occur.
Proof and Reasoning	Students are expected to support their arguments and conclusions with evidence or proof.
Simulations	Students role-play situations or scenarios in order to apply previous learning or find solutions to the problems or situation presented.
Teaching Games	Students participate in a competitive or non-competitive (self or group) game to review previous learning (e.g., "Round the World") or to learn new information.

What Are the Curriculum Modifications?

Now that educational instruction has been described, it is time to go back and look at curriculum to see how it, too, can be modified using additional methods and techniques. June Maker (1983) identifies three components of curriculum—the *content*, the *processes* used to learn, and the *products* or outcomes. The processes, which are the methods that teachers can use for instruction of gifted students, are listed in Table 4.3. A variety of strategies for modifying content and product are appropriate for gifted children, and these are listed in Table 4.4.

As mentioned earlier, the content taught in a curriculum may be composed of the facts and terms of a specific subject, or a series of units or topics that center on a subject area. Content can be the big ideas, concepts, rules, principles, generalizations, or theories of a subject area. Content can also be outcomes or standards for a subject area mandated by a local school board, a state department of education, or a national organization or educational agency.

The *product* component of a curriculum is the actual criterion used to indicate that students have learned the knowledge (content) and skills (process) of the curriculum. In addition to a test or paper, some examples of possible products could include a poem, chart, video, skit, debate, or diorama. The criterion performance or achievement might be designed by a teacher or by the school.

Although you will soon apply these curriculum strategies to your own child in a later chapter, it is important to become acquainted with the possibilities available to you. All of them may be used someday in your child's classroom *instead* of the general curriculum. Looking at these three curriculum components (content, process, product) and modifying them appropriately to match your child's needs are the next steps in changing a gifted child's curriculum *content, tasks,* or *products* she is assigned.

Table 4.4. Content and Product Modifications for Gifted Children

Content Modification Strategy	Definition	Product Modification Strategy	Definition
• Abstraction	Going beyond surface information; symbolism, underlying meaning of content	• Real World Problems or Situations	Providing learners with a problem or situation to solve or work on that is relevant to their own lives
• Complexity	Providing more difficult and intricately detailed content	• Real Audiences	Providing children with experts in a field the child is studying to evaluate child's work; presenting work to a live audience
• Variety	Connecting content and ideas across disciplines	• Transformations	Encouraging nontraditional products and performance that require transforming what has been learned into some visual, dramatic, or other useful form
• Organization	Changing the sequence for how content is taught		
• Study of People	Relating content to the people in the field, famous people, human situations and problems		
• Method of Inquiry	Relating content to how things work, methods that are used in field		

How Do These Modifications Apply to Gifted Children?

This detailed examination of curriculum and instruction can be a little overwhelming. As shown above, there are so many options and strategies available for educational enhancement that often it can be difficult to see how they all really apply to your child. Let us practice with the children we met earlier in Chapter 2.

Each of those children had different intellectual levels, learning strengths, learning preferences, and interests outside and inside school, so each one may require different educational instruction and curriculum. Keep in mind that that these children are composite examples, and the educational matches made for them here may be altered for your own child depending on additional information. For the moment, though, just observe which characteristics and personalities match up best with each instruction and curriculum option. Because you have already examined your child's personality in the previous chapter, soon you will be able to find appropriate educational options that best match his strengths and other characteristics. Please consult the glossary at the end of this chapter if any terms are unfamiliar.

Table 4.5. The Match of Gifted Characteristics and Gifted Provisions

Rob "The Brain" Characteristics	Educational Need/Provision
• Contemplation/ Time to Reflect	• Flexible Project Deadlines
• Thinks in Analogies	• Subject Integration
• Loves to Learn	• Conceptual Discussions, Enrichment Opportunities
• Concentration	• Complex Tasks

Table 4.5. The Match of Gifted Characteristics and Gifted Provisions (continued)

Rob "The Brain" Characteristics	Educational Need/Provision
• Memory	• Complex Tasks, Abstract Thinking, Early Exposure to the Basics
• Problem-Finding	• Problem-Solving Skills Training
• Accelerated Cognitive Development	• Abstract Thinking Tasks, Early Content Mastery, Ability Grouping, Compacting

Maria "The Specialist" Characteristics	Educational Need/Provision
• Intense, Focused Interest and Skill Set	• Mentorship, One-on-One Tutoring, Talent Grouping, Performance Grouping, Compacting
• Intense, Focused Motivation to Learn	• Talent Development
• Self-Criticism	• Individualized Benchmark Setting, Independent Study
• Need to Achieve	• Systematic Feedback, Personal Goal-Setting
• Concentration	• Complex Tasks
• Memory	• Complex Tasks, Early Exposure to the Basics in Specific Talent Area
• Love of Learning	• Conceptual Discussions in Specific Talent Area

Jamal "The Creative Spirit" Characteristics	Educational Need/Provision
• Flexibility	• Open-Endedness, Dilemma Discussions
• Individual Structuring	• Open-Endedness, Creative Problem Solving, Creative Skills Training, Real World Problem Solving
• Risk-Taking	• Personal Goal-Setting, Planning Techniques
• Tolerance for Ambiguity	• Independent Study, Time Management/ Organizational Skills Training

Table 4.5. The Match of Gifted Characteristics and Gifted Provisions *(continued)*

Jamal "The Creative Spirit" Characteristics	Educational Need/Provision
• Flexibility	• Open-Endedness, Dilemma Discussions
• Individual Structuring	• Open-Endedness, Creative Problem Solving, Creative Skills Training, Real World Problem Solving
• Risk-Taking	• Personal Goal-Setting, Planning Techniques
• Tolerance for Ambiguity	• Independent Study, Time Management/ Organizational Skills Training
• Positive Self-Concept	• Group Skills Training
• Inner Locus of Control	• Personal Goal-Setting, Individualized Benchmark Setting
Nicole "The Social Leader" Characteristics	**Educational Need/Provision**
• Backwards Planning	• Planning Techniques, Real World Problems
• Scanning	• Complex Tasks
• Need to Achieve	• Systematic Feedback, Personal Goal-Setting
• Social Cognition	• Group Skills Training, Social Issues/ Dilemma Discussions, Communication Skills Training
• Emotional Stability	• Time Management/Organizational Skills Training, Self-Concept Development
• Perspective-Taking	• Intuitive Expression, Conflict Resolution Tasks
Thao "The Artiste Extraordinaire" Characteristics	**Educational Need/Provision**
• Intense, Focused Interest and Skill Set	• Mentorship, One-on-One Tutoring, Talent Grouping, Talent Exhibition
• Intense, Focused Motivation to Learn	• Talent Development, Subject Integration

Table 4.5. The Match of Gifted Characteristics and Gifted Provisions *(continued)*

Thao "The Artiste Extraordinaire" Characteristics	Educational Need/Provision
• Self-Criticism	• Individualized Benchmark Setting, Independent Study
• Intense Concentration in Art Form	• Complex Tasks, Compacting
• Cognitive Verbal, Visual Matching	• Intuitive Expression, Visualization

Is This Enough or Just a Start?

The descriptive glossary of definitions in Table 4.6 at the end of the chapter, along with the information in Tables 4.3 and 4.4, offers many more options than just those listed for the five high potential children in Table 4.5. As Table 4.6 demonstrates, these educational options could be ones that involve changes in instructional management, modifications in instructional delivery, adaptations through process modification, changes in product modification, or general curriculum modification.

With so many options, how do we know we have picked the right ones? How do we know when we have selected options that will make a difference for a particular child? How do we ensure that Rob gets his craving for new ideas and knowledge filled? How do we make sure Maria picks up the math she needs while learning more about her passion area? How do we ensure that Jamal focuses in on some subject area or field that allows him to extend and enhance his creativity? How do we make certain that Nicole does come to value academic learning, not just all of the other experiences taking place at school? How do we guarantee that Thao is given a balanced education, including one in the cultural arts—history, criticism, and aesthetics of his art form?

On the one hand, you may fear the school has not done enough for your child. On the other hand, when an educational plan becomes too complex and specific, there is less chance that a teacher can carry it out, especially considering his or her other responsibilities. The educational plan has to prioritize and include the most important options, but at the same time take into account that not all of it will get done each year. The plan is something to be revisited on a regular basis in order to decide if it needs to be reprioritized and changed.

Here are some guidelines for setting priorities in educational planning.

Guideline 1. Does it Provide for Academic Progress?

The enhancement of your child's specific gift or talent is the most important educational priority. In other words, if your child is very advanced in mathematics, you will want to request options that will allow your child to extend his math skills and knowledge. If your child is reading well beyond his grade level reading curriculum, you will request options that will allow him to read at the depth and breadth he needs. The academic outcomes in your child's talent areas may include good grades, good scores on tests of achievement and mastery, transformational products or performances, as well as positive academic self-esteem. The key is to provide enhancement that stretches the child beyond what you—and the child—think he is capable of doing. Choosing appropriate management strategies and delivery techniques, coupled with curriculum, process, and product modifications, that allow him to stretch educationally, should be the first priority.

Guideline 2. Does it Remediate Academic Weakness?

The second priority for an educational plan is for it to help the child learn—or relearn or remediate—what she hasn't fully mastered. If a child, for example, has wonderful creative writing abilities, but can't master spelling or capitalization, her ultimate development as a creative writer will be seriously handicapped. The key with her remediation, however, is not to call it or make it the "enrichment" a child receives. The spelling should represent a separate set of "catch up" activities that the child will work on regularly in her own time and which will be checked regularly by a parent or her teachers.

Guideline 3. Does it Enhance Psychological Adjustment?

It is very important that your child's level of self-esteem, motivation to learn, self-efficacy, anxiety, and nervousness also become part of the input as you plan educational options for him. Recent researchers, such as Katharine Hoekman (1998) in Australia, have found that the best way to maintain a gifted child's positive self-concept, motivation to learn, and readiness for new cognitive challenges is for the child to have taken on a challenge he didn't think could be done and then succeed. Dr. Hoekman found much higher levels of anxiety, nervousness, and negative self-esteem among those bright children who have literally never been challenged. This brings us back to the importance of Guideline 1: Academic Progress.

Guideline 4. Does it Provide for Socialization?

Although this goal should not replace the others listed above, finding opportunities for the gifted child to relate to others is yet another positive outcome to consider in educational planning. The key is to not let this goal supplant the others. Far too many teachers, especially those in the primary grades (and again at the middle school level) justify the absence of academic challenge by saying, "This is a year for social development," or "My primary goal is for all of my children to get along." Certainly no one wants war zones for classrooms, but socialization is too often used as a rationalization—or an excuse—for not keeping bright children challenged.

In some cases, by the time they enter kindergarten, gifted children are already processing so differently from their agemates that they may *never* be able to socialize well with age peers. Unfortunately, schools have often seen this as the problem of the bright child, rather than a "problem" of the school's own grouping practices, i.e., grouping children by age.

You will rarely, if ever, hear adults say to a regular ability child, "You need to learn how to get along with children who are gifted." Yet parents of bright children often hear, "Your child needs to learn how to get along with others who are not so bright."

Now that you have a general idea of the "what" you will be trying to include in your child's educational plan, it is time to become much more concrete about what education plans should and should not contain. The next few chapters will explain your next steps in developing an educational plan for your gifted/talented child. Read on!

Table 4.6. Definitions of Gifted Options

Key: IM–Instructional Management; ID–Instructional Delivery; CM–Curriculum Modification; PM–Process Modification; PrM–Product Modification

Ability or Achievement Grouping: Children of high ability or with high achievement levels are put into a separate group for differentiating their instruction. Can be full or part-time, permanent or flexible sorting. **IM**

Abstract Content: Content that goes beyond surface detail and facts to underlying concepts, generalizations, and symbolism. **CM**

Accelerated Pace of Presentation: Substantial increase in tempo of content presentation and acquisition. **ID/PM**

Advanced Placement or International Baccalaureate Courses: Provision of course with advanced or accelerated content at the secondary school level, affording student opportunity to "test out" of or be given credit for completion of college-level coursework. **IM**

Cluster Grouping: Identify and place top 5-8 high ability students in the same grade level in one class with a teacher who likes them, is trained to work with them, and devotes proportional class time to differentiating for them. **IM**

Table 4.6. Definitions of Gifted Options *(continued)*

Key: IM–Instructional Management; ID–Instructional Delivery; CM–Curriculum Modification; PM–Process Modification; PrM–Product Modification

Communication Skills Training: Training in how to express oneself appropriately for full understanding of intention and acceptance of other perspectives. **CM**

Compacted Curriculum/Compacting: Streamlining the regular curriculum to "buy time" for enrichment, accelerated content, and independent study. Usually involves pre-assessment or pre-test of what the student has already mastered. **IM**

Complex Tasks: Providing multiple-step projects for advanced knowledge and skill acquisition. **CM**

Conceptual Discussions: High level discussions of themes, concepts, generalizations, issues, and problems, rather than review of facts, terms, details. **ID**

Concurrent Enrollment: Allowing students to attend classes in more than one building level during the same school year. **IM**

Cooperative Learning Groups: Providing grouped activities for the purpose of developing peer interaction skills and cooperation. May be like- or mixed-ability groups. **IM**

Creative Problem Solving Practice: Training in the six-step Parnes process for identifying a problem, generating possible solutions, selecting the "best" solution, and implementing that solution is the basis for the Future Problem Solving program. **CM**

Creative Skills Training: Training and practice in various creative thinking skills, such as fluency, flexibility, elaboration, risk-taking, SCAMPER, synectics, morphologies, analogies, imagination. **CM**

Credit by Examination: Provision of testing programs whereby the student, after successful completion of a test, will be offered a specified number of course credits. The College Level Examinations Program (CLEP) is the program widely used at the university level. **IM**

Credit for Prior Learning: Allowing students to demonstrate mastery of previously learned material through some form of assessment; same as "testing out." **IM**

Critical Skills Training: Training in critical thinking skills, such as cause and effect, sorting of relevant data, induction, deduction, generalization, etc. **CM**

Table 4.6. Definitions of Gifted Options *(continued)*

Key: IM–Instructional Management; ID–Instructional Delivery; CM–Curriculum Modification; PM–Process Modification; PrM–Product Modification

Cross-Grade/Cross-Age Grouping: Grouping children by their achievement level in a subject area rather than by grade or age level. Currently known as multi-age classrooms. **IM**

Cultural Enrichment in the Arts: Providing knowledge and skills in art, music, theater, dance, creative writing, graphics, particularly the history, aesthetics, and criticism aspects of these art forms. **CM**

Dilemmas, Conflict Resolution Tasks: Providing hypothetical and real ethical dilemmas and conflicts in behavior/intent for discussion, solution, simulation exercises, etc. **CM**

Early Admission to College: Permitting a student to enter college as a full-time student without completion of a high school diploma. **IM**

Early Content Mastery: Giving students access to knowledge and concepts in a content area considerably before expected grade- or age-level expectations. **CM**

Early Entrance to School: Allowing selected gifted children showing readiness to perform schoolwork to enter kindergarten or first grade 1-2 years earlier than the usual beginning age. **IM**

Early Exposure to the Basics: Access to the basic knowledge and skills of the range of academic subject areas considerably before expected age or grade. **CM**

Flexible Project Deadlines: Occasional renegotiation of when projects or assignments will be due, especially when high quality work has already been shown. **ID/PM**

Flexible Tasks: Allowing students to structure their own projects and investigations according to their strengths and interests. **ID/PrM**

Grade-Skipping: Double promoting a student such that he/she bypasses one or more grade levels. **IM**

Grade Telescoping ("Rapid Progress"): Shortening the time of progressing through a school level, such as junior or senior high by one year, while still covering all curriculum. **IM**

Group Skills Training: Training in how to work and communicate as a member of a group, either as leader or participant. **CM**

Table 4.6. Definitions of Gifted Options *(continued)*

Key: IM–Instructional Management; ID–Instructional Delivery; CM–Curriculum Modification; PM–Process Modification; PrM–Product Modification

Higher Order Thinking Skills: Questioning in discussions or providing activities based on processing that requires analysis, synthesis, evaluation, or other critical thinking skills. **PM**

Independent Study Projects: Structured projects agreed upon by student and supervising teacher that allow a student to individually investigate an area of high interest or to advance knowledge. **IM**

Individual Educational/Learning Plans (IEP or ILP or EP): Provision of formal written plan for managing and delivering the curriculum for a child with extraordinary differences in ability or educational needs. **IM**

Individualized "Benchmark" Setting: Working with an individual student to set performance outcomes for the student's next product or performance. **IM**

Intuitive Expression Practice: Providing tasks in which students put themselves "in the shoes of" another person, situation, object through guided imagery, role-playing, etc. **PM**

Learning Contracts: Student and teacher jointly develop a contract for accomplishment of learning outcome(s); often involves a streamlining of regular classwork. **ID**

Like-Ability Cooperative Learning: Organizing groups of learners in three- to four-member teams of like ability and adjusting the group task accordingly. **IM**

Magnet School: Provision of a separate school focused on a specific subject area or areas (arts, math, etc.) or on a specific group of students (academically gifted or mathematically talented) with students gifted in that area. **IM**

Mentoring: Establishment of one-to-one relationship between student and outside-of-school expert in a specific topic area or career. **IM**

Multi-Grade/Multi-Age Classes: Combining two or three grade levels into one classroom and placing the brightest children as the youngest children in the class. **IM**

Non-Graded Classes: Placing learners in a classroom without regard to age or grade and allowing them to work through the materials at a pace and level appropriate to their individual ability and motivational levels. **IM**

Table 4.6. Definitions of Gifted Options *(continued)*

Key: IM–Instructional Management; ID–Instructional Delivery; CM–Curriculum Modification; PM–Process Modification; PrM–Product Modification

One-on-One Tutoring/Mentoring: Placing a gifted student with a personal instructor who will offer curriculum at the appropriate level and pace. **IM**

Open-Ended Assignments: Providing students with tasks and work that do not have single right answers or outcomes. The task may have timelines and a sequence of activities to be accomplished, but outcomes will vary for each student. **PrM**

Organizational Management Training: Training in how to break down projects and goals into manageable and sequential steps and to estimate the time needed to accomplish these steps. **CM**

Partial Day/Send-Out Grouping: Removal of gifted children from a regular classroom for a specified period of time each day or week to work with trained specialist on differentiated curriculum. **IM**

Personal Goal Setting: Teaching students to identify personal goals and how to prioritize time and activities to reach those goals. **ID/PM**

Planning Techniques: Training students in "backwards planning," task analysis, flowcharting, etc. to break down projects and goals into intermediate, manageable sequences of time-related steps. **CM**

Problem-Based Learning: Providing students with unstructured problems or situations for which they must discover the answers, solutions, concepts, or draw conclusions and generalizations. **ID**

Problem-Solving Skills Training: Providing students with problem-solving strategies matched to differing problem types. **PM**

Proof and Reasoning: Requiring students to cite their evidence to support ideas or concepts they generate. **PM**

"Real Audience" Feedback: Using out-of-school experts to evaluate student work in a specialized area of study. **PrM**

Real-Life/"Real World" Learning Experiences: Provision of tasks, projects that relate to current issues and problems in society or student's own world. **PrM**

Regrouping by Performance Level for Specific Subject Instruction: A form of grouping, usually sorted for once a year, that delivers appropriately differentiated curriculum to students at a specific ability or achievement level. **IM**

Table 4.6. Definitions of Gifted Options *(continued)*

Key: IM–Instructional Management; ID–Instructional Delivery; CM–Curriculum Modification; PM–Process Modification; PrM–Product Modification

School for the Gifted: Provision of a separate school with admission requirements that students be identified or "certified" as gifted. **IM**

School-within-a-School: Gifted students are placed in self-contained classes at every grade level in an otherwise heterogeneous school. **IM**

Self-Concept Development: Provision of activities, discussion for the development of self-awareness, self-confidence, and improvement of self-esteem. **CM**

Self-Direction Training: Training in autonomous learning skills, independent thinking, and personal goal setting. **CM**

Service Learning Projects: Provision of academic credit for student volunteer work on community and welfare projects. **CM**

Single-Subject Acceleration: Allowing students to move more quickly through the progression of skills and content mastery in one subject where great advancement or proficiency has been observed; other subjects may be at grade level. **IM**

Social Issues Discussions: Provision of current events, political, philosophical, and social issues for discussion. **CM**

Study of People: Relating a topic of study to the famous people and human issues within that field. **CM**

Subject Integration/"Thematic Approach:" Uniting two or more disciplines and their content through a conceptual theme, such as "origins" or "change" or "friendship." **CM**

Systematic Feedback: Consistent, regular evaluations of student's products, performance, knowledge acquisition for both corrective and reinforcement purposes. **PM**

Systematic Feedback: Consistent, regular evaluations of student's products, performance, knowledge acquisition for corrective and reinforcement purposes. **PM**

Talent/Ability Grouping: Grouping students of like ability or like interest on a regular basis during the school day for pursuit of advanced knowledge in a specific content area. **IM**

Table 4.6. Definitions of Gifted Options *(continued)*

Key: IM–Instructional Management; ID–Instructional Delivery; CM–Curriculum Modification; PM–Process Modification; PrM–Product Modification

Talent Development: Provision of experiences for an individual student with demonstrated high performance or potential in a specific area either through individual work or with a group of students with like talent. **IM**

Talent Exhibition: Providing the venue in which a student may demonstrate individual talents (academic or artistic), such as concert, show, competition, fair, etc. **PrM**

Talent Search Programs: Provision of highly challenging, accelerated learning experiences, usually on a college campus in specific talent area (math, writing) for highly talented students. **IM**

Telescoping of Learning Time: Any technique that shortens the amount of time a student is provided to acquire content and skills, i.e., rapid progress, acceleration, compacting, tempo; can be subject specific or across a grade level. **IM**

Time Management Training: Training in how to make the best use of time available through prioritizing of academic and personal goals. **CM**

Tracking or Full-Time Ability Grouping: Sorting students, usually once a year, by ability level and then scheduling all of their academic (sometimes nonacademic) classes together. **IM**

Transformational Products: Requiring students to show how to use what they have learned by creating a "product" in a nontraditional, often visual medium. **PrM**

Visualization Techniques: Providing students with role-play scenarios or guided imagery that encourages them to create images in their minds. **PM**

Within-Class Ability/Performance Grouping: Sorting of students, topic-by-topic or subject-by-subject within one classroom for the provision of differentiated learning for each group. **IM**

Summary

There are many instructional techniques that a school can use to deliver curriculum (content) to the students. More importantly, there are a variety of ways in which a school can modify the curriculum to make it more appropriate for gifted learners. These modifications include changes in the content itself; changes in the products, performances, or expectations for gifted learners; and changes in the ways teachers actually work with gifted learners. An important part of any educational plan should be outlining as specifically as possible the actual content, process, and product modifications that the gifted child needs in order to have her potential fully developed.

Key Points

- Curriculum is the content, or "what" a school chooses to teach its students.

- Instructional techniques refer to "how" the school and its teachers actually deliver the curriculum.

- Instruction involves making three kinds of decisions:

  1. management—that is, how the children will be organized for learning most effectively.

  2. delivery—that is, what forms the actual instruction will take.

  3. process—that is, how the teacher will teach and how learners will be encouraged to learn.

- Gifted learners have a greater need for their curriculum content, learning processes, and performance or product expectations to be modified.

- Content modifications can include adding (or sub-stituting) abstractions, complexity, variety, organi-zation, study of people, methods of inquiry, and a variety of forms of subject-based acceleration.

- Process modifications can include adding (or substi-tuting) higher-order thinking, open-endedness, group process, freedom of choice, proof and reason-ing, pacing, and flexibility.

- Product modifications can include transformations, real world problems, and real audiences as the ways students might use or demonstrate what they have learned.

5

Subject-Based Acceleration: Which Option Matches Which Child Best at What Age?

Currently, Justin is a nine-year-old third grader whose physical build and coordination are fairly average for third grade. He is a science buff, and he has two close friends in his class who share his intense interest in science. His outside reading is advanced and revolves around exploration of new topics, particularly in the life sciences. His teacher is more than willing to encourage and enrich him in science, if only she knew what to do. Justin's math is also quite advanced (more than two years ahead of his age peers), as is his reading level. His written expression seems to be right at grade level, and his cursive handwriting attempts are very frustrating for both him and his teacher.

Outside of school, Justin's parents have enrolled him in regular science museum classes and have helped him set up a menagerie of small animals in his room. Justin is a keen observer of animal behavior and has attempted to replicate some of the behavioral experiments of Pavlov. Lives of the Cell, *an adult science book by Lewis Thomas, has been Justin's favorite book for the past six months.*

In recent months, Justin has become increasingly less motivated to turn in assignments in all of his classes, including science. Both his teacher and his parents are concerned about beginning patterns of non-producing underachievement.

Thinking that Justin may be bored with the basic third-grade curriculum and may need more advanced work, his parents asked the school whether he should be moved ahead a grade.

Justin's teacher and principal decided to put together a child study team to decide the best course for his future schooling. The first two meetings were spent discussing whether Justin should be skipped to fourth grade for the remainder of the current year or be skipped to fifth grade at the beginning of the next school year. It was ultimately decided that his overall achievement levels, particularly in written language skills, did not warrant a full grade-skip. Justin was a better candidate for subject-based acceleration, especially since the school was not organized for either multi-grade placement or non-graded classes, nor were there sufficient third graders at Justin's ability level to warrant grade telescoping.

At the third team meeting, several subject-based acceleration options were proposed as solutions for Justin's current educational needs, because testing in science, math, and reading (his strongest subjects) showed that he was several grade levels ahead of his third-grade classmates in these areas. Ultimately, a plan was developed that allowed Justin's curriculum to be advanced in these three subjects. The science test determined that Justin's current science knowledge was already at a sixth-grade level. As a result, the school's science specialist agreed to individually mentor Justin two times a week and help him progress through seventh-grade science by the end of the year. In the area of mathematics, Justin's regular third-grade teacher agreed to compact his curriculum by providing him with a more advanced level of math during the regular math time. Justin would work independently on his personal math assignments, but would check with his teacher twice a week for feedback and introduction of new concepts. The district reading specialist agreed to compile a list of high-level books in science for Justin, which would replace his regular reading curriculum whenever pre-testing showed mastery of third-grade reading skills.

The child study team also made plans for Justin to enroll in on-line advanced and accelerated classes in math and sci-

ence when he entered fourth grade. Both Justin and his parents were pleased with this plan.

Were Justin's Options Appropriate?

Justin and his parents were excited by the advanced curriculum he would receive with this plan. It didn't take his parents much time at all to see that Justin's motivation and excitement for learning quickly re-ignited once he began receiving educational content that was appropriately challenging. They did, however, lay out a "T Chart" (a lists of pros and cons), shown in Table 5.1, to make sure they were looking at all possible consequences of the educational decisions being made about their son.

Table 5.1. Justin's T Chart of Subject Acceleration and Compacting

Option	Positives	Negatives
Subject Acceleration in Science and Mathematics	• Chance for exposure to advanced content and skills in specific area of talents and interest • Chance that learning will be more effective because of the faster pacing, less likelihood of developing sloppy habits and diminished persistence • School recognition of his talent • Strengthening of his academic self-esteem because the school chose to do something different with him	• He will not work with agemates on grouped science activities • He will be expected to do much of the work on his own without teacher supervision • Classmates will wonder why he doesn't do the same work they do • May lessen his social self-esteem if classmates treat him as "weird" • Will lack chance to compare his performance in science to others, thereby gaining an inaccurate perception of what he is capable of

Table 5.1. Justin's T Chart of Subject Acceleration and Compacting *(continued)*		
Option	**Positives**	**Negatives**
Compacting in Mathematics and Reading	• Opportunity to master the "basics" of science early so that he can get to the advanced levels earlier • Chance for exposure to advanced content and skills in mathematics • Chance for exposure to subject matter of interest in reading • Elimination of needless repetition of content previously mastered • Teacher recognition of his strengths • Strengthening of his academic self-esteem • For reading, he is provided with balance between work he needs to learn with peers and his own needs for advanced work • Possible prevention of non-production and underachievement	• Because it is always "hard," he may feel he is not as good in it as he originally thought • He will not work with agemates on grouped math tasks • He will be expected to do much of his math on his own without teacher supervision, although teacher is in the room • Classmates may wonder why he doesn't do the same work they do • He will lack chance to compare his performance in math to others • Classmates may not so readily include him in reading discussions and tasks, just because he is not always there • Because his work is always "hard," he may feel he is not as good in math as he originally thought • He may feel "scattered" by frequent changes in how reading is approached

After considering the pros and cons in Table 5.1, Justin's parents decided he would be fine with the subject acceleration in science, despite some possible negative social interaction implications, because he was already used to working on his own at home with his experiments. His close, personal friendships with the other two boys in his class would allow his social life to continue even if this would not take place during science periods. Having his reading and mathematics curriculum compacted would still allow Justin to have some time with his friends, working on concepts and skills he has not yet mastered. His self-directedness (as when he worked on science experiments at home) would work in his favor at school and would keep him from feeling "scattered" when his assignments were modified. Justin and his parents decided that—based on his current grade level, knowledge, and age—the plan was a reasonable one. Justin's parents also knew that if any of these educational and curriculum modifications did not work, they could request another child-study team meeting.

What Are Subject-Based Acceleration Options?

Justin's plan incorporated two different subject-based acceleration options: 1) *single-subject acceleration* in science, and 2) *compacting his curriculum* in both reading and mathematics. These options (or curriculum modifications) allowed him to be exposed to knowledge and skills in these three subject areas when he was developmentally ready. *Subject-based acceleration* can be defined as *any option that allows a gifted student to gain exposure to advanced content and skills beyond the average curriculum standards that are expected for a certain age or grade level.*

The most common subject-based acceleration options are:

- Early Entrance to Kindergarten or First Grade
- Compacting Curriculum
- Single-Subject Acceleration

- Concurrent Enrollment
- Talent Search Programs
- Correspondence Courses
- Independent Study
- Distance Learning
- Advanced Placement Courses
- International Baccalaureate Program
- College-Credit-in-the-School Programs
- Mentorships
- Post-Secondary Options

For the remainder of this chapter, these options will be considered in light of: 1) what each potentially provides for students with gifts and talents, 2) what the research says about each one, 3) when each is most appropriate for a child, 4) considerations that schools and parents must keep in mind when matching a child to the option, and 5) how to decide if the option is successful and should be continued.

Early Entrance to School

Early entrance to school is the practice of admitting a child to school at an age earlier than allowed by the school or school district policy. Early entrance could be as "small" as allowing a child to enter kindergarten a few days or weeks earlier than the mandated age, rather than waiting until the next year, or it could be as "large" an acceleration as allowing a child who normally would be starting kindergarten to enter first grade instead. Early entrance could also mean allowing a four-year-old child to enter kindergarten or allowing a kindergartener to move to first grade halfway through the year.

For any of these cases, the child is unlikely to experience any additional acceleration beyond the early entry unless the teacher has other bright children in the class or has had some special training in how to differentiate curriculum and instruction for bright children. If the early entrance is handled well, neither the school nor the teacher will draw attention to the child's younger age, nor will the child's parents.

What the Research Says about Early Entrance

From 1910 to 1940 in the United States, early entrance in school was a common practice. When parents were ready to send their child to school, they did. Because kindergartens were not consistently established as the first year of school, children often entered first grade with no one very concerned about the child's developmental level, abilities, or social and emotional maturity.

Not surprisingly, the consequences of early entry for these *unselected,* or rather randomly selected, children were frequently negative. Children often did not thrive in the educational environment—academically, socially, or emotionally. Before long, early entrance was seen as negative and harmful. Even as recently as 1991, Eric Jones and Tom Southern surveyed K-3 parents and teachers and discovered that attitudes toward early entrance were still fairly negative, particularly regarding social and emotional issues. Negative attitudes prevailed even when teachers had experienced success with an early entrance child in their classroom. Teachers tended to see successful early entrance children as "exceptions," not the general rule.

As Nancy Robinson and Linda Weimer (1991) explain in their work, there are four different bodies of research regarding early entrance to school. One body of research examines teachers' and administrators' *attitudes* about early entry. A second body of research looks at *unselected* children—that is, children who entered school early and thus were comparatively younger than their classmates in kindergarten or first grade, but who were *not* identified as high ability or high potential. A third body of research focuses on selected children—that is, *gifted* children who entered school early. (Of course, these studies are the most relevant for examining whether early entrance should be used with gifted children.) Finally, the fourth area of research contains *retrospective* studies—that is, looking back at what happened to early entrants over the course of their K-12 school years.

My synthesis of the best evidence located 68 individual studies of early entrance (1919-1981) and 13 reviews of research on the subject (1933-1990). In only two of the 13 reviews of research did the authors—when they drew their conclusions— make any distinction between unselected (non-gifted) and selected (gifted) children. It is interesting, too, that approximately two-thirds of the reviews occurred during the 1960s—a time when the practice was already being discouraged by educators.

As for the 68 individual studies, all were supposed to be contained in the various reviews of research; however, these studies were never consistently included. Of these 68 investigations, 43 looked at unselected children rather than children who had been identified as gifted. Further, 37 of the studies based their conclusions on subjective or opinion results, and only six of the 43 offered data-based results.

There were 49 studies that used a retrospective approach, and 19 of these studies looked at children who had been selected for their advanced ability and high potential. The remaining 30 studies used unselected samples—that is, children who had entered school early without clear academic criteria or evidence of high intellectual potential. All 49 studies focused on what happened to the children over the course of their schooling.

For selected children—that is, gifted children between the ages three and six—the academic effect size was about a half-year's jump in achievement. That is, gifted children who were allowed early entrance were on the average six months ahead in their achievement as compared to their age peers. In addition, both socialization and self-esteem improved slightly. For unselected children, there was no merit academically, and there were some social and emotional difficulties if they did enter school early. No studies addressed the issue of whether girls were more successful with early entry than boys, although there were several opinion articles (usually referring to unselected children) in which the authors argued that boys might find early entrance more detrimental than girls.

Unquestionably, when a gifted child enters school early, the teacher plays a crucial role in helping the child adjust. He must talk to her occasionally about how she likes the class. If the teacher sees any teasing going on, like "Ginnie is a whole year younger—she's too little to be in kindergarten," he can talk with the other students to help them understand the situation better. One advantage of early entrance is that when the child starts at the beginning of the school year with the others in the class, no issue needs to be made about the fact that she is younger.

When is Early Entrance Appropriate?

The gifted child who likely will benefit most from early entrance will have many of the characteristics outlined in this table.

Table 5.2. Candidate for Early Entrance			
Cognitive Functioning	**Personal Characteristics**	**Learning Preferences**	**Interests**
Is processing and achieving well above age peers	*Is independent and motivated*	*Enjoys visual and small motor activities*	*Likes academic work and has exhausted what preschool can offer*
• Scores as moderately or highly gifted on individual intelligence test (>130)	• Wants to start school • Is highly motivated to learn • Is comfortable with older children • Has longer attention span than age peers	• Has preference for reading and/or math activities • Demonstrates consistent participation in small motor activities and close-range visual tasks	• Likes reading activities • Likes math activities • Had wide-ranging interests in previous preschool situations

Table 5.2. Candidate for Early Entrance *(continued)*

Cognitive Functioning	Personal Characteristics	Learning Preferences	Interests
Is processing and achieving well above age peers	*Is independent and motivated*	*Enjoys visual and small motor activities*	*Likes academic work and has exhausted what preschool can offer*
• Shows readiness for reading and good math reasoning, or is already reading and calculating	• Is socially mature, emotionally stable, perceptive, confident • Is independent in action	• Likes being challenged and perceives school as a place to learn	

How Parents and Educators Will Know if Early Entrance Is Working

Evaluation of the effects of an early entry decision needs to occur frequently during the first two to three months of the transition to ensure successful adaptation of the child (and the teacher) to the new situation and setting. All members of the child study team who helped make the decision for early entrance should be a part of this monitoring. A wise approach is to consider this time a "trial period" which can be offered to the child with the understanding that if it is not working, a change can be made. After the first few months, monitoring should focus on the achievement of the child at the end of the first full year in school, and relevant data should be collected, including an interview with both the child and the teacher. Parents and school administrators should ask themselves these questions:

1. Did the child progress as well as the brighter students in the class in most academic areas?

2. Was the child comfortable with the school routine and teacher?

3. Has the child made friends within the class?

4. Does the child see himself generally as a "good" learner?

If parents and school personnel can answer "yes" to these questions based on the child's current achievement and information from the teachers, then early entrance has worked well and needs little further monitoring.

Compacting the Curriculum

Although this practice has been around for several decades, the term "compacting" was first defined by Joseph Renzulli and Linda Smith in 1978. Compacting means streamlining or shortening the regular school curriculum in a specific subject area by pre-assessing the gifted child to discover what she has already mastered in the curriculum, and then replacing the areas mastered with replacement learning experiences or curricula that are new or more appropriate. What makes compacting different from subject acceleration is that the child's actual levels of subject mastery are assessed, and this becomes the basis for what the child will learn next. Curriculum compacting therefore involves both diagnosis (pre-testing or assessing what is already known) and prescription (replacement experience planning). In the last century, and up until 1978, this procedure was called "compression," because it was seen to reduce the number of times children would repeat or review what they already knew.

What the Research Says about Curriculum Compacting

Curriculum compacting has become increasingly important for gifted children due to the slower learning pace in most classrooms and the reduced level of curriculum complexity that so often occurs. Current studies have found that 75-85%

of elementary school students of average or above average ability can pass subject *pre-tests* with 92-93% accuracy. Similar findings have been found for fourth, eighth, and eleventh graders in science and social studies curricula in several states. This means that grade-level curriculum is often too basic and unchallenging for bright learners, as well as for many other learners. Clearly the typical curriculum—at least as reflected in the pre-tests—is set at a low level that would suggest that unless new material is added, gifted children will be stuck in a situation where they are repeating information they already know during virtually all of their time in the classroom. Compacting the curriculum is one form of acceleration that can provide them with more learning and stimulation.

Drs. Joseph Renzulli and Sally Reis (1992) directed a large national study, which found that elementary teachers could eliminate—with no detrimental effects on the students' measures of achievement—up to 40-50% of the regular curriculum in language arts and mathematics for the top 10-15% of students. Up to 80% of the curriculum at grade level could be eliminated for extremely bright students.

In a startling national report (*A Nation at Risk,* 1981), former Education Secretary Terrel Bell stated that the difficulty levels of current textbooks have declined by two grade levels during the past decade and a half. Since that report and others like it, this distressing trend has sometimes been referred to as the "dumbing down of curriculum." These findings add support to the option of curriculum compacting, which would allow brighter children to advance to a level of work that is actually challenging to them. To not do so will waste both their time and ability.

Curriculum compacting for students requires several steps to successfully put into practice. A teacher must first identify what essential information she wants her students to learn in the particular subject or subject area. Then she must develop pre-tests—ways to assess how much of this essential information has already been mastered by the advanced students targeted for this pre-assessment. It is important to note that the assessment does not necessarily need to be an objective, paper and pencil test. Pre-testing assessment can be done through 1) informal discussions with the child, 2) having the child brainstorm what she already knows on a topic, 3) reviewing the child's previous performance in the subject area, 4) conducting a formal interview with the child, or 5) observing how the child performs on a particular task representing learning outcomes in the area.

Next, the educator develops one or more criteria, along with the level of achievement she will accept as "evidence" that the child has mastered the essential outcomes. For example, if the child scores at least 85% on this test, that constitutes reasonable mastery. Pre-test assessments, formal or informal, are then administered to the child (or children), and—where a child demonstrates mastery—a plan is developed for replacing the time thus "gained." Often, this plan also accounts for how specific gaps in the child's learning will be remediated during this time. Examples of what these plans look like and what they might encompass can be found in publications by Renzulli and Reis (1992) and Winebrenner (1990).

It is possible to do too much compacting, however. I was involved in an extensive compaction and enrichment project for students in a small, rural school district. Fourth-grade teachers from each school in the district designed pre-assessments and compacting plans for *all* academic areas. Each teacher was assigned to a specific subject area so that all areas would be covered, and with monthly planning meetings, each teacher used the compacting plan and the corresponding enrichment activities in his/her classroom.

This compacting method continued until January of the school year, when the teachers reported that students were "stressed" because of the fast pace of their learning. Apparently, being compacted and enriched or accelerated in *all* academic areas *all* of the time didn't allow the children sufficient time to just sit back and "digest" what they were learning. Through trial and error over the course of the year, it was determined that alternating two areas for compacting and enrichment per month was enough to keep students motivated, alert, and relatively stress-free.

My search for actual research studies that document the effects of curriculum compacting located 10 studies, done from 1959-1992. All but two of these studies examined the effects on gifted children in grade levels from K-6. The academic effect for K-6 gifted students was very positive when replacement activities in math or science were appropriately presented. This means that when high potential students were excused from reviewing what they already knew and started at the point at which they did not know math and science, and then proceeded at a faster pace than "normal" for a regular classroom, they achieved an additional four-fifths of a year's curriculum for each year they participated in this type of curriculum modification. In the case of subjects such as math and science where skills and concepts build on each other sequentially, the replacement activities used are often accelerated. In other words, the children are allowed to move ahead in their science and math learning, even if that means moving into the next school year's work.

One study of fourth-grade students examined the effects of compacting in language arts, reading, science, math, and social studies, but in this study, the replacement activities involved fewer accelerative options; instead, the replacement activities were ones involving enrichment, peer tutoring, cooperative learning tasks, and correcting class papers. Not surprisingly, a smaller effect on achievement was reported. Even so, some academic gains were made, particularly if the replacement activities involved exposure to content that was more complex (i.e., broader and deeper), considered appropriate for high ability students.

None of the research studies reported possible social or emotional effects for either acceleration or enrichment replacement activities involved with compacting. One could predict, however, that a child who is regularly challenged through compacted curriculum would maintain a positive attitude toward learning and toward the subject area and would feel competent as a learner. On the other hand, if compacting is only used for an individual child, opportunities for socializing with his age peers will be fewer as he works farther ahead in the curriculum. For a child with less than satisfactory social skills, this could be a concern.

As a remedy for this loss of social interaction, Dr. Sally Reis and her associates at the University of Connecticut have developed the idea of *group* compacting plans, which would allow several students with high ability in the same area to learn together. This form of compacting, if studies are ever conducted on it, may prove helpful for the social interactions for gifted learners.

Which Children Need Curriculum Compacting?

The gifted child most likely to be successful with compacted curriculum will have many of the following characteristics listed in the chart below.

Table 5.3. Candidate for Curriculum Compacting			
Cognitive Functioning	**Personal Characteristics**	**Learning Preferences**	**Interests**
Is achieving at a substantially higher level than most of classmates	*Demonstrates motivation to learn, persistence, independence*	*Exhibits willingness to work alone or in small groups on self-instructional tasks*	*Demonstrates interest in compacted area and boredom with routine learning*
• Pre-assessment demonstrates mastery at or above established criterion level on topic or subject-specific measure of outcomes (usually > 85%)	• Is highly motivated to learn in compacted area • Has strong achievement need • Is persistent in assigned tasks and own interests	• Has preference for challenge and skipping what is already known • Prefers individual and small group projects	• Has high interest in compacted area • Has wide-ranging academic interests • Shows a lack of patience with routine academic tasks

Cognitive Functioning	Personal Characteristics	Learning Preferences	Interests
Table 5.3. Candidate for Curriculum Compacting *(continued)*			
Is achieving at a substantially higher level than most of classmates	*Demonstrates motivation to learn, persistence, independence*	*Exhibits willingness to work alone or in small groups on self-instructional tasks*	*Demonstrates interest in compacted area and boredom with routine learning*
	• Is independent in thought and action, self-directed in learning • Makes connections, associations easily • Demonstrates confidence • Is intense and focused when learning • Processes information quickly	• Prefers self-instructional learning and independent study • Dislikes drill and recitation, whole class learning experiences, and peer tutoring	

How Can We Monitor the Success of Curriculum Compacting?

The child's progress should be monitored frequently, particularly concerning the replacement curriculum experiences. If the child does not continue to advance in her learning, begins to exhibit disruptive behavior during replacement activity time, or demonstrates increased stress or unhappiness at being separated from what the rest of the class is doing, then the compacting plan should be gradually and gracefully phased out.

Curriculum compacting should be systematically considered for most gifted children in third grade or higher. Some younger children who have strong skills for self-direction, however, will also benefit from this option. Once gifted students reach a place where they can choose advanced levels in their classes, compacting is not so necessary.

If teachers and parents can say "yes" to the following questions, then curriculum compacting has probably been a successful educational option for the child.

1. Is the child progressing satisfactorily on the replacement activities or tasks assigned?

2. Does the child express personal satisfaction with what she is learning?

3. Does the child continue to maintain satisfactory and appropriate social relationships within her classroom peers?

4. Has the child managed to remediate most "gaps" in knowledge that were identified through the use of pre-assessment test on a specific subject?

5. Does the child wish to continue to have curriculum compacted in the subject area?

Single-Subject Acceleration

Single-subject acceleration curriculum modification allows a gifted student—where substantial advancement or proficiency has been observed in a particular area—to bypass, skip, or move more rapidly through the usual progression of skills and content mastery in that single subject area. In most cases, the student continues to progress in other subjects at the regular pace of those "regular" classes.

For the purposes of this chapter, single-subject acceleration is defined as the delivery of the curriculum by either physically moving the child into a higher grade level within the same building for instruction or by having him work with the higher grade level curriculum in his own age-based classroom.

This usually means that a child is allowed to work on curriculum in a specific area, such as math or science, that is one, two, or three or more years ahead of the child's actual grade level. The child *may* go to another classroom—in a higher grade level—to do this, or more likely, the advanced curriculum will be given to the child to work on independently in his own classroom with occasional help from his grade-level teacher or perhaps under supervision from the higher grade-level teacher. Single-subject acceleration is related to— but is different from—curriculum compacting. Both allow the child to avoid repetition of the grade-level curriculum he has already mastered. Compacting usually provides enrichment that is broader and deeper in most subjects; however, compacting may also involve working ahead and actually may become subject acceleration. Subject acceleration involves working on curriculum that ordinarily would be found at a higher grade level.

I worked with a fourth-grade boy who was systematically accelerated, subject by subject, in every academic subject area. The cumulative effect of these single-subject accelerations allowed him to complete all of his sixth-grade work by the end of his fourth-grade year. This was preferred by the child and his parents rather than a single grade-skip of two years, which would have put him in junior high two years early. This example illustrates subject acceleration that is so extensive that it almost qualifies for grade-based acceleration (grade-skipping). The approach helped his parents delay a grade-skipping decision until they felt he was ready for it.

Subject acceleration can also be thought of as a more generic term for many of the separate options included in this chapter. Talent Search programs, Advanced Placement, Concurrent Enrollment, even Mentorships and Post-Secondary Options are all ways to deliver advanced content and skills beyond age- and grade-level expectations in a different kind of program option. In each case, the student is allowed to move at a rapid pace through curriculum content and work well beyond her actual grade level in a specific area.

What the Research Says about Single-Subject Acceleration

In my synthesis of the best research evidence on single-subject acceleration, I located 21 studies, ranging from 1959-1987. All but one study looked at this practice with gifted children in grades two to twelve. Most of the studies examined acceleration in mathematics, two studies examined acceleration in reading, and two looked at subject acceleration in science. These studies showed that the academic achievement gains of the students were very positive—about three-fifths of a year's additional educational growth for each year that the students were engaged in subject acceleration.

There were no studies that measured the social effects of subject acceleration. Two studies looked at psychological adjustment and found that anxiety level declined, but also that academic self-concept declined somewhat. Whether or not this mixed outcome would be found in other programs is uncertain. More research is needed before it can be assumed that single-subject acceleration causes a slight decline in self-esteem. Such studies should particularly focus on the way the programs are run, who leads them, and how expectations for performance are communicated to students.

With Which Children Is Single-Subject Acceleration Appropriate?

The gifted child most likely to be successful with single-subject acceleration will have many of the characteristics listed in the following table.

Table 5.4. Candidate for Single-Subject Acceleration

Cognitive Functioning	Personal Characteristics	Learning Preferences	Interests
Is processing and achieving well beyond others at same grade level in a specific subject area	*Is self-directed, independent, and motivated to learn*	*Enjoys individual learning and challenge in learning experiences*	*Strong interest in specific academic area with little time to supplement learning outside of school time*
• Has above average ability • Is achieving 2+ grade levels beyond current grade in specific subject area • Possesses strong achievement need • Shows learning strengths in planning, learning, and communication precision	• Is independent in thought and action • Is persistent in own interests, assigned tasks • Enjoys school and learning • Makes connections and associations • Is a fast processor and retains information easily • Is socially mature, emotionally stable, perceptive, confident, and shows a willingness to take risks	• Has strong preference for independent study, self-instructional materials • Demonstrates preference for challenge and fast pacing of instruction • Likes being in competitive situations	• Has intense interest in specific academic area • Has extensive involvement in a variety of out-of-school interests

Monitoring Children in Single-Subject Acceleration

Monitoring the child participating in single-subject acceleration should be frequent throughout the first semester. This will ensure that the child is keeping up, is actually learning the new skills and knowledge base adequately, and is working effectively alone (or in the older class).

If parents and school can answer "yes" to the five questions below, single-subject acceleration is probably working successfully for the child.

1. Is the student "keeping up" with expectations for the older class materials?

2. Is the student "comfortable" with where and how she is learning?

3. Has the student sufficient opportunity to interact with classmates (either the older ones or like-age ones)?

4. Are the teachers providing sufficient supervision of the student's work?

5. Does the student wish to continue learning in this manner?

Concurrent Enrollment

Concurrent enrollment, sometimes called "dual enrollment," refers to the practice of allowing a high potential student to attend classes in more than one building level during the same school year. For example, a junior high or middle school student might attend high school for part of the school day, or a high school student might attend college for part of the day, but will also attend his "regular" level classes for a part of each day.

Concurrent enrollment is most easily carried out when the buildings for the two levels are physically close together, so that the student can just walk from a class in one building to a class in the other. It is also helpful if the school district has transportation available between buildings that are not physically close. Large districts with extensive magnet school programs, for example, often have this type of transportation plan already in place. Perhaps the most critical issue involving the success of the concurrent (or dual) enrollment program is whether or not the student can move gracefully within two schools' schedules without having to show up late for classes already in progress.

One way to facilitate programs of this sort is to devote one-half day to one building level and one-half day to another. For example, a high school student might attend a local community college for math and science instruction each morning but return to high school in the afternoon for social studies, English, and foreign language classes. The lunch hour is used for both travel and lunch. Some of the most successful concurrent enrollment programs that I have observed offered this option to a small group of students who were transported as a group from one building to another and enjoyed some socialization with each other during the travel and lunch times.

What Research Says about Concurrent Enrollment

My synthesis of research on concurrent enrollment located 36 studies from 1959-1988. All of the studies except one included gifted students. Half of the studies looked at concurrent enrollment during the junior high or middle level school years, and half were studies of high school students attending college on a part-time basis. The academic gains across these studies were small but positive. Unfortunately, the majority of studies that measured academic achievement used current-grade-level tests of achievement to compare the concurrent enrollment students with their agemates in high school. In other words, eighth graders who took a ninth-grade course were still being measured with an eighth-grade achievement test. They were never tested on new content they may have learned in the more challenging course. With appropriate measures of what was learned, it is likely that subject-accelerated students would make substantial academic gains. Further research needs to be done to test this hypothesis.

The effect of concurrent enrollment on social skills for both middle school and high school gifted students was negligible in these studies. In other words, these students socialized in much the same way at both buildings as students who stayed at only one building level. The effect on emotional status, however, was very positive, with the greatest gains being exhibited in overall self-esteem, behavioral conduct, and views of themselves as creative thinkers.

With Which Students Is Concurrent Enrollment Appropriate?

Because of the daily exposure to advanced content and older peers, a gifted learner should have the characteristics below.

Table 5.5. Candidate for Concurrent Enrollment			
Cognitive Functioning	**Personal Characteristics**	**Learning Preferences**	**Interests**
Is processing and achieving well beyond others at same grade level in a specific academic area	*Is independent, self-directed, and motivated to learn*	*Enjoys a variety of delivery methods and challenge in learning experiences*	*Strong interest in specific academic area with little time to supplement learning outside of school time*
• Has above average ability • Is achieving 2+ grade levels beyond current grade in specific subject area • Possesses strong achievement need • Shows strength in planning and communication precision	• Enjoys school and learning • Shows independence in thought and action • Is persistent in own interests, assigned tasks • Is accepting of others, yet dominant • Is socially mature, emotionally stable, perceptive, confident, self-aware	• Has strong preferences for most forms of instructional delivery, except independent study • Prefers challenging, fast-paced instruction • Enjoys competitive situations	• Has intense interest in specific academic area • Has wide-ranging academic interests • Is actively involved in a variety of out-of-school activities • Shows little enthusiasm for the extra-curriculars offered at current building level

How Can We Monitor the Success of Concurrent Enrollment?

At the elementary or middle school levels, frequent monitoring of this acceleration option is critical, particularly during the first term. In a high school-to-college option, collection of interview and achievement information is not so critical at the beginning. End of the semester information is probably sufficient.

If the school, student, and parents can answer "yes" to the following questions, then concurrent enrollment is a successful option for the student.

1. Does the student think he has "done well" in the higher-level class(es)? Is he willing to live with somewhat lower grades that might be forthcoming from a more competitive setting at the higher level of schooling?

2. Do the student's grades in the higher-level course(s) suggest satisfactory progress for his level of ability?

3. Has the student been able to make social contacts at the higher level while maintaining friendships at the lower school level?

4. Is the student interested in continuing with this option?

Talent Search Programs

The idea for Talent Search programs was initially proposed and conceived by Professor Julian Stanley at Johns Hopkins University as an option for highly gifted middle school or junior high students who performed well on the Scholastic Aptitude Test (SAT) at a significantly earlier age than when the test would normally be taken (high school). In 1974, The Center for Talented Youth (CTY) began offering the Baltimore, Maryland, schools advanced classes in mathematics, science, the classics (Greek and Latin), German, and writing. These courses were offered throughout the school year, after the regular school day or on Saturdays on the college campus, and were offered more extensively in summer.

Since CTY began, other Talent Search programs have proliferated, including the Rocky Mountain Talent Search in Denver, Colorado, the Midwest Talent Search in St. Paul, Minnesota, the Wisconsin Center for Academically Talented Youth, the Center for Talent Development at Northwestern University in Evanston, Illinois, the Center for Academic Precocity at Arizona State University in Tempe, Arizona, and the Duke University Talent Search program in Durham, North Carolina. Since 1974, literally thousands of gifted middle school students each year have pursued advanced high school and college-level coursework on these college campuses outside of their regular school time, often just for the sheer joy of learning something new and challenging.

In order to qualify for these programs, students must be in the top 1% of performance when compared to their age peers. The Educational Testing Service has established norms for grades seven through eight performance on the SAT and the American College Testing examination (ACT), and over 140,000 younger students take these tests annually. A listing of Talent Search programs offered is shown in Table 5.6 along with addresses and contact information.

Table 5.6. Some Talent Search and Other Accelerated Programs

Center for Talented Youth (CTY) Johns Hopkins University

Institute for the Academic Advancement of Youth
 Johns Hopkins University
 3400 N. Charles Street
 Baltimore, MD 21218
 410-516-0337
 //jhunix.hcf.jhu.edu/~ewt2

Program

• Talent Search summer programs

• Expository Writing Tutorial-by-mail program

• SMPY math, science, English year-long programs

• *Imagine* magazine for GT learners

Duke University Talent Identification Program (TIP)

Duke University
 1121 W. Main Street
 Suite 100
 Durham, NC 27701
 919-683-1400
 tip@duke.edu

Program

• Talent Search summer programs

• Scholar weekends during year

• Learn-on-your-own program: Graphics Calculator Program

Educational Program for Gifted Youth (EPGY), Stanford University

Ventura Hall
 Stanford, CA 94305
 415-723-0512
 ravaglia@csli.stanford.edu

Program

• Distance learning via computer in mathematics, science, humanities,
 year-long

Table 5.6. Some Talent Search and Other Accelerated Programs *(continued)*

Northwestern Center for Talent Development (CTD)

Northwestern University
  617 Dartmouth Place
  Evanston, IL 60208
  708-491-3782
  //ctdnet.nwm.edu

Program

- Talent Search summer programs
- Expository Writing Tutorial-by-mail program
- Midwest Talent Search Program
- Talent Search summer programs

University of Minnesota Program of Teaching for Youth who are Mathematically Precocious (UMPTYMP)

Vincent Hall 115
  206 Church Street S.E.
  Minneapolis, MN 55455
  612-625-2861
  keynes@math.umn.edu

Program

- Explore Testing
- Year-long mathematics programs

Wisconsin CTY (WCATY)

2909 Landmark Place
  Madison, WI 53713
  608-271-1617
  eschatz@madison.tds.net

Program

- Talent Search summer programs (3-12) for Wisconsin citizens only

What the Research Says about Talent Search Programs

The majority of research that exists on this option has been produced at Johns Hopkins, Northwestern, and Duke Universities. Much of the case study research at Johns Hopkins has focused on academic outcomes, and although there were no mathematical calculations of effectiveness, this research clearly suggests substantial academic gains for these bright students in their specific areas of expertise. The Northwestern University research, primarily under the auspices of Paula Olzewski-Kubilius, has focused on the social and emotional adjustments of these students during their on-campus experiences. Similarly, Duke University's Talent Identification Program has reported extensively on the personal characteristics and family demographics of the students who choose to participate there. Both the Northwestern and Duke programs report that students thrive socially and emotionally in these Talent Search opportunities.

My own research with the Wisconsin Center for Academically Talented Youth (WCATY) in Madison, Wisconsin—one replication of a Talent Search summer program—found that these students attended the program primarily to learn what they have no opportunity to learn during the regular school year in their home schools. They left very satisfied with their academic experiences, but even more so with the social relationships and lasting friendships that they formed during the few weeks they were together on campus. This option is particularly beneficial to a gifted student from a small or rural community where she is less likely to find others as academically advanced as herself.

Which Students Are Appropriate for Talent Search Programs?

The gifted learner most likely to be successful with Talent Search learning will have the characteristics listed in Table 5.7.

Table 5.7. Candidate for Talent Search Programs

Cognitive Functioning	Personal Characteristics	Learning Preferences	Interests
Is processing and achieving well beyond grade-level peers	*Accepting of self and others, independent, and mature*	*Enjoys a variety of delivery methods and challenge in learning experiences*	*Strong interest in specific academic area with little time to supplement learning outside of school*
• Scores in upper 3% of ability and specific academic achievement on group tests • Scores in 99th percentile of performance with chronological peers on SAT or ACT • Shows strength in learning, motivation, leadership, communication expression, and communication precision	• Has strong need to achieve • Is independent in thought and action • Has strong enjoyment of school, but is frustrated with repetitive tasks • Is socially mature, emotionally stable, self-aware, and accepting of others • Shows persistence in own interests • Is self-directed and self-sufficient, with an inner locus of control	• Has strong preferences for most forms of instructional delivery • Prefers challenging, fast-paced instruction • Is comfortable in competitive situations • Enjoys working with others of like ability	• Has intense interest in specific academic area • Has wide-ranging academic interests • Is actively involved in a variety of out-of-school interests • Participates actively in general extra-curriculars offered at current building level

Was the Talent Search Program Successful for the Student?

Most of the research on Talent Search programs is based on the attitudes of talented students about the courses in which they have enrolled and the benefits of taking advanced studies on a college campus. Since Talent Search options are handled entirely outside of the general school, parents are the ones who will monitor the outcomes of this option. If your child answers "yes" to the questions below, the Talent Search program was probably a successful option for her.

1. Would she like to do it again?
2. Did she "fit in" and make new friends?
3. Were the studies sufficiently challenging?
4. Did she develop new interests or possible new areas to study and explore?

Correspondence Courses, Distance Learning, and Independent Study

These options are courses that a gifted student takes outside of regular school time either for personal interest or for credit. A middle school or high school student who is extremely advanced as a writer, for example, might take a writing course on-line via computer or through a college independent study or correspondence course catalog. A high school student who has exhausted what her high school can offer her in a specific subject might sign up to take a university course by correspondence or on-line.

As access to the Internet becomes increasingly affordable for families, high potential students have a variety of college-level or advanced courses from which to choose. Stanford

University's Educational Programs for Gifted Youth (EPGY), for example, offers an extensive menu of mathematics, science, and writing courses whose instructors provide personal feedback on students' assignments via Internet. Presently designed for middle and high school students, this distance learning program is expected to expand in the next few years. (See Table 5.8 for more details.)

What the Research Says about Distance Learning or Correspondence Courses

No actual systematic research has been conducted on the effects of distance learning or correspondence courses. To date, the reporting of effects is anecdotal or descriptive only. Julian Stanley (1992) tracked how students who enrolled in Center for Talented Youth correspondence courses have fared, and concluded that this option is less satisfactory than part-time college enrollment due to the need for 1) greater self-discipline to finish assignments, and 2) lack of immediate feedback by an instructor on assignments. On-line programs, such as Educational Programs for Gifted Youth (EPGY) may avoid these problems, because individual instructors are assigned to students on-line, and feedback is relatively prompt.

With Which Students Are Independent Learning Options Appropriate?

The gifted student who will succeed in distance learning or correspondence classes for advanced coursework will have the following characteristics.

Table 5.8. Candidate for Distance/Independent Learning Options

Cognitive Functioning	Personal Characteristics	Learning Preferences	Interests
Is processing and achieving well beyond grade-level peers in a specific academic area	*Self-directed, independent, and motivated to learn*	*Enjoys a variety of delivery methods and challenge in learning experiences*	*Strong interest in specific academic area with time to supplement learning outside of school*
• Has above average ability • Is achieving beyond current grade in specific subject area • Possesses strong achievement need • Shows strength in planning and communication precision	• Shows independence in thought and action • Is persistent in own interests, assigned tasks • Enjoys learning • Is good at structuring and organizing tasks and own time • Is socially mature, emotionally stable	• Strongly prefers independent study and self-instructional materials • Prefers challenging, fast-paced instruction	• Has intense interest in specific academic area • Has wide-ranging academic interests • Is involved in a variety of out-of-school interests • Does not find the general extra-curriculars in school very interesting

How Can Parents and Teachers Judge the Success of Distance Learning?

If a teacher or counselor at the child's school is aware that the student is involved in distance learning activities, it is important for the school to help the student find time to work on assignments while there and to offer support to ensure follow-through. If the school, student, and parents can answer "yes" to the following questions, then distance learning and correspondence classes can be considered successful educational options.

1. Did the student actually complete the course?

2. Do the student's grades in the course(s) reflect satisfactory progress for his level of ability?

3. Is the student interested in continuing with this option?

Advanced Placement/International Baccalaureate Programs

This option generally refers to courses with advanced or accelerated, college-level content, offered usually at the high school, which afford the student an opportunity to "test out" of or earn credit for completion of college-level coursework by passing an examination.

The Advanced Placement Program was established in 1957 by the College Board of the United States. Currently, the program offers advanced curriculum and external examinations in 16 different subjects—as well as to become an "Advanced Placement Scholar"—by successful performance on six AP examinations before the completion of high school. In order for a high school to offer an Advanced Placement course, the instructor must attend extensive training in the content area and learn instructional strategies for teaching the course at an appropriately advanced level. In other words, specially trained high school teachers offer college-level courses in a subject area and prepare students to pass stringent college-level examinations in that area.

This option is widely used; approximately 10,000 high schools in the U.S. currently offer AP courses. Educational researcher Michael Pyryt (1992) reported that in 1991 alone, 535,191 students, representing 65 countries, took AP exams, and 64% of these students received a grade of 3 (Pass) or higher. Currently, approximately 1,200 colleges and universities award credit for AP exams taken in high school and in some cases allow students to enter their freshman year with sophomore standing, depending on the number of AP exams passed and the scores achieved.

Another program with rigorous curriculum standards is the International Baccalaureate (IB) program, first established in Europe in the 1950s. The IB diploma, which allows a student admission to virtually any university in the world, requires fluency in a foreign language and four years of a laboratory science, among other courses. Several selective universities in the U.S. readily accept students for enrollment as second year students upon successful acquisition of the IB Diploma (achieved by scoring 7s on IB exams in prescribed academic areas).

The way AP and IB programs usually work is that a trained instructor offers the advanced coursework during the high school day. The student chooses to register for advanced class instead of a "regular" high school course. For example, the student registers for AP American History rather than regular eleventh-grade History, or for AP Physics rather than twelfth-grade Physics. Over the course of the year, the student actively experiences college-level curriculum and learns appropriate test-taking skills to perform successfully on the two to three-hour standardized exams offered at the end of the school year.

Interestingly, recent reports suggest that the AP and IB examinations are the only national or international tests that have not been "dumbed down" since their inception. It is just as difficult today to pass one of these exams as it was when the testing programs were first developed. The same cannot be said for the Scholastic Aptitude Test, the American College Testing exam, or the large number of ability and achievement tests that have been developed and revised over the years.

What the Research Says about Advanced Placement Programs

The synthesis that I conducted of this body of research revealed 22 studies on Advanced Placement and International

Baccalaureate programs, plus a few precursors of these popular programs; the studies dated from 1944-1986. All of the studies compared the college grade-point averages of two groups of students attending the same college—high potential students who did not take AP or IB classes in high school, and high potential students who did take AP/IB classes. The academic gains for the students in these studies was positive, even though most of the colleges involved in these studies were highly selective colleges and universities. One would suspect that all of the students who were ultimately accepted to these colleges must have taken some kind of accelerated or honors courses in high school to have even been considered by the college. This makes the academic gains found for AP programs and IB programs even more remarkable.

The social effect of AP and IB programs was also moderately positive, indicating that these students tended to participate in extra-curricular activities, often taking leadership roles somewhat more extensively than did their non-AP/IB peers at the college level, and they felt more positive about their social competence. No differences in overall self-esteem, autonomy, or ethics were found when these students were compared to other high potential students without AP/IP coursework.

Survey research done in 1991 on the long-term effects shows that AP students are more likely to apply to selective colleges, graduate early, and to pursue an academic or scientific career. Furthermore, a 1990 study conducted at Johns Hopkins University found that the number of AP credits a college awarded students was the most important predictor of students' first semester grade-point average, cumulative college grade point, number of semesters on the Dean's list, and whether or not students graduated with honors. Thus, if a gifted student earned four credits based on his high school AP test scores, that student was likely to continue to achieve at high levels in college as shown by grades, being on the Dean's list, and receiving honors at graduation.

Who Is Most Likely to Benefit from AP and IB Program Participation?

A gifted student who will thrive in these high powered, academically rigorous classes with motivated peers and who will perform well on high level external examinations will have most of the characteristics listed in Table 5.9.

Table 5.9. Candidate for AP/IB Programs

Cognitive Functioning	Personal Characteristics	Learning Preferences	Interests
Is processing and achieving beyond grade-level peers in specific academic areas	*Is self-directed, independent, and motivated to learn*	*Enjoys a variety of delivery methods, challenge in learning experiences, and learning with like ability peers*	*Strong interest in specific academic area with little time to supplement learning outside of school*
• Has above average ability • Is achieving beyond grade-level peers in specific academic area • Possesses strong characteristics in learning, motivation, communication expression, communication precision, and planning	• Is independent in thought and action with an inner locus of control • Persists in own interests and assigned tasks • Is accepting of others • Is perceptive, verbal, reflective, dominant • Makes ready associations, retains information easily • Is socially mature, emotionally stable • Likes taking cognitive risks	• Prefers learning through lecture, discussion, small group projects • Is comfortable in challenging, in-depth, fast-paced learning experiences • Is comfortable in competitive situations	• Has intense interest in specific academic area • Has wide-ranging academic interests • Is actively involved in a variety of out-of-school interests • Participates actively in general extra-curricular activities offered at school

Monitoring AP and IB Programs

Normal teacher monitoring of AP and IB task completion and test performance should be sufficient for evaluation of course/program outcomes. In addition, teachers and parents can ask their student the following questions:

1. Does the student feel that she is making satisfactory progress in the class?

2. Does the student feel the course materials are interesting, motivating, and at the right level of difficulty?

3. Does the student think she is learning more than she would in some other course at the high school?

4. Does the student think she has a good chance to pass the exam at a level that will earn college credits at a college of her choice?

5. Does the student feel she fits in with others in the class?

College-in-the-Schools

This option refers to the practice of allowing local colleges or universities to offer college-level coursework on the high school campus. Often, these classes are co-taught by a college professor and a high school instructor, although some variations in instruction can also take place—e.g., a college professor can teach the course alone at the high school, or a high school teacher trained in the college course can teach it by himself at the high school.

Frequently these classes are offered before or after school, rather than in the middle of the school day. Students who enroll pay a nominal fee for the course and texts, and when they "pass" the course, the local college offers college credit, usually accepted only at that college or within the same college system, such as community colleges throughout the state. Sometimes this type of coursework is used as a recruiting effort on the part of local community and state colleges. Generally, these courses are offered to students who have exhausted the regular curriculum at the high school.

What the Research Says about College-in-the-Schools

Only one study regarding this specific option was located, and it reported small, positive effects for participating students similar to the effects found for the concurrent enrollment option. Much of the research on Advanced Placement and subject acceleration could be applied to the College-in-the-Schools program, however. These options are similar in that they give students exposure to advanced content and skills, group them by ability and achievement for instruction, and provide external evaluations that lead to college credit.

Who Will Benefit from College-in-the-Schools?

A gifted learner likely to be successful in a College-in-the-Schools program will have the characteristics shown in the Table 5.10.

Table 5.10. Candidate for College-in-the-Schools			
Cognitive Functioning	**Personal Characteristics**	**Learning Preferences**	**Interests**
Is processing and achieving well beyond grade-level peers in a specific academic area	*Is self-directed, independent, and motivated to learn*	*Enjoys a variety of delivery methods and challenge in learning experiences*	*Strong interest in specific academic area with little time to supplement learning outside of school*
• Has above-average ability • Is achieving 2+ grade levels beyond current grade in specific subject area • Possesses strong achievement need • Shows strength in learning, planning, and communication precision	• Is independent in thought and action • Persists in own interests, assigned tasks • Is accepting of others • Enjoys school and learning • Is socially mature, emotionally stable	• Has strong preferences for lecture, discussion, and projects • Feels comfortable in challenging, fast-paced learning experiences • Likes participating in competitive situations	• Has intense interest in specific academic area • Has wide-ranging academic interests • Is actively involved in a variety of out-of-school interests • Participates actively in general extra-curriculars offered at current building level

Monitoring College-in-the-Schools Participants

It is important to frequently monitor the student's academic progress, class participation, and personal satisfaction with this academic option. By the end of the first semester, data from test scores, project performance, and interviews should allow parents and the school to answer the following questions:

1. Does the student feel that he is making satisfactory progress in the class?

2. Does the student indicate that the course materials are interesting, motivating, and at the right level of difficulty?

3. Does the student think he is learning more than would be possible in some other course offered at the high school?

4. Does the student feel that he fits in with others in the class?

Mentorships

Mentorships or internships for gifted learners refer to the practice of placing a student with an expert or professional for the purpose of exploring and advancing a specific interest/proficiency that cannot be provided within the regular educational setting. This implies that true mentorships do not occur until a gifted student has exhausted what her current school system can provide in the student's intense area of interest. There are other kinds of mentorships available which would be suitable to regular learners too, such as mentorships that reinforce what a student is currently learning or that are offered in addition to the student's coursework. But mentorships that push the gifted student forward in her learning are what make this option a form of subject-based acceleration appropriate for gifted learners.

Often, mentorships include a complex admission policy to ensure that the student knows what she wants to study but isn't able to study through the school system. Jill Reilly (1992), author of a widely used handbook for setting up mentorship programs in schools, believes that before students engage in this option, they should be taught interviewing skills, study skills, and communication skills in order to ensure that neither the busy mentor's time nor the student's time will be wasted. There also must be some supervision of the mentorship meetings held and the assignments given to the student by the school to ensure that neither party is letting down its side of the partnership. Mentorship programs often require students to keep a log of activities for accountability and for teacher comment, as well as for logging the hours worked.

Paul, an eleventh grader, was extremely interested in biochemical physiology and had taken all of the life science and physiology courses offered at his high school. He applied for a mentorship and was placed with a university professor working on synthetic blood substitutes. The mentorship went on for a year, with the first several months devoted to Paul meeting weekly with his mentor to discuss the reading assignments he had been given by the professor. Most of these readings were research reports of the professor's own work. When the mentor was convinced that Paul understood the mechanisms of what was being done, Paul was invited into the lab and given personalized training in lab work procedures, such as titrations.

Over the course of the year, the two developed a close relationship, to the point where they could crack "inside" jokes about what certain test tubes contained. They developed their own shorthand form of language and formed a lasting friendship, despite differences in age. Paul continued to work as a lab assistant in the summers and ultimately entered the biomedical sciences program at the university in order to continue his work with the professor. He is currently doing doctoral work in synthetic blood substitutes.

What the Research Says about Mentorships

I was able to locate 13 studies on mentorship programs. The studies all involved high school or adult mentorships, except for one study of a mentorship program for grades five through seven. Three studies that did not look at high potential individuals were eliminated from the analysis. The remaining studies looked at one-year to three-year mentorships, with two of the studies reporting retrospectively 22 years after the mentorships occurred. The academic effects of mentorships for students were very large—approximately a one-half year gain—in the specific subject area. There was also substantial improvement in socialization and self-esteem of participating students. Across the board, this form of individualized subject acceleration clearly produces substantial gains for the gifted student academically, socially, and emotionally.

Which Students Will Benefit from Mentorship?

The learner most likely to succeed in such a one-on-one mentorship will have many of the traits listed in Table 5.11.

Table 5.11. Candidate for Mentorship Experience			
Cognitive Functioning	**Personal Characteristics**	**Learning Preferences**	**Interests**
Is processing and achieving well beyond grade-level peers in a specific academic area	*Is self-directed, independent, and motivated to learn*	*Enjoys a variety of delivery methods and challenge in learning experiences*	*Strong interest in specific academic area with little time to supplement learning outside of school*
• Has above-average ability • Is achieving 2+ grade levels beyond current grade in specific subject area • Possesses strong achievement need • Shows strength in learning, planning, and communication precision	• Is independent in thought and action • Persists in own interests, assigned tasks • Is accepting of others • Enjoys school and learning • Is focused and intense when learning	• Has strong preferences for lecture, discussion, and projects • Is comfortable in challenging, fast-paced learning experiences	• Has intense interest in specific academic area • Has wide-ranging academic interests

Monitoring the Mentorship Experience

General monitoring of a mentorship is crucial during its first few weeks to ensure that the student is relating well to both his regular school responsibilities and his mentorship responsibilities. End of the semester information should focus on academic performance in school, but additional information should be collected about the student's response when he is with the mentor, how well he is achieving with the activities the mentor has planned, and how consistently the two have been able to meet. In many cases, the school will have a coordinator who checks in regularly with the mentor and the student to ensure that the two "connect" both academically and personally. If not, both teachers and parents should check for this. If the school, student, and parents can answer "yes" to these questions, then the mentorship is successful.

1. Does the student think that she has "done well" in the mentorship activity?

2. Do the student's grades in his regular program suggest satisfactory progress for her level of ability?

3. Has the student been able to relate well to the mentor?

4. Does the student feel that the time involved has been "worth it"?

5. Is the student interested in continuing with this option?

Post-Secondary Options

Post-secondary options are a variation of the concurrent enrollment option mentioned earlier. Post-secondary options allow gifted students who have completed all available coursework at their high school in a specific academic area to take courses at a local college for simultaneous high school and college credit. In some cases, the high school will be required to pay college tuition for the student from state monies provided for the student's "seat time" at the high school—a factor that discourages some high schools from wanting to participate in this option. For some students near the end of their high school years, this option allows them to continue being mentally challenged while still actively engaging in the social life and extracurricular activities of their senior year in high school. Post-secondary options can be considered a variation of concurrent enrollment when a student does attend both high school and college part time, but many students participate in post-secondary options full time as well. Unlike concurrent enrollment, post-secondary options are usually a state-legislated option and may not be available in every state. At last count, 20 states offered this option.

Possible problems may occur with this option in issues such as transportation, scheduling conflicts, and less time for social interactions in either setting. In post-secondary options, students generally provide their own transportation and must arrange schedules that suit both settings. However, the positives with this option are that 1) the student gets a chance to sample college life without living away from home; 2) the student begins to acquire college credits early, which will allow him more time later for advanced work or electives of interest; and 3) the student doesn't become bored or restless with his current education because it is too easy.

What the Research Says about Post-Secondary Options

Because this type of state-funded program is currently offered in less than half of the states, little research has been conducted to evaluate its educational effects on participants. Because it is a variation of concurrent enrollment, one might infer that the same positive academic (small) and psychological (substantial) effects would occur. Solano and George (1976) looked at the grade-point averages of 131 high school students who were enrolled in college science and mathematics courses for credit while they were high school students. The students achieved a mean grade-point average of 3.59 on a four-point scale across 277 different college courses. Although this result does not translate into an academic effect because there is no comparison group, there is no question that these high school students were successful in their part-time college courses.

With What Students Are Post-Secondary Options Appropriate?

The gifted high school student most likely to benefit from post-secondary options will have the characteristics and behaviors listed in the Table 5.12.

Table 5.12. Candidate for Post-Secondary Options

Cognitive Functioning	Personal Characteristics	Learning Preferences	Interests
Is processing and achieving well beyond grade-level peers in a specific academic area	*Is self-directed, independent, and motivated to learn*	*Enjoys a variety of delivery methods and challenge in learning experiences*	*Strong interest in specific academic area with little time to supplement learning outside of school*
• Has above-average ability • Is achieving 2+ grade levels beyond current grade level in specific subject area • Has strong achievement need	• Is independent in thought and action • Persists in own interests, assigned tasks • Thinks abstractly, yet is focused and retains information easily	• Has strong preferences for most forms of delivery, except independent study • Is comfortable in challenging, fast-paced learning experiences	• Has intense interest in specific academic area • Has wide-ranging academic interests

Cognitive Functioning	Personal Characteristics	Learning Preferences	Interests
Is processing and achieving well beyond grade-level peers in a specific academic area	*Is self-directed, independent, and motivated to learn*	*Enjoys a variety of delivery methods and challenge in learning experiences*	*Strong interest in specific academic area with little time to supplement learning outside of school*
• Shows strength in learning, planning, and communication precision	• Is self-aware, confident, socially mature, and emotionally stable • Is accepting of others, perceptive, dominant • Enjoys school and learning	• Prefers competitive situations in which to test self	• Is actively involved in a variety of out-of-school interests • Does not show great interest in the general extra-curricular programs offered at school

Table 5.12. Candidate for Post-Secondary Options *(continued)*

Monitoring the Post-Secondary Experience

General monitoring of the post-secondary option is crucial during the student's first term of college enrollment to ensure that she is fitting in to both settings. End of the semester information should focus on academic performance in both settings and class participation levels as reported by the respective instructors. If the school, student, and parents can answer "yes" to the following questions, then the option can be considered successful.

1. Does the student think she has "done well" in the college class(es)? Is she willing to live with somewhat lower grades that might result from a more competitive setting at a higher level of instruction?

2. Do the student's grades in the college course(s) suggest satisfactory progress for her level of ability?

3. Has the student been able to make any social contacts at the college while maintaining friendships at the high school?

4. Is the student interested in continuing with this option?

When to Use Subject-Based Acceleration

Since this chapter is the first of three describing the "when" of educational planning, Table 5.13 is included to provide a helpful summary of when subject-based acceleration options can be offered to gifted students based on their ages and grades. Care must be taken, however, to look closely at the cognitive functioning, learning strengths, learning preferences, and interests of the gifted child, in addition to developmental age or grade when recommending one option over another.

Table 5.13. When to Consider Subject-Based Acceleration Options

Option	Age Range	Grade Range
Early Entrance to School	3-6	K-1
Compacting	5-18 *9-14	K-12 *3-8
Single-Subject Acceleration	6-18 *6-14	1-12 *1-8
Testing Out	7-22 *18-22	2-13 *13
Concurrent Enrollment	8-18 *11-18	2-12 *5-12
Talent Search	9-18	3-12

Table 5.13. When to Consider Subject-Based Acceleration Options *(continued)*

Option	Age Range	Grade Range
Correspondence/Distance Learning	9-18	3-12
	*12-18	*7-12
Independent Study	9-18	3-12
	*9-14	*3-8
Advanced Placement/	14-18	8-12
International Baccalaureate	*16-18	*10-12
College-in-the-Schools	15-18	9-12
	*17-18	*11-12
Mentorships	15-18	9-12
	*17-18	*11-12
Post-Secondary Options	15-18	9-12
	*17-18	*11-12

*Typical, most appropriate age and grade ranges according to research

Which of These Children Should Be Subject-Based Accelerated?

You have just read about 12 forms of subject-based acceleration, and it was a lot to digest. Do you want to test whether all this information makes sense for you? If so, try the following exercise.

For the three children described below, mark with a "c" or an "f" which of the following options should be considered. The "c" stands for the child's current grade level, and the "f" stands for his or her future schooling. Leave blank any option that you feel would not apply. The correct answers are shown at the end of the quiz.

Table 5.14. A Quiz on Subject-Based Acceleration

Characteristics of the Child	Choice Options: Subject-Based Acceleration
TERONE: Will turn five after the mandated time for kindergarten entry. IQ of 145. Has been reading since age three. Is currently learning multiplication facts. Strong reading interest in science. Poor physical coordination, but average fine-motor skills. Language abilities unknown at this time.	_____ Early Entrance _____ Compacting _____ Testing Out _____ Single-Subject Acceleration _____ Talent Search _____ Concurrent Enrollment _____ Advanced Placement _____ College-in-the-Schools _____ Mentorship _____ Post-Secondary Options _____ Correspondence Course
MING-LEE: Currently in sixth grade. IQ of 140. Is at eighth-grade level in math and science and at seventh-grade level in oral and written language achievement. Strong interest in reading and foreign language. Has sister in seventh grade.	_____ Early Entrance _____ Compacting _____ Testing Out _____ Single-Subject Acceleration _____ Talent Search _____ Concurrent Enrollment _____ Advanced Placement _____ College-in-the-Schools _____ Mentorship _____ Post-Secondary Options _____ Correspondence Course

Table 5.14. A Quiz on Subject-Based Acceleration *(continued)*	
Characteristics of the Child	**Choice Options:** **Subject-Based Acceleration**
STEFAN: Currently in tenth grade and taking honors courses in all academic areas. IQ of 135. Strongest interest is in science, but shows extraordinary ability in math as well. Has "A" average in high school. Actively involved in baseball, chess, math team, and band.	_____ Early Entrance _____ Compacting _____ Testing Out _____ Single-Subject Acceleration _____ Talent Search _____ Concurrent Enrollment _____ Advanced Placement _____ College-in-the-Schools _____ Mentorship _____ Post-Secondary Options _____ Correspondence Course

Table 5.15. Answers to the Quiz on Subject-Based Acceleration

Characteristics of the Child	Choice Options: Subject-Based Acceleration	
TERONE: Will not turn five until after the mandated time for kindergarten entry. IQ of 145. Has been reading since age three. Is currently learning multiplication facts. Strong reading interest in science. Poor physical coordination, but average fine-motor skills. Language abilities unknown at this time.	c	Early Entrance
	c	Compacting
	f	Testing Out
	c	Single-Subject Acceleration
	f	Talent Search
	f	Concurrent Enrollment
	f	Advanced Placement
	f	College-in-the-Schools
	f	Mentorship
	f	Post-Secondary Options
	f	Correspondence Course
MING-LEE: Currently in sixth grade. IQ of 140. Is at eighth-grade level in math and science and at seventh-grade level in oral and written language achievement. Strong interest in reading and foreign language. Has sister in seventh grade.		Early Entrance
	c	Compacting
	c	Testing Out
	c	Single-Subject Acceleration
	c	Talent Search
	c	Concurrent Enrollment
	f	Advanced Placement
	f	College-in-the-Schools
	f	Mentorship
	f	Post-Secondary Options
	c	Correspondence Course

Table 5.15. Answers to the Quiz on Subject-Based Acceleration *(continued)*	
Characteristics of the Child	**Choice Options: Subject-Based Acceleration**
STEFAN: Currently in tenth grade and taking honors courses in all academic areas. IQ of 135. Strongest interest is in science, but shows extraordinary ability in math as well. Has "A" average in high school. Actively involved in baseball, chess, math team, and band.	_____ Early Entrance _c_ Compacting _c_ Testing Out _c_ Single-Subject Acceleration _____ Talent Search _c_ Concurrent Enrollment _c_ Advanced Placement _c_ College-in-the-Schools _c_ Mentorship _c_ Post-Secondary Options _c_ Correspondence Course

Summary

There are 12 different forms of subject-based acceleration that can be offered to allow the gifted learner to be exposed to advanced knowledge and skills before the usual age or grade level. In general, some type of subject-based acceleration should be seriously considered for every student with high ability who is performing beyond current grade level. Many of these options require students to have strong independent learning skills so that they can pursue advanced learning at their own pace and level of complexity. Several options allow bright students to pursue advanced learning at an appropriate level and pace as part of a group of like-ability/like-interest learners. Careful attention to attitudes, interests, personalities, and motivational levels of individual gifted students will indicate which options among these alternatives are most likely to work for a student.

Key Points

- Subject-based acceleration provides gifted students exposure to advanced knowledge and skills before their expected age or grade level.

- In the early years, early entrance to school, compacting, and single-subject acceleration may be the most appropriate choices for a gifted child.

- In the middle years, many more options can be offered, including testing out, concurrent enrollment, independent study, and Talent Search programs.

- During high school years, options such as correspondence courses, Advanced Placement, International Baccalaureate, college-in-the-schools, mentorships, and post-secondary options can be offered to gifted learners.

- In extensive examination of the research, every type of subject-based acceleration has been found to result in at least small, positive academic gains. Some of the options resulted in quite dramatic academic gains.

- Some options, such as concurrent enrollment and mentorships, have also shown substantial gains in students' self-esteem and self-efficacy.

- Mentorships show substantial improvements in socialization for gifted learners, while other options, such as early entrance to school, Talent Search, and AP/IB programs, show modest improvements in social skills.

6

Grade-Based Acceleration: Which Option Matches Which Child Best at What Age?

Beth was 14 years old and in eighth grade at a suburban middle school when I first met her. She had just received her scores on the Scholastic Aptitude Test (SAT), a test normally taken by high school seniors in preparation for college entrance. She and her parents were quite surprised by her scores—she had scored 680 on the Verbal and 690 on the Quantitative sections of the test out of a possible 800 for each section. In light of her superior performance on this test taken four years early, the family wanted to know what they should ask the high school to do for their daughter. Beth expressed a strong interest in science and math and "hoped" the high school would let her take more challenging classes in those subjects. It was also clear, based on her high verbal score, that she did not need ninth- or tenth-grade English classes. I agreed to work with the high school to see what kind of an individualized curriculum we could design for Beth. Child study team meetings were convened and included a school counselor, the department heads of English, science, math, and social studies, the Assistant Principal, and me.

During the first three meetings, I shared research results on the effects of acceleration programs for very bright students. What the teachers and administrators learned was that the research clearly showed that no matter what form of accelera-

tion we might plan for Beth, the academic gains would be very positive, and that her social adjustment and self-esteem would not suffer from a more fast-paced, complex program of studies. Then the six of us got down to the business of designing a program for Beth. In the end, the school agreed to offer a program where Beth would:

- *attend high school all four years.*
- *take two trimesters of the basic writing and communication courses for ninth grade, after which she could elect to take any literature course from any year.*
- *take a math placement test to determine which math courses she could take, but not be advanced beyond the tenth-grade course in her first year.*
- *take the required ninth-grade earth science with other ninth graders.*
- *test out of any or all of the required social studies courses in order to replace them with substitutes of her own choosing.*

Beth and her parents rejected this plan. They felt it left no educational alternative for her except to continue to move slowly through the required courses, which she felt she had already mastered. They chose, instead, to have Beth attend the Program for the Exceptionally Gifted (PEG Program) at Mary Baldwin College, a program designed for gifted students like Beth who are well advanced beyond their peers in high school. There, Beth was able to complete four years of high school and four years of undergraduate college in four years. She was one of 30 other girls as bright as she, and she felt very much at home. Beth left her family and home four years earlier than she and her parents had expected, but for the first time in her life, she was literally surrounded by other very bright (and sociable) girls. She graduated with honors from Mary Baldwin, earned a graduate degree, and today is a very successful technical writer in the sciences.

Lateesha

The superintendent of a small school district called me to ask if I would help them make some decisions regarding a fourth-grade student named Lateesha. The school had given her the Wechsler Intelligence Scale for Children (WISC-III), and she had scored at the very top of the test. They had also administered the sixth-grade version of the Stanford Achievement Test, on which she had scored in the 90th percentile or higher on every sub-test, even though she currently was in fourth grade. The school system wanted to know how to keep Lateesha in their school rather than see her parents remove her to a private school, which the parents perceived as more academically rigorous.

Lateesha's parents, the school principals of the intermediate school (grades three through four) and the middle school (grades five through eight), her current fourth-grade teacher, the middle school gifted services coordinator, and I met to discuss possible educational plans for Lateesha. Over the course of three meetings in the spring of that year, we decided that Lateesha would:

- *skip fifth grade and begin middle school in the fall as a sixth grader.*

- *attend seventh-grade honors English classes.*

- *take German at the high school (instead of Spanish, which was offered to all students in the middle school—Lateesha had already studied Spanish over two summers in a foreign language camp).*

- *have a compacted curriculum in sixth-grade social studies, completing what she didn't know of it in the first semester and then doing an independent study on U.S. History (17th-18th centuries) in the second semester.*

- *be allowed to test out of whatever mathematics and science curriculum she had already mastered as the units of study occurred, and then spend her extra time on other enrichments in those areas.*

Lateesha's parents were pleased with the plan, and it was implemented fully the following fall. When her seventh-grade English teacher noted that Lateesha did not write fluently, plans were made for Lateesha to work with the gifted resource teacher weekly to improve her writing fluency. This resource teacher also helped Lateesha develop time-management skills to accomplish her varied assignments at different grade levels as she moved daily between school buildings. Lateesha reported that she felt very challenged by her studies but was concerned that she was missing out on the opportunity to make sixth-grade friends. The resource teacher encouraged her to join a book discussion group held at lunchtime that was made up of highly motivated readers. Although the math compacting continued and Lateesha worked much of the time on her own, compacting in science was stopped so that she could have some small group experiences in the science classroom with her sixth-grade classmates, even though it meant she wasn't progressing as quickly in science as she could have. By the end of the year, she had two close friends who loved to read the same books she did, and she was well accepted in all of her classes. A similar plan, without the grade-skip, was developed for the next year.

Openness, Flexibility, and Responsiveness

What happened within one school system to Beth may seem disappointing and even shocking. Despite knowing the very positive effects of accelerating Beth's academic program, the school chose to be inflexible in most subject areas. They were not willing to listen and learn about, and from, the research evidence. Reading Beth's story is not a very good endorsement of the "public school's willingness to accommodate gifted students." But when we add Lateesha's very different story to this mix, it is clear that the public schools can provide a good program with just a little bit of extra effort, and can thereby meet the needs of very gifted young learners such as Beth and Lateesha.

Beth's Choice: Pros and Cons

Beth and her parents spent many hours discussing the pros and cons of early admission to college—that is, attending the combined high school/college program at the age of 14. Perhaps they developed a chart similar to the one you see in Table 6.1 listing possible arguments both for and against this form of grade-based acceleration. At that time, however, they did not have the research that might support or refute these possibilities. Later in this chapter, you will read about the body of research that genuinely supports acceleration.

Table 6.1. Early Admission to College

Positives of Early Admission to College	Negatives of Early Admission to College
• Tangible recognition of extraordinary ability, therefore stronger academic self-esteem developed	• May become a specialist or take on a very narrow course of study too early, without broad enough foundational knowledge
• Chance for exposure to new content and skills, therefore increased motivation for learning and for taking on longer-term preparations for professional career	• May require leaving home, living on own considerably earlier
• More efficient use of school time, therefore less chance for frustration and boredom	• May be exposed to an "older" lifestyle (drinking, driving, dating) considerably earlier
• Chance that learning will be more effective since more accelerated; less likelihood that sloppy habits, lessened persistence, and inaccurate perceptions of the effort learning takes will be formed	• May be unprepared for the rigors of note-taking, test-taking for advanced content at this higher level of schooling

Table 6.1. Early Admission to College
(continued)

Positives of Early Admission to College	Negatives of Early Admission to College
• Earlier entry into productive career path; more chance for financial success, and scholarly productivity	• May find advanced work too difficult for maturity level and may become "mediocre" when compared to new peers
• Chance for increased productivity, since for many fields, the innovations occur during the early years of individual's career	• May have less opportunity to develop leadership skills because may be perceived as different or "immature" by older peers
• Chance for true peer interaction, thus fewer feelings of isolation, alienation, and differentness	• May require commitment too early to a career before experiencing "real life"
• Regular school won't have to expend effort and funds on individualizing, therefore less tax burden on general public	• May restrict exposure to life experiences usually acquired outside of the regular school curriculum

Lateesha's Choice: Pros and Cons

Lateesha and her parents also spent many hours discussing skipping a full grade—particularly whether she would feel comfortable taking advanced classes at a variety of grade levels in her new school. In the previous chapter, we discussed the subject acceleration that Lateesha would experience in English, as well as concurrent enrollment in German, compacting in social studies, mathematics, and science, and independent study in U.S. History. These options were needed to ensure that Lateesha would continue to advance at the level of complexity she needed once the grade-skip was put into place. The following chart of pros and cons developed by Lateesha and her parents lists their ideas concerning grade-skipping. Several of the pros and cons are the same as for Beth, but some are different.

Table 6.2. Grade-Skipping Pros and Cons

Positives of Early Grade-Skipping	Negatives of Early Grade-Skipping
• Tangible recognition of extraordinary ability, therefore stronger academic self-esteem developed	• Advanced work may be too difficult for maturity level and he/she becomes mediocre in comparison to new peers
• Chance for exposure to more advanced content and skills, therefore increased motivation for learning	• May not have all of the advanced skills needed to work easily at the next grade level in every subject area
• More efficient use of school time, therefore less chance for frustration and boredom	• May be exposed to "older" lifestyle and behaviors, perhaps growing up too fast
• Chance that learning will be more effective since more accelerated; less likelihood that sloppy habits and lessened persistence will occur	• May require making a new set of friends
• Chance for true peer interaction, therefore fewer feelings of isolation, alienation, and differentness	• May have less opportunity to develop leadership skills because perceived as different and "immature" by older peers
• Regular school won't have to expend effort and funds on individualizing, therefore less tax burden on general public	• Rarely is a grade-skip enough for a gifted learner. The school may need to do more, and it may cost additional money

What Are Grade-Based Acceleration Options?

Lateesha and Beth provide examples of two grade-based acceleration options. Beth's grade-based acceleration option was *early admission to college*, while Lateesha participated in the grade-based acceleration known as *grade-skipping*. Basically, grade-based acceleration can be defined as *any option that shortens the number of years a child spends in mastering the K-12 curriculum.* Early admission to high school or college and grade-skipping are different forms of grade-based acceleration because both shorten the number of years a student will spend in the K-12 school system.

In Chapter 5, we discussed at length the reasons that acceleration—whether grade-based or subject-based—is important for some gifted children, particularly the highly gifted. To summarize, the most important reasons are:

- Gifted children learn faster, and actually learn more accurately, when they are taught at a faster pace.

- Gifted children may spend from three to six years of their school lives learning nothing new.

- Gifted children who are not challenged can become discouraged with their abilities and purposely "dumb down" to become underachievers.

- Gifted children enjoy and are motivated by academic challenge.

- It is not equitable for gifted children to expect them to spend their time waiting for others to "catch up."

This chapter will describe six specific types of grade-based acceleration options that are sometimes used in schools to help gifted children keep progressing at a rate that better matches their capabilities. Each option listed is simply a different way to manage or facilitate the acceleration. These options include:

- Grade-Skipping
- Non-Graded Classes
- Multi-Grade Classes
- Grade Telescoping
- Credit for Prior Learning/Testing Out
- Early Admission to College

The next few pages will: 1) present each option, 2) include what the research says about each option, 3) list considerations parents and teachers might need to keep in mind, and 4) describe ways to tell whether the form of acceleration being used is successful. These options are described in the order of the ages at which they might be appropriate for a gifted learner.

Grade-Skipping

Grade-skipping, sometimes called "double promotion," involves cutting a full year from the usual number of years typically required to progress from kindergarten to high school graduation. This type of acceleration is more frequently considered—when it is considered at all—in the earlier years of a child's schooling, perhaps because the beginning levels of learning are more basic and it is much easier to see when a child has mastered those levels and is ready to move on to the next grade.

The child who has skipped one grade will work full time with other children—who are usually a year older—on the regular curriculum for his new grade level. If the teacher enriches or extends the curriculum for brighter students at this grade level, then the child could become a part of that effort; if the teacher does not enrich, then the child would work with the regular curriculum at the same pace as other children in the class.

For schools with limited resources, grade-skipping is a cost-effective way to move a child along, particularly when the school cannot provide significant academic enrichment or differentiation at the current grade level. However, it is probably the accelerative option with the worst reputation. The bad reputation is almost wholly undeserved. The argument against grade-skipping that is most often given by educators is that the child's social and emotional development will be irreparably harmed if the child is put in a class with older students. Years of research and follow-up studies done on gifted children who have been grade-skipped show that this is simply not true.

What Does the Research Show?

In my synthesis of the research on grade-skipping, I located 32 research studies for the years 1917-1981. These studies examined how students who were accelerated performed academically after the acceleration. According to these studies, the effect on academic progress was very positive. More than one additional year's achievement was gained as a result of the grade-skip, and the students performed at least as well as their older-aged gifted peers in the new grade level. In addition, there also was a strong improvement in social adjustment, and a small gain in self-esteem.

The positive social adjustment effect of grade-skipping was surprising, particularly since social adjustment concerns are the reasons most often cited by principals and teachers for not supporting grade-skipping. It is noteworthy that when these children do move to the higher grade, they are, in fact, *more* likely to make friends, perhaps because the older children may have similar interests or are slightly more socially mature. The small but positive improvement in self-esteem also seems to disprove the myths surrounding grade-skipping. These children do *not* lose confidence in themselves even though they have to work a little harder to compete with older children.

The myths connected with grade-skipping and some other forms of acceleration have been thoroughly researched by Tom Southern and Eric Jones. In their book, *The Academic Acceleration of Gifted Children* (1991), they noted that school personnel were more likely than parents to believe grade-skipping would be detrimental, even though the research was extraordinarily consistent in showing strong academic, social, and emotional benefits from using this form of acceleration for gifted children.

Susan Assouline and her colleagues at the Belin-Blank Center at the University of Iowa developed a comprehensive and effective instrument for determining a child's suitability for grade-skipping. The *Iowa Acceleration Scale* (Assouline, Colangelo, Lupkowski-Shoplik, & Lipscomb, 1998), or IAS, is a tool that can help parents and educators take a sensible, objective approach to decisions about grade-skipping on a child-by-child basis. Based on the research literature and 10 years of pilot testing and refinement, the systematic and objective approach of the IAS makes it an extremely valuable tool for parents and school personnel considering this option for a gifted child. The IAS can be ordered from Great Potential Press, whose address is listed in Appendix B. A powerful message of the IAS, however, is that there are some "critical factors" which warn educators and parents that in certain situations, grade-skipping is *not* a good idea. These four critical situations are:

- When the child's ability is less than one standard deviation above the mean (the child scores less than 115 on an intelligence test).

- When the child would be moved up into the same grade as an older sibling (sibling rivalry could worsen and self-esteem could go down).

- When the student is currently in the same grade as a sibling (for the same reasons given above).

- When the student does not want to be grade-skipped, regardless of the reason (there is a lower chance of success).

These four critical factors are the best place to begin the process of deciding whether or not to grade-skip. If any of the four factors are answered with "yes," then the discussion of grade-skipping should be postponed and other alternatives explored.

The key to success with grade-skipping lies in the careful study of the child who is being proposed for a grade-skip. The IAS helps parents and educators collect and then discuss and assign a rating to information on the child's cognitive function (ability and achievement), school history, and other school and academic factors, such as motivation to learn, attendance, siblings' grade levels, self-concept, and extracurricular participation. Information on the student's interpersonal skills is also gathered through questions about maturity, and peer and teacher relationships, as well as estimates of the attitude and support for the acceleration by both the school and the parents. The IAS provides questions in all of the above areas that a school team should answer when considering acceleration for a child. If the IAS had been available for use during the team meeting about Beth, the girl described at the beginning of this chapter, perhaps the evidence of a need for skipping one or more grades would have been more obvious.

Pessimistic beliefs of educators regarding grade-skipping can often be traced to anecdotal "evidence" or a story they heard about someone who had a negative experience. For example, "Mary skipped second grade and then dropped out of school at 14, and it's all because she skipped a grade." Or, "Nadia was skipped and then had trouble making friends in college." Or, "Mark was skipped and never became involved in high school sports." It is more likely that Mary's shortened schooling, Nadia's lack of a social life, and Mark's lack of participation in sports were due to other factors than just the grade-skip decision alone. If parents and educators keep the IAS's four critical factors in mind and take care to determine the most appropriate time for a grade-skip, grade-skips will almost always be successful.

In general, the earlier the grade-skip, the better. Grade-skipping a child early—such as in kindergarten or first grade—helps prevent potential social issues, because the child is exposed to only one peer group from the beginning of his school career instead of two. Another good time to consider a grade-skip, according to the *Iowa Acceleration Scale* research, is when the child will be transitioning to a new building level, such as from elementary to middle school, or from middle school to high school. There is a minimum of social trauma because the child goes about making new friends in the new building level along with all other students transitioning into that building. Regardless of when the grade-skip occurs, whatever parents and educators can do to help the child make the transition with a minimum of extra attention, the better the child's chances to be accepted by his new peers.

For some highly gifted children (those with IQ scores 150+), more than one grade-skip may be needed. Such a child might skip two or even more grades during the course of her schooling, though not necessarily all at one time. Skipping two or more grades is often called "radical acceleration." The research on radical acceleration is not as clear, probably because there are so few documented cases. In some instances, a radical grade-skip could be done all at once; for example, a child in first grade could be skipped to third grade in March, near the end of the school year, and then would move on into fourth grade in the following fall. This would represent skipping two grades. In other cases, the radical grade-skip could be done more gradually in an "every other year" fashion. For example, Josh might skip second grade and go from first to third; then he might skip fifth grade, going from fourth to sixth grade. Then finally he might skip eighth grade, going from seventh to ninth. Radical acceleration is certainly not appropriate for all gifted children, but in the case of a highly gifted child, it may be the only way to keep the child interested and challenged in school.

An every other year option is likely to cause less public attention around the decision than the former, because each grade-skip is "only" for one year. Too often, having a child skip several grades at one time may result in media coverage and can bring undue attention to the child and the decision.

Media coverage shouldn't be a "bad" thing (it certainly isn't in sports), but too often the media have exploited highly gifted children, portraying them almost as "freaks." Reporters will list all the advanced things the child knows, and then find some "problem" with the child. For example, "Tim studies nuclear physics at age 12, but looks forlornly out his window at home wishing for friends to play with...." This sort of media coverage simply exploits the child for sensationalism in the news. No child needs this kind of publicity. The less fuss and attention drawn to grade-skipping or any other acceleration option by teachers, parents, and others who know the child, the better it will be for the child, his teacher, and his future relationships with friends.

Who Is Likely to Benefit from Grade-Skipping?

The gifted child most likely to benefit from exposure to advanced curriculum and the opportunity to socialize with somewhat older children through grade-skipping will have many of the characteristics listed in the chart below.

Table 6.3. Candidate for Grade-Skipping			
Cognitive Functioning	**Personal Characteristics**	**Learning Preferences**	**Interests**
Is processing and achieving well beyond grade-level peers in a specific academic area	*Is self-directed, independent, and motivated to learn*	*Prefers to work at own pace, though not necessarily alone*	*Likes academic work as well as time to pursue more school studies outside of school time*
• Scores well on an individual IQ test (>130) • Is 2+ years ahead on achievement test grade-equivalent scores • Is frustrated with slow pace of regular classroom instruction at current grade level	• Is independent in thought and action • Persists in assigned and self-selected tasks • Enjoys school and learning • Socially mature	• Prefers fast-paced, challenging learning experiences • Enjoys self-instructional materials for learning • Enjoys working with small groups of like ability	• Has wide-ranging interests • Is actively involved in variety of activities and hobbies outside of school

Monitoring the Success of Grade-Skipping

The first full year of grade-skipping should receive regular and careful attention. If a child is not completely sure she wants to skip a grade, sometimes a "trial period" is offered. The child can try it for two to three months and then tell the team whether or not she wishes to continue. Evaluation of the child's adjustment to the grade-skip during the first few months is probably the most important evaluation to make, and the *Iowa Acceleration Scale* has guidelines for monitoring the acceleration. After the critical first year of the grade-skip, attention should shift to what additional educational options might be appropriately offered to the child.

In addition to checking on the child's achievement and attitudes about learning and school, the following questions should be asked. If parents and school can answer "yes" to these questions, then the grade-skip can be considered successful.

1. Did the child progress farther in most academic areas than would be expected if she had stayed at the lower grade level?

2. Is the child comfortable with the new setting and teacher(s)?

3. Has the child made friends in the new class?

4. Does the child wish to continue in the advanced grade?

Non-Graded Classes

Non-graded classes do not refer to the absence of As and Bs, but instead refer to classes in which students are grouped in a way other than by a grade level or age. In a non-graded classroom, students are placed in a classroom according to their approximate level of achievement, regardless of their age or actual grade level. When this option is used, it usually is a school-wide practice, and not one just to benefit gifted children. Advocates propose that it benefits all children because it is based on each child's readiness to learn in different subjects.

Over the decades, other terms have been used to describe non-graded classes—continuous progress, individually guided education, ungraded schools, cross-age grouping, multi-grade classrooms, multi-age classes, and individualized or adaptive learning, to name a few. About once every 15 years, the non-graded approach is touted as a panacea and then disappears again about five years later as a "management nightmare for teachers."

A truly non-graded class will have children of different ages working in small groups, or alone, on a wide variety of tasks during each subject area period. The teacher moves from student to student and from group to group as questions are raised, but everyone is working at a different place in the curriculum. Small groups are formed when children are at the same place in the curriculum, but depending on how long it takes for mastery, that small group may still be there a week later or a new group may have been formed.

Readers may be familiar with the Montessori School model, created decades ago by Maria Montessori in Italy. Her vision of the classroom and the teacher's role closely parallels what occurs in the non-graded classroom. In both the Montessori and public non-graded schools, children are allowed to move ahead through the curriculum when readiness and motivation are exhibited.

In a non-graded classroom, the teacher's primary duties are to introduce new concepts, ideas, and skills as each child is ready for them, give practice tasks to the child to let him apply the new information, and then evaluate each child's progress. Pacing is very flexible. Whole-class discussion, drills, and recitation are rare. Brighter and younger children may race through curriculum that is two or three grade levels ahead of usual age-level performance, while other learners may move more slowly than the expected pace for their age or grade level in order to master the information. In this model, children are rarely grouped by ability; instead, they may be grouped with others who are in the same place in the curriculum, or they may just group themselves based on their own personal preference.

Here is a brief example of possible outcomes for this type of option. In this case, the "non-grading" (and consequent individualizing) took place in just one subject, and the children were all approximately the same age, but what happened is probably typical of what might be expected when non-grading occurs.

A fourth-grade teacher I was working with in a small-town school decided to allow all 28 of her children to move at their own pace in mathematics. Since she used non-grading only in mathematics, this is just a partial example of what true non-grading would be like. At the beginning of the school year, she administered end-of-chapter math tests to every student and stopped testing at the chapter where each student scored below 80%. She discovered that there were 16 chapters of difference in achievement levels between her lowest and highest students. Some children were still working on second-grade math concepts, some were well into the fourth-grade concepts. She then began her non-grading experiment. Each child was first introduced to the "new" concept or skill of the chapter he or she was ready for, was given a packet of practice examples, and was told to come to her with questions and also when ready to take the end-of-chapter test for that set of concepts.

The teacher moved continuously through the classroom during each math period and found she spent about 90% of her time helping the slower math students with additional explanations, re-teaching, and with staying on task. She usually saw her more average and brighter students only when they were ready to be tested and introduced to the next concept. With her reapportionment of time and individualized teaching approach, this teacher discovered at the end of the year that now 33 chapters of difference existed between her lowest and highest students.

Next year's teacher would have an even more diverse class in concept and skill development. Fortunately, the teachers in this school were trained and prepared to continue with this style of learning in mathematics.

How did this type of educational experience affect the children's learning? *All* of the slower students made considerably greater progress in their math concepts that year when compared to their progress in previous years. At the same time, the brightest students were allowed to go beyond the usual limits and ceilings placed on them in class and were happily engaged in sixth- and seventh-grade skills by year's end. This example of non-grading in just one subject makes this option seem very close to single-subject acceleration, which you read about in the previous chapter. But true non-grading uses this approach with the whole school curriculum. Thus, if a child makes similar progress in all academic areas, he can shorten considerably the number of years he will spend in the K-12 system.

Bright children in the class described above loved the faster pace, the control over when and how much they could learn in math, and the frequent feedback on progress (tests). There was nothing holding them back from learning as much as they wanted. They didn't have to wait for others; they could learn at their own pace. The slower students were given more time and help, so everyone seemed to benefit. Ten years later, this teacher is still using this non-graded approach every year with her fourth-grade class.

If non-graded classes were applied to all subject areas, the brighter children could accomplish the requirements of the regular curriculum in significantly fewer years and be ready to move through the K-12 system substantially faster than the majority of learners in school. When this scenario is applied to the curriculum for every subject, this option could be called a type of grade-based acceleration. One could even think of non-graded classes as a subtle form of grade-skipping. The child progresses through the grade levels without any sort of formal grade-skip decision, and no curriculum at a specific grade-level is totally skipped.

What Research Says about Non-Graded Classrooms

The fourth-grade math scenario just described represents only one example of the effects of limited non-graded classes. Schools would not want to reorganize themselves into this model based on one piece of evidence. Fortunately, 20 separate research studies have been conducted on non-graded classes since 1924. Of this number, nine reported general outcomes for all ability levels or were case studies without control group comparisons and without specific measurement of changes in academic achievement, socialization, or psychological adjustment. Even so, these studies generally supported the concept of non-graded classes.

The remaining 11 studies ultimately were included in my analysis of the research. These studies showed that the average academic growth effect for the participating children was substantial and positive, and there was no indication of self-esteem or psychological adjustment difficulties. More specifically, gifted children showed an additional two-fifths (40%) of a year's achievement for each year they were placed in non-graded classrooms. There was literally no difference in the self-esteem (academic or social) of gifted children in non-graded classes as compared to gifted children who were in regular classes. Although none of these studies reported the socialization effects of being in such a classroom, anecdotal evidence suggests that children tend to socialize with those who are working on a similar level of tasks within a small group rather than across all ability levels in the class.

Who Is Most Likely to Benefit from Non-Graded Classrooms?

The gifted child who is most likely to benefit from the self-directed pacing and advanced content found in non-graded classes will have the characteristics shown in the chart below.

You will note that many of these characteristics are the same as those required for grade-skipping as well as for other options described later, since many of these educational options overlap and combine similar ideas. Though repetitive, these fundamental characteristics are included with each option to ensure that they are not overlooked.

Table 6.4. Candidate for Non-Graded Classrooms			
Cognitive Functioning	**Personal Characteristics**	**Learning Preferences**	**Interests**
Needs more to learn in a year than the typical one-year curriculum can offer	*Is independent and persistent*	*Prefers to work alone and at own pace*	*Likes academic work*
• Has above-average ability • Is advanced beyond grade level in most academic areas • Is frustrated with pace of regular classroom instruction at grade level	• Independent in thought and action • Persistent in assigned tasks • Motivated to learn; enjoys school • Socially mature • Accepting of others	• Prefers discussion, peer tutoring, group projects • Likes to work with self-instructional materials	• Has wide-ranging interests • Is actively involved in variety of activities and hobbies outside of school

Monitoring the Success of Non-Graded Classrooms

Parents and teachers should conduct yearly evaluations of how well the non-graded option has "fit" the needs of the child. In addition to measuring actual achievement gains, it is important to ask the child about how well she thinks she is doing academically and socially, whether she has opportunities for social interaction, and whether she is generally enjoying the non-graded option. The non-graded option should be recommended for an additional year if parents and school can answer "yes" to the following questions.

1. Did the child progress farther in most academic areas than would have occurred in a graded classroom?

2. Did the child express satisfaction with what she learned for the year?

3. Does the child have ideas for what and how much she would like to accomplish next year?

4. Is she confident of her ability to learn on her own?

5. Is the child confident of her ability to make friends in the class?

6. Does the child wish to continue this kind of placement?

Multi-Grade Classes

Multi-grade classes, sometimes called "combination classes," share some common traits with non-graded classes but may cover a more limited curriculum in a single year. Often schools will create two-grade combinations, such as first-second, third-fourth, fifth-sixth, or seventh-eighth, but only rarely do they consider the abilities of the children placed in these classes. Instead, the two-grade classroom will often be made up of children of all levels of ability. This option usually occurs because the school has too many or too few children at some grade levels to constitute a full class at grade level. Typically, this option allows children to stay with the same teacher for a second year.

A variation of the multi-grade class would be the "multi-age" class, in which *more* than two grade levels have been combined in a single setting. No matter how many grades are included, the multi-grade classroom is usually a school-wide decision, and not one put into place solely to benefit children who are gifted.

A multi-grade class that *does* consider the educational needs of gifted children will have small groups of children working with the teacher in specific subject areas. In this sort of class, the younger grade-level students will be the brightest ones at that grade level, while the older students will be closer to average in their ability and achievement. The teacher works with one mixed-age group of children that have been selected by how far they have already progressed in that curriculum area (i.e., within-class performance grouping); meanwhile, the rest of the class will work individually or in small groups on a different set of assigned tasks in that same subject area—perhaps to practice skills and content taught when *they* worked with the teacher in a small group. Little whole-class discussion occurs, particularly in math and reading, but there may be whole-group interactions in science and social studies, where the content may represent a mix of the two years' curriculum in those areas—a selection of the "best" non-repetitive topics.

Multi-grade classes can be considered a form of grade-based acceleration because they eliminate the lock-step curriculum for every subject. If the model is used school wide, the brighter children can accomplish the requirements of the regular curriculum, two years at a time, in significantly fewer years and be ready to move beyond the K-12 system earlier than usual. As a result, multi-grade classes can lead to the option of grade-skipping discussed earlier in this chapter.

The key in multi-grade classes, however, is that the gifted student must be placed in the younger of the two combined grade levels each year he is involved. If a child was a first grader in a first/second-grade combination, then for the next year he must be a second grader in a second/third-grade combination, and so forth. By the second year in such a system, the teacher will need to provide enrichments and extensions in most academic areas in order to keep gifted learners appropriately challenged and motivated to learn (if the child has not been moved on to the next combinations grade). In theory, this sounds workable, but in practice, there are few multi-grade schools that consistently offer overlapping multi-grade classes (e.g., grades one-two, two-three, three-four, etc.) This means the gifted child will need to change multi-grade classes each year—go from the one-two class in year one to the three-four class in year two, and so on.

What Does the Research Say about Multi-Grade Classes?

Since 1990, there have been five studies and two meta-analyses conducted on the effects of multi-grade (also called multi-level) classes. None of the studies reported separately on the effects for gifted learners, however. This means that there is no definitive "yes" or "no" for this option when it comes to offering it to gifted children.

Overall, results have been somewhat contradictory. In some studies, when multi-grade teaching is combined with multiple methods for teaching reading, primary students accomplished an additional two years' growth in reading. But Veenman (1995), in a meta-analysis of all studies of multi-level or multi-grade classes, concluded that there were no differences in achievement or non-cognitive effects when multi-grade classes were compared to single-grade classes.

Common sense might suggest that for gifted children, exposure to two years' curriculum for each year in school would be advantageous, but the key to success is to ensure proper implementation. The gifted child would always need to be one of the youngest in the combination of grade levels.

The gifted child most likely to benefit from exposure to multi-grade curriculum and the opportunity to socialize with somewhat older children will probably exhibit characteristics and behaviors like those in Table 6.5.

Cognitive Functioning	Personal Characteristics	Learning Preferences	Interests
Needs more to learn in a year than the typical one-year curriculum can offer	*Is independent and persistent*	*Likes working alone and with others*	*Likes academic work but wants to use outside time on other activities*
• Has above-average ability • Is advanced beyond grade level in most academic areas • Is outstanding reader with high verbal ability • Is frustrated with the pace of regular classroom instruction at the present grade level • Has long attention span in areas of interest	• Independent in thought and action • Persistent in assigned and self-selected tasks • Accepting of others • Socially mature, emotionally controlled • Enjoys school and learning	• Prefers to work alone or in small groups with others of like ability • Prefers to work with self-instructional materials	• Has wide-ranging interests • Is actively involved in variety of activities and hobbies outside of school

Table 6.5. Candidate for Multi-Grade Classes

Monitoring the Success of Multi-Grade Classes

In a yearly review, parents and the school should evaluate how well the multi-grade option has "fit" the needs of the child by interviewing the child about social interactions as well as looking at actual achievement gains. Has the child made "older" friends? Has she felt accepted within the classroom? Whether the multi-grade option is to be recommended for the next year will depend on the answers to the following questions:

1. Did the child progress farther in most academic areas than would have occurred if in a single-grade classroom?

2. Did the child express satisfaction with what she learned for the year?

3. Did the child make friends within the class?

4. Does the child believe she had enough attention from the teacher so that she could learn as rapidly as she wishes?

5. Does the child wish to continue with multi-grade placement?

Grade Telescoping

Grade telescoping, also called "rapid progress," involves allowing a child—or preferably, a group of children of the same age—to complete the school's curriculum of *several* years in one year's less time. For example, a middle school student could complete the three years' curriculum of middle school in two years, perhaps attending summer school in between the two years to keep up the learning pace. He could do this by working on his own in the library for math, moving in and out of science and social studies classes offered in all three years as he masters what is being taught in each of them, and/or working with a teacher specialist on a regular basis to cover all of the concepts, skills, and literature of three years of language-arts curriculum. Or he could be part of a group of able students who are provided with the three-year's curriculum at a faster pace (e.g., two-year's time) by a separate set of teachers for each area of the curriculum.

Grade telescoping requires the school to look carefully at its curriculum, to eliminate repetition, to limit practice of already mastered skills and concepts, and to step up considerably the pace of learning. Usually, the child is not allowed to skip *any* subject areas of curriculum, but will move more rapidly through them.

Grade telescoping is particularly effective when a small group of bright children work through the curriculum together. For example, a small group of gifted fifth-grade students is supervised in each subject area by a teacher perhaps one to two times a week, and the students are given tasks to accomplish before the next meeting. The group then works on the tasks—both together and independently—supporting each other and asking for help only when no one in the group understands the materials being studied.

This option has been widely used in some Australian school systems. In Melbourne, for example, students who attend University High School—a selective (college prep) school for grades seven through twelve—can choose to complete six years' curriculum in four, five, or six years. Different teachers are assigned to the three options so that pacing can be adjusted for the curriculum to be covered in the differing time spans. Evaluations of students in the two telescoped groups (the four-year and five-year students) have shown no substantial differences in overall achievement (performance on university entrance exams) when compared to the students who moved at the traditional six-year pace. This means that students can move on to the challenges that they will find in college a few years earlier, with less risk of underachievement or declining motivation to learn. The evaluation showed that participation in extracurricular activities by the faster-paced students was no different than for other students, and the telescoped students were as socially and emotionally adjusted. The accelerated students scored just as high, or in some cases, even higher, on the state of Victoria's university entrance exams and were just as readily accepted into the university system upon graduation. In other words, we cannot say whether grade telescoping is either beneficial or harmful to the students. It seems to be a good option to keep advanced learners working at faster levels, but it doesn't make them learn more or better. The ultimate benefit may be that it keeps bright students positively engaged in school and learning.

Successful grade telescoping requires careful study of the curriculum to ensure that the accelerated pacing leaves no gaps in a student's knowledge and skills. Likewise, the student must have a "supervisor" to coordinate information from the subject-area teachers, to get feedback on the student's performance, and to ensure that the student works up to speed. If a student grade telescopes alone without others in a group, there is a real question about how to provide social outlets for her during school time. There is a possible danger that the child might focus only on studies and neglect chances for friendships with peers. A counselor should be specially assigned to monitor social development and participation in school, social, and extracurricular activities.

What Does the Research Say about Grade Telescoping?

My research on grade telescoping located 28 studies, ranging from 1918-1982. Most of the studies took place in either the 1930s or the 1960s. All but three of the studies used some measure of giftedness as a criterion for student placement in the program. Six of the studies documented telescoping for elementary aged children who completed two years' curriculum in one year's time. The other studies were equally divided among telescoping in middle school/junior high years and high school years. Sample sizes ranged from 15 students in one study to 1,027 students in the largest study.

For this type of acceleration, the academic effects for these children were large and positive, accounting for about three-fifths (60%) of a year's additional gain for each year students in the studies were telescoped. No difference in social adjustment was reported, but there was a small, positive effect on measures of self-esteem and perceived pressure to achieve. These results established that the gifted children made great academic gains with grade telescoping, felt slightly better about themselves as learners, and did not lose out socially. It appears that grade telescoping allowed a group of gifted learners to maintain the socialization they needed at school. However, it would be difficult to know how a single child doing this option alone might be affected socially.

Grade telescoping should raise increasing interest among parents and teachers of gifted children in light of the troubling current trend in middle school philosophy and programming to stress the importance of social adjustment, with much less emphasis on cognitive development, knowledge, or skill acquisition. Recent articles (not research) justify this trend by saying that because middle school children are developing so rapidly in their physical and emotional domains, they do not have the capacity to develop their minds to a higher order. Whether or not these arguments are valid, it is clear that educators at this level are concerned about socialization.

The research on gifted children does not support this viewpoint. Research clearly shows that it is the thinking and learning of bright children—not their socialization—that is developed and accelerated throughout their youth. The brighter they are, the more likely they are to enter the stage of abstract and logical thinking—also called the Piagetian Formal Operations stage—by middle school age (Carter & Ormrod, 1982). Consequently, the lack of attention middle schools are placing on advanced thinking during this critical period is actually detrimental to the cognitive growth of gifted youngsters. If gifted learners are ready to think more abstractly about complex ideas, how will it benefit them to just lie back and socialize for three years instead of concentrating on advancing their curriculum? Grade telescoping in the middle school years—that is, completing the three years' work in two years' time—might be just the educational solution needed. This option does require considerable reorganization of the school itself. Nonetheless, it is one good solution for gifted children traversing those middle school years.

At the high school level, telescoping may be of particular value to a gifted student if the school is unable to offer accelerated and honors courses in most subject areas, or cannot provide the scheduling flexibility for students to take advanced courses outside of the high school during school time, or if the school does not have a pro-academic climate for learning. For example, a high school student who telescopes might take some courses through independent study or correspondence, thereby earning credits at a faster pace. Some high schools also accept on-line computer classes, and these might be a part of his telescoped program as well. In other words, for grade telescoping to work as a grade-based acceleration option, an individual student might need to use some subject-based acceleration options as well.

Who Is Most Likely to Benefit from a Telescoped Curriculum?

The gifted learner who is most likely to benefit from a telescoped curriculum should possess the characteristics in Table 6.6.

Table 6.6. Candidate for Telescoped Curriculum			
Cognitive Functioning	**Personal Characteristics**	**Learning Preferences**	**Interests**
Is processing and achieving well above most others at current grade level	*Is independent and motivated*	*Prefers to work at own pace, but not necessarily alone*	*Likes academic work*
• Has above-average ability • Has mastered grade-equivalent curriculum	• Wants to learn at a faster pace • Is focused when learning and retains information easily	• Prefers fast-paced, challenging content • Prefers self-instructional materials	• Has wide-ranging interests

Table 6.6. Candidate for Telescoped Curriculum
(continued)

Cognitive Functioning	Personal Characteristics	Learning Preferences	Interests
Is processing and achieving well above most others at current grade level	*Is independent and motivated*	*Prefers to work at own pace, but not necessarily alone*	*Likes academic work*
• Is frustrated with pace of regular classroom instruction at grade level	• Has strong achievement need • Takes risks willingly and is confident • Is an abstract and perceptive thinker • Persists in assigned tasks and own interests • Is independent in thought and action • Is socially mature, emotionally stable, and accepting of others	• Enjoys working in like-ability or like-interest groups	• Is actively involved in variety of activities and hobbies outside of school

Monitoring the Success of Grade Telescoping

Achievement, socialization, and self-esteem are all critical for the success of grade telescoping. Each year, information should be gathered to ensure that the student is keeping up with the faster pace of exposure to new curriculum and is generally participating in socialization through extracurricular activities. Care should be taken to keep the student involved in the general school routine and to ensure that the student is not basically isolated from regular contact with teachers and other students. The telescoping option is successful if the following conditions are satisfied.

1. Did the child accomplish approximately one and a half year's curriculum for each year in the option?

2. Does the child feel connected to fellow students and teachers?

3. Does the child like the faster pace of learning? Or is she feeling pressure to achieve that is uncomfortable?

4. Does the child wish to continue with this kind of placement?

Testing Out

Testing out has also been called "credit by examination" or "placement testing." It differs from compacting (described in a previous chapter) in that the assessments for this option are formal and objective in nature, and no replacement learning experiences are added to the curriculum.

The testing-out option is exercised by a student when he is allowed to complete a test in a subject area that covers one semester or one year of work. If he scores at an acceptable criterion for showing mastery to the school or teacher (usually a score of 80-85% or above), then the student is allowed to move into a higher level course, or he can use the earned time to pursue a different subject.

In elementary or middle school, moving to a higher-level class is much more likely. But once the student is in high school or college, testing out can signal the end of study in that specific subject area, either because the school has nothing further to offer the student or because the student has no deep, continuing interest in that subject area and prefers to pursue something of greater interest. Gifted students who are repeatedly allowed to test out in areas where they have already mastered the knowledge and skills are often able to complete the K-12 curriculum in considerably fewer years than the typical 13. This form of grade-based acceleration, then, will end up shortening the number of years in school in the same way as a grade-skip does.

With the current national interest in having schools teach to state-mandated standards and to be assessed on those standards (sometimes called "outcomes-based education"), the option of testing out has become increasingly popular. Most of the subject standards—whether developed by states or by national associations—are actually minimum standards geared to the average or below-average learner. Thus, the tests used represent an effort by the schools to bring up the learning of those who might have previously failed to meet the standards or "slipped through the cracks." Little systematic attention by state education departments and local school districts has been given to the appropriateness of—or the challenge levels of—these standards for bright students. As a result, gifted children are often able to "pass" the standards being used to demonstrate mastery several years in advance of the stated grade level.

At the college level, testing out has been big business for decades. High school students come to college with widely varying educational backgrounds. Students from small schools may not have had a broad offering of advanced coursework available to them, and remediation or "catch up" may be needed. College placement tests are used widely in language arts, mathematics, and foreign language; the test results provide college counselors with the information they need to place students in an appropriate level of coursework.

On the other hand, students from larger schools may come to college having received a full range of advanced and accelerated coursework. The College Level Examination Program (CLEP) test allows these students to show what they already know about a subject. College advisors can then move students ahead to more advanced coursework.

On entering college, Marta, for example, takes the CLEP and/or university exams for music theory (she has played piano and violin since age six), German (she completed four years of German in two years' time in high school), and math. Her scores on the CLEP exams tell the university that she should be awarded six credits (the equivalent of the first two courses) in music theory, 16 credits of German (the first four courses), and placement in Honors Calculus II. In order to be given these credits toward graduation, she must enroll in and complete the next level music theory, German, and math courses. After completing these higher-level courses, Marta can either continue in these three subject areas or be finished with required work in those areas and move on to other subjects of interest.

What Does the Research Say about Testing Out?

The best evidence on testing out, according to my synthesis of research, is located in 13 studies between 1935-1985. All of these studies were conducted on college students, with sample sizes ranging from 79 to 11,082 students, and all involved gifted students. The studies showed a substantial and positive academic achievement effect size. Students gained about three-fifths of a year's additional achievement in the specific area covered by the exam. None of the studies measured the social or psychological effects of credit by examination, but anecdotal evidence provided in several studies suggested that self-rated socialization and psychological adjustment were slightly less positive for those who tested out compared to non-testers. Perhaps finding themselves in tougher courses than other freshmen prompted slight feelings of inadequacy, which may have led to less time socializing and more time studying to "keep up." On the other hand, students may simply *think* that their time must be spent this way, rather than it being an actual necessity.

One study on credit by examination compared the effects of students who tested out of one subject area with those who tested out in three to four areas. The social and emotional effects, anecdotally related, were substantially more positive for those college students who tested out of *more* areas, suggesting that they were probably brighter and less worried about keeping up with others. Socialization problems, then, may be merely in the "eye of the beholder."

It is a concern that no research on testing out or receiving credit for prior learning exists for gifted children younger than college age. Perhaps more studies will be done soon. Common sense would suggest that academic effects would be similar to what was found for college students, but more research is needed on this very important grade-based acceleration option.

Who Is Most Likely to Benefit from Testing Out?

The gifted learner most likely to benefit from testing out of classes in content they have already mastered will have the characteristics listed in Table 6.7.

Table 6.7. Candidate for Testing Out			
Cognitive Functioning	**Personal Characteristics**	**Learning Preferences**	**Interests**
Is processing and achieving well above most others at chronological age	*Is independent and motivated*	*Prefers to work at own pace, but not necessarily alone*	*Likes academic work*
• Has above-average ability • Is 2+ years advanced in grade-equivalent curriculum	• Independent in thought and action • Motivated to learn; enjoys school	• Prefers fast-paced, challenging learning experiences	• Has strong interest in one or more specific subject areas

Table 6.7. Candidate for Testing Out

(continued)

Cognitive Functioning	Personal Characteristics	Learning Preferences	Interests
Is processing and achieving well above most others at chrono-logical age	*Is independent and motivated*	*Prefers to work at own pace, but not necessarily alone*	*Likes academic work*
• Is frustrated with the pace of regular classroom instruction in a specific subject area	• Self-accepting	• Prefers work with self-instructional materials or working in small like-ability groups	• Is actively involved in a variety of activities and hobbies outside of school

Monitoring the Testing-Out Option

It is particularly important to examine the effects of testing out at the end of the first term after the child has been placed in a more advanced curriculum. From that point on, whatever else has been offered in the new setting is probably more important in the long term than the effects of testing out. After collecting current achievement and interview data, parents and school can evaluate the testing-out option by asking the following questions.

1. Did the student make satisfactory progress in the new, advanced course/class placement?

2. Is the student comfortable with the new setting and teacher(s)?

3. Has she made friends within the new class?

4. Is she experiencing any gaps in her learning in the subject area in which she tested out?

5. Is she ready to test out in another subject area?

Early Admission to College

Beth's story at the beginning of this chapter accurately described this option, but in fact, many early admissions to college do not involve such a radical acceleration as Beth's. There is substantial research to document students successfully leaving high school after tenth or eleventh grade to enter college at that time, often without any formal graduation from high school. This option, once funded by the Ford Foundation as a way to actively recruit bright students to enter college early, was particularly popular during two periods of our nation's recent history: 1940-1942, and again in 1949. There was a belief that bright students would be the best military leaders; hence the need to get their preparatory training over more quickly. At present, early entrance to college is used by gifted students who believe that high school has little more to offer them.

Students who have been admitted early to college typically participate in the regular university curriculum and work with others who are older than they. No additional curriculum enrichment takes place—at least not systematically—except for possible enrollment in honors classes at the college level.

Research on Early Admission to College

To synthesize the research on early admission to college, I located 37 studies done between 1923-1988. All but 10 of these studies tracked the specific outcomes of this option for identified gifted students. The academic effect was moderately powerful and positive. By making the move early to college, these students showed about one-third of an additional year's gain. No substantial problems were noted in socialization, although the students in the studies in the 1940s and 1950s reported that they did not spend as much time socializing as they perceived other students did. The psychological effect, though small, was positive, as rated by the students' college advisors.

The specific studies that have considered Beth's somewhat radical form of early admission to college have produced some interesting findings. For example, the Early Entrance Program (EEP), established in 1977 at the University of Washington in Seattle, and the Study for Mathematically Precocious Youth (SMPY) program, established in 1971 at Johns Hopkins in Maryland, have conducted many studies—both by case study and by comparison—on early entrance to college. Only a few differences were found between the young early entrants and their older college classmates. The early entrance students were less conforming, less assertive, and tended to get higher grades than their older peers who had entered college at a more traditional age. There were no indications of emotional maladjustment among these students who were radically accelerated.

In a slightly different set of studies, Cornell (1987) documented somewhat lower levels of self-esteem and social mobility among young women who were early entrants to the Mary Baldwin College PEG program as compared with same-age intellectual peers who did not enroll in such a radically accelerated program. It is possible, however, the students' self-esteem was not lower, but was simply more realistic. That is, students like Beth were confronted for the first time with others who were also truly achieving and processing at the same level and pace. After years of being the superlative performer, this new situation might cause a student like Beth to readjust her academic self-concept to a more realistic level for the situation.

Such early entrance programs clearly provide ample opportunities to interact with true peers, perhaps for the first time for some gifted students. Longer-term studies on these early entrance students suggest that they tend to socialize with other early entrants at least for the first two years at college, and then as their studies become even more advanced, they interact with a wider selection of older companions as well.

Perhaps even more reassuring to parents and students who are considering early college entrance are the follow-up reports of what many of these early entrants—even if they were radically accelerated—do after earning their Bachelor's degree. Brody and Stanley (1991) report, "rarely does a student who graduates from college several years earlier than typical immediately go to work in a permanent career" (p. 118). Most enter some form of graduate study, which has the benefit of giving them more vocationally productive years at a young age and thus increases the likelihood that they will be more effective over the length of their career. Some of them return for a second Bachelor's degree in a very different course of study. Others accept fellowships to study abroad, and some go on to participate in volunteer experiences, internships, and even to travel the world with the time they have saved by going to college early.

Who Is Most Likely to Benefit from Early Admission to College?

The gifted student most likely to benefit from early admission to college is one who has characteristics listed in Table 6.8.

Table 6.8. Candidate for Early Admission to College			
Cognitive Functioning	**Personal Characteristics**	**Learning Preferences**	**Interests**
Is processing and achieving well above most others at current grade level in high school	*Is independent and motivated*	*Prefers to work at own pace, but not necessarily alone*	*Likes academic work and doesn't have strong interest in school extracurricular activities*
• Scores in the highly gifted range on an intelligence test (highly gifted range of 150+ for radical early admission)	• Independent in thought and action • Motivated to learn; enjoys school • Socially mature	• Prefers fast-paced, challenging content	• Has strong interest in at least one academic area

Table 6.8. Candidate for Early Admission to College *(continued)*

Cognitive Functioning	Personal Characteristics	Learning Preferences	Interests
Is processing and achieving well above most others at current grade level in high school	*Is independent and motivated*	*Prefers to work at own pace, but not necessarily alone*	*Likes academic work and doesn't have strong interest in school extracurricular activities*
• Has completed some advanced level coursework while in high school, such as AP courses • Scores highly (>650 verbal and math) on SAT or ACT exams taken prior to eleventh grade • Is frustrated with pace of regular classroom instruction at grade level	• Accepting of others • Self-confident • Thrives in competitive situations	• Prefers to work with self-instructional materials, lecture, individual projects, and discussion • Will not "regret" leaving the social atmosphere of high school nor missing the high school graduation ceremony	• Has some involvement in activities and hobbies outside of school

Monitoring Early Admission to College

The end of the first semester after early admission to college is a particularly important time for evaluation. It is helpful for early admission students to have a college advisor to talk to, particularly during the first year.

It is particularly critical to look at the student's study habits. Has she been able to acquire appropriate study and test-taking skills for the new environment? Often, early admission is the first time bright students are forced to really study something they don't know, and they may not have learned how to study or to organize their time to study. Likewise, has she been able to create a life for herself beyond her books? In addition to the student's achievement, the following questions should be asked to provide guidelines to parents and teachers—as well as to the student— concerning whether the decision to accelerate is successful.

1. Is the student satisfied with her grades in enrolled courses?

2. Is she comfortable with the new setting and instructors(s)?

3. Has the student made friends?

4. Does the student participate in college activities outside of class attendance?

5. Does the student wish to continue with this kind of placement?

What Grade-Based Acceleration Options Are Best for Which Ages?

We have presented six different acceleration options and have noted what the research says about each. But how do we decide *which* option to use for *which* child? And at what age?

Table 6.9 matches appropriate ages and grades with the various grade-based acceleration options for gifted and talented students. As noted in the previous chapter on subject-based acceleration, however, care must be taken to look closely at the cognitive functioning, learning strengths, learning preferences, and interests of each gifted child—in addition to his developmental age or grade—when recommending one option over another.

Table 6.9. When to Consider Grade-Based Acceleration Options

Option	Age Range	Grade Range
Grade-Skipping	6-18	K-12
Non-Graded Classrooms	5-18 *9-14	K-12 *3-8
Multi-Grade/Age Classrooms	6-18 *6-14	1-12 *1-8
Grade Telescoping	12-18	6-12
Testing Out	7-22 *18-22	2-13 *13
Early Admission to College	14-18	8-12

* Indicates typical, most appropriate age and grade ranges, according to research

Another Quiz: Which of These Children Should Be Grade-Based Accelerated?

Just as for subject-based forms of acceleration, you have now acquired new knowledge about grade-based acceleration options. It may be helpful for you to test your understanding with the following quiz. Based on the information you read in this chapter, which of these children should be grade-based accelerated—Kaley and/or Tomas and/or Jasmin? Which grade-based acceleration option would you recommend? You can check your answers at the end of the chapter.

Currently in fourth grade, Kaley goes to fifth grade for science and reading. She is making good progress working independently on the sixth-grade math curriculum, and she will have completed it by the end of the year. Her intelligence test scores are in the highly gifted range (159 IQ). She has made good friends with two other bright girls in fifth grade and plays with them outside of school as well. She has difficulty being accepted by her fourth-grade classmates. She generally works independently and has interests and concerns that are not shared by these age peers. She often describes her classmates as "babyish." The other students don't like that she is different and call her "weird," but this does not particularly disturb her at the present time. She takes violin lessons outside of school and plays with a local youth orchestra, where she is concertmistress. She is generally positive about her abilities and has good self-esteem. She doesn't mind school, but wishes she could have more time to socialize with her fifth-grade friends. She is the oldest child in her family.

SHOULD SHE ACCELERATE?   Yes   No
WHAT FORM(S) OF ACCELERATION WOULD BE BEST?

Currently, Tomas is taking the last of his high school math in a local program, even though he is only in eighth grade. Even though math is his "thing," Tomas also performs above eighth-grade level in all of his other courses and is taking enriched classes offered in English, science, and social studies at his local high school. When he was in fourth grade, the psychologist reported his IQ as 135, in the gifted range. He has performed in the school play this past year and is on the school's soccer team, where he is one of the better players. He recently took the SAT exams designed for eleventh- and twelfth-grade students and scored 590 on the verbal portion and 750 on the math portion of the exam out of a possible 800 for each section. He is looking for-

ward to playing on the soccer team at the high school and has already been "recruited" by the coach there. His high school has a strong theater program, and he hopes to participate in that as well. Tomas is an only child of parents who strongly value education. He gets along well with children of all ages and truly enjoys his social interactions at school and on the soccer field. At the same time, though, he loves his enriched and accelerated classes, particularly in math.

SHOULD HE ACCELERATE? **Yes** **No**
WHAT FORM(S) OF ACCELERATION WOULD BE BEST?

Jasmin

Currently in tenth grade, Jasmin is enrolled in four Advanced Placement courses (Calculus, Chemistry, English Literature, American History)—a first for the school, which usually requires students to be in eleventh grade before taking AP classes. She is doing well in her classes, but is concerned about what she will study next year. She works on the school literary magazine and is a photographer on the school newspaper, which means she regularly makes contact with a wide variety of students. She frequently complains that the kids her age "are so immature." When she was tested in the primary grades, her IQ was measured at 149, in the highly gifted range. She is well-organized in all she does. She thinks and acts independently, and she has never had a need for a large group of friends. She has mentioned to her counselor that she would like to leave high school early and go to the local university.

SHOULD SHE ACCELERATE? **Yes** **No**
WHAT FORM(S) OF ACCELERATION WOULD BE BEST?

Answers to the Quiz

Kaley should probably be *grade-skipped* into fifth grade immediately. When she and her bright friends make the transition to middle school, *grade telescoping* should be considered.

Tomas is a better candidate for *subject-based acceleration* than for grade-based acceleration. This will allow him to participate fully in the arts and sports he loves. He should be allowed to try to test out of any subjects he chooses at the high school level, thereby giving him time to pursue theater and soccer even more fully. He should be encouraged to take *Advanced Placement* and accelerated courses, and provisions should be made for him to take his mathematics through *correspondence courses* or *concurrent enrollment* at the local college.

Jasmin should be allowed to *enter college early*, beginning with her eleventh grade year. It is imperative that she take the SAT or ACT as early as possible so that she can apply to colleges, preferably ones in the area. She might want to consider commuting from home for her first couple of years at college to ease her transition away from home until she decides if she wants to transfer to a more selective university or continue where she is.

Summary

There are at least six different ways, listed below, that the number of years a gifted child spends in the K-12 school system can be shortened. For many bright children, grade-based acceleration can be a solution, especially those who find school too slow and stilted, who are very independent and persistent, and who are highly motivated when there are regular opportunities to tackle difficult and new knowledge and skills. Care must be taken, however, to ensure that the child's level of cognitive functioning, personality, school-related attitudes, and motivation support this acceleration.

Key Points

- Grade-based acceleration is defined as any practice that shortens the number of years a student participates in the K-12 school system.
- Six forms of grade-based acceleration that are supported by research are:
  - grade-skipping.
  - grade telescoping.
  - non-graded classes.
  - multi-grade classes.
  - testing out (credit by examination).
  - early admission to college.
- Grade-based acceleration options that may be more effective for younger gifted learners include non-graded classes, multi-grade classes, and grade-skipping.
- Options that may be more effective for gifted learners in the middle years include grade telescoping, testing out, and grade-skipping.
- High school grade-based acceleration options include testing out, grade telescoping, and early admission to college.
- Grade-based acceleration may not be desirable for every gifted learner, but with careful appraisal of the "whole" child, it will become clear whether this option will be a successful decision or not.

7

Program Provisions (Grouping) within the School

A Scenario: What Would You Do?

Suppose you are a sixth-grade teacher in a K-6 school. You have 28 children in your class, two of whom are gifted. You cannot arrange for the two gifted students to take classes at the junior high because the junior high is 10 miles away, and transportation is impossible. It is up to you and your fellow teachers to somehow differentiate the general academic curriculum for these bright students. Should you each try to work with these two students individually when you can find time, or is there a better way to manage their instruction? List the steps you could take to ensure that these students get appropriate challenge and access to differentiated curriculum and instruction. (One possible set of solutions is provided at the end of this chapter.)

Step 1: _____

Step 2: _____

Step 3: _____

Step 4: _____

Step 5: _____

Ways to Manage the Instruction of Gifted Children by Grouping

Chapters 5 and 6 presented a variety of ways to make individual enrichment and acceleration decisions for children who are significantly beyond their agemates and who are learning significantly faster than their grade-level peers. Only a few of the options provided ways for these gifted or talented children to work with each other. For example, among the 11 subject-based accelerative options discussed in Chapters 5, only three—*Talent Search* programs, *Advanced Placement* programs, and *college-in-the-school* programs—grouped gifted students together. Among the grade-based accelerative options discussed in Chapter 6, only *multi-grade classes* and *grade telescoping* took into account that the bright children would be grouped together to progress through the option.

Few parents wish to see their child come to school and work alone for the next 13 years of school. At the same time, neither do most parents of gifted children wish to see their child work exclusively at the average pace of mixed-ability groups for the next 13 years of school. Peer relations are important; so is learning to work in groups. In fact, there is an amazingly large body of research—over 1,500 different studies—on the variety of forms that grouping can take, though only a small number of these studies examine the effects of grouping on children who are gifted or talented. Most of the studies that have looked at gifted children support specific types of grouping. And certainly, school is the place where grouping that is beneficial to gifted children can most easily occur. The remainder of this chapter, then, will be devoted to describing the research on grouping practices as it applies to gifted children, K-12.

Two broad categories of grouping are 1) *small group* and 2) *whole class*.

Each of these broad categories can have significant variations. Small groups for gifted children may take any one of the following forms:

1. A "dyad" of two students, often grouped for joint projects or peer tutoring.

2. A "cluster" of five to eight students, usually grouped within one classroom for the purposes of academic differentiation of curriculum.

3. An "enrichment grouping" of eight to 12 students either in a *pull-out grouping* or a *within-class grouping*.

4. A regrouping of students based on performance level in specific subject areas, either with all students at the same grade levels or across grade levels.

Whole class groups typically are of only two general types: either the groups are *mixed-ability* (heterogeneous) or *like-ability* (homogeneous).

The history of grouping practices in schools has been controversial, with strong opinions for and against it. However, an understanding of the research, which will be described later, will clarify the concerns.

The first documented research on gifted programming occurred in 1878 in the St. Louis, Missouri school system. Since then, educators have at various times looked upon the ability grouping of bright children both favorably and unfavorably.

Arguments in favor of some form of grouping of gifted children by ability or performance are these:

1. It is easier to provide different materials and instructional strategies because the learning group is smaller and more homogeneous.

2. The learning climate is more pro-academic and supports intellectual endeavors.

3. Social interactions and friendship choices are more easily made when other students are intellectual peers.

4. Because bright children will "bounce" ideas off each other and "spark" one another, they will develop further cognitively and socially if they are with peers of similar abilities or interests.

Arguments opposing ability- or performance-based grouping for gifted children are most often these:

1. Grouping creates elitist attitudes among the children, the parents, or both.

2. When gifted children are grouped separately for instruction, the class tends to get divided along racial or economic lines.

3. Grouping gifted children together prevents other children from access to "high end" learning.

4. Stronger teachers get the gifted classes; poorer teachers get the lower ability groups.

5. The self-esteem of lower ability children can be damaged because they are excluded.

6. Gifted children can serve as models or examples for less able children and can help teach them.

There are still educators today, unfamiliar with the research on gifted students, who believe grouping gifted students together is elitist or detrimental to other students in some way. In fact, as we will see, the research shows that grouping is positive for gifted students.

Forms of Grouping

Various forms of grouping, and what the research actually says about each, will first be listed, then described in detail, followed by a discussion of the implications for families.

The most frequent forms of grouping for high ability children are:

- Whole class strategies
  - o Full-time ability classes or "tracks"
    - ◆ Special schools for the gifted
    - ◆ Full-time gifted programs or classes
    - ◆ School-within-a-school
  - o Untracked whole class instruction, "default" option
- Small group strategies
  - o Pull-out gifted groups
  - o Cluster grouping
  - o Regrouping by ability/achievement level for specific subject instruction
  - o Within-class ability/achievement level grouping
  - o Like-ability cooperative grouping
  - o Cross-grade grouping by achievement level
  - o Peer tutoring dyads
  - o Mixed-ability cooperative grouping ("Default" option)

Whole-Class Strategies

Full-Time Ability Grouping/Tracking

Full-time ability grouping, sometimes called "tracking," has been roundly criticized by some in recent years. In essence, it is the practice of grouping children by their performance on tests of ability or achievement into different curriculum levels.

In the earliest forms of tracking, the brightest students or the ones most advanced in their achievement were placed in the top track (sometimes called the "college prep" or "college bound" track). Those in the middle of the ability or achievement continuum were placed in the average or "general" track, and those who performed poorly on such tests were placed in the remedial or "vocational" track.

Once placed, students took all of their classes within their track, regardless of how uneven their own abilities or performances might be. (Think of Maria in Chapter 1 who showed some very advanced abilities, and others that were average.) Once placed within a track, it was almost impossible to move to a higher track. For example, a student might perform extremely well in the middle track, but to move up to a higher track, he would not only have to be doing well in his current track, but also would have to pick up the work of the next track to "catch up"—a nearly impossible task. This kind of inflexible tracking had the danger of becoming a permanent and rigid demarcation of students. If teacher and student attitudes were not carefully monitored in schools, it became a way of labeling students' worth as well. Jeannie Oakes (1985), in her landmark book, *Keeping Track*, clearly describes the potential emotional turmoil that rigid and inflexible tracking could cause.

But tracking as described by Oakes in 1985 had little to do with educating gifted and talented children. Gifted children, in fact, were found at all levels. If they were achieving at high levels, they might be placed in the top track (and a lot of them were), but if they were underachieving, they could easily have been found in the middle or lower tracks, depending on how severe their underachievement.

Some variations of tracking do deal directly with gifted children, however, and these have been studied in the literature, particularly with regard to full-time ability grouping. The most frequent of these variations are special schools for the gifted and other full-time gifted programs, sometimes called a school-within-a-school.

Special Schools for the Gifted

Special schools for the gifted exist in various parts of the United States, and many have been around for 50 or more years. To mention a few, Los Angeles has the Mirman School, a private school for the gifted; New York City, Salt Lake City, St. Paul, and Tucson have public magnet schools for the academically gifted; in the Denver area there are no less than eight private and public schools for the academically or creatively gifted; and Michigan has the Roeper City and Country School for the Gifted and Interlochen Pathfinder School and Center for the Arts. All of these schools have consistently high entrance requirements, and all have long waiting lists of gifted children who wish to attend.

Full-Time Gifted Classes or Programs/ School-within-a-School

Full-time gifted programs are more often found in medium to large public school systems. Gifted children from several schools within the district are housed in one building, often called a magnet school, and take all of their classes together there. The building might also house heterogeneous or mixed ability classes, but few of the classes of both groups would be mixed. The full-time program for gifted and talented children operates as a school-within-a-school.

One of the most collaborative versions of this school structure can be found in northern Minnesota in a medium-sized rural district. All of the gifted children from schools in the district are transported daily to a central school, the "magnet" school. One classroom per grade level in which these gifted children are placed is taught by a trained gifted specialist. The specialist trades roles in her area of expertise at that grade level with other teachers who may have different areas of expertise. For example, a third-grade teacher with a strong background in science teaches all of the science classes to all students in the gifted magnet school, and one of her colleagues teaches all students the social studies classes, appropriately differentiated. The students from the entire school are mixed together heterogeneously for art, music, physical education, recess, and lunchtimes. Thus, gifted children are with other gifted students for the academic areas, such as math, reading, and social studies, but are mixed with all students for other subjects, allowing for socialization across all groups of students.

Full-time gifted programs, also called self-contained gifted programs, may also occur in each school of a larger district, rather than having the gifted students congregated in only one district school. Usually, this depends on whether sufficient numbers of bright students are located in that school to make a full class of 18 to 20 students.

What Research Says about Full-Time Grouping

Over the past 15 years, nine analyses of the large body of research on full-time grouping have been conducted. Four of these studies have compiled and looked at studies of full-time ability grouping, or tracking. That is, the achievement levels of students in three-tracked schools (the letters XYZ were used to denote the different tracks) were compared to the achievement levels of students in untracked schools. Robert Slavin (1987), who conducted many of these syntheses, concluded that the academic effect size of tracking is zero. That is, students who are tracked do no better or worse than students in untracked schools. But wait; let's look further.

The question for the readers of this book is what happens academically, socially, and/or emotionally to *gifted or talented children* in these two management systems. It is clear that the answer cannot be found in these XYZ studies because of a fundamental flaw in that research. The flaw is that standardized achievement tests were used in most of these studies. Thus, if a gifted child were tested before being tracked and scored near the ceiling of the test (97th-99th percentile), and then the child's achievement was measured a year later—again scoring at or near the ceiling of the test—the effect size would of course look as though no growth had taken place. In other words, there would be no clear picture of any progress the gifted child made in either kind of school system—tracked or untracked—because the test used to judge academic progress did not have a high enough ceiling to indicate the gifted child's actual achievement progress. Just as in ability testing, without a high enough ceiling, we have no true measure of what the child knows or can do.

Two other researchers, James and Chen-Lin Kulik (1982; 1984; 1987; 1989), have conducted several analyses of a second body of studies on tracking—called the ability comparison studies. In these studies, actual levels of achievement of students with varying abilities were compared in the two kinds of schools—tracked and untracked. The Kuliks' analyses showed that gifted children in a full-time gifted placement (special school, full-time program, or school-within-a-school) when compared to equally gifted students in mixed ability classes (untracked), showed an academic effect that was both substantial and positive. Almost a half-year's additional academic progress was found for each year the gifted children were in the full-time program at the elementary level (K-6). Gifted students in full-time programs at the secondary level (grades 7-12), made one-third of a year's progress.

Unfortunately, most of these studies looked only at the grouping strategy itself and paid little attention to actual teaching differences between the full-time gifted group and the mixed-ability classes. Thus, it is difficult to know what portion of these gains were a result of the children's interactions with each other and what portion could be attributed to differences in curriculum. James Kulik (1992) has argued quite cogently that the latter is more likely the greater influence on overall academic gain.

The Kuliks (1985) also examined the research on tracking and self-esteem of high-ability students. They found that when high achieving students are placed in full-time tracks with others of like-ability, their self-esteem was somewhat lower than for brighter students in untracked classes. (This fits with what was discussed earlier on some forms of acceleration in Chapters 5 and 6.) The Kuliks also found that students in an ability-group setting—regardless of the track—were substantially more motivated toward subject areas than were students who were not ability-grouped. This suggests that if motivation can be improved by ability grouping, then students might work a little harder, and ultimately there might be some improvements in overall achievement for all tracks!

In 1992, Cornell and Delcourt directly compared five different types of ability-grouping programs for gifted children—special schools, regrouped classes, pull-out groups, within-class grouping, and no program at all. Substantial positive effects in achievement in most academic core areas were found for students in special schools when compared to students' achievement in the other four options that had less than full-time grouping.

It seems that the arguments opposing full-time grouping for gifted children are based more on an educator's personal philosophy than on research results. Primarily, teachers and many parents are concerned that placing a gifted child in such a setting will not prepare him to interact well with children of other ability levels. They are concerned that it may lead the gifted child to have unrealistic views of what another child knows and can do. In truth, ability grouping is more likely to make the gifted child more aware that there are other children as bright or brighter than he is. Furthermore, because his cognitive needs are being met consistently, the gifted child may then be more willing to interact socially with children of all ability levels in extracurricular activities outside of school.

The greatest deterrent to full-time ability-group placements, however, may be practical rather than philosophical. There are not many full-time gifted programs around, and programs that do exist have long waiting lists for entrance. If you are fortunate enough to have such an option available in your locale, you may wish to put your child on the waiting list. The academic and motivational benefits alone may make it worthwhile. It is also likely that your child will form meaningful friendships with others of similar interests and abilities—relationships that may last a lifetime. If your child does attend a full-time gifted program, however, it will be important to provide experiences outside of school that allow him to interact freely with others of varying abilities, whether in sports, music, or arts groups, in community and religious organizations, through work experiences, or in community and neighborhood projects.

Who Is Likely to Benefit from Full-Time Grouping?

The gifted children who will benefit from full-time gifted grouping will have the characteristics listed below.

Table 7.1. Candidate for Full-Time Grouping			
Cognitive Functioning	**Personal Characteristics**	**Learning Preferences**	**Interests**
Is processing and achieving well above most others at current grade level	*Is academically motivated*	*Prefers to work at a fast pace, though not necessarily alone*	*Likes academic work and even pursues it outside of school time*
• Scores well on an individual IQ test (>130) • Is advanced in achievement beyond grade level • Is frustrated with slow pace of regular classroom instruction at current grade level	• Enjoys school • Accepting of others • Self-accepting • Comfortable in competitive situations • Intellectually curious	• Prefers fast-paced, challenging learning experiences • Enjoys working with small groups of like ability	• Has wide-ranging interests • Is actively involved in variety of activities and hobbies outside of school

Untracked Whole-Class Instruction: The "Default" Option

Heterogeneous grouping is the classic view of what teachers do in schools. That is, they present a lesson for the whole class, with little or no differentiation for either lower or higher ability students. All students are given the same tasks that allow them to practice the concept being presented until it is mastered. To measure mastery, a test—either diagnostic or final—is administered, and grades are then assigned based on how well the student performs on the test. This organizational model is *not* an appropriate option for gifted learners!

Robert Slavin raised concerns with this method as early as 1987 by describing a phenomenon he called the "Robin Hood Effect." He argued that any time all learners are taught until all of them master a particular concept or area, the amount of content covered is necessarily decreased. The overall achievement of average and higher ability students will decline because of this lack of additional exposure to new content, but lower ability students will rise in achievement due to increased time for them to review and practice skills.

Slavin cited researchers of the 1960s and 1970s who documented that there is a "steering group" of learners to whom teachers aim their level of instruction during whole class or group-paced instruction. Even though teachers think they are teaching to the middle, Slavin noted that the steering group generally represents the 19th to 23rd percentile of ability in the class—far too low for the majority of the learners in the class. Hence, although the few students in those percentile ranges may rise somewhat in their mastery of classroom materials, it is probably at the expense of the majority of the learners in the class.

What Does the Research Say about Whole Group Class Instruction?

The effects of whole-group, heterogeneous instruction almost have to be studied in reverse, because in most of the gifted education research, whole-group instruction has represented the control or comparison group rather than the group primarily being studied. Thus, any time an effect size is reported for the curriculum strategy, it also reports the achievement level for whole-group instruction, but as a control group. For example, if full-time ability grouping shows a half-year's additional gain, and the full-time group is being compared to the whole-class option, then equally gifted children in the whole-class option did not make this gain!

In general, the research studies show almost no instances in which whole-group instruction of students of heterogeneous ability is more beneficial for gifted children than some form of differentiated small group instruction. If educators should want to level the playing field of achievement so that all become mediocre in their output, then whole-group instruction is the answer! However, it should be noted that no society has been valued for its level of mediocrity.

As an illustration, I was involved some years ago in a three-year evaluation of a special school that intended to teach the same curriculum to all students, but each student could learn at his or her own pace. Students had their own computers with most of the curriculum tasks on them; students were expected to complete these tasks while teachers circulated to help those who needed help. Any other enrichment offered to students was offered at the same level for all students.

At the end of the first year of this study, all of the children had actually declined in their math skills. However, the lower ability students, who had received the major share of teachers' time, had made some gains in other academic areas. The students of average ability generally maintained their progress in the other areas, but the higher ability students significantly declined in *all* academic areas. By the end of the third year, the lower ability students were continuing to improve in their achievement, and the average ability students were now declining at a rate steeper than the gain being made by the slow ones. The high ability students—those who still remained in the school—continued to decline significantly in all academic areas.

What this says about whole-group instruction—that is, offering the same curriculum to all students and then presenting that curriculum at a pace so it can be mastered by all students— is that few students, except those with exceptionally low ability, will benefit. Some students, especially those whose learning preferences lean toward lecture and discussion, may enjoy this form of instruction, but even for them, the outcome is not promising. They may enjoy school more, but they will not benefit academically from the time spent in this type of classroom.

One interesting study by Chauvet and Blatchford in 1993 found that *any* form of small grouping—whether teacher-selected mixed-ability, like-ability, or friendship grouping— was better than whole-class instruction. And among the three small grouping choices previously mentioned, like-ability groups were superior in achievement to groups based on friendships, but friendship groupings were superior to mixed-ability groups assigned by the teachers.

At the beginning of this section, you read the words "default option," meaning that whole-class instruction is the approach that educators use unless some specific alternative action is taken. Regrettably, this default option is the most prevalent mode of instruction used in American schools today. At the elementary level, you may find some teachers who try to differentiate their teaching to fit different levels of ability among their students. But in general, teachers aim to teach "the third-grade curriculum" to all third graders, the "fourth-grade curriculum" to all fourth graders, and so on. That most often means that if an advanced student has already mastered the grade-level curriculum, he will be offered little or nothing more for the rest of the year—an incredible waste of learning time and student potential.

In the middle and senior grade levels, this "default option" is even more uniform. Not only do teachers rigidly stick to the "grade-based curriculum" notion of using whole-group instruction, but also consistently add "content-presentation-via-lecture" to the whole group at one time as well. Students are "taught" to take notes as dictated by the teacher and then are tested on these notes. Little, if any, differences in methods of instruction, content, or skills are offered to students with gifts and talents. There is a feeling among all too many educators that what they offer in the classroom is not only necessary, but also is sufficient for all learners.

Small Group Strategies

Pull-Out Groups

In the early 1980s, June Cox, Neil Daniel, and Bruce Boston conducted the Richardson Study, the most recent attempt to survey gifted program practices in the United States. The researchers found that nearly 80% of all gifted programs surveyed at that time used pull-out groups to deliver differentiated educational experiences to gifted children, and this option is still widely practiced today. Also known as "send-out" or "resource" programs, pull-out groups usually remove children from regular classroom work for a specified number of hours per week. During this time, they meet with a gifted specialist teacher and with other gifted children (of similar or varied ages) to engage in enrichment or extension activities, which may or may not be related to what is going on in the regular classroom.

Most pull-out programs meet one to two hours weekly. Some pull-out program times are as short as one hour per week, and others may be as much as one to two days per week. At the elementary level, the pull-out times are usually scheduled for the same time each week so that grade-level teachers and the students can plan accordingly. Classroom teachers, especially those who support programming for the gifted, will be careful not to give tests, offer special events, or introduce new topics during that one- to two-hour period that the gifted child is in the pull-out program. Teachers often use the time to help the remainder of the class practice skills they have not yet mastered—something the gifted child does not need.

Cox, et al. (1985) found that pull-out programs were generally less effective academically than most other grouping options for gifted students. In fact, they found problems with pull-out programs. Sometimes, children who are pulled out are required to make up work they missed while at the pull-out class. Another common problem is that the gifted specialist teacher may be isolated from interactions with other teachers in the schools or may not have adequate planning time to communicate with fellow teachers. The specialist teacher and the program may be resented by other educators because they get the "best" students; the curriculum may be considered "fluff"; or other teachers may feel that important class work is being missed, and that they could teach these children as well as the specialist.

Cox, et al. recommend that for pull-out programs to work, time must be provided for the gifted teacher specialist to interact with the other teachers and to relate the curriculum extensions to the work that is being done in the regular classroom. Pull-out options are not commonly used in high schools, primarily because it is assumed that the wide variety of advanced course offerings in language arts, math, science, music, art, and drama will meet the needs of most gifted students looking for challenge in their areas of interest. Scheduling any sort of pull-out program at the middle school or high school is difficult because students have so many different teachers for their classes. Offering a pull-out class at the secondary level often requires masterful scheduling and a flurry of memos to teachers and participants reminding them of the erratic schedules that occur. Few content-oriented teachers in the middle or high school are willing to release gifted students once each week for a pull-out, particularly since it may not be connected with their content area. Hence, pull-outs at the middle and high school levels are often non-content-specific and might be offered only for five or six weeks rotating through class periods—for example, first period in the first week, second period in the second week, and so on. Activities or topics offered each week must be fairly self-contained, because students may not be able to leave specific classes on the designated day if a test or lab is scheduled.

What Does the Research Say about Pull-Out Programs?

In 1990, Vicky Vaughn, under the guidance of John Feldhusen and Bill Asher at Purdue University, conducted a synthesis of the research studies on pull-out programs. Despite the widespread use of this form of gifted instructional management, only nine studies at that time actually measured the effects of pull-outs.

The research showed that substantial academic gains were made when the regular curriculum was systematically extended in the pull-out program. Gains in critical and creative thinking also were found when those skills were emphasized for an entire year in the pull-out program. Gifted students engaged in the pull-out program also showed slight positive gains in self-esteem.

The studies included in this synthesis of research may have been unique, because too often, the typical pull-out program does not have a single focus or outcome and is not coordinated with the regular curriculum. Instead, the pull-out program becomes a potpourri, doing critical-thinking for a few weeks, followed by a study of mythology, followed by a little creative problem solving. It is highly unlikely that any substantial academic effects will be found for this form of pull-out grouping as it is ordinarily practiced.

In Cornell and Delcourt's study (1992) that compared the achievement and affective outcomes of a variety of gifted grouping options (including special schools, special advanced classes, within-class grouping, pull-out programs, and no program), pull-out programs showed somewhat better achievement in reading, social studies, and science, and only slightly better achievement in math than within-class grouping or no program options at all. This makes it imperative for schools that use pull-out as a program option for gifted children to think through carefully what the focus of the pull-out will be and then to follow through on that, if academic gains are sought.

Cornell and Delcourt also found that general self-worth and academic self-concept were not as high for students in pull-out programs as for children in the regular class, but that their general self-worth was slightly higher than for bright children in special classes or special schools. What this may suggest is that when gifted children have prolonged time with each other in challenging situations, they may not feel as positively about their capabilities or general self-worth as when they spend less time there and are comparing themselves with all ability levels. As parents and teachers, it is important to decide how great a role measures of self-worth should play. Is the goal to produce bright students with a realistic picture of their capabilities in the larger scheme or things? Or is the goal to produce bright students who may or may not be living up to their elevated self-perceptions? Should they be encouraged to stretch their potential such that they need to study, or should they essentially be allowed to coast through their school years, getting good grades with little effort?

One issue not thoroughly explored through research but which is often broached in the general literature is the impact a pull-out program makes on educators' and parents' perspectives. Too often, the pull-out program is perceived by a school principal, teachers, and sometimes even parents as "the gifted program." The assumption is that, because the school offers this once-a-week program, the gifted childrens' academic and self-esteem needs have been met. Yet with some reflection, it should be clear that a "program" of one or two hours a week or even one or two days a week does not account for the majority of the gifted child's academic time in school. The gifted child is a gifted child all day every day, not just on the day she goes to the pull-out class. If such a child spends most of her time in the regular classroom where she is asked to learn only what others are learning at the traditional pace, and if she can only expect, at most, 16% of that time (Renzulli, et al., 1994) to be engaged in any form of enrichment, then advanced learning at her level is remarkably limited, regardless of the pull-out program.

The best type of pull-out program is one that exists as a supplementary program to support and extend a truly differentiated curriculum than is already being offered daily to gifted or talented students in the regular classroom. Perhaps you should think of it as an option that you might request, but only after direct, daily, differentiated curriculum and instruction is already in place for your child. It will be important, too, to specify what the focus of the pull-out "curriculum" should be and to ensure that the pull-out program activities are connected with what is going on the regular classroom. You will learn more about this in the next chapter on curriculum for the gifted.

Who Is Likely to Benefit from Pull-Out Programs?

Gifted students who are most likely to benefit from open-ended tasks, challenging instruction, and working in small like-ability groups should have the characteristics in Table 7.2.

Table 7.2. Candidate for Pull-Out Programs

Cognitive Functioning	Personal Characteristics	Learning Preferences	Interests
Is processing and achieving well above most others at current grade level	*Is academically motivated*	*Prefers to work at a fast pace, though not necessarily alone*	*Likes academic work and even pursues it outside of school time*
• Achieves at a high level in specific domain extended in pull-out • Is advanced in academic achievement beyond grade level • Is frustrated with slow pace of regular classroom instruction at current grade level	• Enjoys school • Motivated to learn • Self-accepting • Accepting of others • Independent in thought	• Prefers fast-paced, challenging learning experiences • Enjoys working with small groups of like ability	• Has wide-ranging interests • Has high interest in domain covered in pull-out • Is actively involved in variety of activities and hobbies outside of school

Cluster Grouping

Cluster grouping refers to the practice of identifying the top five to eight academically talented (or intellectually gifted) students at a grade level and placing them in the same classroom at that grade level with a teacher best suited and qualified to work with gifted students. Such a teacher is one who 1) likes to work with gifted children, 2) is trained or is willing to acquire special training to work with gifted children, and 3) will actually spend a proportionate amount of instructional time with this small cluster group. This teacher will have the same class size as all other teachers at that grade level and will typically have a heterogeneous mix of abilities for the remainder of her student load. If she has a class of 24 and eight are in the gifted cluster, she will use approximately one-third of her instructional time offering differentiated learning experiences for the cluster and using appropriately modified instructional delivery and methods.

The cluster group will have daily blocks of time when those students work both with intellectual peers and with chronological peers. Academic subjects for the cluster group students will be delivered at an appropriately challenging level and pace. The cluster group students will have the opportunity to interact with students of all ability levels in their classroom in non-academic areas.

This method of managing instruction for gifted or talented children makes good sense in practical terms. It is difficult for a teacher to justify spending large proportions of class time differentiating instruction for only one or two children. But eight children are enough of a "critical mass" that they cannot be ignored. In fact, it will take a creative teacher to keep up with them!

Who should be grouped into such a cluster? Should they be grouped because they have the potential to be tops in all academic areas? Or should they be grouped because they are demonstrating a specific talent, such as math or reading, or are ahead of others in most academic areas?

At the beginning of this section, you may have noted a distinction between the academically talented as a cluster *or* the intellectually gifted as a cluster. Recalling the discussion of Gagné's theory in Chapter 2, the "talented" cluster would include the most advanced learners at a grade level—those farthest ahead in their academic work. The differentiation for this group would probably include a great deal of subject-based acceleration in math, science, social studies, and language arts/English. Students would be identified for this "talent cluster" through their performances on achievement tests, preferably out-of-level tests. Compacting the curriculum would be the first step for any differentiation developed for them (more about compacting in later chapters).

The "gifted cluster" might look somewhat different. The children in this cluster group will be identified by their general capacity to reason conceptually, think abstractly, and solve problems. Differentiation for this group should be based more on in-depth learning, independent study, exposure to higher order knowledge, and problem-based learning than on acceleration of subject matter. In some cases, the children in a "gifted" cluster might *not* be the most advanced workers at a grade level since the cluster could include gifted children who are underachieving. Allowing the underachievers to participate in the cluster will nurture their motivation to learn and to become excited by challenge.

This clarification between these two cluster types is critical to the success of the practice. If both types of children are included in the same cluster, the academic growth we would expect from ability grouping may be hindered. The intellectually gifted children may "drop out" if the learning is too fast-paced and doesn't allow time for reflection and analysis, while the academically talented children may "drop out" if the curriculum is so slow that they feel they are not progressing rapidly enough in their achievement. And of course, the mix of carefully selected students with a teacher who will work with them effectively is of primary importance to make this management strategy work.

Research on Cluster Grouping

The first research on cluster grouping, reported in 1986 by Barbara LeRose, reflected on the effects of the "Lighthouse Project" which began in Racine, Wisconsin in 1974. In this comparative study, test performances were measured for gifted children who were grouped in clusters and for equally gifted children who were placed in accelerated classes. Both groups received the same differentiated curriculum. The cluster group scored significantly higher on tests of verbal creativity than the accelerated students, leading one to conclude that more frequent opportunities for verbal interaction with intellectual peers may have occurred for the smaller group housed together with one teacher on a daily basis.

James and Chen-Lin Kulik have conducted several analyses of the existing research on the various forms of ability grouping. In two of their studies, they examined the academic effects of clustering gifted students within classes. They found very strong, positive academic gains, suggesting that clustered gifted students actually achieve approximately 60% more grade-equivalent knowledge and skills than equally gifted children who have not been clustered.

One study not included in the Kuliks' meta-analysis compared the achievement test results for two different graduating classes at each of two schools in small rural districts (Gentry & Owen, 1999). In one district, high achieving students were cluster grouped for grades three through five; in the comparison district, other provisions, such as in-class enrichment and pull-out programs, were offered to high achieving students in grades three through five. The clustered students showed small, positive academic gains even when their comparison group was being enriched in some other fashion. Although these findings are considerably less dramatic than previous research, they do suggest that cluster grouping may be superior to other forms of flexible grouping for students with academic talents. Gentry and Owen found, however, that the training of teachers was critical if cluster grouping was to meet the academic needs of high achieving students.

The research results suggest that this practice is one you will definitely want to consider. However, you will need to ask the school which kind of clustering they use—gifted or talented. Then, if that model matches your child's strengths, you may want to request your child's inclusion. In a cluster group, your child will have a chance for prolonged interaction and cognitive stimulation with other students of similar ability or with high achieving peers in a supportive learning climate, yet also will have some daily time with children of all ability levels.

Who Is Most Likely to Benefit from Cluster Grouping?

Students who will benefit from cluster grouping will have characteristics listed in Table 7.3.

Table 7.3. Candidate for Cluster Grouping

Cognitive Functioning	Personal Characteristics	Learning Preferences	Interests
Is processing and achieving well above most others at current grade level	*Is academically motivated*	*Prefers to work at a fast pace, though not necessarily alone*	*Likes academic work and even pursues it outside of school time*
• Scores well on an individual IQ test (>130) **OR** • Advanced in academic achievement beyond grade level • Is frustrated with slow pace of regular classroom instruction at current grade level **OR** • Is frustrated with the lack of time for thinking about what has been learned and learning in depth	• Enjoys school **OR** • Is non-productive in school work despite evidence that academic skills are in place	• Prefers fast-paced, challenging learning experiences **OR** • Prefers flexible timelines for learning • Enjoys working with small groups of like ability	• Has wide-ranging interests • Is actively involved in variety of activities and hobbies outside of school

Regrouping for Specific Subject Instruction

In regrouping, students who are gifted in an area such as mathematics are grouped with similarly gifted students. At the elementary school level, regrouping is most often a school-wide or grade-wide decision, such that the subject area to be regrouped—such as reading, math, science, or social studies—is taught by all teachers at the same time of day. Students are sorted by their current level of ability or performance in that subject and go to one teacher responsible for their level during that subject area time. Whereas full-time ability grouping does the same thing for all academic and non-academic study areas, regrouping usually occurs only for one or two subject areas such as reading or math. The child studies other subjects in mixed-ability classes.

Regrouping might work at the elementary level like this. At 10:00 a.m., time for reading, all fourth-grade students line up at their respective classroom doors to proceed to their respective performance-level reading classes. Advanced readers go to the classroom taught by Teacher C, average readers go to the class taught by Teacher B, and the lower readers stay in the room with Teacher A. In some schools, this grouping continues throughout the year; in others, the groups stay until the next set of achievement test scores are reported.

At the junior and senior high level, students go to their scheduled regrouped classes during specified periods of the day, for example, Honors English, General English, or Remedial English. In many cases, school counselors have sorted students, usually on the basis of prior teachers' recommendations and placement or achievement test scores. Thus, students are placed—at least theoretically—according to their actual level of performance. For example, a student whose math skills are lagging behind his English skills might be in Honors English but in General Math. Unless the junior high school is extraordinarily large, however, students who are placed in one honors class may end up being placed in other honors classes as well, even if they would be better off in another level of instruction. Much depends on how well the person in charge of scheduling can arrange the schedule.

A few years ago, I conducted an extensive evaluation of one junior high school in a large urban school district. All 1,400 students were individually placed in appropriately regrouped classes for all four academic core areas. Impressively, two school counselors and the schedulers had found ways to make it possible for a student advanced in science and math, but average in other subjects, to be placed in the honors sections for two subjects and in general classes for others. If their performance warranted it, some students were placed in all four honors regrouped classes.

The school was recognized in the district as a magnet school for "academically gifted," and this school did attract a large proportion of bright students in the district. Because the school managed to regroup all of its students appropriately, it was able to report that over 90% of the students were placed in at least one honors class when performance warranted such placement.

Much could be learned by other school schedulers from this school. The schedule itself should never be the rigid "make or break" criterion for deciding if this practice will be instituted in a school, but too often, this has been the case. If the scheduler or his supervisor feels strongly about differential education, then the schedule can be managed so that more advanced classes can be added if needed; if not, then the "complexity of scheduling" is often used as a convenient excuse for why the practice cannot be implemented.

At the high school level, the concept of honors or college prep, general, and remedial classes is often the way regrouping occurs, but just as often, classes are given differential names to describe—as well as disguise—their level of challenge. For example, a student signing up for eleventh-grade chemistry might select from "Theoretical Chemistry" or "General Chemistry" or "Kitchen Chemistry." Students usually self-select into these courses, subject by subject. The hope is that motivated and brighter students will recognize that "Theoretical Chemistry" is where they should be, while students who are not motivated to work hard in science will probably select one of the other options. A similar self-selection process occurs for each academic area. Conceivably, a gifted student might end up taking all high level regrouped classes and thus be informally "tracked" with other high achieving students for the majority of the school day. Practically, though, a gifted student may not be high achieving or motivated in every academic area and would choose the levels where he can realistically succeed. In this case, no "tracking" would have occurred.

Unfortunately, counselors in many schools do not have the "luxury" of meeting individually with students for academic advising prior to registration. So unless parents are able to offer guidance, students may miss important information regarding which courses to take, or they may choose courses to be with friends or to avoid a teacher whose personality they may dislike.

Perhaps the biggest issue from these self-selected options for advanced classes, though, is that of grades and evaluation. Students perceive that it will be more difficult to "ace" the Theoretical Chemistry course and that their grade-point average (GPA) might suffer. On that basis, some bright students who wish to attend highly selective colleges may choose the less challenging version of the science class to ensure getting an "A." Most high school counselors know that highly selective colleges do not make decisions based solely on grade-point averages. In fact, when asked, college admission representatives say that they prefer to see a high school transcript with challenging classes and an occasional B over one that shows top grades in all classes, but few challenging classes. In other words, the colleges do their own weighting of grades and other factors, which include participation in extracurricular activities and the student essay, in which the student introduces herself to the college.

Some high schools have weighted grades. In a system of weighted grades, a B received in an honors class would equal an A in a more general class in terms of school GPA and class ranking. However, since most selective colleges do their own weighting of students' grades, the weighted grade serves mostly to rank the student among his peers in the high school rather than aid college admission. Two of my own children graduated with 4.60+ GPAs on a 4.0 scale on university applications for admission, but were not ranked #1 or #2 in their school. For bright students, the short-term recognition of graduating first in one's class may seem important, but such ranking seems to have no long term effects.

What Does the Research Say about Regrouping?

Most of the general research on regrouping for reading and math instruction was reported over a decade ago by Robert Slavin (1987). He reported that it made no difference in overall achievement whether one learned to read and compute in a mixed ability classroom or in a regrouped class. However, Slavin calculated this after eliminating all studies that reported the effects of regrouping *gifted* children. Thus, Slavin's oft-cited research says nothing about the academic effects for gifted children who are regrouped or even tracked.

One study that Slavin included did contain outcomes that were ability-related, and this study seems relevant even though gifted children were not specifically delineated. In that study, the researcher (Provus, 1987) not only regrouped children by their ability levels in reading and math, but also provided differentiated learning materials for each regrouped level. In this case, the effect size for the high achieving groups was substantial and positive—about 80% of an additional year's achievement when compared to equally bright children who had not been regrouped for these subjects.

Ellen Goldring (1990) also conducted a meta-analysis of studies and, unlike Slavin's research, focused on the effects of gifted children in special classes (regrouped) when compared to gifted children in regular classes. The special, regrouped classes produced significant gains in achievement, particularly when these classes were offered in science and social studies. Another study likewise found that high ability students tend to achieve at significantly higher levels in science instruction using computers when they were working with a like-ability group than when they were working alone (Berge, 1990). These studies support the commonly held notion that gifted students will "bounce" ideas off of each other and thus learn even more than what is being formally presented to them.

In 1993, Hacker and Rowe studied nine Australian schools that changed from ability-grouped classes to mixed-ability ones. The quality of classroom interactions in science at the high school level declined not only for high ability students, but also for low ability students. The high ability students had fewer opportunities to discuss and use higher order thinking, and the lower ability students participated less and acted out more in the mixed ability settings.

Dewey Cornell and Marcie Delcourt (1992), in a large, national study, reported strong support for special regrouped classes for gifted learners. They studied 1,178 gifted students in five different kinds of programs for the gifted: 1) separate schools; 2) regrouped classes in reading, math, science, and social studies; 3) pull-out classes; 4) within-class grouping for subject area instruction; and 5) no program at all. All of the students were measured on the *Iowa Tests of Basic Skills* and the *Harter Self-Perception Profile*.

All of the regrouped classes in reading and some areas of math, social studies, and science showed substantial academic gains overall. When these special classes were compared with pull-out groups, within-class groups, and no program at all, the regrouped classes still produced higher gains. The only option that was generally superior to regrouping for subject area achievement was special schools—an option that has already been described.

Although self-perceptions by these students were generally positive no matter which program type, academic self-concept was significantly higher for students enrolled in no program at all, followed by those in pull-out programs. As mentioned earlier, a possible reason is that when bright students are placed with others of like-ability and similar performance levels, they may feel less like an academic "star," but they may be developing a much more realistic picture of their capabilities!

When parents are considering which management strategy to request of the schools for their child, there is ample evidence to suggest that regrouping in their child's talent area(s) will be beneficial. The biggest obstacle to this option is the current structure of the school. If the school has already sorted various levels of coursework, the request can be easily granted. If not, then you might be asking the school to reorganize—not a request that will go over positively!

Who Is Most Likely to Benefit from Regrouped Classes?

Students who will benefit from like-ability interactions in regrouped classes will have characteristics listed in Table 7.4.

Table 7.4. Candidate for Regrouped Classes

Cognitive Functioning	Personal Characteristics	Learning Preferences	Interests
Is processing and achieving well above most others at current grade level	*Is academically motivated*	*Prefers to work at a fast pace, though not necessarily alone*	*Likes academic work and even pursues it outside of school time*
• Is advanced in academic achievement beyond grade level in the area of the regrouped class • Is frustrated with slow pace of regular classroom instruction at current grade level	• Enjoys school • Is motivated to learn • Self-accepting • Independent in thought	• Prefers fast-paced, challenging learning experiences • Enjoys working with small groups of like ability	• Has high interest in domain of regrouped class • Is actively involved in variety of activities and hobbies outside of school

Within-Class Grouping

At the elementary level, a teacher using within-class grouping will divide the class into smaller groups for instruction in reading or math according to their abilities (gifts) or performance (talents) in those areas. Each group will be named something not descriptive of a level, such as birds' names, colors, names of countries or cities, and so forth. Each group then spends a proportionate amount of the subject area instructional time working directly with the teacher—usually at least once each day—while the other groups work by themselves on other assigned tasks.

At the secondary level, within-class grouping is used less regularly, in part because of the complexity of management. The typical high school teacher has five to six classes per day in different subjects, each a class of 20 to 30 students. Even so, a teacher may decide to divide a class period into smaller groups if the students differ markedly in their background knowledge and skill regarding a specific topic. The more widely diverse the abilities within a classroom, the more necessary this sort of grouping may become. Tasks and assignments may be differentiated for different small groups so that all learners can move forward at their own levels in the topic being learned.

Whether at the elementary or secondary level, within-class grouping may have merit even though the teacher may feel scattered by having to cater to several different groups. Students in the same group will benefit from working with each other, or they may seek help from others in their group when the teacher is not readily available. Likewise, students benefit more from a smaller teacher-to-student ratio than would be the case with whole group instruction.

Research on Within-Class Grouping

Slavin's (1987; 1990) research looked at both elementary and secondary research on within-class grouping. At the elementary level, he found no comparative studies in reading where effect sizes could be calculated—surprising since within-class grouping has been a method for teaching reading for decades! Slavin did, however, find several studies of within-class grouping in mathematics, and for these, the academic gain was substantial.

He found that children's attitudes toward the subjects in which they were grouped were substantially more positive, particularly when that grouping occurred for science or social studies.

James Kulik's (1992) analysis of the various forms of grouping concluded that within-class grouping has clear and positive academic effects for gifted children, and that it does not entail additional curriculum adjustment at the elementary level by the teacher.

A different finding, however, occurred in Cornell and Delcourt's previously discussed study (1992) conducted for the National Research Center on Gifted and Talented. They found that within-class grouping did *not* result in higher student achievement in reading or math as compared with having no program at all for gifted students, and in science and social studies, within-class grouping was even somewhat less effective than having no gifted program at all.

It is difficult to understand why Cornell and Delcourt did not find a difference. Perhaps a small portion of the teacher's time for instruction is less beneficial for gifted students than letting them learn the information totally on their own. Or perhaps teachers are unable to prepare adequately differentiated tasks for gifted children grouped within the class because of the many curriculum adjustments that must take place for all groups. It is likely that one of these possibilities is the explanation rather than that the grouping is ineffective or contributes to a decline in student achievement.

Despite the questions raised about the effectiveness of within-class grouping for gifted children, Cornell and Delcourt's research is clear; grouping options for instruction—other than within-class grouping—do result in marked gains over within-class grouping. Gifted and talented students who learn in pull-out, regrouped, and separate school classes all performed significantly higher than those who were within-class grouped in reading, math, science, and social studies. If teachers and schools persist in using within-class grouping, they will need to provide adequate time and teacher training for preparing differentiated learning experiences for these groups and will need to monitor the achievement of all of the students who participate in this option.

Who Is Most Likely to Benefit from Within-Class Grouping?

Students who will benefit from within-class grouping for differentiated instruction will have the characteristics listed in Table 7.5.

Table 7.5. Candidate for Within-Class Grouping

Cognitive Functioning	Personal Characteristics	Learning Preferences	Interests
Is processing and achieving well above most others at current grade level	*Is academically motivated*	*Prefers to work at a fast pace, though not necessarily alone*	*Likes academic work and even pursues it outside of school time*
• Is ahead on achievement test grade-equivalent scores • Is frustrated with slow pace of whole group instruction or cooperative learning at current grade level	• Enjoys school • Motivated to learn • Persistent in assigned tasks • Independent in thought and action	• Prefers fast-paced, challenging learning experiences • Enjoys working with small groups of like ability • Enjoys working on assigned tasks without teacher supervision at times	• Has wide-ranging interests • Is actively involved in variety of activities and hobbies outside of school

As a parent, the practice of within-class ability or performance grouping is one you may wish to request when other forms of grouping are not possible within the school's structure. Within-class grouping will only work, however, when there are several other advanced children in your child's class to form a group. The next practice you will read about may be your alternative of "last resort" when there are three or fewer gifted children like your own in a classroom.

Like-Ability Cooperative Grouping

Like-ability cooperative learning found some popularity in the 1990s. In this option, a teacher selects into groups three or four students who are processing or performing at approximately the same level. The groups work together on materials or tasks differentiated for their level of performance or ability. Each student takes a test at the end, but evaluations of how each individual contributed to the shared learning are a part of each student's grade as well.

The research is just beginning to be published on this practice. Although there is a wealth of research on cooperative learning, it seldom has examined the effect on students of like-ability. Instead, research has focused on the effects when three or four students of *varying* abilities work together on a shared task and are given a "group" grade for their work.

Because of this, I studied like-ability cooperative learning with high achieving English students enrolled in Advanced Placement English classes (Rogers, 1993). The classroom teacher, who had two periods of this class, designed a 21-day unit on American novels and a second 21-day unit on American poets for these advanced learners.

For the novel unit, students in the fifth-period class were trained to work in cooperative groups. The teacher randomly assigned all class members to four-person, like-ability groups. Each group was to read the selected novel and then to discuss meaning and significance over the course of two weeks. Subsequently, each student wrote a paper analyzing some aspect of the novel. First drafts of each paper were read by the student's cooperative group members who suggested changes, revisions, and clarifications. Each student then wrote a final paper to turn in on the final day of the unit.

Meanwhile, the sixth-period class progressed through the reading and discussion of the novel using whole class instruction with teacher lecture and discussion. After two weeks, each student wrote a first draft of a paper and had a short conference with the teacher about changes, revisions, and clarifications. For both classes at the end of the three-week unit, students' names and class periods were removed from their papers, and the papers were read by three individuals (the AP teacher, the school's gifted coordinator, and me) and were rated on 14 criteria.

After 21 days, the previous teaching strategies for the classes were reversed for a poetry unit. Now the sixth-period class learned in like-ability cooperative groups, while the fifth-period class was teacher-directed in approach. The papers were again read and evaluated "blind"—that is, with no student names—by the three co-researchers.

The results showed that the papers produced in like-ability cooperative settings were more grammatically accurate, arguments were more logical, and conclusions were more elaborative and fully developed than were the papers produced in the teacher-directed classes. Students' attitudes toward cooperative learning similarly improved after participation in the like-ability cooperative groups.

What the Research Says about Cooperative Grouping

The largest study of like-ability cooperative grouping completed thus far was conducted by the National Research Center on the Gifted and Talented (Reis, et al., 1994). Both quantitative and qualitative effects were measured for mixed-ability and like-ability cooperative learning groups of fourth-grade students in eight districts representing the Northeast, Central, and Western regions of the U.S. There were 262 mixed-ability cooperative triads (that is, one high, one low, one average student) and 262 like-ability triads (triads consisting of high ability, low ability, or average ability students).

Academic achievement in the science or math units did not differ for either form of cooperative grouping, and there were no differences in how well students liked each other after being grouped. It is likely that if the actual math and science units had been more challenging, some differences in achievement might have been documented. There may have been a "ceiling level" to the materials being learned that didn't allow for a true measure of academic progress for the higher ability students.

In all triads—whether mixed-ability or like-ability—high ability students' capabilities were viewed more favorably than other students. However, average and low ability students viewed other average and low ability students' capabilities more favorably when they were in like-ability groups, and viewed them less favorably when they were in mixed-ability groups. In both triad types, self-esteem remained steady for high ability students, but the self-esteem of other ability levels declined when in mixed-ability triads.

What this research suggests is that high potential students are neither harmed nor helped in academic areas by any form of cooperative learning, although the social effects of either form (like- or mixed-ability groups) may be beneficial. The question then becomes, do the social benefits outweigh the bright student's need for academic challenge, and if so, how much of their time should be spent on this type of socialization in school?

It is my opinion that this option is one to consider for your child *only* when other forms of longer-term ability grouping are not possible within the school's structure *and* if there are only a very few advanced learners in your child's classroom. If cooperative learning is a regular strategy used by the classroom teacher, then request that your child be grouped with other bright students on cooperative tasks that involve review or previous learning or the learning of easy content. By grouping brighter students together, the teachers can give the group a more challenging task to work on while other groups review or learn the "basics." This may result in differentiated and more challenging cooperative tasks being given to your child and her like-ability peers to work on. Without differentiation, like-ability cooperative learning will probably not result in improved overall academic achievement.

Cross-Grade Grouping

Cross-grade grouping, sometimes called cross-age grouping, is a variation of regrouping for specific instruction. In this case, an elementary school must have a schedule such that *all* grade levels teach reading or math or science or social studies at the same time of day. Thus, when it's 10:00 a.m. at the elementary school, all children line up at their doors for reading and proceed to the class of their current level of achievement, regardless of grade level. Thus, Cameron, who is reading at sixth-grade level but is in third grade, goes to the sixth-grade classroom for reading, and Yolanda, who is in sixth grade but is reading at fourth-grade level, goes to the fourth-grade class for her instruction in reading. The key to this option is that there are no ceilings or basements for what children can or cannot learn at a specific grade level—a philosophy that could reap substantial benefits for academically talented children.

Cross-grade grouping at the middle school and high school levels is less often a school-wide program. Courses are frequently offered at these levels that are open to any student in that school, regardless of actual grade level. A ninth-grade student who is extraordinarily advanced in math can take Calculus along with the few eleventh graders and many twelfth graders who are enrolled. If she is also advanced in language, she could register for a special seminar on 19th century British Literature, normally a twelfth-grade course, rather than sitting through the ninth-grade Introduction to Literature. One of my daughters, in her freshman year of high school, found that she was with other freshmen for only two of her seven daily classes. From her perspective, it was a year of great social interaction and stimulating learning!

In contrast to the elementary school, cross-grade grouping at the secondary level is a variation of subject acceleration. Hence, much of what the research says about subject acceleration could also apply here as well. At the elementary level, however, although some acceleration takes place, children are expected to complete the "regular" curriculum of the grade level in which they have been placed. A very bright third grader, then, may be working with very average sixth graders in the same class on the same materials. For some students, this can work, especially when there is no other option a school will consider, but in general, gifted children in these regular classes will feel isolated from others who think and analyze quickly the way they do. Thus, cross-grade grouping for gifted learners may not be much help in providing time needed for true peer interaction.

What the Research Says about Cross-Grading

Robert Slavin (1987), in his formal synthesis of this body of research, found that cross-grade grouping had a substantial and positive academic effect for reading and math across all ability levels when compared to children in whole class reading and math instruction. My research on gifted students instructed in non-graded classes (see Chapter 6) likewise showed a positive academic effect.

Unfortunately, there is no research yet on the social and emotional effects of cross-grading. How do older children feel about their learning abilities when they are grouped with younger students in their classes? And how do younger, bright children feel about being placed in classes with older learners of average ability? Are they intimidated, or do their egos expand by their placement in a higher grade? Do they enjoy the interactions with different ages? Further research is needed.

At the secondary level, Slavin (1987) found no difference in academics, perhaps because studies at secondary building levels are confounded by scheduling issues. Rarely can a secondary school maintain a school policy in which all classes at the school can offer cross-grading options. Hence, students will be working in cross-graded math but might be in an enriched, regrouped science class. Another possible reason Slavin found no difference is that achievement tests are administered less frequently at high school levels; course grades become the primary measure of achievement. Student grade-point averages, because of the more subjective nature of grades, are a much more difficult measure of achievement when one is trying to show differences from method to method.

Cross-grade grouping for specific classes in which your child's talent lies will almost certainly improve academic performance; however, it may not give your child the interaction with true peers that he needs as well. You should probably formally request this option only when other forms of ability or performance grouping are not available, or if your child's academic abilities are truly well beyond those of his gifted or talented classmates.

Peer Tutoring Dyads

Since the mid-1980s, this grouping strategy has been researched extensively, particularly in the areas of reading, science, mathematics, and computers. The strategy most often involves teacher selection of a dyad of two students—one "high" and one "low" or "average" student—to work together on the mastery of specific academic tasks. The rationale for such pairing is that the higher student will be able to teach, or re-teach, the task to the lower student. A variation of the practice is to place students of similar ability in pairs to work jointly on mastery of differentiated academic tasks; there, a "higher performing" dyad would be given a more challenging task to work on than a "lower performing" dyad.

The mixed-pair practice has been used extensively at all building levels, elementary, middle/junior high, and senior high. Most research studies, however, have examined elementary applications; few studies have focused on middle school dyads. In general, the like-ability variation of this practice occurs more frequently at the high school level in classes that already are regrouped by achievement or ability levels.

What Does Research Say about Peer Tutoring Dyads?

Early research suggested that lower ability students would achieve at higher levels when tutored by high ability peers. This would make sense, in view of Herbert Walberg's (1984) comprehensive analysis of tutoring in general (adult working with a child), which indicated that tutoring afforded greater opportunities for focused re-teaching than could take place in traditional classrooms. Walberg found that tutoring produced a sizeable academic effect—more than twice as much learned by the student being tutored as was possible in more traditional settings!

Since 1990, the research on *mixed-ability* peer tutoring dyads has concluded that the lower ability member of the dyad remains longer "on task," speaks up more often to clarify or to understand materials, behaves more appropriately (less acting out), and achieves more than when instructed in more traditional methods. For the higher achieving student in these dyads, there were no more differences in achievement or behavior than when they received traditional instruction.

Several studies have reported different results, however, for *like-ability* dyads. When both students in the dyad are of high ability, this teaching approach results in significantly higher achievement and more pro-academic interactions (giving and receiving help) for the pairs. However, low ability students in *like-ability* dyads felt less positive about their abilities (Carter & Jones, 1993).

The final word, then, on peer tutoring as a strategy for developing gifts and talents would be that like-ability or like-interest dyads typically produce higher achievement than when a high potential student works alone. However, using the bright child to tutor another child of lower ability does *not* increase the bright child's achievement. Peer tutoring using mixed-ability dyads will only enhance the achievement and behavior of the lower ability student.

Is there a happy medium? Perhaps looking at the tasks given to a mixed- or like-ability dyad is the best way of sorting through the differential effects of peer tutoring. If the task involves work that one member of the pair knows and the other doesn't, probably neither child will benefit. The "knower," not being a trained teacher, will merely give the "non-knower" the information to be copied and turned in, and she will learn nothing new for herself. For this kind of task, using the child as a second teacher may be pure exploitation of the bright child. For low level or mastery tasks, it would be wiser to pair the dyads for like-ability, so that two children working at approximately the same level are given a task that will stretch them, no matter how different the actual level of difficulty may be in other dyads.

In other words, less able pairs of students should work on tasks appropriate for their level of understanding and skill, and more able dyads should work on more difficult tasks. However, when the task given to a mixed dyad is a problem-based investigation, is open-ended, or requires higher order thinking skills, there is a chance that both members will benefit from having to work out solutions, even if the brighter member may not get as much from the experience as the less able member.

Mixed-Ability Cooperative Grouping: A "Default" Option

Heterogeneous grouping for cooperative learning has been a widely adopted educational reform in recent years, often hailed as being beneficial for *all* children. On the other hand, many parents worry that their children are being slowed in their learning because the schools' focus is on socializing children and teaching to the average or mid-range child.

Mixed ability cooperative learning has taken several different forms since its insurgence in the mid-1970s. For David and Roger Johnson, this practice involves each teacher selecting heterogeneous student groups, with each group consisting of four students—one high, one low, and two average ability. Each group is then given a task to work on together toward final assessment for mastery. Although each group member will take his or her own individual test at the end, the test performances of all the group members are averaged together, and all group members are assigned that same final grade. Thus, the higher ability members must ensure that all members learn the task.

This can be called the "sink or swim" method of cooperative learning. Each member of the group feels the pressure to succeed. In more recent variations, the Johnsons have tried to differentiate roles within the group and have experimented with how higher order thinking tasks might produce academic benefit for all group members.

Robert Slavin (1990) has experimented with four forms of "Student Team Learning" (STL) methods of heterogeneous grouping for cooperative learning. One or more of these approaches may be used in your child's school.

For Student Team Achievement Divisions (STAD), mixed ability teams (containing one high, one low, and two average-ability students) stay together for a variety of tasks over a longer period of time. After a month or so, the students are reshuffled into a new mixed-ability team. Each team works together on teacher-directed tasks to prepare for its final assessment. The goal is to be the "best" team in the class—the one with the most points when assessment time comes. Each student takes an individual test or assessment when the practice period is complete, and each student's score is added to other students' scores to result in a team score. Grades are then assigned based on the summed scores, not an individual score.

"Teams-Games-Tournaments" (TGT) cooperative learning also involves mixed-ability teams preparing cooperatively for a final "tournament," in which the high ability members of each team compete against all other high ability members in the class on a more challenging task or set of questions; meanwhile, low ability members of each team compete against low ability members of other teams on less challenging tasks or questions. Winners at each ability-sorted "table" bring home bonus points to their cooperative teams. Scores for each team are summed, and a winning team is declared. Re-sorting by ability for future tournaments is based on the winners, who go "up" a table, and losers, who go "down" a table, in subsequent competitions.

Team-Assisted Individualization (TAI) is Slavin's third form of cooperative learning. Four-member mixed-ability teams are allowed to progress through programmed materials at their respective individual paces, and teammates check each other's work. Each member takes end-of-unit quizzes when individual materials have been mastered, and points are awarded on a weekly basis for the total number of units each team completes, creating a team score.

The final form of cooperative learning devised by Slavin and his associates is Cooperative Integrated Reading and Composition (CIRC). Here, mixed-ability teams are organized in groups of three, called triads. While the teacher works on reading with the high ability member of each triad, the other two members of each team are helping each other progress through an activity sequence, which involves oral reading, comprehension, writing, and basal-text-reading workshops. Then the teacher works with the middle ability member of each triad while the other two members of each group help one another. Each triad member, in turn, works with the teacher in ability-sorted small groups, and each has opportunities to get help from other team members in between. Team members check each other's work on these activities.

Sharan (1988) has developed "Group Investigation" as another form of cooperative learning. Mixed-ability groups plan and carry out integrated study projects that focus on acquisition of new information, analysis, and synthesis through a six-stage process of investigatory learning. The knowledge base that is covered tends to be more "higher order" (i.e., more complex, such as studying the history of a country or the biology of a forest, not map skills or math facts) than for other forms of cooperative grouping.

Kagan (1984) and Aronson (1987) have built on this idea of more integrative tasks with their complementary forms of cooperative grouping. Mixed-ability *teams* each take responsibility for a different subtopic of a larger content area, and each team is responsible to teach this subtopic to all other teams in the class (Kagan's "Co-op Co-op"), *or* each mixed-ability *team member* becomes responsible for a subtopic of the group topic and teaches it to the rest of the *team*. The team, in turn, teaches its topic to the rest of the class (Aronson's "Jigsaw Methods"). Other variations of mixed-ability teaming for higher level math, such as in "Groups of Four" (Burns, 1981), and general science and math for ESL students using such programs as "Descubrimiento" (Cohen, 1986) have also been devised.

What the Research Says about Mixed-Ability Cooperative Grouping

Robert Slavin's (1990) analysis of the research on mixed-ability cooperative learning is extensive and systematic. In 68 studies, the overall effect size across all forms of cooperative learning was a small but positive gain in achievement. However, the greatest positive effects were found for two of his own forms, Teams-Games-Tournaments (TGT) and Student Team Achievement Divisions (STAD). With its combination of cooperative preparation, ability-grouped assessment, and diagnosis-prescription (reward and punishment), all organized around determining the "top" class team (competition), TGT produced substantial positive academic gains across all ability levels, and STAD produced a smaller but positive effect as well. This suggests that the elements of competition and individual accountability, when added to cooperative preparation, can produce at least a small, positive gain in achievement for all. None of the other forms of cooperative learning showed achievement gains for children at any level of ability.

In terms of non-cognitive outcomes, Slavin's review of research (1990) shows that when mixed-ability cooperative learning is used for a majority of class time, there is 1) an increase in cross-racial friendships, 2) an improvement in classroom acceptance for and the academic performance of students with mental or physical disabilities, 3) an increase in a positive learning environment, 4) general movement toward an *internal* locus of control in which students believe they are in control of their own success or failure, and 5) a general increase in liking classmates and in altruism. The studies are inconsistent on whether students enjoy what they are studying, spend more time on task, improve their self-esteem, or feel more accepted by their peers.

It should be noted once again that Slavin's studies of mixed-ability cooperative grouping seldom have focused on gifted students. The few studies that reported the effects of this kind of grouping on gifted students initially reported that they did better academically in cooperative groups. However, more recent analysis of the quality of this research suggests that there was no improvement in achievement at best, and at worst, there was substantial alienation or isolation of the gifted student from other group members.

What was said previously about mixed dyads and the tasks assigned probably applies for this series of options. Mixed-ability groups should include gifted students in the mix *only* when the tasks themselves are higher order and complex investigations, problem-based learning tasks, or open-ended tasks.

You probably noticed at the beginning of this section that this option was called a "default" option. This means that you will not have to ask the school for it. Mixed-ability cooperative learning will probably be available to your child without your input. If this is the only grouping option offered to your child at this time, your job will be to ask teachers to look more closely at the *type* of cooperative task they are using with students; you may want to request that your child be placed in a cooperative group with other students of like ability and that differentiated tasks be provided, particularly when the general task is to review previously learned information or to acquire low-level facts, terms, and concepts.

As you have already surmised, this is probably not an option you will need to request from the school because it is already in place. It will be your job to figure out alternatives to the "default" option of mixed-ability instructional grouping. Specifically, you will need to consider which forms of grouping and acceleration would allow your gifted child to make the progress he is capable of making for the year.

Table 7.6 summarizes program provisions for gifted students in the schools and attempts to identify particular characteristics of cognitive functioning, personal characteristics, learning preferences, and interests that would make some options more advisable than others for your child. The table also includes the school structures needed for various options.

Table 7.6. School Instructional Management Provisions and their Impact on Gifted Students

Provision	Academic Benefits?	Social Benefits?	Emotional Benefits?	Needed School Structure or Organization	Personal Characteristics Necessary
Pull-Out Groups	Yes	Yes	Yes	Part- or full-time trained gifted specialist; resource room to hold classes; materials and resources budget; connection between regular curriculum and what is provided in pull-out setting; regular teachers must be supportive of pull-out importance for gifted children	CF: Gifted or talented, depending on what focus of pull-out is PC: Motivated to learn; independent in action; persistent; comfortable with other gifted children LP: Likes independent study, discussion, and small group work; likes learning in depth or breadth; likes challenge; creative I: Wide-ranging interests; not interested in routine work in classroom

CF=Cognitive Functioning level; PC=Personal Characteristics; LP=Learning Preferences; I=Interests

Table 7.6. School Instructional Management Provisions and their Impact on Gifted Students (*continued*)

Provision	Academic Benefits?	Social Benefits?	Emotional Benefits?	Needed School Structure or Organization	Personal Characteristics Necessary
Cluster Grouping	Yes	--	--	One trained (gifted specialist) teacher per grade level; sufficient students (5-8) at each grade level to cluster them; commitment to divide time proportionately for differentiation; remaining teachers must support cluster teacher concept; cluster concept must be carefully explained to all parents in the school so that misconceptions don't arise	CF: One of top 5-8 gifted or talented students at grade level, depending on which will be focus of cluster PC: Motivated to learn; independent in thought and action; sensitive to others; persistent; comfortable with agemates, regardless of ability level LP: Likes small group work, self-instructional materials, projects; likes challenge I: Not interested in routine work in classroom; likes academics

CF=Cognitive Functioning level; PC=Personal Characteristics; LP=Learning Preferences; I=Interests

Table 7.6. School Instructional Management Provisions and their Impact on Gifted Students *(continued)*

Provision	Academic Benefits?	Social Benefits?	Emotional Benefits?	Needed School Structure or Organization	Personal Characteristics Necessary
Regrouping for Specific Instruction	Yes	--	--	Regrouped curriculum scheduled at same time across a grade level; teacher knows curriculum area well and likes working with advanced students; materials and resources budget; curriculum is differentiated in difficulty, coverage, expectations for performance and pacing	CF: Talented or high performing in regrouped curriculum area PC: Motivated in curriculum area LP: Likes challenge and fast-paced learning I: Likes curriculum area
Within-Class Grouping	Yes	--	--	Sufficient students (6-12) to form a small group within classroom; teacher commitment to differentiate in difficulty, coverage, expectations, and pacing; fairly well-behaved class of students generally	CF: Talented or high performing in grouped curriculum area PC: Independent in thought and action; persistent; focused LP: Likes small group work, self-instructional materials, projects; likes challenge I: Not interested in routine work in classroom; likes curriculum area

CF=Cognitive Functioning level; PC=Personal Characteristics; LP=Learning Preferences; I=Interests

Table 7.6. School Instructional Management Provisions and their Impact on Gifted Students *(continued)*

Provision	Academic Benefits?	Social Benefits?	Emotional Benefits?	Needed School Structure or Organization	Personal Characteristics Necessary
Like-Ability Cooperative Grouping	Yes	Yes	Yes	Sufficient students (3-4) to form one group at least; teacher willingness to differentiate in difficulty, coverage, and expectations	CF: Talented or high performing in grouped curriculum area PC: Independent in thought and action; persistent; focused LP: Likes small group work, self-instructional materials, projects; likes challenge I: Not interested in routine work in classroom; likes curriculum area

CF=Cognitive Functioning level; PC=Personal Characteristics; LP=Learning Preferences; I=Interests

Table 7.6. School Instructional Management Provisions and their Impact on Gifted Students (*continued*)

Provision	Academic Benefits?	Social Benefits?	Emotional Benefits?	Needed School Structure or Organization	Personal Characteristics Necessary
Cross-Grade Grouping	Yes	Yes	Yes	Cross-graded curriculum scheduled at same time across all grade levels in school; teachers comfortable with multi-age groups; curriculum is "articulated" carefully; teachers can work with all abilities at a performance level	CF: High performing at appropriate cross-graded level of curriculum area PC: Persistent; comfortable with children of all ages and abilities; independent; motivated to learn LP: Likes challenges; likes learning in depth and breath I: Likes curriculum area; studies on own outside of school in curriculum area
Peer Tutoring Dyads	No	–	No	Teacher comfort with allowing students to learn from each other; teacher knowledge of actual skill and knowledge levels of individual students in class; teacher comfort with allowing gifted students to work together	CF: High performing in grouped curriculum area PC: Independent in thought and action; persistent; focused LP: Likes peer learning, self-instructional materials, projects; like challenge, learning in depth and breath, discussion I: Likes curriculum areas; studies on own outside of school in curriculum area

CF=Cognitive Functioning level; PC=Personal Characteristics; LP=Learning Preferences; I=Interests

Table 7.6. School Instructional Management Provisions and their Impact on Gifted Students *(continued)*

Provision	Academic Benefits?	Social Benefits?	Emotional Benefits?	Needed School Structure or Organization	Personal Characteristics Necessary
Mixed-Ability Cooperative Grouping	No	Yes	Yes	Teacher comfort with allowing students to learn from each other; fairly well-behaved class of students generally	CF: None needed PC: Focused; sociable; motivated to learn LP: Likes peer learning, projects, discussion I: Likes curriculum area
Schools for the Gifted	Yes	Yes	Yes	School (private or public) located nearby; teachers and administrators trained in gifted education; adequate materials and resources to differentiate for difficulty, coverage, and pacing	CF: Highly gifted or talented intellectually or academically PC: Persistent; focused; motivated to learn LP: Likes challenge; likes learning in depth and breadth; deals well in competitive situations; thrives with fast pacing, craves new knowledge and skills; thrives when with others like self I: Likes academic learning; not interested in routine work in classroom; wide-ranging OR very focused interests outside of school

CF=Cognitive Functioning level; PC=Personal Characteristics; LP=Learning Preferences; I=Interests

Table 7.6. School Instructional Management Provisions and their Impact on Gifted Students *(continued)*

Provision	Academic Benefits?	Social Benefits?	Emotional Benefits?	Needed School Structure or Organization	Personal Characteristics Necessary
Full-Time Gifted Program/ School-within-a-School	Yes	Yes	Yes	Sufficient gifted or talented students to comprise one classroom per grade level; one teacher at each grade level trained in gifted education; teacher comfort with allowing gifted students to work together.	CF: Highly gifted or talented intellectually or academically PC: Motivated to learn; persistent; focused LP: Likes challenge; likes learning in depth and breadth; deals well in competitive situations; thrives with fast pacing; craves new knowledge and skills; thrives when with others like self I: Likes academic learning; not interested in routine work in classroom; wide-ranging OR very focused interests outside of school

CF=Cognitive Functioning level; PC=Personal Characteristics; LP=Learning Preferences; I=Interests

Priorities for In-School Provisions

After studying the summary in Table 7.6, you may find this next section repetitive. But if you dislike tables and charts, perhaps the following recommendations will be helpful, since they list guidelines concerning what to ask the school to provide in order to meet the educational needs of your child. These guidelines are listed in a general order of importance. Your own child's needs, however, may dictate a different order for your requests.

1. **Grouping is important.** Teachers and parents must find ways to allow gifted or talented students to spend the majority of their learning time in the academic core areas with others of like abilities and interests. Although self-contained grouping, such as a special school for the gifted or a full-time gifted program, may not be the answer or even a possibility, you should be able to expect a third to a half year's additional achievement per year as a minimum standard of what you could expect bright children to accomplish no matter what their management or grouping arrangement. In other words, for each year in school, gifted students should be given the chance to accomplish 15-18 months' work in academic core areas as compared with the regular curriculum. It is crucial to carefully monitor this rate of academic progress through out-of-level achievement tests.

2. **Cluster grouping as an option.** Cluster grouping and regrouped classes for all academic core areas may be suitable substitutes for full-time placement in a gifted program or school. Care must be taken, however, concerning what type of cluster is established and to ensure that placement in advanced regrouped classes is due to the student's actual performance, not just scheduling because a class is available at an open slot in the course schedule.

3. **Curriculum matters.** No matter what the grouping arrangement chosen for the academic core areas, attention must be focused on what will be taught and to what level of depth. Ultimately, the curriculum is probably more important than how the children are grouped. (The next chapter will address this issue in depth.)

4. **Pull-out programs are not enough.** Pull-out programs should be used with care. It is the focus of the pull-out program that is critical. The greatest achievement gains will be found for pull-out programs that extend the general classroom curriculum in *specific* academic areas. Likewise, the pull-out can probably never be considered sufficient differentiation for gifted or talented children. Their needs are *every day* in almost *every academic area.* A pull-out experience once or twice a week will not, by itself, suffice.

5. **Within-class grouping is not sufficient.** Within-class grouping, like-ability cooperative learning, and like-ability peer tutoring dyads should be used when no other forms of grouping are possible in a school setting. They can be beneficial for gifted children if the curriculum is appropriately differentiated, but too often, teachers are not trained, nor do they have the time to do this well on a daily basis. Likewise, the group in which the gifted or talented child or children find themselves may have a wide range of ability. Hence, the child may not be stretched as fully as needed in such an arrangement.

6. **Enrichment is usually inadequate.** Do not expect that enrichment will take place with any regularity in a school that expects *all* teachers to enrich in their respective classrooms. Any enrichment provided will be infrequent and more likely "busy work," rather than differentiated learning tasks and experiences.

7. **Dyads should be used sparingly.** Teachers should use mixed-ability dyads and grouping for open-ended or problem-based tasks *only*, not for convergent, repetitive, or mastery learning tasks.

8. **Mixed-ability cooperative learning is appropriate only in certain situations.** Teachers should use mixed-ability cooperative learning only for occasional socialization or for open-ended or problem-based tasks. It is not appropriate for convergent, repetitive, or mastery learning tasks.

9. **Be cautious in accepting whole-class instruction.** Whole-class instruction should be used rarely, if at all, with gifted or talented children. The pacing and instruction will not be suitable for effective retention of what is learned. If whole-class instruction were offered as the mode of delivery for an out-of-level (i.e., cross-graded) class, it might be used successfully with gifted or talented children.

When They Say..., What Will You Say?

As a conclusion to this chapter, and to ensure that what you have read makes sense, write down the responses you would *now* give to claims made by anti-grouping advocates and educators (see Table 7.7). Realize that you will never really have time to prepare the "perfect" answer when someone says such things to you. There will be further chances to practice in the coming chapters as well. Possible answers are listed in Table 7.8.

Table 7.7. When They Say..., What Will You Say?

They Say...	You Say...
Ability grouping isn't a "picture" of the real world. Students need to learn to get along with others at all levels of ability.	
Ability-grouping is elitist and undemocratic.	
The "good" teachers get the "good" students. The lower ability students get the "bad" teachers.	
Ability grouping removes role models that "at risk" students need to succeed.	
Ability grouping is racist.	
It's rigid; once you're in one group level, you can't move up.	
Low level students' self-esteem is damaged, sometimes irreparably.	
The achievement of low-level and average students is limited.	
Too much time in low-level groups is spent on discipline.	
Grouping is espoused only by the politically and socially powerful parents of high ability students.	
Without brighter students in a class, the quality of discussion goes way down.	

Table 7.8. What You Might Say...Possible Responses

They Say...	You Say...
Ability grouping isn't a "picture" of the real world. Students need to learn to get along with others at all levels of ability.	Actually, as adults, we are grouped by the jobs we take, the amount of education we acquire, and we are most likely to group ourselves with others who are about as smart as we are and who share common interests with us. We rarely experience "mixed-ability" grouping in the adult world.
Ability-grouping is elitist and undemocratic.	If careful placement in groups has taken place, such that one's actual level of ability or performance is the major criterion for placement, then it is an equitable strategy. The point of being grouped is to be learning at the level one is capable of. One group is not "better" than another, just more appropriate for meeting specific educational needs. If one group gets a reputation as "better," then the school needs to deal with this attitudinal issue.
The "good" teachers get the "good" students. The lower ability students get the "bad" teachers.	Being in the high achieving group does not mean the students are "good" or "better" than others— just different. Teacher selection is at issue here, not grouping itself. Administrators should match teachers to the students with whom they work best. Why are inadequate or unskilled teachers allowed to even be in the school system?

Table 7.8. What You Might Say...Possible Responses *(continued)*

They Say...	You Say...
Ability grouping removes role models that "at risk" students need to succeed.	Schunk and Bandura have shown that a person chooses a role model from those who they perceive to be similar to themselves in capability but who are experiencing some success. Rarely does a low achieving student choose a gifted child as his or her role model.
Ability grouping is racist.	The general tracking research has documented that there are significantly fewer than expected minority children (except Asians) in higher achieving groups and significantly more than expected minority children in lower achieving groups. This is not the fault of grouping or placement, but may reflect how ability or achievement is being measured. It may be more important to change the measures and placement procedures than to eliminate the groups themselves.
It's rigid; once you're in one group level, you can't move up.	For full-time ability grouping (tracking), this is true. But this doesn't have to be the case with other forms of grouping by ability or achievement level. Regular monitoring of students' performances may make it possible for them to move from group to group within the school year as topics and units of instruction change.
Low level students' self-esteem is damaged, sometimes irreparably.	The Kulik studies have established that just the opposite is true. In low track classes, low ability students are less likely to be intimated by the fast thinkers and will be afforded more chances to be called on and to answer questions.

Table 7.8. What You Might Say...Possible Responses (continued)

They Say...	You Say...
The achievement of low level and average students is limited.	If care is taken about what is taught and to what level of difficulty, then the ultimate achievement we could expect from lower and average ability students should not be limited. Every child must be challenged at his or her own level of need for challenge. It is unrealistic, however, to believe that all students will ultimately be capable of the same level and depth of learning. Furthermore, the differences are what make this a vibrant and interesting society.
Too much time in low-level groups is spent on discipline.	Oakes' own observations of low-track classrooms found no significant differences in the amount of time spent on disciplinary issues, actual instructional time, or on exposure to higher order thinking. The only significant difference for low-level groups was in homework expectations—significantly less time was required for homework in low-level classes.
Grouping is espoused only by the politically and socially powerful parents of high ability students.	Actually, the parents of gifted children are a lot less well-trained and less well-organized for advocacy than are parents of special education children. Parents of gifted children are often regular volunteers and supporters of the school and therefore may be seen to have a direct influence on school decisions. They have very little political power, as shown by the number of states in the U.S. which have no mandate that gifted children be served and which don't require specialized training for teachers who work with children.

Table 7.8. What You Might Say...Possible Responses *(continued)*	
They Say...	**You Say...**
Without brighter students in a class, the quality of discussion goes way down.	Bright children are sent to school to be fully educated, not to act on behalf of the teacher or to make a teacher's life or discussion quality more positive. Their needs to learn are every bit as important as the needs of all other children. To prevent them from leaving a classroom so that they can receive special needed services is an exploitation of their abilities for the benefit of the teacher and the rest of the class.

A Possible Set of Steps for a Teacher

How would a teacher know which kinds of instructional grouping to use? At the beginning of this chapter, you were asked to pretend you were the teacher of a sixth-grade class, and to plan how you would provide for the special gifts and talents of your students. The chapter then described certain instructional management practices you might want to request for your child. Here are steps the teacher could take that will help determine the best or most practical grouping practice(s) to use with a given group of gifted students.

Step 1: First, the teacher must ascertain the capabilities of the students. It will be necessary to assess the two to three bright children per classroom on their current mastery levels in reading, language arts (including spelling), science, and math. Use out-of-level assessments if they do better than 85% on grade-level assessments.

Step 2:   Next, the teacher should determine if there is a sufficient number of students to form a cluster in one or more academic areas. If a group of five to eight children who are considerably ahead of the other children in all of these areas is found, these children should be regrouped to form a *cluster* in one classroom, so that they can learn together and so that all academic areas will be differentiated by that one teacher. These children will benefit from being grouped with others who learn like they do.

Step 3:   If the bright children are gifted in different areas, a single cluster might not be the best instructional strategy. If a group of three to four children are found who are ahead in math, and a different three to four are found who are ahead in reading, and so forth, regroup these children for each specific subject by assigning them to one grade-level teacher who will be responsible for differentiating that subject as a *within-class group*.

Step 4:   If the group of gifted children is ahead in one subject area only, then use a *pull-out* grouping run by a gifted specialist to differentiate for that subject on a *daily basis* (even if only a half hour daily).

Step 5:   If the school administration will not collaborate on differentiating through grouping, then *pair* or *group* the two or three bright students in each class and let them proceed through self-instructional materials on their own with one or two supervisory sessions per week.

Summary

There are a variety of whole-group and small-group instructional practices used with gifted and talented learners. Research shows that these practices differ in their academic, social, and emotional effects. In general, gifted learners learn best when they spend the majority of their academic learning time with others who have similar learning characteristics or in some sort of ability grouping, whether this means being placed in a special school full-time or being placed in a smaller like-ability group or cluster of five to eight children for academic learning on a daily basis. In general, the more time gifted children have to learn with other gifted children, the greater the academic benefits. According to the research, even some time spent together in learning is preferable to no time with other students of like ability.

Key Points

- Whole-class or whole-group strategies for managing the instruction of gifted learners can take two distinct forms:
  - A whole mixed-ability class (for example, an entire typical third grade) that learns the same materials and learning tasks at the same time. This form, often called a heterogeneous classroom, does not aid the learning of gifted children in any way.
  - The whole group/class is sorted by ability or achievement level, one level to a class, each one using experiences appropriate to its needs. This form, which involves sorting, shows positive academic, social, and emotional benefits for gifted learners.

- The grouping of classes by ability level as a way of instructional management can take several forms:
  o A special school for the gifted.
  o A school-within-a-school.
  o Full-time gifted program.
  o Self-contained classroom.

- Small group strategies for managing the instruction of learners takes many forms, including:
  o Pull-out classes.
  o Cluster grouping.
  o Regrouping for specific subject instruction.
  o Within-class grouping.
  o Like-ability cooperative tasks.
  o Cross-grade grouping.
  o Peer tutoring dyads.
  o Mixed-ability cooperative learning.

- Of the small group strategies, cluster grouping and regrouping have the most powerful academic effects, followed by cross-grading, pull-out classes, within-class grouping, like-ability dyads, and cooperative tasks.

8

More Program Provisions in School

What Would You Do for Hannah?

Hannah

Pretend you are a "better than average" fourth-grade teacher and you are concerned about one of your students. Hannah is a popular fourth grader who gets along well at school and with her teachers at all times, and she seems to look forward to school each day. She does well in all of her subjects, but some of her teachers (and you, too) suspect that there is more she could be doing, if only the teachers could find time to provide her with more challenging curriculum. Currently, when Hannah finishes her assignments, she alternates between doing extra sheets with the same kinds of learning tasks she just finished or helping others in her class who are having difficulty with those tasks. She doesn't seem to mind doing these things, but you have noticed that she less and less frequently finishes her work early and that her work seems to be less carefully done when it is turned in. What should you do?

In-School Enrichment Options for Gifted Children

Hannah's work slow-down and beginning symptoms of carelessness foreshadow some possible underachievement or non-production in years to come unless the school can provide challenges that will excite her curiosity and motivate her to keep her interested in learning. Third and fourth grades seem to be the first trouble spots for many gifted children. By the fourth grade, they have experienced several years of coming to school, putting forward very little effort, and getting amply rewarded for it. Gradually, the message they receive is that they can come to school and do well without really having to try. Many times, these bright children look around and notice that their class-mates, who are working more slowly, are not having to do as much work as they do. Therefore, as a first step toward later underachievement, they slow down their pace. If, when they finish, another task much the same as the already completed one is given, why would they want to finish quickly?

The second stage of underachievement often follows quickly. If they are frequently told how "good" their work is, even when they know they didn't put out their best effort, these children become less committed to doing their best work. You may recall from Chapter 1 that what these children wanted from their teachers was consistent, realistic feedback. Without such feedback, bright students may see many of their assignments as irrelevant and unimportant.

Some form of enrichment is certainly necessary for Hannah and others like her. This enrichment can take many forms: 1) *exposure* beyond the regular curriculum—to new ideas, skills, and concepts not encountered before; 2) *extension* of the regular curriculum—going more broadly and deeply into the ideas already introduced in that curriculum; and 3) *concept development*—using a concept introduced within the regular curriculum and exploring its meaning and implications fully. No matter what forms of enrichment the teacher decides to use, the key to enrichment lies in the maxim "HOTS not MOTS." In other words, whatever curriculum challenge the teacher offers, it must incorporate *Higher Order Thinking Skills* (HOTS), not *More of the Same* (MOTS).

What is exposure enrichment? Are there prepared materials a teacher can purchase or adapt? Must the enrichment always take place at school? Shouldn't all children enjoy and benefit from participating in exposure enrichment?

The answers to these questions are both simple and complex. For the first question, exposure enrichment can come from almost anywhere, but it MUST, according to both Joseph Renzulli and John Feldhusen, be based on the gifted child's interests. Hence, if a teacher or parent has an inkling of something that interests the child, the basis for an exposure enrichment experience is established. Renzulli and Feldhusen have argued, therefore, that often this means we must attract the child or children through a variety of short-term experiences, and then observe how interested or involved the child becomes.

Renzulli (1977) developed his *Interest-a-lyzer* to aid in narrowing down possible exposure experiences that might be considered the first step. The child is asked to rate preferences for various roles in several simulated situations. For example, "The school is putting on a play. Which three roles would you like to play?" The various potential responses are then keyed to the following domains: 1) fine arts/crafts; 2) performing arts; 3) literary/writing; 4) science/technical; 5) mathematics; 6) athletics; 7) business; 8) managerial; 9) government/law; and 10) history. Additionally, Renzulli has included a wide variety of possible enrichment experiences in which the child rates how frequently he has engaged in those experiences, and which five experiences are ones that he has not experienced but would like to experience right away. This list of experiences has been included as a "starter" list for exposure enrichments at the end of this chapter. My *Interest Inventory* (Rogers, 2001) in Chapter 3 (also in Appendix A) will give teachers and parents ideas for additional exposure enrichments that might be offered in school.

Although a child's interest is a good starting point for exposure enrichment, a second component is needed to make it "appropriate" for gifted children. General classroom enrichment includes any activity that excites, stimulates, and interests most children in the classroom. No distinction is made in how the enrichment will be provided for students with differing abilities or needs. Everyone participates. General classroom enrichment activities would include field trips, resource speakers, demonstrations, hands-on activities, class projects or plays, newspapers, etc. In truth, no child should be denied such activities. What makes an enrichment activity particularly "appropriate" for a child with gifts or talents, according to Harry Passow (1996), is when all of the following three questions are answered with "no":

1. Is this an activity every child *should* be doing?
2. Is this an activity every child *would like* to do?
3. Is this an activity that every child is *capable* of doing?

If we answer "yes" to any of these questions, then the enrichment is probably not advanced or differentiated enough to be specifically appropriate for gifted learners. Take, for example, calculus. Every student does not need to master calculus in order to succeed in the adult world. Not every student would want to learn calculus, and for some students, learning calculus is not even possible due to lack of ability or understanding in math. But calculus is suitable as differentiated curriculum for learners who are gifted in mathematics.

In Chapter 4, you learned—in general terms—what educational planning entails: curriculum, instruction, instructional delivery, and program planning for enrichment and acceleration. You also began to explore the process of matching a child's specific gifts and talents to the wide range of options available. In Chapters 5 and 6, you focused on when a gifted child should encounter the wide variety of acceleration options—when to speed up, when to maintain, when to forge ahead. In Chapter 7, you began to understand the nitty gritty of managing your child's educational needs in a school setting— for example, when a child should be grouped with other bright children and when she should be grouped with all other children for optimal learning. That leaves this chapter to explore the details of delivering "appropriately" enriched instruction and curriculum within the school setting. Again, we will focus on the things you should ask for in the school setting, but we will also look at what the research has to say about instructional delivery, modification, and differentiation.

The Essentials of Gifted Provisions in Schools

In 1998, I conducted an exhaustive review of the research on gifted education practices to discover what constituted appropriate options for gifted students. In the past few chapters, you have seen what that research has to say about acceleration and grouping. Now is the time to add the last pieces to the puzzle. Table 8.1 lists those practices that are essential for students with gifts and talents in the school setting, as well as those practices that are essential for all students and therefore must also be included in the educational plan of the gifted child. In most cases, these all-student essentials are regularly provided for in schools, but when budgets get tight, or when schools are off on the latest reform "bandwagon," some of these essentials may be missed. Therefore, when building your educational plan, you will want to check with the school to ensure that the all-student essentials are covered during the time your child is involved with her regular classroom and engaging with all students.

At the same time, it will be necessary to figure out when each set of essentials is truly needed for your child. He may not need every essential every year, but there may be critical periods as you look at his current behavior, learning preferences, and interests when some of these essentials become a priority.

Your educational plan will probably have two parts. The first will be a set of recommendations for the next year of school; the second will be your longer-term recommendations, such as what should be accomplished for your child while he is in the primary and intermediate grades or while he is in the middle school/junior high years of his schooling. Spend some time now looking at these essentials while thinking about the specific characteristics of your own child. Once you have looked at what the research says about these essentials, you will be ready to outline your child's educational plan.

Table 8.1. Essentials for a Positive School Experience

Essentials for Students with Gifts or Talents	Essentials for All Students
Accelerated pace when learning new concepts in math and science	*Discussion* to reflect orally on information and concepts learned
Discovery learning to find information, solutions, answers for self, actively	*Drill and recitation* to review previously mastered materials
Like-ability small group projects to learn how to participate without being "leader"	*Flexible project deadlines* to allow for contingencies and different learning styles
Independent study to learn how to manage research without teacher direction	*Flexible task requirements* and parameters gauged to individual abilities
One-on-one tutoring for talent development	*Higher order thinking skills* (HOTS) to practice with knowledge acquired and understood
Self-instructional materials to learn how to manage own time and learning	*Individual projects,* often teacher-chosen, to develop individual accountability
Proof and reasoning practice to learn to support own ideas, solutions adequately	*Inquiry learning* led by teacher to draw conclusions about what has been learned

Table 8.1. Essentials for a Positive School Experience *(continued)*

Essentials for Students with Gifts or Talents	Essentials for All Students
Teaching games to acquire new learning in competitive and non-competitive situations	*Teaching games* to review previous learning under competitive conditions
Compacting of previously mastered info, replacement with more complex content	*Compacting* of previously mastered info, followed by applications for this learning
Abstract content to learn how to reflect on deeper meanings and ideas	*Learning contracts* to negotiate and be responsible for own learning
Consistent challenge through explorations of greater breadth, depth in concept	*Lecture* to learn how to process auditory information for acquisition and retention
Interdisciplinary connections among disciplines organized by theme, concept	*One-on-one tutoring* for remediation
Telescoping of learning time to maintain concentration and focus on new learning	*Open-ended problems*, projects to encourage divergent thinking, production
Method of inquiry to learn to relate content to the methods, techniques of production	*Problem-based learning* tasks related to the "real world"
Real audiences to be given realistic feedback from experts	*Simulations* to apply previous learning to new problems, situations
Transformative products to learn how to transform info into visual, useful forms	*Study of people* to relate content to human situations, issues, and problems
Performance grouping to be differentiated in complexity, pacing, coverage in domain	*Communication skills* training to learn to express self appropriately, accurately
Conceptual discussion to explore themes, generalizations, issues, problems	*Creative problem-solving* practice to learn structure for solving ambiguous problems
Dilemmas, conflict resolution to solve hypothetical and real ethical issues	*Creative skills* training to practice thinking skills for divergent production

Table 8.1. Essentials for a Positive School Experience *(continued)*

Essentials for Students with Gifts or Talents	Essentials for All Students
Early content mastery to develop foundation for more complex learning	*Critical skills* training to practice thinking skills for problem solving, etc.
Individualized benchmark setting to plan and monitor performance goals short term	*Arts training* in history, aesthetics, criticism of all art domains
Whole-to-part learning of new concepts, knowledge, and skills	*Intuitive expression* practice to develop empathy, sensitivity to others
Talent development focus to extend, elaborate on given gifts of student	*Organization, time management training* to learn how to accomplish goals, projects
Talent exhibition to allow demonstration of high performance and potential	*Personal goal setting* to identify personal goals and priorities
Literary "Classics" to expand foundations of thinking	*Planning techniques training* to learn how to carry out projects, tasks, plans
"World's Great Ideas" to expand foundations of thinking	*Problem-solving skills* training to learn problem and solution finding
	Self-concept development to understand own strengths and talents
	Self-direction training to learn autonomy and independent skills
	Service learning projects to learn how to contribute to community at large
	Social issues discussions on current events, social, political, philosophical issues
	Systematic feedback for regular, honest monitoring of student work, progress

Instructional Delivery Options for Students with Gifts and Talents

Projects and Self-Direction

In the late 1970s and throughout the 1980s, the research in gifted education focused on learning preferences of the gifted and found that the pattern of preference for gifted students was consistently and significantly different than those for the regular student population. Gifted and talented students repeatedly indicated that they prefer to structure the tasks on which they work and to set their own deadlines instead of having the teacher assign tasks and deadlines (Dunn & Dunn, 1984; Renzulli & Smith, 1978; Stewart, 1980). They prefer working on projects alone or with one like-ability peer, and gifted students who teach each other either through tutoring dyads or projects show academic benefits (Kingsley, 1986; Johnsen-Harris, 1983).

When asked how they like to learn, gifted children strongly prefer self-instructional tasks, games, or simulations—all with new content acquisition as the goal. Their greatest preference is for independent study projects that are reading-based or content acquisition-based. Their greatest interest in learning is to "learn something new and different," rather than to do hands-on learning without learning something new. Furthermore, high achieving students generally learn more and retain information more accurately when allowed to self-pace learning tasks that are relatively structured (Whitener, 1989), such as is the case for most self-instructional materials, games, and simulations. This applies to the critical importance of providing structure for independent study projects (Treffinger, 1986) that allow gifted students to broaden their content base and teach them task completion (Stedtnitz & Speck, 1986), while exploring real world investigations and solutions (Starko, 1988).

Of course, as Barbe (1982) noted, preferring specific practices or instructional delivery media does not necessarily coincide with what the child needs educationally. On the other hand, matching a child's preferences for how she learns with how the curriculum is actually delivered almost certainly will enhance the child's motivation to learn so that attitudes toward school remain positive. Positive attitudes and motivation are important if the child is to reach higher achievement. There is some research to support that gifted students' learning styles and preferences should be considered when developing educationally sound curriculum and program policies for them (Shore, Cornell, Robinson, & Ward, 1991).

How and when do projects and independent study opportunities fit into the picture of a gifted child's enrichment? A teacher can provide exposure enrichment for children like Hannah by having her work with a small group of three or four other bright students to learn about tessellations in math (and art), or seashells in science, or Clara Barton and the Red Cross in social studies, or to compare the various Harry Potter books in reading. None of these projects is directly connected to the regular curriculum, but each project may help to develop a new interest in this group of students. Hannah could also do some independent study work with any of these topics for her exposure enrichment. Truthfully, if Hannah were to explore artistic variations of tessellations when she finished her math early, her teacher would probably not see such a slow down in her overall production!

Projects and independent study also work well for the delivery of extension curriculum. For example, students in the regular class might be reading a book by Gary Paulsen, but Hannah and her small group of advanced readers might do a comparative author study of three Gary Paulsen books to determine whether he uses similar literary devices and themes in his other works. Each member of Hannah's group could do a short-term independent study to locate yet another author who uses a Paulsen theme but who develops it in a completely different way. Hannah has now elaborated on, and extended, the initial learning and concepts provided by the regular reading curriculum.

For concept development curriculum enrichment, projects or independent study can be used. Hannah and her group might be given a reading list of "classic" books on a Paulsen theme (for example, humans vs. nature) from which they draw some conclusions about the treatment of this same theme by other authors during different periods of history and across different cultures. Judith Halsted's book, *Some of My Best Friends Are Books: Guiding Gifted Readers from Pre-School to High School* (1994, 2002), would be a good starting place for developing such a thematic list of books.

Lecture, Discussion, Mentoring, and Tutoring

Gifted students most often have learning styles that are multi-modal—both visual *and* auditory—in their preferences for acquiring and processing new information (Dunn & Dunn, 1984). This would suggest that lecture situations should require visual support through use of overhead transparencies, charts, maps, films, diagrams, or videos for information delivered orally.

The Dunns also found that not all gifted children enjoy discussion as a way of learning. Students who are primarily auditory learners tend to prefer discussion, but it is not a favorite learning style for the more visual learners. In general, a preference for discussion was not significantly more positive than for the general population. Nevertheless, Shore, Cornell, Robinson, and Ward (1991) found research indicating that gifted learners prefer complex verbal responses such as through discussions that focus on dilemmas and conflict resolution. Conceptual discussions that explore higher level themes, issues, and problems satisfy the research-supported practice of providing a qualitatively different, abstract curriculum for gifted learners.

The value of mentorships in academic, social, and psychological areas was substantiated (Rogers, 1991) in Chapter 5, especially at the secondary level. Bloom concluded in his longitudinal research on talent development (1982) that one-on-one tutoring for the purposes of talent development, and not remediation, results in the likelihood of eminence in academic, athletic, and arts domains. The key to both mentorships and tutoring, however, is selection of the "right" person to be the mentor or tutor. This person should have an accurate perception of the child's talent and needs for development and be able to shape the learning to match the child's set of needs. The mentor or tutor must also be a powerful teacher-communicator who has carefully articulated the benchmarks of progress toward which the gifted child will work.

Lecture and discussion lend themselves easily to the delivery of exposure enrichment. Speakers can be invited to introduce students to new topics of interest, which can then be followed by more work in the new topic area. Field trips, films, and videos can also be used as "lecture" in an introductory way. For extension enrichment, resource speakers and materials may be used to elaborate further on what is being covered in class. For example, in science, the whole class might be learning about the human skeleton. For extension, the teacher invites a forensic pathologist to talk to a group of advanced science students about how x-rays and autopsy results help to identify unknown murder victims; the specialist might go on to explain how to reconstruct a human's outward appearance just by building up clay on a skull!

Discussion is also a viable medium for extension enrichment. A teacher can work with the smaller group or the individual gifted students and ask higher order, exploratory questions, or broach the ethical or social issues of the general topic so that the group can go farther with the ideas and concepts previously introduced. This medium also works well for concept development—getting the gifted students to go farther with the initial concept or idea learned. For example, if the forensic specialist showed the students examples of heads reconstructed from skulls, she might get them to figure out just how accurate such a reconstruction might conceivably be—that is, how much estimation or guesswork is required along the way which could lead to inaccuracies in the reconstruction. Students might also explore through discussion with the specialist what percentage of reconstructions result in identification and actual criminal apprehension, and how much of a state's public safety budget is spent on improving such forensics in the various investigation branches.

Mentorships and tutoring for talent development are most likely to be extension and concept development enrichment options. Usually, only when a gifted child has mastered what can be learned on a topic in the school setting should he be paired with a mentor or tutor for further work in that area of passion. Sometimes, however, mentorships and tutoring can be ways to enhance motivation for a student who is otherwise withdrawing from academic participation.

Pacing and Time Telescoping

Dr. Brian Start of the University of Melbourne has spent the last 10 years measuring the comparative learning rates of children of varying abilities and has concluded that the learning rate of children above 130 IQ (gifted) is approximately eight times faster than for children below 70 IQ (mildly mentally impaired) (Start, 1995). Professor Julian Stanley and his colleagues at Johns Hopkins have suggested that mathematically precocious students are significantly more likely to retain science and mathematics content accurately when it has been presented two to three times faster than the "normal" pace of a traditional mixed-ability class (Stanley, 1993).

Further, Stanley has found that gifted students are significantly more likely to forget or mislearn science and mathematics content when they are forced to review and drill with it more than two to three times. In other words, the constant repetition of the regular classroom, so necessary for mastery among the general population, is actually detrimental to long-term storage and retrieval of technical content for gifted students.

Some preliminary work at the Center for Talented Youth at Johns Hopkins (Durden, 1992) suggests that this need for less repetition and drill may also hold true in the areas of foreign language learning, literature, and writing. The implications seem clear that curriculum compacting should be an integral part of any educational plan for gifted students since compacting eliminates unneeded repetition of information and concepts already mastered, buying time for advanced explorations and investigations. Research on the academic effects of compacting was presented in Chapter 5.

Sternberg (1985) has labeled gifted learners as "decontextualists" in the way they process information. In other words, when they acquire new information, they tend to chunk it in large "contexts" and then store it that way in long-term memory. When asked to retrieve such information to use in solving a math problem, for example, gifted children can quickly pull out the large chunk and retrieve the solution, but may be unable to break down the larger chunk to tell how they came to the solution. This certainly has implications for the need to restructure how gifted students acquire information. It suggests that they are most likely to benefit from learning the whole of a concept initially, with subsequent practice thereafter to help them see the parts of this whole. When this idea of whole-to-part learning is added to the need for rapid presentation pace to match the gifted learner's learning rate, it is easy to see why the Study for Mathematically Precocious Youth, and all its replications across the country, has worked so successfully with gifted learners for some 30 years.

Pacing, telescoping of learning time, and whole-to-part learning are most likely to be considered in the extension and concept development forms of enrichment. That is not to say one cannot speed up the pace of presentation for an exposure enrichment opportunity as well. Suppose gifted math students are invited to stay after school for a two-hour session learning about fractals and their applications in nature. The session is organized so that the students quickly learn what a fractal is, are given a few examples of fractals, and then are asked to find their own examples of fractals in everyday life and nature.

Critical and Creative Thinking Skills

Although the research suggests that higher order thinking skills and creative thinking skills are important for all learners, it seems these skills are essential for gifted learners. A few research studies point out that gifted students tend to use higher order thinking more frequently and appropriately even without direct training, yet they tend to benefit significantly more from such skills training when it is offered (Nasca, 1985; Redfield & Rousseau, 1981). Joseph Renzulli (1978) has offered a taxonomy of 255 critical and creative thinking skills that he considers essential for the full development of a gifted learner. A copy, which you may wish to share with your child's teachers, can be obtained by contacting Creative Learning Press in Mansfield Center, Connecticut.

A related aspect with regard to critical thinking skills is the need to teach gifted students to cite their proof and support their arguments. James and Shelagh Gallagher (1994) suggest that many gifted children never learn to give reasons to support their arguments and may use their advanced language skills to camouflage what they don't understand correctly or well. This can easily lead to development of sloppy thinking habits, particularly when it occurs several years in a row in school.

Regarding creativity, divergent thinking, and problem solving, Dunn and Griggs (1985), in their extensive learning preferences comparisons, concluded that academically and intellectually gifted students often are uncomfortable in taking risks or in dealing with ambiguity and unstructured problems. Torrance (1986) showed that creative thinking performance can be improved in students who are gifted—intellectually or creatively—by using direct instruction in creative thinking skills and by using creative problem-solving structures. Clearly, there is a need for teaching creative thinking and encouraging divergent production, but the question is whether that need is any greater for the gifted than for the general population. Tannenbaum (1981) has argued that such training would allow the gifted to make unique contributions to society, but the research on whether this is more likely to happen among the gifted is still unanswered.

Specific training for critical and creative thinking fits well within exposure enrichment activities. Many critical thinking programs are available, but one of the best is the set of conceptual reasoning and critical thinking skills described by Richard Paul (1998). This set includes process skills—such as recognizing the meaning of a concept, how it is ordered and structured—and practice in identifying frame of reference, end in view, question at issue, assumptions, inferences, and implications. Gifted students, grades two through seven, have practiced using Richard Paul's thinking skills while learning language arts, social studies, and science units through the College of William and Mary. The children are asked, for example, to read an original document from colonial times, identify the assumptions of the author, and discuss the implications of this document on life today (Van Tassel-Baska, 2000).

Teaching gifted children how to do synectics (Gordon, 1980), SCAMPER (Eberle, 1987), or "forced relationships" (Feldhusen & Treffinger, 1985)—three very different divergent thinking skills for generating ideas—are other excellent examples of exposure. Synectics involves using analogies and metaphors to help the child analyze problems from different viewpoints. In forced relationships—making connections between very unlike things—a child might be asked to find some way to use both a spoon and a rope to create a new tool. For SCAMPER—transforming a product or idea in seven different steps—the child might be given a toy and told to make modifications to it according to the SCAMPER acronym:

Substitute parts, Combine with other parts, Adapt to a different setting or use, Modify, Minify, Magnify some part of it, Put to other uses, Eliminate some part, and Rearrange or Reverse parts of it. To change a teddy bear, for example, I might decide to make it very tiny (minify) and make its eyes glow and buzz (substitute and combine); then I could give it a voice that would remind its owner about what she had to do today (put to other uses, adapt to different setting).

It is important that a child learn these kinds of creative, divergent thinking skills—which are not content-based—before moving on toward extension or concept development enrichment experiences, which are content-based. In other words, exposure enrichments are crucial as a gifted child's first enrichment experiences.

Discovery, Inquiry, and In-Depth Topic Development

Teachers and parents can be trained in special classes or by involvement in national creativity programs such as *Odyssey of the Mind, Destination Imagination, Future Problem Solving,* and *Invention Convention.* Such enrichment activities can be extremely rewarding.

Jerome Bruner's (1960) espousal of discovery learning resulted in the classic interdisciplinary curriculum *Man: A Course of Study* (MACOS). This curriculum provided elementary students of all ability levels with a dizzying array of content resources and guided them toward discovering "what makes humans human." Teachers were trained to provide structured learning sessions during which students learned about a wide variety of animal and primitive cultures. Bruner labeled this instructional method "guided discovery," and this curriculum was the national rage for a full decade in the 1970s. As a nationally disseminated curriculum, MACOS was thoroughly evaluated, and several research studies documented its efficacy with learners. At the time, the curriculum raised controversies.

Many of the concepts were considered too advanced or sensitive for most young learners.

Gifted learners were the primary recipients of this highly abstract, conceptual curriculum. After several years, teachers retired it from use, claiming it was too "difficult" or controversial for the majority of their learners and required too much time for the general population of learners to "discover" the concepts being taught. However, not only did gifted learners show significant motivation to learn with this curriculum, but they also drew the appropriate generalizations and conclusions about humanity. For gifted students, it was unfortunate that the Bruner curriculum was dropped.

Much of the current discussion about inquiry learning and problem-based learning represents an extension of Bruner's work of the 1960s. Although inquiry and problem-based methods parallel the "principles of gifted education" (Callahan, 1985), there is no research to suggest that the practices are critical only to gifted learners. Success with inquiry and problem-based learning has resulted in improved achievement for all learners (Van Tassel-Baska, 1999).

Dr. James Campbell (1988) also found in studying "award winning" mathematics programs, such as Math Olympiad, that problem-oriented independent study, when regularly scheduled, was the factor that each of these programs had in common. In most cases, no textbooks or exams were given; rather, each student was assigned stimulating open-ended problems for homework. For example, students might study the water of their local river to determine whether it was polluted and, if so, what factors were contributing to the pollution. During the course of their research, they would learn how to take water samples, how to use local records concerning the waste management procedures of industries, and the monitoring efforts by industries and environmental groups.

In-depth topic exploration and concept development can refer to a variety of activities, including learning facts and intricacies of a subject, developing related thinking skills, and finding connections among ideas in the topic domain. Freeman (1985) and Van Tassel-Baska (1985) have argued that gifted children, by their nature, want to "know all there is about a subject" and therefore "crave depth." Approaches that allow students to learn in depth can improve achievement and motivation for gifted learners in many formats—when studies of history, advanced mathematics, philosophy, and philology are delivered via seminar (Barbe & Malone, 1985; Feldhusen & Reilly, 1983), "Type III Enrichment" (students' self-selected, first-hand investigations into real-world problems) (Olenchak & Renzulli, 1989) is used, or when Talent Search opportunities involve subject acceleration (Stanley, 1985). Approaches like these allow bright students to address topics in depth with others who are like-minded and who have the same high interest in learning about the topic.

Discovery and inquiry as methods of learning lend themselves to exposure enrichment quite well. They become the means by which gifted children learn about new areas they may find interesting. *Man: A Course of Study*, described earlier, might be a good example of curriculum that could be used to extend the regular social studies curriculum on cultures for gifted learners. Discovery and inquiry may also be the means for exploring a concept fully and in depth, which means concept development enrichment can be offered through these delivery methods.

Talent Exhibition/Competition

This topic heading refers to programs in which gifted children compete or perform to exhibit their talent or other special achievements. A music recital or participation in a competitive spelling bee or Math Olympiad are some examples. The research in these areas is a bit thin, but common sense may make up for what the research does not say. Bloom's longitudinal study on talent development in young children (1982) pointed out that a key to later eminence in a talent field was whether the child with talent was provided with frequent "benchmarks of progress," such as an exhibition or competition. In piano, the exhibition could be yearly piano competitions, as well as recitals. Among swimmers, it might be frequent swimming meets. Bloom argued that it isn't the competition involved in these exhibitions that leads to ultimate success in the domain, but rather that the child and his teacher view the exhibition as a benchmark—an up-to-date picture of how much the child has accomplished since the previous exhibition. This, in turn, helps the child and his teacher plan for the next benchmark.

Although Bloom's work referred specifically to exhibitions and competitions that occurred outside of school, similar benchmarks can be arranged within the school setting. A child with extraordinary talent in piano or drawing may not learn much new in the way of talent development in the school setting. He will probably receive private lessons outside of school, which account for his actual progress, but he can show his latest efforts and have them appreciated by others, both adults and children, in school. The school could have a talent show or could just highlight the child's talent in an assembly or art display. The product or performance may be the only form of talent development in which the school can engage. The message that the talented child should receive is that school is a secure place in which to develop, and that educators accept student "differences," even if they cannot directly provide the extended knowledge and skills that his particular talent should receive.

For the gifted child with extraordinary talent in areas of mathematics, writing, science, chess, or knowledge acquisition, a talent exhibition in that area becomes the competition. The child has a chance to show her latest efforts or "gains" and to have them appreciated by others at school. In many cases, these core academic talents can be developed by the schools if educators care about seeing the talents developed. At the very least, academic competitions give the talented child a chance to find out how she is doing compared to other children talented in the same domain. They become the important benchmarks of progress for such a child.

Drs. Frances Karnes and Tracy Riley have published a comprehensive book, *Competitions: Maximizing Your Abilities* (1999), which describes 275 different academic, fine and performing arts, leadership, and service learning competitions. Likewise, Drs. Mary Tallent-Runnels and Ann Candler-Lotven have written *Academic Competitions for Gifted Students* (1999). Some of the hundreds of competitions suggested in these two books, which can best be supervised and administered through the schools, have been listed in Table 8.2. If your school is not currently participating in these programs, you may ask the school to provide one or more of these programs for your child and for others in the school who have similar talents. In Chapter 9, we will list some competitions and opportunities that may be more appropriate outside of school.

Table 8.2. Academic Competitions for Students

Competition	Contact	Age Level	Activity
Academic Games Tournament	Academic Games League P.O. Box 17563 West Palm Beach, FL 33406	10-18	Team tournaments in math, language arts, and social studies
Academic Triathlon	Academic Triathlon 15612 Highway 7 Minnetonka, MN 55345	10-18	Team competition in three creative events
Advanced Placement Scholar Awards	Educational Testing Services Box 6671 Princeton, NJ 08541	14-18	Score of 3+ on 3-6 AP exams; two levels of awards
All USA High School Academic Team Competition	USA Today 1000 Wilson Blvd. Arlington, VA 22229	14-18	Recognition based on principal/counselor nominations
American Computer Science League Competition	American Computer Science League Box 40118 Providence, RI 02940	12-18	Team competitions in computer knowledge, skill, programming
American Express Geography Competition	American Express Geography P.O. Box 672227 Marietta, GA 30067	12-18	Individual or team production of essay solution to geographic problem

Table 8.2. Academic Competitions for Students *(continued)*

Competition	Contact	Age Level	Activity
American Mathematics Competitions	AMC-University of Nebraska 1740 Vine Street Lincoln, NE 68588	12-18	Individual math exams
BOOK IT National Reading Incentive Program	Pizza Hut, BOOK IT P.O. Box 2999 Wichita, KS 67201	5-10	Classroom competition in reading goals
Continental Mathematics League	CML Box 2196 St. James, NY 11780	7-18	Math meets for teams of students
Creative Writing Essay Contest	Modern Woodmen of America 1701 1st Avenue, Box #2005 Rock Island, IL 61204	11-15	Writing competition through participating schools
Destination Imagination	Destination Imagination P.O. Box 547 Glassboro, NJ 08028-0547 www.destinationimagination.org	6-18	Team competitions in a variety of creative areas
ERECTOR Challenge	ERECTOR Set Company 1675 Broadway, 31st Floor New York, NY 10019	8+	Class competitions in design using given set of materials

Table 8.2. Academic Competitions for Students *(continued)*

Competition	Contact	Age Level	Activity
Future Problem Solving Bowl	FPS Program 318 W. Ann Street Ann Arbor, MI 48103	10-18	Team competitions in problem solving and scenario writing
Global Challenge	National Mathematics League P.O. Box 9459 Coral Gables, FL 33075	12-18	Individual, team national exam in current events, geography
HOBY Sophomore Leadership Seminars Los Angeles, CA 90024	Hugh O'Brian Youth Foundation 10880 Wilshire, #1103	15	School selected individual leader attends national seminar
International Science and Engineering Fair	Science Services 1719 N Street NW Washington, DC 20036	14-21	Team competitions in 13 science areas
Kids Are Authors	Trumpet Book Fairs 801 94th Avenue N. St Petersburg, FL 33702	5-13	Team picture book production competition
Knowledge Masters	Academic Hallmarks P.O. Box 998 Durango, CO 81320	11-18	Team competition via computer on academic achievement

Table 8.2. Academic Competitions for Students *(continued)*

Competition	Contact	Age Level	Activity
MATHCOUNTS Foundation	MATHCOUNTS Foundation 1420 King Street Alexandria, VA 22314	12-14	Team and individual competitions
Mathematical Olympiads	Mathematical Olympiads 125 Merle Avenue Oceanside, NY 11572	6-12	Team competitions
Merlyn's Pen Contest and Critique	Merlyn's Pen P.O. Box 910 East Greenwich, RI 02818	11-18	Submission of school magazine for critique of design, art, writing
National Academic Team Challenge	Foundation for Scholastic Advancement P.O. Box 3340 Iowa City, IA 52244	14-18	Team competitions in English, math, history, and sciences
National Americanism Essay Contest	AMVETS 4647 Forbes Blvd. Lanham, MD 20706	12-18	School-sponsored essay competitions
National Council of Teachers of English Writing Awards	NCTE 1111 W. Kenyon Road Urbana, IL 61801	16-17	Teacher nomination and writing sample competition

Table 8.2. Academic Competitions for Students *(continued)*

Competition	Contact	Age Level	Activity
National Current Events League	NCEL Box 2196 St. James, NY 11780	7-18	Team meets competition
National Engineering Design Challenge	Junior Engineering Society 1420 King Street, #405 Alexandria, VA 22314	14-18	Team competition in engineering design
National Federation of Press Women High School Journalism Contest	NFPW Box 99 Blue Springs, MO 64013	14-18	Journalism competition through participating schools
National Geography Bee	National Geographic Society 1145 17th Street NW Washington, DC 20036	9-14	National meets competition
National Geography Olympiad	National Geography Olympiad Box 2196 St. James, NY 11780	7-18	National exams in geography
National German Standardized Testing	American Association of German Teachers 112 Haddontowne Court Cherry Hill, NJ 08034	16+	Foreign language competition

Table 8.2. Academic Competitions for Students *(continued)*

Competition	Contact	Age Level	Activity
National Greek Examination	University of Massachusetts Box 33905 Amherst, MA 01003	14-18	Foreign language competition
National High School Oratorical Competition	American Legion Headquarters P.O. Box 1055 Indianapolis, IN 49206	14-18	Prepared oration competition
National History Day Contest	National History Day, Inc. University of Maryland College Park, MD 20742	11-18	Individual research/performance competitions
National Junior Classical League Contest	Miami University Oxford, OH 45056	14-18	Classical languages and cultures competition
National Junior Forensic League	NFL Box 38 Ripon, WI 54971	11-14	Debate and speech competition for grades 6-9
National Language Arts Olympiad	NLAO Box 2196 St. James, NY 11780	7-18	Language arts achievement test competition

Table 8.2. Academic Competitions for Students *(continued)*

Competition	Contact	Age Level	Activity
National Latin Exam	National Latin Exam Box 95, Miami University Oxford, OH 45056	14-18	Foreign language competition
National Mathematics League Competitions	National Mathematics League P.O. Box 94459 Coral Springs, FL 33075	12-18	Team mathematics competitions
National Peace Essay Contest	U.S. Institute of Peace 1550 M Street, #700 Washington, DC 20005	14-18	Writing competition in civics, politics, history, international affairs
National Social Studies Olympiad	National Social Studies Olympiad Box 2196 St. James, NY 11780	7-18	National exams in social studies
National Spelling Bee	Scripps Howard P.O. Box 5380 Cincinnati, OH 45201	6-15	National spelling competition
National Teen Business Plan Competition	Income of Her Own P.O. Box 987 Santa Barbara, CA 93102	13-19	Preparation of entrepreneurial business plan

Table 8.2. Academic Competitions for Students *(continued)*

Competition	Contact	Age Level	Activity
National Two-Dimensional Art Contest	Francis Hook Fund P.O. Box 597346 Chicago, IL 60659	6-18	Individual art work submission
Paul A. Witty Outstanding Literature Award	International Reading Association Texas Christian University Fort Worth, TX 76129	6-18	Writing sample competition
Physics Bowl	American Association of Physics Teachers 1 Physics Ellipse College Park, MD 20740	17-18	National exams in physics
Pledge and Promise Environmental Awards	Sea World Education Department 7007 Sea World Drive Orlando, FL 32821	5-18	Team environmental action service project competition
Promising Young Writers Program	NCTE 1111 W. Kenyon Road Urbana, IL 61801	12-13	Teacher nomination and writing sample competition
Science Olympiad	Science Olympiad 704 N. Bradford Street Dover, DE 19904	5-18	32 individual and team events in a variety of science areas

Table 8.2. Academic Competitions for Students *(continued)*

Competition	Contact	Age Level	Activity
Space Science Student Involvement Program	National Science Teachers Association 1840 Wilson Blvd. Arlington, VA 22201	8-18	Competitions in five space science areas
Stock Market Game	Stock Market Game 120 Broadway New York, NY 10271	10-18	Team competition in stock investment simulation
Tests of Engineering Aptitude, Mathematics and Science (TEAMS)	Junior Engineering Society 1420 King Street, #405 Alexandria, VA 22314	14-18	Team competition in real-world engineering problems
U.S. Academic Decathlon	U.S. Academic Decathlon 11145 183rd Street El Cerritos, CA 90701	14-18	Team competition in 10 scholastic events
U.S. National Chemistry Olympiad	American Chemical Society 1155 16th Street NW Washington, DC 20036	14-18	Individual examination on national test
U.S. Savings Bonds National Student Poster Contest	Department of Treasury Bureau of Public Debt Washington, DC 20226	9-12	Poster contest on theme of "saving"

Table 8.2. Academic Competitions for Students *(continued)*

Competition	Contact	Age Level	Activity
USA Computing Olympiad	University of Wisconsin 900 Wood Road Kenosha, WI 53141	14-18	Team competition to attend International Olympiad in Informatics
WordMasters Challenge	WordMasters 213 E. Allendale Avenue Allendale, NJ 07401	8-14	Vocabulary and verbal reasoning competition
Young Inventors and Creators Program	National Inventive Thinking P.O. Box 836202 Richardson, TX 75083	12-18	Individual competitions in seven invention and six creative arts categories

Content and Curriculum Modification Provisions

Multidisciplinary Learning

Gifted learners tend to make connections between new and prior learning more frequently than other children (Rabinowitz & Glaser, 1985; Rogers,1986; Simon & Simon, 1980). This would certainly support the necessity of enrichment experiences for gifted learners that incorporate multiple disciplines. In 1980, Goldberg, Passow, and Lorge suggested the use of seminars organized around issues, problems or people as a way to teach interdisciplinary or multidisciplinary learning. Certainly, the evaluation studies of Bruner's MACOS support this form of curriculum for enhancing the achievement of gifted learners, even if the curriculum itself focused on the science and social studies disciplines. In a formative article in 1985, Kersh and Reisman described how to develop such curricula for gifted learners. They suggest that the student's area of strength or talent be the starting point, and then this becomes linked with one or more additional disciplines through symmetry, patterns, constraints, variations, and transformations.

Modifying a curriculum to be multidisciplinary will probably be most useful in the exposure and extension forms of enrichment for gifted students. Linking different disciplines will engage the interests of students in the exposure experiences. For example, a child like Maria knows all there is to know about the history of the Civil War in 1861-1865 in the United States. Through exposure enrichment, she links the aftermath of the war to the Civil Rights movement of the 1960s and affirmative action in the 1970s, as she connects with sociology, business, government, and current events. Her interests broaden as a result.

If our goal is to *extend* Maria's knowledge of the Civil War, a multidisciplinary curriculum approach offers many options for further learning. Maria may begin with a "web" of linking disciplines, each of which becomes an area of further study for her. An example of this can be seen in Figure 8.1.

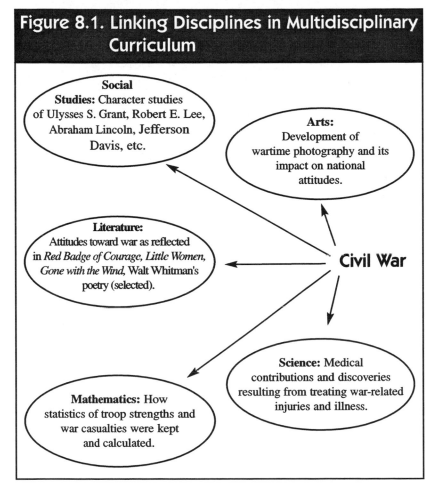

Figure 8.1. Linking Disciplines in Multidisciplinary Curriculum

Social Studies: Character studies of Ulysses S. Grant, Robert E. Lee, Abraham Lincoln, Jefferson Davis, etc.

Arts: Development of wartime photography and its impact on national attitudes.

Literature: Attitudes toward war as reflected in *Red Badge of Courage, Little Women, Gone with the Wind,* Walt Whitman's poetry (selected).

Civil War

Science: Medical contributions and discoveries resulting from treating war-related injuries and illness.

Mathematics: How statistics of troop strengths and war casualties were kept and calculated.

The ultimate form of enrichment—concept development—will probably not be best implemented through this curriculum modification. To most thoroughly develop concepts, it is usually necessary to go back to a disciplinary approach. For Maria, this might mean, for example, looking in depth at what role cotton and tobacco played in creating the schism between North and South in the Civil War.

Arts Education

In general, research has suggested that studying the arts results in improvement in abstract thinking, problem solving, skills of observation, self-esteem, and self-expression (e.g., Szekely, 1981; Parker, 1989). Only a little of the research suggests that these outcomes are significantly different for gifted learners.

Artistically gifted learners, however, do benefit from direct and extended training in art production, as well as aesthetics, criticism, and history (Bloom, 1982; Clark & Zimmerman, 1984). Common sense suggests that a more cognitive approach to the arts (aesthetics, criticism, history) will provide for intellectually and academically gifted students as well, and will ensure that they have at least a foundational knowledge of the arts in addition to development of their own specific gifts or talents.

Professor Julian Stanley, a proponent for specific talent development through subject-specific acceleration, argues that *all* gifted students, regardless of talent area, should be given a grounding in *all* of the cultural arts. For him, other enrichment is basically irrelevant (1985).

If the arts are to be "taught" as curriculum for the gifted, they fit primarily into the exposure enrichment experiences for the general population of gifted children. The curriculum will consist of analytical exposure to the best products and performances in all art areas (visual arts, dance, theater, creative writing, music, and graphic media), including their history.

For the child with gifts in the visual or performing arts, extension experiences can be designed to elaborate on knowledge or skills the child has already acquired, particularly by making links among skills and aesthetic concepts across arts disciplines. For example, if the fourth grade is studying American landscape painting as part of their art curriculum, the gifted child can be studying the influences of American Indians and Europeans on American landscape painting as an extension of classroom learning. For this type of gifted child, concept development can also take place through her arts education experiences. The child might study the stylistic influences on one American landscape painter and then try to paint in that style.

In summary, arts education, particularly the history, criticism, and aesthetic principles of the various art forms, is crucial knowledge for gifted children regardless of their area of giftedness. For the child with a talent in a specific arts domain, it is critical to go into more depth within the general arts curriculum. Clearly, the arts must play an important role in the educational development of every child with a gift or talent.

Foundations of Thinking/Qualitatively Different Curriculum

Of course, the fundamental underlying question for everything in this chapter is, "What comprises a 'qualitatively different' curriculum?" Scholars in gifted education have argued that all disciplines need a foundational base of knowledge (Van Tassel-Baska, 1985; Ward, 1980), but little research has focused on the specifics of this base. Professor Jerome Bruner's research would suggest that this base be composed of the "big ideas" or concepts of each discipline, but others, such as Dr. Sandra Kaplan and Professor Mortimer Adler, have suggested that the "big ideas" or concepts should be universal and more abstract. Professor Joyce Van Tassel-Baska and her colleagues at the College of William and Mary have adopted a few of Adler's universal and abstract concepts, such as systems, change, and power, and have used them as the base for highly effective social studies, language arts, and science units. Van Tassel-Baska's own research (2000) has shown improvements in both critical and conceptual thinking with gifted students engaged in these units. Evaluations of the Junior Great Books program of graded literary classics have also shown improvement in critical thinking and attitudes toward reading (Johnson, 1999). At a minimum, the research suggests that there are "lists" of ideas and readings that should be foundational for the gifted child. Perhaps it is time to go back to the summer reading lists and study of the classics often required by private schools!

The foundational base described here is best offered as exposure enrichment, and it should be begun as early as possible in a gifted child's schooling. Much of this base is no longer considered necessary in the general curriculum because it does not contribute directly to the basics of self-sufficiency in the modern world of work. Schools currently struggle with meeting standards imposed on them from national and state levels through mandatory yearly assessments. A classical education is no longer the goal of American schools, nor in many cases is it considered "politically correct." Hence, perhaps a suitable place to offer it may be as supplementary experiences in the exposure sense to gifted learners who have already achieved the standards of the regular curriculum in school.

Table 8.3 lists a compilation of Kaplan's, Adler's, Van Tassel-Baska's and my ideas as foundation concepts to which gifted children should be exposed. In addition, Halsted's books, *Some of My Best Friends Are Books* (1994) and *Some of My Best Friends Are Books, 2nd Ed.* (2002), offer summaries and annotations of several hundred literary classics in a wide variety of literary genre that are "required" reading for gifted readers. These sources can provide enough exposure opportunities in school for gifted learners for most of their K-12 career!

The research on gifted students' learning preferences pointed out one additional way in which curriculum can be modified. Gifted boys, in particular, and to some extent, girls, were found to be motivated by learning about how things work and the ways professionals work (Maker, 1983). Again, Bruner's evaluations of MACOS suggest that these children thrive when they use the methods of anthropologists and animal behaviorists in active discovery learning. Maker termed this curriculum modification Study of Methods (or Methods of Inquiry). It is certainly a modification that can be adapted for almost every discipline included in the "foundational base" that a school will provide as exposure enrichment for gifted students.

The learning preferences research also found that gifted girls, in particular, and to some extent, boys, are motivated by learning about famous people, career paths, and people-oriented issues in various content areas (Maker, 1983). This suggests that at a minimum, units on biographical reading and character study will appeal as exposure enrichment for gifted learners and should probably be included in the foundational base that schools are asked to provide for gifted students.

Table 8.3. Foundation Concepts for Gifted Learners		
Concepts		
Power	Death	Leisure
Change	Ownership	Work
Courage	Life	Freedom
Commitment	Peace	Conflict
Family	Responsibility	Violence
Love	Invincibility	Sound
System	Religion	Hate
Creation	Silence	Wisdom
Morality	Evaluation	Energy
Friendship	Communication	Conservation
Pollution	Tradition	Emotion
Tradition	Destruction	Law and Order
Happiness	Understanding	Suffering
Truth	Knowledge	Supernatural
Beauty	Ignorance	Spirituality
Justice	Equality	Loyalty
Healing	Invention	Infinity
Evil	Immortality	Adaptation
Good	Tolerance	Exploration
Time	Fairness	Magic
Eternity	Education	Values
Survival	Ethics	Growth

Product Transformations, Real Audiences

The issue of teaching "real world" problems was discussed in a previous section of this chapter (see Projects). Professionals generally agree that "real-world" instruction in schools is needed, especially for gifted learners (Haensly & Roberts, 1983), but there is little research literature on the effects of requiring "real world" products from gifted students. Dr. Alane Starko (1996) evaluated high ability children engaged in four years of the Renzulli and Reis (1985) Schoolwide Enrichment Model program with its focus on Type 3 "real world," in-depth investigations, and she found that these children improved in creativity, productivity, and learning motivation.

Maker (1983) suggested that "real world" products should be evaluated by "real audiences," that is, experts in the fields that incorporate such products. Although no direct research on the impact of such a practice can be found, indirect results, particularly through mentorships, suggests that the realistic, systematic feedback provided by the mentor or "expert" contributes to the achievement and self-efficacy of gifted students. To add to this, the research of Dr. Katherine Hoekman and her colleagues (Hoekman, McCormick, & Gross, 1998) on self-esteem has shown that expectations for performance and product must be specific and high, such that the gifted producer experiences some temporary "dissonance" (i.e., thinks he may not be able to do it) and then actually does accomplish the task. Hoekman has found significant improvement in academic self-esteem when this occurs.

Highly challenging real world problems and products evaluated by "experts" in the respective field(s) of these problems and products can occur primarily with extension and concept development enrichment. For example, suppose the gifted child has learned about genetically linked chronic diseases as a part of science and health in the regular curriculum. For extension, she is then encouraged to learn about the experimental techniques being developed currently for Alzheimer's disease in order to develop a set of guidelines for when patients should be allowed access to these experimental treatments, creating a prioritized list of needs for differential treatment. For concept development, the gifted student may work with the local research hospital engaging in one of these experimental treatments, finding out first hand what the impact of this treatment is on patients' physical and psychological states.

In general, it is important to provide gifted students with a wide variety of problems on which to work. These problems, whether using non-traditional media or focusing on real world issues, should offer an opportunity for the students to use what they have learned, rather than simply to summarize what they have observed or read. Making connections for these students with real world experts to provide them with feedback on their products seems to be critical for their development as well.

Affective Curriculum

Gifted children can find themselves "out of step" with their peers in several areas. They often deal with social and psychological issues connected with the "differences" they have cognitively. They can look around and see that they learn in ways that are different from their peers. They can also often see that their peers do not particularly like this difference. Often, the bright child is sensitive to the feelings of others and is concerned much earlier with moral and ethical issues. Silverman (1993) and Webb, Meckstroth, and Tolan (1982) describe the "asynchrony" that results in conflict for many gifted children—their mind is working at an advanced level, while their feelings and emotions are closer to those experienced by their agemates. There is no question that affective curriculum needs to be a part of what they are offered as curriculum in school.

Such "affective" curriculum should include knowledge and skills in the areas of social relations, personal adjustment, motivation, emotional expression, humanistic values, and moral reasoning. The research on these aspects of curriculum has been

primarily from the counseling perspective, suggesting that counseling with individuals and groups of gifted students does lead to
improvements in the areas listed above. Hoekman's (1998)
research on the part that challenge plays in improving motivation
and positive emotional expression could also be considered as
related to affective curriculum, but little research has directly measured the affective impact of emotion-laden topics in curriculum.

Some curriculum models have integrated affective topics
into their learning course of study. *Junior Great Books* focuses on
character development, *Philosophy for Children* studies moral
and ethical issues, and *Future Problem Solving* teaches children
to solve real-world problems, keeping in mind sociological and
ethical implications of their solutions.

Many curriculum development models have an underlying affective thrust. Jerome Bruner's "structure of the intel-
lect" model focuses on the "big ideas" of a topic, with the ideas
including values, human dilemmas, etc. Hilda Taba proposed
four inquiry strategies with children, one of which is conflict
resolution. Lawrence Kohlberg has a model for moral reasoning, by which children can move forward in their moral reasoning through discussion and exposure to moral and ethical
dilemmas.

Gifted children can gain exposure to affective issues
through the books they read for pleasure. Judith Halsted dis-
cusses the importance of bibliotherapy in *Some of My Best
Friends Are Books: Guiding Gifted Readers from Pre-School
to High School* (1994, 2002). In this approach, the adult and
child or children read a book that addresses an issue—such as
making friends, sensitivity, or using one's ability—and then
the two (or the group) discuss and apply this issue to their own
situation.

Leadership is also an important part of affective education. Drs. Frances Karnes and Jane Chauvin (1999) are rare in
that they have not only developed an instrument to measure
degrees of leadership skill in teens and young adults, but have
used this instrument to measure the impact of leadership skill

development programs. They provide exercises to help students develop leadership skills. They have concluded that substantial improvements in leadership skill can be made through such affective curriculum.

Though curriculum structure is important, the key to affective "improvement" for gifted children lies in the availability of people who represent three kinds of educational supports: 1) a counselor to provide the support and "content" individual gifted students may need for small group affective discussions about social and self-esteem issues; 2) teachers who willingly discuss the big ideas and underlying moral dilemmas of the content they are teaching; and 3) parents who nurture and promote their relationships with their gifted children so that ongoing discussions can occur.

The older the gifted child becomes, the more complex are the emotional issues to be faced. It is helpful to begin including affective learning in the elementary years to prepare the child for ongoing discussions throughout adolescence and to give him the language and the comfort of practice in talking about social and emotional concerns.

Rob, Maria, and Your Gifted Child

The past few chapters have suggested many things that you need to consider for your gifted child. You will need to consider her strengths and preferred learning style. You will need to assess her talents and abilities, interests, and social skills. You will need to determine the level at which she is capable of performing, possibly through out-of-level testing. There are decisions to be made about how you will manage her years in school. Will you accelerate her, either by shortening the years in school or ensuring a chance to learn advanced content and skills at an earlier age? Will you look for ways to have your child grouped with others who learn as she does? And what are the essential elements your child should be learning when she is grouped with her academic peers? You may want to quickly review the summaries of the last four chapters to refresh your understanding of all the choices you have. You may need to re-read some sections. When you are familiar with all of the options, you will be ready for the next exercise.

Below are the "Summary Comments" from the *Data Collectors* for Rob and Maria (Table 8.4), which you first studied in Chapter 3, and a blank *Data Collector* (Table 8.5) for you to complete for your own gifted or talented child. Take the time now to collect the information on *your* child and enter it into the *Data Collector*. Be sure to complete the summaries at the bottom of each column, because you will use them to make the "matches" that your child will need between his or her characteristics and behaviors and school-based options.

From the *Data Collector* information, you will then be ready to make the in-school matches to the educational provisions your child needs. You can start to think about this as you study the *Yearly Educational Planner* as it has been filled out for Rob (Table 8.6) and for Maria (Table 8.7). A blank *Yearly Educational Planner* is provided for your use in Table 8.8, and another is available in the supplementary materials in Appendix A.

Table 8.4. Summary Comments from Rob's and Maria's *Data Collectors*

Comment Category	Rob "The Brain"	Maria "The Specialist"
Cognitive Functioning	Rob is functioning at the 99th percentile of ability and can be considered gifted intellectually, both verbally and non-verbally.	Maria is functioning at the 99th percentile of ability and can be considered gifted, particularly in the verbal domain.
Learning Strengths	Rob shows outstanding strengths in intellectual and academic domains. He is functioning at the gifted level for both age and grade comparisons; he is capable of working beyond grade-level curriculum. His planning and communication skills should be extended.	Maria shows outstanding strengths in reading and writing, and her age and grade comparisons show she is functioning at the gifted level in all areas of the curriculum except mathematics. Her planning and communication precision skills should be extended.
Learning Preferences	Reading and social studies are Rob's strongest preferences, but he is highly motivated in all academic areas. He has a strong preference for self-structured, challenging content acquisition, and also likes interaction in competitions and discussion.	Reading and social studies are Maria's strongest preferences, with less motivation for the other areas. She has a strong preference for learning new content on her own, with strong dislikes for discussion, peer learning, group learning, and review.
Interests	Rob is highly interested by most academic pursuits in school. He has strong outside interests in reading, history, science fiction and fantasy, and in social issues.	Maria's interests in school center around social studies, reading, and language arts, and she is highly motivated in these areas. Her outside interests involve history, research, reading, and participating in service projects within the community.

Table 8.5. *Data Collector*
(also in Chapter 3)

©2000 by Karen B. Rogers

Child _____ Age _____ Gender _____ Date _____

Cognitive Functioning	Learning Strengths	Learning Preferences	Interests
Objective Measures:	Parent Input Intellectual:	Reading	In School Reading
	Academic:	Math	Language Arts
	Creative:	Science	Mathematics
	Social:	Social Studies	Science
	Arts:	Arts	Technology
	Teacher Input	Challenge	Social Studies
Subjective Measures:	Academic	Group Learning	Arts
	Personal	Individual Learning	School Attitude
	Social	New Learning	Outside of School
	Achievement	Old Learning	Building/Crafts
		Lecture	Business
		Discussion	Collections
		Peer Learning	Fine Arts/Design
		Drill and Recitation	Games, Competitions
			History

Table 8.5. *Data Collector* (continued)			
Cognitive Functioning	**Learning Strengths**	**Learning Preferences**	**Interests**
		Projects	Humor
		Independent	Law/Gov't./ Religion
		Study	Nature
		Self-Instruction	Performing Arts
		Games, Competitions	Reading
			Research
			Science
			Sci Fi/Fantasy
			Service/Charity
			Sports
			Technology
			Writing
Comments	**Comments**	**Comments**	**Comments**

Table 8.6. *Yearly Educational Planner*

©2000 by Karen B. Rogers

Child __Rob_____ Age __9-1/2__ Grade __4__ Gender __M__ Date _____

Date Plan Will Begin _____ School _____

School-Based Essential	Domain	How Often	Who and How Managed	Assessment
Academic Progress				
Grade-Skip	General	Next Fall	Principal places Rob in grade 5 class	1-month "grace" period. If teachers and Rob feel it's successful, he continues in grade 5
Compact math, replace with grade 7 math	Math	Each unit or chapter	Math teacher assesses and replaces	Pre-assess math unit. If >85%, he moves to replacement unit. Success at 85%
Compact reading, replace with advanced book list, tiered assignments	Reading	Each unit	Reading teacher assesses regular reading skills. Rob works on own on advanced lists, assignments.	Post-tests on grade 5 reading curriculum Units. Weekly assessment of Rob's progress on replacement experiences
Compact social studies; replace with ancient history	Social studies	Each unit	Social studies teacher assesses s.s. units. Rob works on self instructional ancient history materials.	Post-test on self-instructional course by social studies teacher
Compact science; replace with like-ability group advanced research projects	Science	Each unit	Science teacher assesses science unit	Evaluation of complete research project by science teacher

Table 8.6. *Yearly Educational Planner* (continued)

School-Based Essential	Domain	How Often	Who and How Managed	Assessment
Academic Remediation Participate in scenery and performance of a school play	Arts (theater, fine arts)	One play	Theater teacher after school	Rob decides if experience is enjoyable
Psychological Adjustment Leadership role in school government, conflict resolution program, or service project at school	Self-esteem and leadership	All year	Advisor or Guidance Counselor	Rob decides if experience is worthwhile
Socialization Participation in at least one academic team competition, e.g., Knowledge Bowl, WordMasters, Math Masters	Competition Teamwork	All Year	Competition Coach	Success of team; Rob's enjoyment

Table 8.7. *Yearly Educational Planner*

©2000 by Karen B. Rogers

Child _Maria_____ Age _11__ Grade _5__ Gender _F_ Date _____

Date Plan Will Begin _____ School _____

School-Based Essential	Domain	How Often	Who and How Managed	Assessment
Academic Progress				
History Day - research and performance	Social studies	Jan– April	Social studies teacher	Success in competition
Compact Social Studies; replace with "conflicts" unit (War of Roses; Crimean War, etc.)	Social studies	Each unit	Social studies teacher assesses, supervises Maria's self-study of "conflicts" curriculum	Weekly supervision of Maria's progress in self-study
Compact Reading; replace with advanced book list, tiered assignments	Reading	Each unit	Reading teacher pre-assesses each grade 5 reading unit, supervises Maria's independent work	Weekly supervision of Maria's progress on book list, assignments
Academic Remediation				
Regroup by performance level for math instruction	Math	Whole year	Math teacher of regrouped class	Successful achievement on work
Speech and debate unit or club	Language arts	Season	Speech and Debate Coach	Successful growth, development of communication skills
Psychological Adjustment				
Participate in theater program	Self-esteem	All Year	Theater teacher or coach	Successful participation; Maria's enjoyment

Table 8.7. *Yearly Educational Planner* (continued)				
School-Based Essential	**Domain**	**How Often**	**Who and How Managed**	**Assessment**
Socialization				
Service Learning Project leader	Social studies	All Year	Advisor or counselor	Success of project and Maria's ability to relate to group on the project
Participate in Junior Great Books discussion group	Reading	12 weeks	Discussion leader	Active participation in discussions with group of readers

Table 8.8. *Yearly Educational Planner*

©2000 by Karen B. Rogers

Child _____ Age _____ Gender _____ Date _____

Date Plan Will Begin _____ School _____

School-Based Essential	Domain	How Often	Who and How Managed	Assessment
Academic Progress				
Academic Remediation				
Psychological Adjustment				
Socialization				

Summary

Enrichment for gifted learners has three levels of complexity. The first level is simply *exposure* to new ideas and skills not taught in the regular school curriculum. The second level is fuller development or *extension* of the regular curriculum. A third level can be described as a *full, in-depth mastery* of an area or a concept or body of knowledge only introduced in the regular curriculum. Although all children need and benefit from some forms of enrichment, there are some types of enrichment that must be offered consistently to the gifted and talented students. The research supports the need for these essentials.

Key Points

- Exposure, extension, and concept development represent three levels of enrichment that are necessary and appropriate for gifted and talented learners.
- Some of the essential forms of enrichment for gifted or talented learners include:
  - Self-directed projects.
  - Fast-paced mathematics and science.
  - Whole-to-part discovery of concepts.
  - Critical and creative thinking skills.
  - In-depth topic development.
  - Competitions.
  - Interdisciplinary curriculum.
  - Curriculum that is infused with the arts.
  - The "Classics."
  - Real world problems evaluated by real audiences.

- Once a child's information about cognitive functioning, learning strengths, learning preferences, and interests has been collected, a plan can be developed to cover 1) the child's academic progress (movement forward in talent areas), 2) academic remediation (how the child's gaps in learning and skills will be addressed), and 3) psychological adjustment and socialization.

9
Out-of-School Provisions for Gifted Children

A Conversation

Principal: *Mr. and Mrs. Garcia, I have looked over your proposed educational plan for your daughter, Rosa, and I must say, it is quite ambitious.*

Mr. Garcia: *Yes, it is, but we believe it is important and that she is capable of handling all that it entails. When can the school staff start carrying it out?*

Principal: *I don't see how we can possibly carry this out! We have so many students who might want special attention and we don't have enough money to cater to all of them.*

Mrs. Garcia: *Are there any parts of the plan you think you could carry out for our daughter?*

Principal: *Well, since she is so far ahead of the other second graders in all academic areas, I think we can look at what she might miss if we skipped her in the fall to the fourth grade. I'll ask her teacher to check Rosa's knowledge and achievement against what the third-grade curriculum covers. If there aren't too many holes or gaps, we can consider skipping her one grade.*

Mr. Garcia: *What will you do about any gaps you find?*

Principal: *For the rest of this school year, her current teacher will allow her to work on filling in these gaps when she has completed her regular work. And what the teacher can't get to, you will have to help her finish next summer.*

Mrs. Garcia: *We'll do our part, but it doesn't seem like she should have to do double work to get ready for next year. Can her second-grade curriculum be compacted in those areas where she is already strong and knows the material? For example, she has yet to miss a spelling word all year, but still is required to do the spelling exercises each week. The spelling words are far too easy for her. She also finds math very easy. I'm sure she could test out of most of the math chapters being taught in the next few months. Compacting or allowing her to test out of these two areas would give her extra time to work on her gap areas in the third-grade curriculum.*

Principal: *I'll talk to Rosa's teacher about this possibility. It seems reasonable. It will depend on whether her teacher can find the time to provide extra third-grade material, including tests and a place where Rosa can work on her own quietly. The teacher will have to get access to the units or subjects Rosa needs to be studying. I think I can provide the teacher with a little time to set this up. How does that sound to you?*

Mr. Garcia: *Thank you. It will be a good start. The only other request that I have is for Rosa to be with other bright children in school on some sort of regular basis. She tells us there are no other children who think like she does in her grade. Is that possible?*

Principal: *We no longer offer a pull-out program for our fast and advanced learners. We lost funding last year and had to let the gifted specialist resource teacher go, so I don't think we can meet your request this year. But once we know what next year's budget allocations will be, we may be able to bring the resource program back again next year.*

Mrs. Garcia: *I don't think we should wait until the end of this school year to plan this for next year. I know at least five other very bright children in the other second-grade classes. Couldn't they be clustered together in the same classroom next year?*

Principal: *If we are going to skip Rosa next fall, I don't think I can allow that many children to be skipped just so they can be clustered together for their learning. I think you will just have to be happy with the skip.*

Mr. Garcia: *Grade-skipping will put her closer to the level she should be working on in her learning, but it won't necessarily help her connect with others like herself. Wouldn't it be possible to provide a cluster at each grade level? You must have five or six children at each grade level who are rapid learners like Rosa. That way Rosa could be placed with a fourth-grade teacher who wants to work with these rapid learners and who can get some training in how to work with them effectively. The cost to you would be the training for those five or six teachers who would be the cluster teachers, and it certainly would provide daily challenge for 30 to 48 bright learners in the school. This would be less costly than hiring an additional resource teacher to do pull-out programs for these children.*

Principal: *Let me do some thinking about this and get back to you. I like the idea of staff development, and you are right. For the cost of some training, I can serve a good proportion of our more able students.*

In this example, Rosa's parents got some of what they wanted for their daughter—though not everything—and it is a good beginning for advocacy efforts. This is the kind of conversation with a principal that we hope you can have after reading and studying the information in this book. Parents throughout the country have found that they need to become strong and well-informed advocates in order to get appropriate curriculum services for their gifted children.

In 1995, the U.S. Office of Education Report, titled *National Excellence: A Case for Developing America's Talent*, reported that less than 3 cents of every $100 in education is spent on special programming for gifted and talented learners. Since that time, the $9 million in federal money represented by that statement has been pared down, so that now only 1 cent of $100 is expended. What this means for parents of gifted and talented children is that much of what they will ask the schools to provide is not possible due to budget constraints. Thus, in some schools and school districts, those options that will cost the school little or no money have the best chance of being accepted for the gifted child's educational plan. After all, public schools generally believe that their mission is to provide a basic education, not all the education that might be ideal or optimal for every child, and they plan their expenditures with this in mind.

Much of what parents ask for will likely fall on their shoulders and pocketbook. Is this unfair? For some families, perhaps not, if they can afford the costs of enrichment science and art classes outside of school. But what about families of gifted children who do not have extra resources and who must rely on the schools to provide for their bright children? As discussed earlier, Gallagher (1965) estimated that it costs a school 27% more to fully educate a gifted child as compared to the costs to educate the general population of students. This means that for every $100 a school needs to educate a regular child, it will need $127 to educate the gifted child.

Until state legislators and federal politicians realize, however, that 1) schools in general are under-funded and 2) that *not* educating gifted children is a severe talent loss that impacts our nation's best interests and ability to continue as a world leader, families will still have to muster their own resources to provide the challenge and stimulation that schools cannot, or choose not, to offer. Unfortunately, this also means that many thousands of our nation's gifted and talented but economically disadvantaged children will not have their gifts and talents developed unless by chance or by accident. Therefore, parents will need to find as many inexpensive or free options as possible as resources for their children's education. A few of these possibilities will be covered in the remainder of this chapter.

Regrettably, the message I must pass on to you is this: "Don't rely on or expect the schools to provide for your child's full gifted education. It probably isn't going to happen. Work with the schools to get the best educational provisions you can, but be prepared to do additional enrichment at home or with your own resources as well."

Guidelines for Out-of-School Provisions

The previous chapters describe the optimal programs, structures, and curriculum that gifted and talented children need in their school program for full development of their abilities. The same structures can provide guidelines to help you focus on what educational opportunities you might choose to provide for your child outside of the school program.

1. *Provide advanced learning opportunities, regardless of your child's age, in the specific area or areas in which your child's talents and interests lie.* This does not mean rigidly scheduling activities that fill up your child's time week after week—as in dance lessons, followed by soccer practice on Monday, piano on Tuesday, gymnastics on Wednesday, painting on Thursday, followed by soccer practice again, and so on. Your child will gain more from focusing on one activity at a time, particularly one that actually advances her skill level and her desire to know. If the activity is fairly sedentary (as in piano or computer programming), you may want to add an activity that involves some physical skill, perhaps around a sport such as swimming, cross country, bowling, tennis, or golf, that could provide lifelong fitness as well as leisure-time enjoyment. Once an outside class or activity has finished, you and your child can decide on the next activity together, again based on the child's interests, motivation, and skill level at that time.

2. *Provide opportunities for socialization with others of like ability or interests.* This becomes particularly important if your child has little or no chance to learn with true intellectual equals in school. It is human nature to make connections and lasting friendships among those who think like you and are

interested in similar things. There is nothing elitist about this. It is a simple fact that humans, both adults and children, are most likely to feel comfortable with those who have similar interests.

Outside-of-school enrichment classes are a place for friends; special Saturday classes, conferences, or other gatherings sometimes sponsored by local or state gifted advocacy groups and parent associations are another possibility. The Minnesota Council for the Gifted and Talented for example, offers a yearly Saturday conference with a full day of separate programs for parents and children. While children take classes on telescopes, fossils, or mosaics, parents learn about characteristics of gifted children, intelligence testing, graduation standards, or Talent Search opportunities.

Opportunities to interact with other bright children are also possible in summer school programs for gifted children offered by some school districts, or through Talent Search classes for middle school and high school gifted students held on college campuses during the summer or on Saturdays.

3. *Provide opportunities for socialization with a mix of adults and children of varying abilities and ages.* It is important to give all children the message that they are a part of the human "community" and that they have a responsibility to that greater community. With their natural curiosity, idealism, sensitivity to the needs of others, and problem-solving abilities, gifted children usually enjoy working with others.

Participation in Scouts or other character-building organizations will give your child a broader chance to interact with others who focus on idealist concerns and a chance to see the positive side of human nature, as will participation in community clean-up, fund-raising projects, or church-related activities.

The more widely your child samples possible ways to become involved in the community, the better her chances of finding the "perfect" way to use her talents for the good of humanity—whether that means serving dinners to the poor on Thanksgiving Day or teaching disadvantaged children about art as a museum docent.

4. *Find ways for your child to understand his own identity and uniqueness.* This means that you will need to carve out large blocks of time for your child to work alone or with you on the development of his talent and interests. The two of you will need to find those "benchmarks of progress," either through private competitions, special lessons, mentors/tutors, periods of self-study, or on-line instruction to move him along the path to full talent development.

But there is another side to this development as well—his personal development. You are your child's most important teacher when it comes to confronting the moral and ethical dilemmas of life in general. Not only are you a model through your own behavior of how to resolve such dilemmas, but you must also be ready for freewheeling exploration of the "what ifs" of these dilemmas.

Many gifted children show early concerns for human issues, moral causes, and problems such as war, terrorism, hate, injustice, or pollution, and for many, the need to discuss and think about these concerns is foremost. They need the opportunity to think out and create a rationale for what they would do in such dilemmas long before they may actually be confronted with them in real life. Books may provide neutral territory in which to explore these issues—readings that you and your child can discuss together.

5. *Provide your child with some of the "classics" of literature, philosophy, art, music, and theater.* You are correct in assuming that these classic foundations will not be taught in the schools to any significant degree. So many other areas are now mandated in public education (basic skills, health, drug education, sex education, violence prevention, etc.) that five or six hours a day does not leave teachers with much time or incentive to offer the broad-based curriculum based on the classics that was offered in earlier decades. Even in many college programs, the tendency to get students to "specialize" early means they will probably not have much space in their programs for a wide-ranging, "classical" education, even if they pursue a "liberal arts" education there.

6. *Provide a variety of experiences that build fine-motor skills, dexterity, and spatial visualization.* Although knowledge and information from recent research on the brain and neural pathways is rapidly increasing, it is difficult at this point in time to apply this knowledge directly to the development of your own child's brain. There seems to be evidence to suggest a need to develop "other" parts of the brain (to create new neural pathways).

Instruction in a musical instrument that requires finger dexterity, such as piano, violin, bass, guitar, flute, oboe, clarinet, etc., particularly while learning to read music, should be offered once your child reads comfortably. Developing your child's keyboarding skill on the computer is also important. Lightning speed on the word processor may be the only way your child will be able to get her thoughts down as quickly as they come to her mind, allowing writing and communication expression to become a joy rather than a burden. Learning to orienteer with a compass and a map builds spatial-visual skill, and listening to books or poetry—live or on tape—helps to develop listening as well as visualization skills.

7. *Provide experiences that require memorization and improving the ability to remember.* This is not a skill the schools always offer, but is one that practically guarantees success in higher-level study. Schools are intent on teaching processes and the "hows" of doing things. Time allocated for learning facts, definitions, and terms is minimal.

   The field of knowledge is wide open with lists of things to learn; vocabulary to master; science, history, and social science facts to acquire; and poetry, speech, and prose to recite from memory. Teaching your child a number of different ways to remember information, such as mnemonics, will also help her in later life.

8. *Help your child learn to communicate precisely and expressively.* Communication requires both a strong *reception capacity*, the ability to comprehend what one hears and then interpret it accurately, and *expression component* the ability to share personal reflections, reactions, beliefs, and values in oral and written forms. Children who never have a chance to discuss ideas are at a disadvantage.

   Spending less time watching television and more time listening to the radio or taped books, having regular "book club" discussions within your family, and having regular current events or social/moral issues discussions during family meals will help your child develop these reception and expression capacities. Some families hold regular meetings to help decide who will do which chores and how the family will spend its time together.

9. *Teach your child a variety of problem-solving strategies that will help in social, real world, and academic situations.* Deflecting the negative comments

and actions of others can be "taught" through role play with you as the problem child, or by providing your child with a repertoire of light responses, jokes, and phrases to use.

There are many sources available for teaching your child how to make decisions, from easy decisions such as what to wear tomorrow to choice of college and college major. Books such as *JumpStart: Ideas to Move Your Mind* (Elyé & Southwick, 2000) can provide the basis for discussion and practice.

Likewise, strategies for inductive and deductive reasoning can be taught at home in fun ways. Gifted children are often good problem finders, but they haven't necessarily learned the skills to be good problem solvers.

10. *Help your child feel comfortable in and knowledgeable about the world.* This begins by active description and interpretation of his own backyard, neighborhood, community (behind the scenes), state, country, and even the world, to the extent that family finances allow. Family trips are invaluable. Capturing the perspective of how much is out there can be learned by first seeing Mount Rushmore or Colonial Williamsburg and then reading about them in books.

Exposure to the world must be as much as possible in person, preferably as a family. While your children are still young and in your care, travel our country's highways and see the beautiful national parks. How can your child truly appreciate our nation's remarkable strength without visiting the sources of its history, from battlefields to national archives to the White House? A year spent attending school abroad can help a student expand his world view while still having the support of a host family, or perhaps the entire family can live abroad for a year or more. (Westphal, 2001) Travel you cannot afford can be done with books and videos from the library, but one way or another, your child needs to know how things work, what species live in different locations, and what varying geography looks like.

Talent and Interest Development

Most states have parent or teacher organizations that offer Saturday enrichment programs for gifted and talented children. Later in this chapter, you will find a current listing of parent gifted associations or state departments of education if no parent association exists. Contact the organizations in your state to find out about Saturday and summer gifted programs (See Table 9.1).

The talent areas covered by such programs will vary. Summer "academies" or Saturday programs sponsored by a university or school district will probably offer a great variety of challenging programs in a wide variety of talent areas. Research on these programs shows greater increases in motivation for the talent area and self-efficacy than in academic growth. At a minimum, they may allow your child to find a true peer with similar interests—the start of a lifelong friendship! For many gifted children, this is the first time they have found a real friend.

Several Saturday and summer programs, especially those for middle level and secondary students, have been nationally recognized for their excellence. If you live in the vicinity of one of these programs, you are in luck. You will find a few of these programs listed in Table 9.1. A more comprehensive listing can be obtained by ordering the book *Educational Opportunity Guide* from Duke University (Talent Identification Program, 1121 West Main Street, Suite 100, Durham, NC 27701, 919-683-1400). The book is published frequently, so ask for the most recent update.

Table 9.1. Saturday and Summer Programs for Gifted Students

Program	Contact	Offerings	Qualifications
Advanced Programs for Young Scholars Northwestern State University Natchitoches, LA	800-259-3173	Summer residential programs in humanities, natural sciences, math, computer science, music theater, marine ecology	Grades 8-12 with ACT or SAT scores, letter of recommendation from GT teacher, evidence of high achievement
Bennington College July Program Bennington College Bennington, VT	802-440-4418	Intensive, exploratory courses in arts, humanities, and sciences	Grades 9-12 with transcript, recommendations, parent statement, personal essay
Carnegie Mellon Summer Programs for High School Students Pittsburgh, PA	Undergraduate-admissions@andrew.cmu.edu	Pre-college programs in architecture, art, design, drama, music, advanced placement courses in sciences, math, humanities, and engineering	Grades 11-12 with ACT or SAT scores, letter of recommendation, essay, work sample, transcript
Center for Academic Precocity Summer Programs (Arizona State University) Tempe, AZ	Cap@asu.edu	Enrichment programs in a wide variety of math, technology, science, humanities, and arts courses	Grades K-12; only grades 5-12 are residential; GT recommendation, work samples, test scores, ACT/SAT for older students
Challenges for Youth-TAG Iowa State University Ames, IA	Opptag@IASTATE.edu	3-week accelerated, individualized courses in math and a variety of sciences	Grades 7-10 with ACT or SAT score

Table 9.1. Saturday and Summer Programs for Gifted Students *(continued)*			
Program	**Contact**	**Offerings**	**Qualifications**
Concordia Language Villages Concordia College Moorhead, MN	Clvoffice@ village.cord.edu	1- to 4-week programs in 10 different languages and village or travel experiences	Grades 3-12
Duke Summer Programs Duke University Durham, NC	919-684-3847	Variety of 3-4 week programs in academic areas, graphics calculators, marine science, scientific field studies (national, international)	Grades 7-12 with SAT or ACT score qualifying students as gifted or talented
Early Preparatory Learning Program Wisconsin Center for Gifted Learners Milwaukee, WI	Wcgl@acs. stritch.edu	4-week interdisciplinary programs across seven disciplines	Ages Preschool-14 with test scores, interview, parent/student questionnaires
Future Astronaut Training Program Kansas Cosmosphere and Space Center Hutchinson, KS	800-397-0330	1-week simulated astronaut training, rocketry, astronomy	Grades 8-11 in good physical health

Table 9.1. Saturday and Summer Programs for Gifted Students *(continued)*

Program	Contact	Offerings	Qualifications
GERI Summer Programs (COMET, STAR, PULSAR, NOVA) Purdue University Lafayette, IN	Geri@soe. purdue.edu	1- to 3-week classes in a range of all academic areas	Grades 5-12 with transcript, personal essay, GPA, SAT or ACT scores
Governor's Summer Residential Programs. Nine regional sites in VA	Through local GT coordinator	Variety of science, technology, and arts programs throughout Virginia	Grades 4-12 with teacher recommendation, work samples, GT nomination, test scores
Hopkins Summer Programs Johns Hopkins University Baltimore, MD	www.jhu.edu/ ~sumprog	Courses for college credit in social studies, humanities, sciences, English, and computers	Grades 11-12 with SAT or ACT, personal essay, teacher report, recommendations
Horizons Unlimited G/T Academy University of Oklahoma Norman, OK	Alogan@ou.edu	Variety of computer, sciences, arts, and aerospace studies	Grades 6-8 with personal essay, test scores, report card, GT recommendations

Table 9.1. Saturday and Summer Programs for Gifted Students *(continued)*

Program	Contact	Offerings	Qualifications
Institute for Academic Advancement of Youth California State University Loyola Marymount University Fresno, Los Angeles, CA	410-516-0337	Accelerated courses for high school and college credit in areas such as math, science, humanities, writing - part of Johns Hopkins programs	Grades 7-12 with SAT scores, letter of recommendation, evidence of high achievement
Junior Statesmen Summer School Held at Stanford, Yale, Georgetown, Northwestern, Princeton, and University of Texas	800-334-5353	Advanced Placement government, law, and speech courses taught by nationally recognized leaders in these fields	Grades 10-12 with transcript, essay, letters of recommendation
Marie Walsh Sharpe Art Foundation Colorado Springs, CO	719-635-3220	Intensive visual art studio program with artists-in-residence	Grade 12 with portfolio of artwork, teacher recommendation, personal statement
Missouri Scholars Academy Missouri Dept. of Education Columbia, MO	Dwelch@mail. dese.state.mo.us	Variety of academic, personal development, and recreational programs in 3-week period	Grade 11 with personal essay, PSAT score, GPA, teacher report

Table 9.1. Saturday and Summer Programs for Gifted Students *(continued)*

Program	Contact	Offerings	Qualifications
National Computer Camp Held in Atlanta (GA), Cleveland (OH), Santa Clara (CA), Los Angeles (CA), Fairfield (CT)	Zabinski@ funrsc. fairfield.edu	1-week classes in all levels of educational and recreational computing/ language	Ages 8-18 with interest in computers
National Scholars Academy University of Iowa Iowa City, IA	www.uiowa.edu /~belinctr	1-week program in law, science, writing, mathematics, or engineering	Grades 10-12 with test scores
Pre-College Enrichment Programs Academic Study Associates Held at Amherst, Stanford, University of Massachusetts, Oxford University	ASAProgram@ aol.com	Enrichment courses in sciences, arts, humanities, SAT prep, athletics	Grades 7-12

Table 9.1. Saturday and Summer Programs for Gifted Students *(continued)*			
Program	Contact	Offerings	Qualifications
Pre-College Programs and EFL Brown University Providence, RI	Summer_studies @brown.edu	4- and 7-week pre-college courses in all disciplines	Grades 10-12 with SAT, GPA, teacher report, personal essay, recommendations
Seacamp Big Pine Key, FL	www.seacamp. org	Studies in marine sciences, basic SCUBA diving certification, photography, arts	Grades 7-12 with teacher report and recommendations
Science-by-Mail Boston Museum of Science/NSF	Cotter@a1.mos. org	National pen-pal program of science experiments and research projects	Grades 4-9
Summer Enrichment Program University of Northern Colorado Greeley, CO	970-351-2683	2-week academic program in sciences, arts, social studies areas	Grades 5-10 with teacher, parent, or self-nomination
Summer Enrichment Program University of Oregon Eugene, OR	541-346-1404	30 courses in academic, arts, and creative areas	Grades 7-10 with teacher report, test scores, personal essay

Table 9.1. Saturday and Summer Programs for Gifted Students *(continued)*

Program	Contact	Offerings	Qualifications
Summer Enrichment Program University of Virginia Charlottesville, VA	Curry_sep@ virginia.edu	2-week programs in variety of academic areas	Grades 5-11 with test scores, GT recommendation, teacher report
Summer Institute for the Gifted Held at Drew University (NJ), Bryn Mawr (PA), Oberlin (OH), Vassar (NY), and Pacific Lutheran (WA)	800-735-2030	Variety of academic programs, as well as courses for college credit - run as summer camp	Grades 4-11 with teacher report, test scores, SAT or ACT scores, GT recommendation
Summer Laureate University for Youth University of Arkansas Little Rock, AK	Cjweeks@ualr. edu	3-week enrichment courses in science, languages, social studies, math, arts	Grades 2-8 with test scores, personal essay, teacher report, parent statement
Summer Program for Academically Talented Youth University of Southern Mississippi Hattiesburg, MS	Gifted.studies @usm.edu	Variety of programs in academic areas and leadership studies	Grades 5-12 with teacher report, IQ scores (for some programs)

Table 9.1. Saturday and Summer Programs for Gifted Students *(continued)*

Program	Contact	Offerings	Qualifications
Summer Science, Engineering, Architecture, and Pre-College Enrichment Program Clemson University Clemson, SC	Cnell@ clemson.edu	1- to 3-week courses in areas listed in title of program with college credit for older students	Grades 7-12 with PSAT, GT nomination, recommendations
Summer Stretch Program University of Washington Seattle, WA	Mosolf@u. washington.edu	Intensive 4-week courses for academic credit in literature, sciences, rhetoric, and mathematics	Grades 8-10 with SAT or WPCT test scores
Summer Writing Program Carleton College Northfield, MN	Summer@ carleton.edu	3-week intensive writing seminar for college credit	Grades 11-12
Talented and Gifted Program Southern Methodist University Dallas, TX	Khargrov@mail. smu.edu	Variety of enrichment and pre-college programs in most academic areas	Grades 8-12 with personal essay, teacher report, SAT or ACT scores, GPA

Table 9.1. Saturday and Summer Programs for Gifted Students *(continued)*

Program	Contact	Offerings	Qualifications
Tufts Summer Enrichment Programs Tufts University Boston, MA	www.tufts.edu/ as/summer	Courses for college credit in 40 academic areas	Grade 11-12 with personal essay, recommendations, SAT or ACT scores
WCATY Summer Programs Wisconsin Center for Academically Talented Youth Madison, WI - offered at different regional college campuses	Eschatz @ madison.tds.net	Intensive, fast-paced 3-week courses for academic credit in variety of academic areas	Grades 3-12 with SAT or ACT scores, GT teacher recommendations
Wright State Summer Enrichment Wright State University Dayton, OH	Trenner@ corvus.wright. edu	Variety of arts, creativity, leadership, and academic courses	Grades 7-12 with transcript, personal essay, work sample, GT recommendations

Table 9.2. State Residential and Private Schools for Gifted and Talented Students

School Name	Contact Info	Specialization
Alabama School of Mathematics and Science Mobile, AL	334-441-2120	Grade 11-12 public, residential, coeducational school for math and science talent development
Brevard College School for Gifted Students in the Arts Brevard, NC	704-884-8256	Grades 8-12 private school for students gifted in arts areas
Creative Children's Academy Palatine, IL	847-202-8035	Grades PreK-8 private school for creatively and academically gifted children with interdisciplinary, hands-on, project-oriented curriculum
Early Entrance Program (EEP) University of Washington CSCY Program Seattle, WA	Mosolf@u.washington.edu	Grades 9-12 public day program that allows gifted students to enter college 3-4 years earlier than agemates
Firespark School for Gifted Students in Fine Arts Brenau University Gainesville, GA	Mccord@lib.brenau.edu	Ages 13-18 private school for students gifted in the arts, including writing
Groton School Groton, MA	978-448-7510	Grades 8-12 private school with a special program for gifted and talented students

Table 9.2. State Residential and Private Schools for Gifted and Talented Students
(continued)

School Name	Contact Info	Specialization
Hope Center Children's Program Denver, CO	303-388-4801	Primary private school for gifted, at-risk children
Hunter School for the Gifted New York, NY	212-678-3700	Elementary private school for gifted children; affiliated with Teachers College
Illinois Mathematics and Science Academy Residential High School Aurora, IL	Lsmith@imsa.edu	Grades 10-12 public laboratory school for students gifted in math and science
Indiana Academy for Science, Mathematics and Humanities Muncie, IN	317-285-8105	Grades 11-12 public residential school for students gifted in math, science or the humanities
Lee Academy for Gifted Education Tampa, FL	813-931-3316	Ages 4-17 private school with accelerated curriculum, international connection, and dual university enrollment options
Logan School for Creative Learning Denver, CO	303-340-2444	Grades 1-8 private school for gifted and creative learners with broad-based curriculum
Louisiana School in Math, Science, and the Arts Natchitoches, LA	800-259-3173	Grades 11-12 public residential school for students gifted in math, science or the arts
MacIntosh Academy for the Gifted Littleton, CO	303-794-6222	Grades K-8 private school for gifted students with strong academic focus

Table 9.2. State Residential and Private Schools for Gifted and Talented Students
(continued)

School Name	Contact Info	Specialization
Milton Academy Milton, MA	617-898-2227	Grades 9-12 private school for gifted students with rigorous, wide-ranging curriculum
Mirman School for Gifted Children Los Angeles, CA	310-476-2868	Grades 1-9 private school with wide-ranging curriculum
Mississippi School for Mathematics and Science Columbus, MS	www.msms.doe.k12.ms.us	Grades 11-12 public residential high school for students gifted in math or science
North Carolina School of the Arts Winston-Salem, NC	910-770-3291	Grades 8-12 public training school for students gifted in arts areas
North Carolina School of Science and Mathematics Durham, NC	919-286-3366	Grades 11-12 public residential high school for students gifted in math or sciences
Oklahoma School of Science and Mathematics Oklahoma City, OK	Emanning@ossm.edu	Grades 11-12 public residential high school for students gifted in math or sciences
Phillips Academy Andover, MA	Admissions@andover.edu	Grades 9-12 private school with extremely rigorous curriculum in all academic areas
Phillips Exeter Academy Exeter, NH	Admit@exeter.edu	Grades 9-12 private school with wide-ranging, rigorous curriculum

Table 9.2. State Residential and Private Schools for Gifted and Talented Students
(continued)

School Name	Contact Info	Specialization
Program for the Exceptionally Gifted (PEG) Mary Baldwin College Staunton, VA	PEG@cit.mbc.edu	Grade 9-12 private residential program that allows gifted girls to enter college four years early
Renaissance Academy Colorado Springs, CO	719-475-2510	Grades 1-8 private school with rigorous curriculum for the gifted
Ricks Center for Gifted Children University of Denver Denver, CO	Nhafenst@du.edu	Grades PreK-12 private school with wide-ranging curriculum for students with gifts and talents
Rocky Mountain School for the Gifted and Creative Boulder, CO	303-545-9230	Grades 1-8 private school with individualized curriculum
Roeper School for the Gifted Bloomfield Hills, MI	AYDYO6A@prodigy.com	Grades PreK-12 private school with wide-ranging, challenging curriculum; a day school only
Simon's Rock College of Bard Great Barrington, MA	Admit@simons-rock.edu	Grades 10-11 private university that recruits early-entrance highly gifted students
South Carolina Governor's School for Science and Mathematics Hartsville, SC	Van_sturgeon@scgssm. coker.edu	Grades 11-12 public residential high school for students gifted in math or sciences
St. Andrew's School Middletown, DE	www.st-andrews/ pvt.k12.de.us	Grades 9-12 private school with rigorous curriculum (was depicted in *Dead Poet's Society*)

Table 9.2. State Residential and Private Schools for Gifted and Talented Students
(continued)

School Name	Contact Info	Specialization
St. Anne's School New York City, NY	212-722-1295	Grades 1-12 private school with rigorous curriculum
Taft School Watertown, CT	Admission@taft.pvt.k12.ct.us	Grades 9-12 private school with rigorous, individualized curriculum
Texas Academy of Mathematics and Science	Jones@TAMS.UNT.EDU	Grade 11-12 public residential school in which last two high school years are completed in one year
Thacher School Ojai, CA	Admission@thacher.org	Grades 9-12 private school with rigorous academic and outdoor challenges in its curriculum
Westover School Middlelbury, CT	Admission@westover.pvtk12.ct.us	Grades 9-12 private school for gifted women in academics, engineering, or music
Winston Academy Plantation, FL	Win_lng@msn.com	Ages 10-14 private gifted school with rigorous, individualized curriculum

Current thinking about gifted children with updates on special talent development programs and schools are the typical contents of a variety of magazines and journals to which you can subscribe. *Gifted Child Today* (Prufrock Press) addresses numerous educational issues with some focus on personal and social development concerns. *Parenting for High Potential* (National Association for Gifted Children) is geared to parents of gifted children with a very balanced exploration of educational, personal, and social concerns. *Roeper Review* (Roeper School) is a bit more technical but contains many thought-provoking articles about gifted children's needs, even though it is aimed primarily at educators. Additionally, there are many, many specialty magazines designed to appeal to children with gifts and talents. Table 9.3 lists children's magazines that will be of interest.

Table 9.3. Magazines for Children

Magazine	Publication Address	Content/Interest Areas
3-2-1 Contact	P.O. Box 53051 Boulder, CO 80322	Science/technology in projects, experiments
Calliope: World History for Young People	30 Grove Street, Suite C Peterborough, NH 03458	Five issues per year focus on different theme in history
Chickadee	25 Boxwood Lane Buffalo, NY 14225	Nature and environmental study with some features on other sciences
Cobblestone	30 Grove Street, Suite C Peterborough, NH 03458	U.S. history features
Cricket	315 Fifth St., P.O. Box 300 Peru, IL 61354	Variety of literary genres for children
Current Science	3001 Cindel Drive Delran, NJ 08370	Latest advances in technology and science
Faces: The Magazine about People	30 Grove Street, Suite C Peterborough, NH 03458	Articles, projects on anthropology from the American Museum of Natural History

Table 9.3. Magazines for Children *(continued)*

Magazine	Publication Address	Content/Interest Areas
Imagination	Johns Hopkins Press/CTY 3400 N. Charles Street Baltimore, MD 21218	School-age challenges, articles, stories for highly gifted children
Kid City Magazine	200 Watt Street P.O. Box 53349 Boulder, CO 80322	School-age challenges, stories, articles for Sesame Street graduates
Ladybug: The Magazine for Young Children	315 Fifth Street P.O. Box 300 Peru, IL 61354	Version of Cricket for children ages 2-6
Let's Find Out	Scholastic 730 Broadway New York, NY 10003	Features on all academic areas for older children who can read well
Merlyn's Pen: The National Magazine of Student Writing	Merlyn's Pen, Inc. P.O. Box 910 East Greenwich, RI 02818	Written work and art work by children; middle school or high school editions
Muse	Cricket Magazine, Inc. 315 Fifth Street P.O. Box 300 Peru, IL 61354	Science and arts features of ages 8-14 in conjunction with Smithsonian/ Cricket
National Geographic World	17th & M Streets NW Washington, DC 20036	Science, hobbies, and sports features
Odyssey	30 Grove Street, Suite C Peterborough, NH 03458	Space and astronomy features
OWL: The Discovery Magazine for Children	25 Boxwood Lane Buffalo, NY 14225	Nature magazine published by Young Naturalist Foundation, ages 9-12
Quétal? or Das Rad or Bonjour	Scholastic 730 Broadway New York, NY 10003	Introductory language learning through games, stories, pictures
Ranger Rick	National Wildlife Federation 8925 Leesburg Pike Vienna, VA 22184	Nature study for graduates of *Your Big Backyard*
Scholastic DynaMath	730 Broadway New York, NY 10003	Real world math through activities and games

Table 9.3. Magazines for Children *(continued)*

Magazine	Publication Address	Content/Interest Areas
Sesame Street Magazine	P.O. Box 55518 Boulder, CO 80322	Pre-school challenges, games, projects in math, reading, thinking
Sports Illustrated for Kids	P.O. Box 60001 Tampa, FL 33660-0001	Sports magazine for ages 8-13
Stone Stoup	P.O. Box 83 Santa Cruz, CA 95063	Children's art and writings ages 5-12
Story Art Magazine	National Story League 984 Roelofs Road Yardley, PA 19067	Short story magazine for children and adults
Your Big Backyard	National Wildlife Federation 8925 Leesburg Pike Vienna, VA 22184	Nature study through stories, puzzles, and games
Zillions	Consumers Union/Reports P.O. Box 2015 New York, NY 10703	Consumer Reports for kids by Consumers Union, ages 8-14
Zoobooks	P.O. Box 85384 San Diego, CA 92186	Animal studies

Like-Ability/Interest and Socialization

There will always be the opportunity for your child to find a friend who is a "soul-mate" when she becomes involved in outside-of-school classes or schools as described in the previous section. Keeping that in mind, how will you find *additional* socialization experiences for your child? One way is to contact your state parent association to find out what kinds of conferences or meetings it offers for parents and gifted children, whether or not the association publishes a regular newsletter that lists enrichment experiences offered throughout the state, and whether there are chapter meetings in your area. Table 9.4 lists the associations for each state. In cases where there is no permanent address for the state parent association, the department of education is listed instead. Project Promise at Colorado State University has developed a website that links to ALL state departments of education, including the District of Columbia. The site is: http://promise.cahs.colostate.edu/DOE.html.

Table 9.4. State Gifted Education Information

Alabama Department of Education 3346 Gordon Persons Bldg. P.O. Box 302101 Montgomery, AL 36130-2101 334-242-9700	Alaska (call state ed. organization) Programs for Gifted and Talented Children 801 W. 10th Street, Suite 200 Juneau, AK 99801 907-465-3452
Arizona Department of Education Gifted and Talented Specialist 1535 W. Jefferson Phoenix, AZ 85007 602-542-4361	Arkansas Department of Education Programs for Gifted and Talented #4 Capitol Mall Little Rock, AR 72201 501-682-4475
California State Department of Education Gifted and Talented Programs P.O. Box 944272 Sacramento, CA 94244-2720 916-657-4865	Colorado Department of Education Gifted Specialist 201 E. Colfax Avenue Denver, CO 80203-1704 303-866-6600
Connecticut Association for the Gifted Gifted and Talented Programs P.O. Box 2219 Hartford, CT 06145 860-566-5677	Delaware Department of Education Gifted and Talented Specialist P.O. Box 1402, Federal & Lockerman Streets Dover, DE 19903 302-739-4667
District of Columbia Public Schools Gifted and Talented Department 825 N. Capitol Street NE Washington, DC 20002-4232 800-872-5327	Florida Department of Education Gifted and Talented Programs Turlington Bldg. 325 W. Gaines Street Tallahassee, FL 32399-0400 904-288-3103

Table 9.4. State Gifted Education Information
(continued)

Georgia Department of Education Superintendent's Help Desk 2054 Twin Towers East Atlanta, GA 30334 404-656-2800	Hawaii Gifted Association P.O. Box 22878 Honolulu, HI 96823 808-732-1138
Idaho Department of Education Gifted and Talented Programs P.O. Box 83720 Boise, ID 83720-0027 208-332-6800	Illinois State Board of Education Gifted and Talented Division 100 N. 1st Street Springfield, IL 62777 217-782-4321
Indiana Department of Education Gifted Program Specialist Room 229, State House Indianapolis, IN 46204-2798 317-232-0808	Iowa Talented and Gifted Assoc. 8345 University Blvd., Suite F1 Des Moines, IA 50325 IowaTAG@aol.com 515-225-2323
Kansas State Department of Education Gifted and Talented Programs 120 SE 10th Avenue Topeka, KS 66612-1182 785-296-3201	Kentucky Department of Education Gifted and Talented Division 500 Metro Street Frankfurt, KY 40601 800-533-5372 or 502-564-4770
Louisiana Department of Education Div. of Special Populations P.O. Box 94064 Baton Rouge, LA 70804-9064 225-342-6110	Maine Parents for Gifted/Talented Youth 203 Pine Hill Road Berwick, ME 03901 207-698-7754
Maryland State Department of Education School & Community Outreach 7th Floor 200 W. Baltimore Street Baltimore, MD 21201 888-246-0016 or 410-767-0600	Massachusetts Department of Education Gifted and Talented Programs 350 Main Street Malden, MA 02148-5023 781-338-3000
Michigan Alliance for Gifted Education 3300 Washtenaw, Suite 220 Ann Arbor, MI 48104 734-677-4404	Minnesota Council for Gifted and Talented 5701 Normandale Road Minneapolis, MN 55424 952-927-9546

Table 9.4. State Gifted Education Information

(continued)

Mississippi Department of Education Academic Education P.O. Box 771 Jackson, MS 39205-0771 601-359-3778	Missouri Department of Elementary/Secondary Education Gifted and Talented Programs P.O. Box 480 Jefferson City, MO 65102 572-751-4212
Montana Association for Gifted/Talented Education 1135 Whitefish Stage Kalispell, MT 59901 406-756-5063	Nebraska Department of Education Gifted and Talented Programs 301 Centennial Mall South Lincoln, NE 68509-4987 402-471-2295
Nevada Department of Education Gifted and Talented Programs 700 E. 5th Street Carson City, NV 89701 775-687-9200	New Hampshire Department of Education Gifted and Talented 101 Pleasant Street Concord, NH 03301-3860 603-271-3494
New Jersey State Department of Education Gifted Education Division 100 Riverview Plaza, P.O. Box 500 Trenton, NJ 08625-0500 609-984-1805	New Mexico State Department of Education Gifted and Talented Programs 300 Dan Gaspar Santa Fe, NM 87501-2786 505-827-6683
Advocacy for Gifted Education in State of New York 280 Concorde Avenue Oceanside, NY 11572 516-678-4130	North Carolina Department of Public Instruction Gifted and Talented Education 301 N. Wilmington Street Raleigh, NC 27601-2825 919-715-1246
North Dakota Department of Education Gifted and Talented Programs/Capitol Bldg. 600 E. Boulevard Avenue Dept. 201, Floors 9-11 Bismarck, ND 58505-0440 701-328-2260 or 701-328-4770	Ohio Association for Gifted Children Allen County ESC 204 N. Main Street, Suite 303 Lima, OH 45801 419-222-1836

Table 9.4. State Gifted Education Information
(continued)

Oklahoma State Department of Education Gifted and Talented Programs 2500 N. Lincoln Blvd. Oklahoma City, OK 73105-4599 405-521-3308	Oregon Department of Education Gifted and Talented Division 255 Capitol Street NE Salem, OR 97310-0203 503-378-3569
Pennsylvania Department of Education Gifted and Talented Education 333 Market Street Harrisburg, PA 17126-0333 717-783-6788	Rhode Island Department of Elementary/Secondary Education Gifted and Talented Programs 255 Westminster Street Providence, RI 02903 401-222-4600
South Carolina Department of Education Gifted and Talented Programs 1429 Senate Street Columbia, SC 29204 803-734-6500 (x8355)	South Dakota Association for Gifted Education 2006 Buena Vista Rapid City, SD 57702 605-343-7051
Tennessee Department of Education Gifted & Talented Office 710 James Robertson Parkway Nashville, TN 37243-0375 615-741-2731	Texas Association for the Gifted and Talented 406 E. 11th Street, Suite 310 Austin, TX 78701 512-499-8248
Utah State Office of Education Gifted and Talented Programs 250 E. 500 South Salt Lake City, UT 64111 801-538-7500	Vermont Council for Gifted Education Johnson State College 337 College Hill Johnson, VT 05656 802-635-1321
Virginia Department of Education Gifted Education Div. James Monroe Bldg. 101 N. 14th Street Richmond, VA 23219 800-292-3820	Washington Office of Supt. of Public Instruction Gifted Specialist Old Capitol Bldg., P.O. Box 47200 Olympia, WA 98504-7200 360-753-6738

Table 9.4. State Gifted Education Information
(continued)

West Virginia Department of Education Division of Gifted Education 1900 Kanawha Blvd. E. Charleston, WV 25305 304-558-2696	Wisconsin Association for Gifted & Talented 1608 W. Gloverdale Drive Appleton, WI 54914 920-991-9177
Wyoming Department of Education Gifted/Talented, Hathaway Bldg. 2nd Floor 2300 Capitol Avenue Cheyenne, WY 82002-0050 307-777-7675	Project Promise at Colorado State University has developed a website that links to ALL state departments of education, including the District of Columbia. The site is: http://promise.cahs.colostate.edu/DOE.html.

General Socialization

The *Rogers' Interest Inventory* you previously completed for your child contains numerous projects and activities to help your child engage socially with children of all ages and abilities. Putting on performances, starting a business, or working on a neighborhood clean-up project all provide opportunities for your child to do something worthwhile, satisfying, and entertaining, while simultaneously learning to interact appropriately with other children and adults.

Barbara Lewis has written two wonderful books you may want to order through Free Spirit Press: *The Kids' Guide to Service Projects* (1995) and *The Kids' Guide to Social Action* (1998). Both books contain literally hundreds of ideas for your child's involvement in worthy projects and service to the community. In addition, Table 9.5 lists just a few ideas that you and your child might find appealing and worthwhile.

Table 9.5. Social Action and Service Projects for Children

Project Category	What to Do	Contact
Animals	Raise funds to "adopt" a specific zoo animal and better conditions	Local zoo director or exhibit curator
Community	Conduct a neighborhood drive to collect used household items to distribute to refugee families or to a local shelter	Local social services administrator
The Elderly	Write down an older person's personal history	Local senior citizen center or nursing home
Environment	Raise seedlings to transplant in a local community park, garden, or nature preserve	State or city forester about locations, America the Beautiful Fund (202-638-1649), or Rainforest Alliance (212-677-1900)
Friendship	Start a monthly "get acquainted" lunch period for newcomers	School principal
Health	Volunteer to help at a blood drive	American Red Cross (local chapter) or Public Health Service (202-690-6867)
The Homeless	Hold a clothing drive to collect cold-weather outerwear, such as coats, hats, scarves	Local social services administrator
Hunger	Collect grocery coupons to donate to a local food bank	Local social services administrator or food bank coordinator
Law	Work with student council at school to develop a strong discipline policy. Take it to the school board to enact it as a district policy	School principal and school board members
Literacy	Read to or tutor children in a local homeless shelter	Local shelter coordinator

Table 9.5. Social Action and Service Projects for Children *(continued)*

Project Category	What to Do	Contact
Politics	Work at a polling place during an election	Local League of Women Voters president
Safety	Assist a sports league or after-school sports program by keeping track of equipment, arranging treats, helping with practices	Local athletic association
Special Needs	Raise funds for Braille books for the visually impaired	National Self-Help Clearinghouse (212-642-2944) or Youth Service America (202-296-2992)
Transportation	Raise funds and distribute recyclable leaf bags in poorer neighborhoods	Local social services administrator

Identity and Self-Awareness

There are a variety of ways, both individually and more communally, that your child can become more aware of his abilities and character. Reading inspiring biographies and autobiographies can help him find role models for the person he wishes to become. Table 9.6 lists a few books I have found inspiring.

Table 9.6. Inspiring Biography and Autobiography Selections for Gifted Children

Title	Author	Content
Carry On, Mr. Bowditch	Jean Latham	Story of poorly educated man who finds success in early America
Christabel	Christabel Bielenberg	Life in Nazi Germany
The Exile	Pearl Buck	Biography of Buck's mother as missionary in China
Little House on the Prairie (series)	Laura Ingalls Wilder	Life of Laura from childhood through adulthood in early Midwestern U.S.
Lives of the Noble Greeks and Romans	Plutarch	Fascinating stories of the ancient Greeks and Romans
Madame Curie	Eve Curie	Biography of author's scientist mother
Marco Polo	Gian Ceserani	Story of Polo's explorations to China
The Maus Series: A Survivor's Tale	Art Spiegelman	Series of books in cartoon form about a survivor of the Holocaust
The Microbe Hunters	Paul de Kruif	Life stories of biological scientists
Narrative of the Life of Frederick Douglass	Frederick Douglass	Written by a former slave in 1845 who went on to contribute greatly to U.S. society
Native American Doctor: The Story of Susan LaFlesche	Jeri Ferris	Biography of Omaha American Indian who trained in medicine and returned to her tribe
Queen Victoria	Lytton Strachey	Story of one of the most powerful queens of England
Shakespeare of London	Marchette Chute	Life of one of most famous English dramatists

Table 9.6. Inspiring Biography and Autobiography Selections for Gifted Children *(continued)*

Title	Author	Content
This Boy's Life: A Memoir	Tobias Wolff	Autobiography of famous fiction writer
Where Do You Think You're Going, Christopher Columbus? Or What Happened Next, Paul Revere?	Jean Fritz	Lively biographies of famous individuals

Reading books as "bibliotherapy" may help your child overcome personal issues or even fears and concerns that keep her from learning about herself and her strengths. There are many books that contain annotated lists of appropriate books that deal in healthy ways with a variety of crises that particularly affect gifted children. Two that are particularly helpful are Judith Halsted's *Some of My Best Friends Are Books* (1994, 2002) and Baskin and Harris's *Books for the Gifted Child* (1980). Both identify themes that are of concern to gifted and talented children, and then list books at different age levels that address these themes in positive ways. Halsted, for example, lists books with themes of achievement, aloneness, arrogance, creativity, developing imagination, differentness, drive to understand, identity, intensity, introversion, moral concerns, perfectionism, relationships with others, sensitivity, and using ability. Both books include lists of appropriate reading material across all literary genres, from the classics to poetry, science fiction, nonfiction, picture books, fantasy and mythology, biography, historical fiction, mystery, folk and fairy tales, and realistic (current) fiction.

Table 9.7 lists a few books for different age levels that are "musts" for developing a gifted child's identity and self-awareness. When you think you have exhausted this list and the bibliographies of the two books listed above by Halsted (1994, 2002) and Baskin and Harris (1980), two additional books that will provide additional reading outlets are Kathleen Odean's *Great Books for Boys* and *Great Books for Girls*, each listing over 600 books that are exciting, provide strong role models, and are expansive in their viewpoints.

Table 9.7 A Short List of Good Books for Gifted Students

Title	Author	Age Level	Category/Contents
Harald and the Great Stag	Donald Carrick	K-2	Moral concerns: Stag hunt in medieval England
Island Boy	Barbara Cooney	K-2	Drive to understand: Family life on isolated island off Maine coast
My Friend Jacob	Lucille Clifton	K-2	Relationships with others: Friendship between boys of different races, ability, and ages
Time to Get Out of the Bath, Shirley	John Burningham	K-2	Aloneness: Shirley's imagination as she takes a bath
What Happened to Patrick's Dinosaurs?	Carol Carrick	K-2	Using ability: Imaginative story about the disappearance of dinosaurs
Willaby	Rachel Isadora	K-2	Identity: Young girl's recognition of her drawing ability by her teacher
Caddie Woodlawn	Carol Ryrie Brink	3-5	Moral concerns: Girl's life in pioneer times in Wisconsin
The Eleventh Hour	Graeme Base	3-5	Drive to understand: Horace the Elephant's birthday party surprises
A Girl Called Al	Constance Greene	3-5	Aloneness: Nonconformist girl moves and has to make friends

Table 9.7 A Short List of Good Books for Gifted Students *(continued)*

Title	Author	Age Level	Category/Contents
Harriet the Spy	Louise Fitzhugh	3-5	Using ability: Harriet's notebook of her comments gets taken by her classmates
Part-Time Boy	Elizabeth Billington	3-5	Identity: Introverted boy's summer experiences help him grow
Racso and the Rats of NIMH	Jane Conly	3-5	Relationships with others: Racso tries to fit into the colony of NIMH rats
And This Is Laura	Ellen Conford	6-8	Using ability: Psychic girl discovers value of her gift
The Lemming Condition	Alan Arkin	6-8	Aloneness: Lemming who does not leap into the sea
A String in the Harp	Nancy Bond	6-8	Drive to understand: Young boy finds harp key that takes him back to 6th-Century Wales
The True Confessions of Charlotte Doyle	Avi	6-8	Identity: 13-year-old girl sails from England to America by herself
The Village by the Sea	Paula Fox	6-8	Relationship with others: Emma tries to figure out her family's story
Westmark	Lloyd Alexander	6-8	Moral concerns: Trilogy of books about printer's apprentice in tumultuous kingdom

Table 9.7 A Short List of Good Books for Gifted Students *(continued)*

Title	Author	Age Level	Category/Contents
Anthem	Ayn Rand	9-12	Aloneness: Future world in which man finds he doesn't want to be like everyone else
Bronstein's Children	Phillip Berman	9-12	Moral concerns: East German Jewish boy tries to understand his father's actions after Nazi period
Celine	Brock Cole	9-12	Using ability: High school girl with artistic talent tries to make sense of realities of daily life
Fahrenheit 451	Ray Bradbury	9-12	Drive to understand: Future world in which Montag tries to survive in anti-intellectual world of censorship
The Tempered Wind	Jeanne Dixon	9-12	Relationships with others: Disabled teen finds her place in rural Montana
Very Far Away from Anywhere Else	Ursula LeGuin	9-12	Identity: Nonconformist teen learns how to fit in

The next step is how to persuade your child to read these books. Sometimes gifted children resist reading. Many times, as gifted children grow older, they become entrenched in a single form of literature, such as historical fiction or nonfiction. Likewise, they will tend to have access to current fiction, but will not seek out more traditional classics on their own. It is clear is that these children need to read broadly across all literary genres, because each genre provides differing emotional and intellectual impact on its readers.

There are two tried and true ways to get your child to read across genres. The first is to get two copies of the book and read alongside your child. When you both are done, you can then have some informal discussion about what you read, what was learned, the themes of the book, and its impact. The second way is to read a book aloud to your child at a regular, "special time," either daily or several days a week. As your child grows older, the resistance to this will increase; you may only be "allowed" to do this with the classics.

Some wonderful books by William Russell that provide selections from the classics appropriate for children ages 5-12 may help modify this resistance—*Classics to Read Aloud to Your Children* and *More Classics to Read Aloud to Your Children*. You will find Cervantes, Robert Louis Stevenson, Nathaniel Hawthorne, and Lewis Carroll for "reading level 1 children" (ages 5-8), followed by Mark Twain, Louisa May Alcott, and Robert Frost for "reading level 2 children" (ages 8-11), and Stephen Crane, Jack London, O. Henry, Shakespeare, and Charles Dickens, among others, for ages 11 and up.

In addition to reading, competitions and contests offer another way for your child to find his strengths and interests. Table 9.8 includes some possible competitions that your child can enroll in without being associated with a school or team. Many have been in operation for years and are held in great esteem nationally.

Table 9.8. Competitions and Contests for Talent Areas

Competition	Contact	Age Level	Activity
AAA National Traffic Safety Poster Program	AAA 1000 AA Drive Heathrow, FL 32746	5-18	Submission of original traffic safety slogan and poster for savings bond
Ann Arlys Bowler Poetry Contest	Weekly Reader Corp. 245 Long Hill Road Middletown, CT 06457	9-18	Submission of original poem for cash, publication in *Read* magazine
Annual NewsCurrents Student Editorial Cartoon Contest	Knowledge Unlimited, Inc. P.O. Box 52 Madison, WI 53701	5-18	Submission of original political cartoons for cash, publication in *NewsCurrents*
Arts Recognition and Talent Search	National Foundation for Advancement of Arts 800 Brickell Avenue Miami, FL 33131	17-18	Submission of performance tapes or products in six arts areas for judgment by panel of art experts in respective field
Baker's Plays High School Playwriting Contest	Baker's Plays 100 Chauncy Street Boston, MA 02111	14-18	Submission of original script on high school experience for cash
Cricket League Contest	Cricket League P.O. Box 300 Peru, IL 61354	9-14	Written product based on *Cricket* magazine theme

Table 9.8. Competitions and Contests for Talent Areas *(continued)*

Competition	Contact	Age Level	Activity
Delius Compos, Contest for High School Composers	Delius Association College of Fine Arts Jacksonville, FL 32211	15-18	Submission of original scores for cash prizes
Duracell/NSTA Scholarship Competition	1840 Wilson Blvd. Arlington, VA 22201	14-18	Submission of device that runs on batteries and performs a practical function
Economics in One Easy Lesson Essay Contest	Free Enterprise Institute 9525 Kate Freeway, # 303 Houston, TX 77024	14-18	Submission of essay on given economics theme/questions for cash
Elvis Week Annual Art Exhibit and Contest	Graceland Division of Elvis Presley Enterprises 3734 Elvis Presley Blvd. Memphis, TN 38116	<16	Submission of artwork reflecting Presley or his home for display during Elvis Week at Graceland
Explorers Club Youth Activity Fund	Explorers Club Fund 46 E. 70th Street New York, NY 10021	18-22	Application for grant to cover investigation and field research
Federal Junior Duck Stamp Conservation and Design Program	U.S. Fish & Wildlife Service Federal Duck Stamp Office 1849 C Street NW Washington, DC 20240	5-18	Submission of original stamp design to state sponsor of contest for ribbons

Table 9.8. Competitions and Contests for Talent Areas *(continued)*

Competition	Contact	Age Level	Activity
Firestone Firehawks	Bridgestone/Firestone, Inc. 50 Century Blvd. Nashville, TN 37219	5-15	Application to join club and win trip to Olympic National Park in Washington state
Fischbein Memorial Short Story Writing Contest	Short Story Writing Contest 984 Roelofs Road Yardley, PA 19067	10-18	Submission of original short story for money prize and publication in *Story Art* magazine
Fountainhead College Scholarship Essay Contest	Ayn Rand Institute P.O. Box 6004 Inglewood, CA 90312	16-18	Submission of essay concerning themes in *The Fountainhead* by Ayn Rand for scholarship
Freedoms Foundation National Awards Program	Freedoms Foundation Valley Forge Route 23 Valley Forge, PA 19482	5-18	Submission of essay or speech on citizenship and American rights for savings bond
Guideposts Young Writers Contest	*Guideposts* Magazine 16 E. 34th Street New York, NY 10016	16-18	Submission of original true story about faith-based experience for scholarship and possible publication in *Guideposts* magazine
International Robot Contest	Jake Mendelssohn 190 Mohegan Drive West Hartford, CT 06117	All ages	Submission of fire-fighting robot that can move through a house to extinguish a candle

Table 9.8. Competitions and Contests for Talent Areas *(continued)*

Competition	Contact	Age Level	Activity
International Student Media Festival	Association for Education Communication & Technology AACUPS-2644 Riva Road Annapolis, MD 21401	5-22	Submission of original media production on computer for critique and certificate of recognition
Junior Scholastic Find the Map Man	Junior Scholastic 555 Broadway New York, NY 10012	12-14	Map reading and drawing competition for savings bond and other prizes
Junior Science & Humanities Symposia	Junior Science Academy of Applied Science 98 Washington Street Concord, NH 03301	14-18	Submission of original research paper with focus on impact of results on humanity
"Kids Helping Kids" Greeting Card Contest	UNICEF 333 E. 38th Street New York, NY 10016	5-13	Submission of original greeting card based on given theme for trip to NY
Marie Walsh Sharpe Art Foundation Summer Seminar	MWS Foundation 711 N. Tejon, Suite B Colorado Springs, CO 80903	16-18	Submission of art portfolio for participation in summer seminar participation
Merlyn's Pen: The National Magazine of Student Writing	Merlyn's Pen, Inc. P.O. Box 910 East Greenwich, RI 02818	12-18	Submission of original written work or artwork for publication in middle school or high school

Table 9.8. Competitions and Contests for Talent Areas *(continued)*

Competition	Contact	Age Level	Activity
Mississippi Valley Poetry Contest	North American Literature Escadrille P.O. Box 3188 Rock Island, IL 61204	6-18	Submission of original poetry for cash in different age level divisions
Mothers Against Drunk Driving Annual Poster/ Essay Contest	MADD 5111 E. John Carpenter Freeway Suite 700 Irving, TX 75062	6-18	Submission of posters or essays on given MADD theme for variety of awards
MTNA-CCP/Belwin Student Composition Competition	Music Teachers Association Carew Tower 441 Vine Street, #505 Cincinnati, OH 45202	6-22	Submission of original composition for cash prizes
National Federation of Music Clubs Scholarships and Awards	National Fed. of Music Clubs 1336 N. Delaware Street Indianapolis, IN 46202	16-26	Submission of composition or performance for scholarships
National Peace Essay Contest	National Peace Essay Contest 1550 M Street NE, #700 Washington, DC 2000	14-18	Submission of essay on given topic of peace
National Story League and Keffer Memorial Short Story Writing Contest	Richard Shepherd 984 Roelofs Road Yardley, PA 19067	10-18	Submission of original short story for money prize and publication in *Story Art* magazine

Table 9.8. Competitions and Contests for Talent Areas *(continued)*

Competition	Contact	Age Level	Activity
National Two-Dimensional Art Contest	Frances Hook Scholarship Fund P.O. Box 597346 Chicago, IL 60659	6-18	Submission of original art work for scholarship
National Writing and Art Contest on the Holocaust	U.S. Holocaust Memorial Museum 100 Raoul Wallenberg Place SW Washington, DC 20024	12-18	Submission of original writing or art on theme provided by the museum for prizes and trip
National Written and Illustrated By Awards Contest	National Awards Contest P.O. Box 4469 Kansas City, MO 64127	6-19	Submission of original illustrated book for judgment by Landmark Editions for publishing contract and royalties when published
Olympic Size Morgan Horse Dreams Contest	American Morgan Horse Association P.O. Box 960 Shelburne, VT 05482	<22	Submission of original essay or poem on meaning of contest's name for cash and ribbons
Panasonic Young Soloists Award	Very Special Arts Education Office JFK Center for Performing Arts Washington, DC 20566	<25	Submission of taped performance for scholarship and performance at JFK Center for Performing Arts
Project Learn MS Scholarship Essay Competition	MS Association of America 601 White Horse Pike Oaklyn, NJ 08107	14-18	Submission of essay on topic of multiple sclerosis for cash and scholarships
Publish-a-Book Contest	Raintree/Steck-Vaughn Publishers P.O. Box 27010 Austin, TX 27010	7-12	Submission of original fiction or non-fiction story for cash and free books from publisher

Table 9.8. Competitions and Contests for Talent Areas *(continued)*			
Competition	Contact	Age Level	Activity
Read Magazine Letters about Literature	Letters about Literature 245 Weekly Reader Corp. P.O. Box 2791 Middletown, CT 06457	12-18	Submission of letter about recently read book that elicited strong feelings for cash award and visit to Library of Congress
Respec/Teen Letter Writing Contest	Speak for Yourself Lutheran Brotherhood 625 4th Avenue S. Minneapolis, MN 55415	12-14	Submission of letters to U.S. Representatives on solution for issue confronting young people for savings bond
Scholastic Writing Awards	Scholastic Writing Awards 730 Broadway New York, NY 10003	12-18	Submission of original written work in variety of categories for scholarships and publication in *Scholastic* magazine
Seventeen Magazine Annual Fiction Contest	Seventeen Magazine 850 Third Street New York, NY 10022	13-21	Submission of original fiction short story for cash and possible publication
Smithsonian Summer High School Internship Program	Office of Elementary/Secondary Education A & I 2283, MRC444 Smithsonian Institution Washington, DC 20560	17-18	Application to intern in particular field of study or interest at Smithsonian summer after graduation

Table 9.8. Competitions and Contests for Talent Areas *(continued)*

Competition	Contact	Age Level	Activity
Spider's Corner	*Cricket* Magazine 315 Fifth Street, P.O. Box 300 Peru, IL 61354	6-18	Submission of poem or story for publication in *Spider* magazine (ages 6-9)
SuperScience Blue's Annual Toy Tester Contest	*SuperScience Blue Scholastic Magazine* 555 Broadway New York, NY 10012	9-12	Team competition to improve given simple toy for science toys and books
Tandy Leather Art Scholarship	Tandy Leather Company 1400 Everman Parkway Fort Worth, TX 76104	17-18	Submission of leather work of art for scholarship
Thomas Edison/Max McGraw Scholarship Program	Scholarship Program P.O. Box 380057 East Hartford, CT 06138	14-18	Submission of completed science or engineering project for scholarship and national presentation
TIVY Games National Tournament	TIVY Games National Tournament TIVY Games, Inc. 4341 Will Rogers Parkway Oklahoma, OK 73108	10-14	TIVY club teams compete through game sets at different challenge levels for cash and trophy
United Nations Pilgrimage for Youth	Odd Fellows/Rebekahs P.O. Box 1778 Palm Harbor, FL 34682	16-17	Application for NYC tour with international students of same age

Table 9.8. Competitions and Contests for Talent Areas (continued)

Competition	Contact	Age Level	Activity
U.S. Savings Bond National Student Poster Contest	National Student Poster Contest Savings Bond Marketing Department of Treasury Bureau of Public Debt Washington, DC 20226	9-12	Submission of original poster for U. S. savings bonds for cash
Very Special Arts Young Playwrights Program	Young Playwrights Coordinator J.F. Kennedy Center for Performing Arts Washington, DC 20566	12-18	Submission of original scripts that address some aspect of a disability for production at J.F.K. Center for Performing Arts
Washington Crossing Foundation Scholarship Awards	Washington Crossing Foundation P.O. Box 17 General Defermoy Road Washington Crossing, PA 18977	17-18	Submission of essay on interest in government service for scholarships to college
We Are Writers Too Competition	Creative with Words Publications P.O. Box 223226 Carmel, CA 93922	<19	Submission of original writing or poetry for possible publication
Wendy's: "A Home and Family" Adoption Art Contest	Wendy's International P.O. Box 256 4288 W. Dublin Granville Road Dublin, OH 43017	<18	Submission of original artwork by adopted child only for certificate of merit

Table 9.8. Competitions and Contests for Talent Areas *(continued)*

Competition	Contact	Age Level	Activity
Westinghouse Science Talent Search	Science Talent Search 1719 N Street NW Washington, DC 20036	17-18	Submission of original research report on individual project for scholarship and college admission aid
Young Game Inventors Contest	U.S. Kids P.O. Box 567 Indianapolis, IN 46206	<13	Submission of original board game for variety of prizes, games, and magazine subscriptions
Young Playwrights Festival	Young Playwrights, Inc. 321 W 44th Street, #906 New York, NY 10036	<18	Submission of original script for possible production in New York

A modern way to help your child become self-aware and knowledgeable about himself might be to have him take individualized classes by computer (on-line). Perhaps this is a part of his talent development or just exploration of other areas to see if he is "good" at these things. Parts of this list were shared in the acceleration chapters, because the classes are geared to move at the pace your child chooses. He will be given tasks to complete and submit, but the amount of time he takes to complete them is up to him. He will receive feedback from instructors at the site about his individual work. Table 9.9 lists just a few examples of this fast-growing learning option.

Table 9.9. Tutorial and Correspondence Programs for Gifted Students
Duke Talent Identification Graphics Calculator Program
1121 W. Main Street, Suite 100 Durham, NC 27701 919-683-1400 Tip@duke.edu
Johns Hopkins Center for Talented Youth Expository Writing Tutorials
3400 N. Charles Street Baltimore, MD 21218 410-516-0337 Cty@jhu.edu
Northwestern Center for Talented Youth Expository Writing Tutorials
617 Dartmouth Place Evanston, IL 60208 708-491-3782 Cty@nwu.edu
Stanford Educational Programs for Gifted Youth (EPGY) in computers, mathematics, science, humanities
Stanford University EPGY Ventura Hall Stanford, CA 94305 415-723-0512 Ravaglia@csli.stanford.edu

The Classics

A few more words are needed on what might be considered the "classics" of literature. For the young, early reader, the works of C. S. Lewis (*Narnia Chronicles*), Frank Baum (the *Oz* books, numbering 32 volumes), and Madeline L'Engle's *Meet the Austins* and *A Wrinkle in Time* series are all good. The J. K. Rowling series on *Harry Potter* gives children a glimpse into different forms of giftedness and offers the bright child many "layers" of meaning within exciting and often chilling stories. Stephanie Tolan has written many very sensitive stories with gifted children as protagonists. A mother of a gifted child, Tolan's insight is astonishing. E. L. Konigsberg, who has written such stories as *From the Mixed Up Files of Mrs. Basil Frankweiler* and *George,* also shows a distinct penchant for writing about gifted protagonists in her novels for young readers.

As your child gets older, she will delight in Montgomery's books about *Anne of Green Gables*, a very gifted young orphan, and Judy Blume's books about a variety of gifted youngsters trying to deal with life around them. Of particular interest would be, *Are You There, God? It's Me, Margaret*, in which a young, free-thinking gifted girl tries to figure out her own religious beliefs. After that, your child will be ready for the swashbuckling tales of Alexander Dumas or the often stimulating tales of Charles Dickens.

Obviously, there are all of the fairytales out there, but some care must be taken. If your child has a vivid imagination, many of these stories are violent and cruel, and they may do more harm than good. It is recommended that you reread them yourself before passing them along to your child. There are many choices for introducing you child to the world's different mythologies. Be sure not to stop after Bullfinch's *Greek and Roman Mythology* or a similar compendium has been digested. There are wonderful sources for studying American Indian myths, as well as those of China, India, Russia, and even Hawaii! Table 9.10 includes a few sources that you can search regularly for good books to add to your child's reading of the classics.

Table 9.10. Sources for Finding Good Children's Books

Source	Address	Content
Alibris	www.alibris.com	Company that specializes in finding out-of-print books, both children's and adult
American Library Association	Available at most libraries by request	Publishes yearly list of 75 "notable children's books"
Book Links	434 W. Downers Grove Ave. Aurora, IL 60506	Magazine of American Library Association that highlights books on selected topics and authors
BookFinder	Any library or on CD-ROM at a library	Regularly produced compendium of books categorized by problem, issue, or theme
Children's Book and Music Center	2500 Santa Monica Blvd. Santa Monica, CA 90404 800-443-1856	Good source for hard-to-find and specialty books and tapes for children
Chinaberry Books	2780 Via Orange Way Suite B Spring Valley, CA 91978 800-776-2242	Catalog of 500 children's books and descriptions for toddlers to teens
Five Owls	2004 Sheridan Avenue S. Minneapolis, MN 55405	Articles, bibliographies, reviews on children's literature
The Horn Book Magazine	11 Beacon Street Boston, MA 02108	Reviews, recommendations, articles on children's books
Parents Choice: A Review of Children's Media	Parents Choice Foundation P.O. Box 185 Waban, MA 02168	Reviews of all forms of children's media; also bibliographies, articles
Riverbank Review of Books for Young Readers	University of St. Thomas 1000 LaSalle Avenue MOH217 Minneapolis, MN 55403	Quarterly review of current children's literature

The Great Books Foundation has developed two series of the world's literary classics that may also be useful to your family. The *Junior Great Books* series identifies five or six selections for each grade level that children are to read and discuss with a trained facilitator. The training is available through the foundation for a reasonable cost and is remarkably useful in a variety of ways. If your child's school does not offer this program, you may wish to undergo the training yourself and volunteer to lead such a program in your child's school or a small discussion group outside of school.

For the gifted reader, this series will probably be completed long before the grade-level designations on each set of selections, and your family will be ready for the next *Great Books* series, a complete set of the literary foundations from ancient Greece to the present. Of particular interest, if you can get your hands on it, is the *Syntopticon*, which outlines the major classics of literature throughout human history. There is much for your family to read about and digest through this source, although it is currently out of print, so you may need to search Internet sites or companies that find rare and out-of-print books to get your hands on this series.

The classics of philosophy can be introduced in two ways. First, there is the *Philosophy for Children* program of readings and discussions, developed several years ago by Matthew Lipman. In this program, Lipman uses short stories and books to illustrate the major world philosophies and philosophical ideas without naming the philosophers themselves. A wide variety of discussion materials accompany these readings, which will give you ample assistance in helping your child digest these theories and abstract ideas. Once this series has been completed, George Bernard Shaw's book, *A History of Western Philosophy*, will identify the philosophers by name. Most gifted youngsters are ready for Shaw's book in their early teens, but parents will enjoy it as well. The classics of philosophy can be explored further through the work of Mortimer Adler with his *The World's Great Ideas* books.

Classics, of course, include more than simply books. Introduction to the classics of art, music, theater, and dance are probably best approached as "field trip" experiences, rather than through books. Most art museums have "free days" for visiting their collections. Be sure to take advantage, too, of their visiting exhibitions. In many cases, an artist's body of work can be studied in one visit. Works that you can't visit in person can be explored through art books checked out of your local library. A particularly good series are the *Time-Life* books published in the 1960s on famous artists. Each book contains a timeline of what other artists, writers, and philosophers were doing at the time a particular artist was working, as well as what was happening in science, government and politics, and historically. The message to young gifted readers of this series is that the artists truly reflected culture of that time through their art—a heady idea, indeed!

Music experiences should be carefully chosen. If you are lucky enough to live near an orchestra, be sure to attend the young people's concerts. In these, children are sometimes exposed to the ideas behind the classics performed, and the prices are usually quite reasonable. I look back on many pleasurable hours taking large groups of children to these concerts during the days when my own children were growing up. The school never saw these events as quite "interesting" enough to qualify as a school field trip, yet the explanations and what the children were asked to listen for were absolutely fascinating. If you are not close to an orchestra, you might view the Leonard Bernstein videotapes of the many young people's concerts performed with the New York Philharmonic Orchestra in the 1960s and 1970s. They are on audiotape, videotape, and DVD and can be ordered from any number of mail-order catalogs. They may be available at your local library. The use of young, gifted performers will be fascinating to your child.

Theater performances are also a must for your child, but again, the introduction should be gradual. Starting with Shakespeare is probably not a good idea. You may be fortunate enough to live near a Children's Theater that performs such classics as *Cinderella, The Little Match Girl, Peter Pan, The 500 Hats of Bartholomew Cubbins, A Christmas Carol,* and others. Once your child shows an interest in theater attendance, you may be ready for other plays such as those by Shakespeare, O'Neill, Williams, Chekhov, Moliere, Shaw, and Coward. It can be extremely rewarding if you and your child read the plays together before attending them. This adds more awareness of what actors and the director are trying to do, rather than just trying to figure out what is going to happen in the play.

It is probably good to save plays by Pintner (*Who's Afraid of Virginia Wolfe?*) and Brecht (*Mother Courage*) until the late teens, when a great deal of theater has already been experienced, so that these playwrights don't overly color your child's theater experience as "depressing." All theaters offer student rates, and often family rates, so try to take full advantage of these discounts as you explore the world of theater.

Reading from the classics provides a core knowledge base; as schools become increasingly laden with extra teaching agendas (such as sex education, drug education, character education), there is less and less time to teach the "foundations" of knowledge. One researcher, E. D. Hirsch, has attempted to identify these foundations and has written a series of books to introduce children to this classical foundation. Hirsch's series, entitled *What Every Child Should Know*, was developed for every grade level through grade 12; each book contains the basic ideas, famous people, and events of history, mathematics, science, literature, and the arts to give the reader a solid "arts and sciences" education. Hirsch's work has become the foundation of many "core curriculum" schools, and his books are widely available through bookstores for parents who wish to share such an education with their own child.

Fine-Motor, Spatial, Visualization Skills

Helping your child learn to draw, paint, make craft items, and express herself artistically is a good start toward developing fine-motor, spatial, and visualization skills. Most local art museums offer short-term classes in these areas for a nominal cost. Likewise, learning to play a musical instrument early, one that requires finger dexterity, will greatly help in developing these skills. Most music stores are a good source for beginning lessons. Once your child reaches ages 9 or 10, he can begin to branch out into wind or percussion instruments, if that is where his interest is, and most school music programs offer training as well as low cost instrument rentals so that your child can become a part of organized music groups.

If your child seems to have a strong talent in either art or music, more extensive development may be called for. The National Guild of Community Schools of the Arts Membership Directory lists over 180 schools of the performing arts. You can get a copy of this directory from your local library or write to P.O. Box 8018, Englewood, NJ 07631. Many museums have arts resource centers that can provide you with the names of artists, musicians, arts organizations, and other outlets for further instruction in the arts.

Construction projects and crafts are another avenue for developing fine-motor skills, spatial intelligence, and visualization skills. Ready-made materials and project ideas are available through hobby and craft stores or commercial companies. Several of these are as follows. Your local specialty toy and arts stores may have additional ideas and materials.

- Creative Publications (788 Palomar Avenue, Sunnyvale, CA 94086) has a wonderful inventory of problem-solving visualization materials, including posters, blank game boards, visual challenges, and puzzles, and they can send you a catalog.

- Edmund Scientific sells kits for beginning experimenters, with lenses, prisms, and telescopes (Edmund Scientific, 101 E. Gloucester Pike, Barrington, NJ 08007).

- Learning Things has play and science apparatus, and lots of materials, tools, and supplies for construction projects for children (P.O. Box 436, Arlington, MA 02174).

- Lego Systems (555 Taylor Road, Enfield, CT 06082) also has a complete catalog of Duplo™ and Lego™ sets.

Memorization

Memory is increasingly important as a child progresses through elementary, middle, and high school and then goes on to college. Memory can be developed through practice in wide and varied areas. Astronomy (e.g., learning the names of different groups of stars), sports statistics, English kings and queens, U.S. presidents, the table of chemical elements, battles of the Revolutionary or Civil War, ancient cities and wonders of the world, geographical information, and other historical periods—all offer plentiful opportunities for remembering things. There are many systems for improving one's memory. Learning some of these methods along with your child might be a fascinating pursuit for both of you.

Once your child is "into" memorizing lists of information, she may be ready for memorizing famous poems, speeches, and literary passages. Poets Robert Frost, Langston Hughes, Emily Dickinson, Walt Whitman, William Wordsworth, Walter de la Mare, Edgar Allan Poe, Robert Lewis Stevenson, and A. A. Milne are good ones to start with. The following books contains good children's poems to memorize:

- *I'm Nobody! Who Are You? Poems of Emily Dickinson for Children*, Emily Dickinson, Stemmer House.

- *The Light in the Attic*, Shel Silverstein, Harper & Row.

- *The Nonsense Verse of Edward Lear,* Holbrook Jackson (Ed.), Harmony Books.
- *Poem Stew,* J. B. William Cole (Ed.), Harper Trophy.
- *A Swinger of Birches: Poems of Robert Frost for Young People*, Robert Frost, Stemmer House.
- *Under the Greenwood Tree: Shakespeare for Young People*, Barbara Holdridge (Ed.), Stemmer House.
- *Where the Sidewalk Ends*, Shel Silverstein, Harper & Row.

Various literary magazines listed earlier in this chapter are good sources for current modern poetry that may have potential for memorization. There is also a book by John Hollander titled *Committed to Memory: 100 Best Poems to Memorize*, which covers adult poetry, from the Bible to Shakespeare and many poems in between.

Communication

Your child's communication precision and expression—both verbal and nonverbal—are important life skills to develop. Although futurists talk about the inevitability of voice-activated computers and word processing, the need to write as well as speak will continue to be important to communication, whether face-to-face or via some medium such as a telephone, computer, or...? Facility and fluency are what is called for, so the more practice, the better. Try to set up high interest activities or projects for your child to work on that will build these skills. Many of the things listed by your child on the *Rogers' Interest Inventory* will provide activities to develop your child's communication skills. Some ideas for projects are listed below, but these are just starters for creative ideas you can come up with.

- Write a creative story, play, or poem.
- Print your own newspaper or magazine.
- Take photographs of landscapes, interesting people, unusual objects; enter a photography contest.
- Write your own column for critiquing movies for local newspapers.
- Write a letter to the editor of the local newspaper.
- Write a public official (Mayor, Congressman, etc.) or someone who heads an organization that can make a change.
- Write lyrics or music for a song or musical play.
- Design unusual creations out of paper, wood, or other materials (e.g., costumes, clothes, or furniture).
- Learn another language using audio tapes and/or books.
- Make up your own language.
- Keep a notebook or diary for as long as a year at a time.
- Make and record observations of people or animal behavior on a regular basis.
- Read regularly a new science or literary magazine.
- Make a movie with a home video camera.
- Perform as a comic or member of a comedy team.

If this list has not started your creative juices flowing yet, the following books may provide inspiration.

- *The Bias-Free Word Finder: A Dictionary of Nondiscriminatory Language,* Rosemary Maggio, Beacon Press.

- *A Book of Your Own: Keeping a Diary or Journal,* Carla Stevens, Clarion Books.

- *Caution: This May Be an Advertisement: A Teen Guide to Advertising*, Kathlyn Gay, Franklin Watts.

- *Great Speeches of the 20th Century,* Rhino Records, 800-432-0020.

- *The Kids' Address Book: Over 3000 Addresses of Celebrities, Athletes, Entertainers, and More... Just for Kids!* Michael Levine, Perigree Books.

- *Market Guide for Young Writers,* Kathy Henderson, Writers' Digest Books.

- *Totally Private & Personal: Journaling Ideas for Girls and Young Women,* Jessica Wilber, Free Spirit Press.

- *What! I Have to Give a Speech?* Thomas Murphy, Grayson Bernard Publishing.

- *The Young Person's Guide to Becoming a Writer,* Janet Grant, Free Spirit Press.

Table 9.11 lists many good websites that allow children to communicate in written or interactive form with others of similar interests and skills. This list does not include all of the sites that crop up almost daily (and which disappear almost daily). Even if a site changes its scope by the time you read this book, you can tell by the addresses how to do a search of your own.

Table 9.11. Communication Websites for Children

Website	Address	Content
Deja News	www.dejanews.com	Link to newsgroups for children interested in discussing current events
Institute for Global Communications	www.igc.org	Link to several nets that aggregate articles, headlines, and features on global issues
Netiquette Home Page	www.albion.com/ netiquette	Quiz and rules for communicating on-line, with links to other sites with information about courtesy on the Internet
Peace Pals	Members.aol.com/ pforpeace/peacepals/ index.htm	Site that allows children to correspond with other children around the world
Teen Poetry	www.teenpoetry. studentcenter.org	Three sites that allow teens to "publish" their poetry and receive evaluations from peers
Toastmasters International	www.toastmasters.org	Organization that develops youth leadership by training them to speak effectively
Voices of Youth	www.unicef.org/voy	Site that encourages children to express their opinions about the future
The Web of Culture	www.worldculture.com	Site that encourages cross-cultural communication about religion, holidays, foods, customs, languages
Writes of Passage: The Online Source for Teenagers	www.writes.org	Interactive literary journal for writers between 12-19 from well-known authors
Yahooligans! Hobbies Links	www.yahooligans.com/ Sports_and_Recreation/ Hobbies	Site links about collections, crafts, magic, drama, gardening, pets, etc.
Young Writers' Site of Inkspot Resources	www.inkspot.com/young	Advice, interviews, articles, and links to writing resources for children

Problem Solving

Problem solving is an integral part of what most children learn in school, but too often, the strategies taught in math or in social studies are not so easy to transfer to real life or to human problems and issues. Some wonderful books for children have been written about problem solving in recent years, and you may want to purchase your own copies of them to use over and over again with your child.

Barbara Lewis's book, *What Do You Stand For?* (1997), has wonderful chapters that can help your child come up with solutions to the problems caused by others around him. Chapter topics include: positive attitudes (resiliency, being a good sport, acceptance, and hope); choice and accountability (making good decisions and accepting responsibility); courage (confidence and resolve); endurance (patience and strength in adversity); forgiveness, leadership, peacefulness (conflict resolution, cooperation, compromise); and relationships. The chapter on resourcefulness and ingenuity will provide your child with a wide variety of problem-solving strategies and frames of mind. The book is written in an easy-to-read style, with real life photographs and stories of children who have solved problems that required the characteristics listed in the chapters mentioned. This book provides direct hints about how to resolve problems and is a wonderful source of character-building and self-awareness discussions that you can have with your child as you work through various simulations of character "dilemmas." The chapters on caring, communication, empathy, forgiveness, honesty, health, imagination, justice, and loyalty are particularly thought-provoking.

Other helpful books for developing your child's skills for problem solving in the real world include:

- *The Best Friends Book: True Stories about Real Best Friends; Fun Things to Do with Your Best Friend; Solving Best Friends Problems; Long-Distance Best Friends; Finding New Friends and More!*, Arlene Erlbach, Free Spirit Press.

- *Better Than a Lemonade Stand: Small Business Ideas for Kids*, Daryl Bernstein, Beyond Words Publishing.

- *Creative Problem Solving (PS) for Kids*, B. Stanish and B. Eberle, Prufrock Press.

- *Don't Rant and Rave on Wednesdays: The Children's Anger Control Book*, Adolph Moser, Landmark Editions.

- *Fighting Invisible Tigers: A Stress Management Guide for Teens*, Earl Hipp, Free Spirit Press.

- *The First Honest Book about Lies*, Jonni Kincher, Free Spirit Press.

- *How Do They Do That? Wonders of the Modern World Explained*, Caroline Sutton, Quill Books.

- *How Rude! The Teenagers' Guide to Good Manners, Proper Behavior, and Not Grossing People Out*, Alex Packer, Free Spirit Press.

- *JumpStart: Ideas to Move Your Mind*, Beatrice Elyé with Catherine Southwick, Great Potential Press.

- *Mistakes that Worked*, Charlotte Foltz Jones, Doubleday.

- *People Power: A Look at Nonviolent Action and Defense*, Susan Neiburg Terkel, Dutton.

- *Respecting Our Differences: A Guide to Getting Along in a Changing World*, Lynn Duvall, Free Spirit Press.

- *Stick Up for Yourself! Every Kid's Guide to Personal Power and Positive Self-Esteem*, Gershen Kaufman and Lev Raphael, Free Spirit Publishing.

- *Teaching Values: An Idea Book for Teachers (and Parents)*, Gary Davis, Westwood Publishing Company.

- *Tricks of the Trade for Kids*, Jerry Dunn, Houghton Mifflin.

- *The Ultimate Kids' Club Book: How to Organize, Find Members, Run Meetings, Raise Money, Handle Problems and Much More!*, Melissa Maupin, Free Spirit Press.

- *Values Are Forever: Becoming More Caring and Responsible*, Gary Davis, Westwood Publishing Company.

- *What Would You Do? A Kids' Guide to Tricky and Sticky Situations*, Linda Schwartz, The Learning Works.

Knowledge of the World

Knowledge of the world comes in two ways. The first and best way works for all children, regardless of their gifts and talents—actual "field trips" out in the world! Explorations by you and your child may begin with your own backyard or basement. For example, you might have your child map everything she observes within one square yard of the backyard or list everything she learns from poring over a family scrapbook found in the basement or attic.

Later you will want to take "behind the scenes" tours of places in your own community—from a local bookstore to the library to the grocery store or a fast food store. Many schools plan field trips to factories and manufacturing centers, such as a toy manufacturer or a snack food company. If these are not a part of the regular school routine, try to find opportunities to visit such places. The factories don't have to be large to be educational. One of the most eye-opening—and eye-watering—tours our family took was to visit a small herbal tea factory. The immediate "assault" of the aroma of the mint room will never be forgotten.

An excellent book that gives advice on how to help younger gifted children connect to the world is Jacquelyn Saunders and Pamela Espeland's, *Bringing Out the Best: A Resource Guide for Parents of Young Gifted Children* (1991, Free Spirit Press, Minneapolis, MN). But once your child has learned to read, there is a wonderful assortment of books to help you and your child answer questions about the world. Some beginning books might include:

- Aliki books such as *Fossils Tell of Long Ago* and *Wild and Woolly Mammoths*

- *The Charlie Brown's Super Books of Questions and Answers* series on subjects from Animals to Space to Transportation to People and History to How Things Work

- Jean Fritz's history books for children, *What's the Big Idea, Ben Franklin?; And Then What Happened, Paul Revere; Where Do You Think You're Going, Christopher Columbus?*

- Ruth Heller's science books, including *Chickens Aren't the Only Ones*; *The Reason for a Flower;* and *Plants that Never Ever Bloom*

- Eliot Humberstone's books, *Things That Go; Things Outdoors; Things at Home*

- David Macauley's books on how things were built, including *Pyramid*; *City*; *Cathedral*; *Subway*

- David Macauley's *The Way Things Work* book and CD-ROM

- Richard Maurer's *The NOVA Space Explorers Guide: Where to Go and What to See*

- Scholastic, Inc.'s *Let's Find Out* series
- Paul Showers' *What Happens to a Hamburger?*
- Troll Associates' *Wonders of the World* series
- The Updegraff books on geography, including *Continents and Climates; Mountains and Valleys; Seas and Oceans;* and *Rivers and Lakes*

As the Internet becomes more accessible, there will be more ways to connect and feel comfortable with the way things work than you will have time to explore.

Homeschooling: A Last Resort

You may have noticed in reading this chapter that my discussion of homeschooling as a means for teaching gifted children has been a long time in coming. You have probably guessed correctly that I believe that the tax-supported services of the public school system should be exhausted first before parents take on the role of teaching their children academics. This book has made suggestions for how to persuade your child's school to offer appropriate flexibility and to make the appropriate academic and curriculum decisions for your gifted child. Schools are still the places where you are most likely to find individuals trained to be teachers, who have access to a wide variety of curriculum and instructional strategies, and where there is a chance that other children like your own child will be found.

Regrettably, however, sometimes parents may feel there is no other reasonable option than to homeschool, and the most current research seems to suggest that homeschooled children achieve at least as well, and in some cases better, than their peers who attend school. If the child is a part of the decision to homeschool, he seems to do just fine. Perhaps the most difficult aspect of homeschooling is the extraordinary demands it puts on the parents, who must take on an additional role—that of the child's teacher.

There is some concern about the quality and quantity of materials currently available to homeschooling families. Much of what is available has been written largely for religious or philosophical purposes, and thus may not accurately represent a broad view of commonly understood concepts, historical events, and ideas or beliefs. With careful searching, however, parents may be able to find suitably abstract and complex resources for home use. Most likely, if you do decide to home-school your gifted child or children, you will find yourself quite busy adapting and rewriting the curriculum you find at the homeschool websites or in teacher supply stores.

Many of the resources listed in Table 9.12 have been designed for use by teachers, but can also be used for your child to study independently at home or with a small group of other gifted homeschoolers. The initial purpose of these materials was for bright students to work on by themselves when their regular work was done in class. In a homeschool setting, they may become a major focal point of your child's curriculum and learning. A thoughtful presentation of homeschooling approaches can be found in Lisa Rivero's book *Creative Homeschooling for Gifted Children: A Resource Guide* (2002).

Table 9.12. Potential Resources for Homeschooling Curriculum

Resource	Where Obtained	Contents/Guideline Category
20 Ideas (and 20 More Ideas) for Teaching Gifted Kids in Middle School & High School J. McIntosh	Prufrock Press P.O. Box 8813 Waco, TX 76714	*Like-ability/Socialization:* Small group activities that could be carried out outside of school. Gr. 5-12
100 Amazing Make-it-Yourself Science Fair Projects G. Vecchione	Prufrock Press P.O. Box 8813 Waco, TX 76714	*Fine-motor skills/Spatial:* Imaginative projects to recreate. Gr. 5-12
Amazing (and Simple) Science Experiments with Everyday Materials M. Mandell & E. R. Churchill	Prufrock Press P.O. Box 8813 Waco, TX 76714	*Fine-motor skills/Spatial:* 160 experiments to set up. Gr. 2-8
Brain Twisters & The World's Greatest Brain Bogglers Creative Kids Magazine	Prufrock Press P.O. Box 8813 Waco, TX 76714	*Problem solving:* Puzzles and games to develop logic, critical thinking, problem solving. Gr. 3-12
Challenging Minds, L. Kelly	Prufrock Press P.O. Box 8813 Waco, TX 76714	*Problem solving:* A year's worth of activities to teach thinking and problem-solving skills. Gr. 5-12
Competitions: Maximizing Your Abilities through Academic & Other Competitions F.A. Karnes & T. L. Riley	Prufrock Press P.O. Box 8813 Waco, TX 76714	*Identity:* Information on 275 different competitions in a variety of talent domains with eligibility and contact information. All grades

Table 9.12. Potential Resources for Homeschooling Curriculum (*continued*)

Resource	Where Obtained	Contents/Guideline Category
Coping for Capable Kids L. Cohen & E. Frydenberg	Prufrock Press P.O. Box 8813 Waco, TX 76714	*Identity:* Sections in book for parents and children on solving social problems. Gr. 4-12
CPS for Kids (Be a Problem Solver) B. Stanish & B. Eberle	Prufrock Press P.O. Box 8813 Waco, TX 76714	*Problem solving/Socialization:* Small group six-step process to identify problems and solve 30 different "problem" activities. Gr. 2-8
CPS for Teens P.A. Ewell & D Treffinger	Prufrock Press P.O. Box 8813 Waco, TX 76714	*Problem solving/Socialization:* 31 problems for older students using a six-step problem-solving process. Gr. 4-12
Critical Thinking Activities to Improve Writing Skills K. Baker, et al.	Critical Thinking Press & Software P.O. Box 448 Pacific Grove, CA 93950	*Problem solving:* Four book levels that teach children to analyze problems and produce written solutions. Gr. K-12
Doorways to Decision-Making J.D. Casteel & R. J. Stahl	Prufrock Press P.O. Box 8813 Waco, TX 76714	*Problem solving:* 43 high interest activities to teach children how to resolve disputes and dilemmas. Gr. 4-12
Enhancing Independent Problem Solving in Students W.R. Hresko & S.R. Herron	Prufrock Press P.O. Box 8813 Waco, TX 76714	*Problem solving:* Uses math problems with graphs, charts and measurement as base for learning pattern recognition, planning, and estimation. Gr. 3-5

Table 9.12. Potential Resources for Homeschooling Curriculum *(continued)*

Resource	Where Obtained	Contents/Guideline Category
Getting Kids Published J. Whitfield	Prufrock Press P.O. Box 8813 Waco, TX 76714	*Communication:* Ingenious ways to help children write in products that are publishable. Gr. 3-12
The Gifted Kids' Survival Guide, General and Teen Handbook versions J. Galbraith & J. Delisle	Prufrock Press P.O. Box 8813 Waco, TX 76714	*Identity:* Explorations of what giftedness means, how to deal with school and peer challenges. Ages 6-10, 11-18
Independent Study Program S.K. Johnsen & K. Johnson	Free Spirit Press 217 Fifth Avenue N. Suite 200 Minneapolis, MN 55401	*Interest development:* Teaches eight steps of research with 100 ideas for independent studies and methods. All grade levels
Lateral Thinking Puzzles P. Sloane & D. MacHale	Prufrock Press P.O. Box 8813 Waco, TX 76714	*Problem solving:* Several books of lateral thinking puzzlers. Gr. 3-12
Leadership for Students F.A. Karnes & S. M. Bean	Prufrock Press P.O. Box 8813 Waco, TX 76714	*General socialization:* Techniques of leading a wide variety of learning activities and projects. Gr. 3-12
Market Guide for Young Writers K. Henderson	Prufrock Press P.O. Box 8813 Waco, TX 76714	*Communication/Talent development:* Guide to writing, publishing, and contests for young authors. Gr. 3-12

Table 9.12. Potential Resources for Homeschooling Curriculum *(continued)*

Resource	Where Obtained	Contents/Guideline Category
Mind Benders A. Harnadek	Critical Thinking Press & Software P.O. Box 448 Pacific Grove, CA 93950	*Problem solving:* Three books at different grade levels that teach students to comprehend and organize sets of clues to reach conclusions. Gr. K-12
Psychology for Kids J. Kincher	Free Spirit Press 217 Fifth Avenue N. Suite 200 Minneapolis, MN 55401	*Identity:* Hands-on workbook to promote self-discovery and awareness. Gr. 4-12
Real Life Math Mysteries M. Washington	Prufrock Press P.O. Box 8813 Waco, TX 76714	*Knowledge of world:* Use of problem-solving skills on real world math problems. Gr. 3-12
SET M.J. Falco	SET Enterprises 15402 E. Verbena Drive Fountain Hills, CA 85268	*Visualization:* Game in either computer disk or card form that requires perceptual problem solving. All grade levels
Simulation Series C. Beeler	Prufrock Press P.O. Box 8813 Waco, TX 76714	*Like-ability socialization:* Six books of simulations covering environment, western exploration, advertising, and history. Gr. 4-12
Stories with Holes N. Levy	NL Associates P.O. Box 1199 Hightstown, NJ 08520	*Problem solving:* Ten volumes of mysteries for which student must ask questions answered "yes" or "no" to solve mystery. Gr. 3-12

Table 9.12. Potential Resources for Homeschooling Curriculum *(continued)*

Resource	Where Obtained	Contents/Guideline Category
Super Sentences S. Winebrenner	Prufrock Press P.O. Box 8813 Waco, TX 76714	*Communication:* 22 vocabulary-building activities requiring application of reading and language skills. Gr. 3-12
Survival Guide for Parents of Gifted Kids S. Walker	Free Spirit Press 217 Fifth Avenue N. Suite 200 Minneapolis, MN 55401	*Identity:* Valuable guidebook for parents about challenges, problems gifted children face. All grade levels
A Teen's Guide to Getting Published D. & J. Dunn	Prufrock Press P.O. Box 8813 Waco, TX 76714	*Communication:* Specifics of writing for publication for advanced writers. Gr. 4-12
Visual Thinking Puzzles (and Optical Picture Puzzles) N. Levy	NL Associates P.O. Box 1199 Hightstown, NJ 08520	*Visualization:* Two books of visual and spatial problems. Gr. 3-12
Writing with Authors K. Johnson	Prufrock Press P.O. Box 8813 Waco, TX 76714	*Communication:* 20 authors teach lessons on how to write. Gr. 2-8
You Decide G. & A. Smith	Prufrock Press P.O. Box 8813 Waco, TX 76714	*Problem solving/Like-ability socialization:* Role-play and critical analysis of Bill of Rights dilemmas. Gr. 7-12

Summary

No matter how well developed and reasonable the educational plan, it will probably not be fully implemented by the school for reasons of time or money or both. It will be important for parents to take on whatever aspects that the school cannot carry out. In addition, parents of a gifted or talented child have a number of tasks they must address in helping their child develop fully in mind, body, and spirit.

Key Points

- There are ten essentials that parents must try to provide for their gifted child outside of school time, all of which emphasize talent development, social adjustment, skill-building, and knowledge of the world.

- Talent development, as well as interest development and self-awareness, must be the primary thrust of parents' efforts.

- Providing like-ability and mixed-age/mixed-ability social outlets is essential for the gifted child's future ability to function in the world.

- Knowledge of the world and the classics are two areas not fully covered in school curriculum which must be supplemented at home.

- Dexterity, spatial visualization, social problem solving, and memory must also be taught outside of school if children are to receive adequate exposure to these skills.

10

Developing Your Child's Plan and What Happens Next

Scenario

Marcelo

Last year Marcelo, as a 10-year-old fourth grader, was functioning at very high levels in his small K-6 private school. His third-grade teacher realized how motivated Marcelo was by the "difficult" work he chose for himself, so he decided to find out how much of the school's curriculum Marcelo really had already "mastered." As a result of both formal and informal assessments measuring what Marcelo already knew and could do, it was clear that Marcelo was working on sixth-grade curriculum in all the academic content areas, but he continued to participate in P.E., art, and music with his fourth-grade agemates. His teachers saw him as happy, a self-starter, sociable, and very motivated by difficult and challenging tasks. His only notable academic weakness was in written expression; Marcelo did not enjoy expressing his ideas in essay form because his handwriting is poor. Outside of school, Marcelo kept busy reading in his favorite areas—space science, chemistry and nuclear physics (including the Fermi Newsletter). *He balanced his active academic life with swimming, outdoor activities with his family, singing in the church choir, and computer graphics. The school staff expressed concern, however, about what they could do for Marcelo the next year when he would need seventh- and eighth-grade curriculum—not easily accessible from the elementary school. With this in mind, Marcelo's parents presented a proposed educational plan to the district middle school, grades six through eight. They wanted him to begin sixth grade there, despite the fact that he had already mastered much of the sixth grade curriculum. They asked that his curriculum be compacted in mathematics and science—his two "favorite" academic areas—and that he be allowed to work on his own in those areas. The school agreed to let him enter sixth grade, a one-year grade-skip, but took a "wait and see" approach to the parents' request for independent study to compact his math and science.*

Marcelo entered the sixth grade, a very loud, boisterous class of students who had known each other for years. On the first day of school, his locker was broken into and his gym shoes were stolen. He was forced to go to gym class in his socks, which was a distinct embarrassment. When he returned to the locker room after gym, his regular shoes had been stolen as well. As the weeks went by, Marcelo withdrew from others more and more. The sixth-grade boys either ignored him or verbally taunted him for being smart and "geeky." As time went on, Marcelo found ingenious ways to retaliate, often getting in trouble for his misdeeds. His only friend in school was a boy with severe physical and mental disabilities, which also resulted in taunts from the "popular" crowd. Marcelo helped the boy get to his classes and eat at lunchtime. In his own classes, Marcelo answered the questions his teachers posed in only the most simplistic ways. He often refused to turn in English assignments. He was clearly unhappy with his situation, and the school stated they would do nothing to accommodate his need for challenge until he could get his "behavior" in order. They were not convinced that he was "that bright." In their words, Marcelo had gotten off "on the wrong foot" in this school, and they felt it was Marcelo's own responsibility to fix it.

If one considers the theory behind the current "middle school philosophy," the school's attitude and response to

Marcelo and his parents is not surprising. According to various middle school "experts," this age is a time for cognitive consolidation because the mind, they say, is on a developmental plateau; these pre-teens need to develop their social skills so they can grow into their next "stages." Marcelo's outward behaviors in class only reinforced this belief for his teachers, so they expressed real concern that he was not "developing" socially in the expected manner. In fact, they wanted Marcelo tested for the Emotional and Behaviorally Disordered class. They felt that until Marcelo got "on the right track" socially and emotionally, there was nothing they could or should do for his cognitive development. Their belief was that if he really had the potential to begin with, then his cognitive development would come at the appropriate time anyway.

What went wrong? Was Marcelo's educational plan a mistake? Was the school's philosophy wrong? Was there a mismatch between Marcelo's needs and the atmosphere into which he was placed? And now, with all of these problems, can the situation be corrected and improved? Has this gifted young man's self-esteem been permanently damaged?

The Essential Elements of an Educational Plan

Before continuing Marcelo's saga, it is important to review the basic elements any educational plan must contain (see Table 10.1). An education plan must be detailed and specific about what steps will be taken to continue the gifted child's *academic progress and talent development*. These steps are the heart of the plan and should account for approximately 60-65% of the effort the school will expend on the gifted child's behalf.

This piece of the plan—which contains decisions for instructional management and delivery, curriculum adaptation, and acceleration—must be carefully spelled out. Further adaptation listed in the plan should indicate the name of the person who will be responsible for implementing and for monitoring its success.

As a check and balance, each adaptation must be thoroughly explainable by a particular need of the student—that is, it must match or correspond to one or more specific cognitive functioning levels, learning strengths, learning preferences, personality characteristics/behaviors, in-school interests, or outside interests of the child. All of these aspects of the child should be "matched" with one option or another of the educational plan. Until that is done, the academic progress portion of the plan is not complete. For example, if a child like Marcelo is working well beyond the next grade level in his school work, prefers older friends, works well on his own, and has expressed an interest in skipping a grade, then a grade-skip is probably an option that matches these characteristics. Were all of Marcelo's needs matched with a corresponding option?

The second aspect of the plan consists of actions to be taken that will help the child *remediate any weaknesses or issues* that he may have. It is expected that this piece of the plan will account for no more than 10% of the child's work time in school. The "weaknesses" may be academic, social, emotional, or motivational, but a specific plan must be listed for working on each of these weaknesses. Marcelo, for example would need assistance in writing or learning keyboarding to use in writing essays. Or perhaps if the child dislikes working with a mixed ability group on a project, then his listed goal or "remediation" plan may entail a teacher finding an open-ended task for such a group to work on and for which there is individual accountability rather than a "sink or swim" cooperative group approach to evaluation. It is hoped through this approach that the child will learn that the product of the group can sometimes be "better" than what one does alone and that all members of the group can benefit from sharing their perspectives and efforts.

The third aspect of the educational plan includes *provisions for the psychological adjustment* of the child. How can the school help the child continue to be motivated to learn and to feel good about himself as a person, a learner, and as a social being? Would small group discussions on self-awareness be helpful? Would a few short talks with a school counselor help the child get himself "on track" or become adjusted to the routines and expectations of the school setting? No more than 5-10% of the school's effort would probably be expended in this area, but that small amount might make all the difference in whether a child proceeds without psychological damage in what often can seem like a hostile environment for gifted students.

The final aspect of the plan will *help the child adjust socially*, both with his intellectual peers as well as with his age peers. What co-curricular activities might the child be steered toward? Is there a pull-out program in which the child can participate? Marcelo's plan needed to include provisions for participation in a science or other club he would enjoy. The child's learning preferences, interests both in and out of school, and personality characteristics will provide clues for what forms this socialization will take. A child like Marcelo who loves simulations and games and has a strong interest in science might find the "right" kind of socialization by joining a Knowledge Bowl team as the "science" expert or working with a group of students on a Science-by-Mail project.

This part of the plan will account for approximately 20% of the child's activities, with the focus being more on providing time to interact with like-ability peers than with agemates.

Table 10.1 shows the basic structure of a simple education plan for a student like Marcelo. Table 10.2 shows Marcelo's plan and why it didn't work. It needed more detail and more provisions. Notice that nothing was planned for Marcelo's psychological or social adjustment, nor to remediate his writing difficulties.

Table 10.1 *Yearly Educational Planner:* School

©2000 by Karen B. Rogers

Child _____ Age _____ Gender _____ Date _____

Date Plan Will Begin _____ School _____

School-Based Essential	Domain	How Often	Who and How Managed	Assessment
Academic Progress				
Academic Remediation				
Psychological Adjustment				
Socialization				

As the format in Table 10.1 shows, the educational plan should be proposed for one year and then be revisited to see if it is still "working" in each succeeding year. The "School-Based Essential" information can come from various sources. Specific ideas for these essential steps can come from Table 8.1 in Chapter 8, for example, or the specific research-based practices described in detail in Chapters 4, 5, 6, and 7. These essential steps should be chosen for their appropriateness for the child for this year, for this time, and for their feasibility within the specific school setting. These essentials may be varied with each year, so that across the K-12 span, the child will ultimately access all of the essentials that research suggests a gifted child needs.

The column in Table 10.1 labeled "Domain" refers to the specific subject or talent area in which an essential is to be implemented, particularly for the Academic Progress and Remediation rows of the plan. A domain may include all academic areas, or it may be a single specific academic (such as math or reading) or a non-academic subject area such as art or music. For socialization, specifying whether the domain will be with like-ability peers or age peers is probably specific enough. The child's interest around which the planned measure will be centered might also be specified, for example with like-ability science peers (for socialization activity) or age peer student government (for socialization or leadership activity).

The "How Often?" column should delineate the frequency with which the essential adaptation will occur, including estimated hours per day or week, number of weeks, or whether this will be done throughout the year. "Who and How Managed" should name the person who will be responsible for this aspect of the plan and how that person will carry it out, for example by providing the child with extra resource material.

The final column on "Assessment" should indicate how the school will monitor the implementation and effectiveness of the measure proposed. Will the child's grades be monitored? Will the child be interviewed? Will her teachers be asked to comment on how it is going? Will her achievement test score gains be the ultimate "proof" or "record" of the success of her plan?

Creating the Plan: Your Turn

Because your own child's plan is so important, you may wish to practice writing plans for some hypothetical case studies first. In Chapter 8, you went through some initial steps of an educational plan for Maria and for Rob. Now, see if you can figure out what to do about Marcelo, the young man described in the beginning of this chapter. His plan is outlined in Table 10.2. It is remarkably empty, isn't it? You have already read about what went wrong, and you know about his interests, preferences, and personality. Refer to the first pages of this chapter if you have forgotten them. After reviewing Marcelo's academic strengths and weaknesses and his situation and looking at the "bare-bones" plan that was drawn up for him, consider what can be done at this point to rectify it. Must Marcelo start over in a new setting? Fill in your ideas for Marcelo's *Yearly Educational Planner* in the boxes of Table 10.2.

Table 10.2. *Yearly Educational Planner*

©2000 by Karen B. Rogers

Child ___Marcelo___ Age _10_ Gender _M_ Date _____

Date Plan Will Begin _____ School _____

School-Based Essential	Domain	How Often	Who and How Managed	Assessment
Academic Progress Placement in sixth grade middle school	All academic areas	Full year, daily	Principal supervision of class scheduler	Satisfactory grades and achievement test scores
Academic Remediation				
Psychological Adjustment				
Socialization				

For his academic progress, what will you add to ensure that Marcelo begins to learn "new" content during the rest of his sixth-grade year? Will he be rescheduled into seventh-grade math and science classes for a "fresh start" on content acquisition, as well as finding like-ability or like-interest peers? For language arts, should he be regrouped with advanced English students and placed in an interdisciplinary social studies course on "futuristics"(a combination of science and social issues)? Once his academic progress has been considered, are there areas where he needs some remediation? At this point, the school may not know what Marcelo's gaps are, but as his progress is monitored, the remediation portion of the plan can be added as needed.

Psychological adjustment is an essential part of Marcelo's plan. Six weeks of twice-weekly meetings with a school counselor may help him overcome the retaliatory responses he has exhibited and learn strategies for deflecting the negative behaviors and attitudes of others in the school. Marcelo's socialization will be helped most if he can be placed regularly with other bright students who are either from older grades or from his same grade. Encouragement to join the science club or the MathMasters team might be a start. Volunteer tutoring, such as with special needs students in the school, might be another avenue for him to feel socially accepted in the school. Did you think of some similar activities to put in the Educational Plan in Table 10.2?

You may wish to try writing an Educational Plan for one more child—this time with more information from the *Data Collector* in summary form—before you sit down to create your own child's yearly educational plan. Choose either Tanya or Carson from the case studies below, and try to include all of the feasible educational options they would benefit from during the next year's school program. Use the information in Tables 10.3 and 10.4 to help you write out your Yearly Educational Plan for Tanya and Carson. You can write your Educational Plan using the outline in Table 10.5.

Table 10.3. *Data Collector* Summary

Case Study ___Tanya___ Age __9 yrs., 5 mos.__ Grade _4__

Cognitive Functioning:
- Highly gifted range of ability (WISC-3 FS=154; all 19s on six verbal subtests; three 19s on performance subtests)
- Outstanding range of achievement (ITBS Grade 6 total score battery 99th percentile; also 99th percentile on all composite scores)

Learning Strengths:
- "Superior" for Learning, Communication Precision, Communication Expression, Planning
- Reading and writing are strongest academic areas

Learning Preferences:
- Independent study, programmed instruction, teaching games, group projects, peer teaching; does NOT like discussion

Behavior:
- Perceptive, sensitive to problems, independent in thoughts, independent in actions, socially mature, persistent in assigned tasks, flexible; NOT persistent in own interests, nor popular

Outside Interests:
- Often reads 20-30 hours per week
- Piano, riding, scouts, collections, computer games

School Interests:
- History
- Science

Table 10.3. *Data Collector* Summary

Case Study *Carson*   Age _5 yrs., 2 mos._ Grade _K_

Cognitive Functioning:
- Highly gifted range of ability (Slosson score=158)
- Outstanding range of achievement (SAT Grade 3 score total battery 99th percentile; GE 2:7 in math; 3:5 in reading, spelling)
- Has completed all grade one district standards

Learning Strengths:
- "Superior" for all Renzulli scales except Motivation and Planning (i.e., Learning, Creativity, Leadership, Artistic, Musical, Communication Precision, Dramatic, Communication Expression)
- Reading and math are strongest academic areas

Learning Preferences:
- Peer teaching, teaching games, independent study, group projects, drill and recitation; NOT discussion

Behavior:
- Curious, self-accepting, accepting of others, persistent in assigned tasks; NOT persistent in own interests

Outside Interests:
- Reads 10-15 hours per week, collections, computer games

School Interests:
- Science
- Performing arts (magic)
- Crafts

Table 10.5. *Yearly Educational Planner*

©2000 by Karen B. Rogers

Child _____ Age _____ Gender _____ Date _____

Date Plan Will Begin _____ School _____

School-Based Essential	Domain	How Often	Who and How Managed	Assessment
Academic Progress				
Academic Remediation				
Psychological Adjustment				
Socialization				

When you have completed your educational plan for Tanya or Carson in Table 10.5, you may wish to check it against the plans I developed for each of them at the end of this chapter (see Tables 10.6 and 10.7). If the match with your plan looks good, and particularly if you think your plan is better than the ones at the end of the chapter, you are ready to compose a plan for your own child.

Your Educational Plan for Your Child

By now, you have gathered a great amount of information about your child. The *Parent Inventory for Finding Potential*, the *Teacher Inventory of Learning Strengths*, and the *Rogers' Interest Inventory* have all helped you understand your child. Perhaps you have used some of the other checklists contained in the Supplementary Materials listed in Appendix A, such as *Attitudes about School and Learning, Reading/Language Interest and Attitudes, Science Interest and Attitudes*, etc. You have summarized your findings in your *Data Collector*. You have organized all of the information about your child's level of cognitive functioning, learning strengths, learning preferences, personality characteristics/behaviors, in-school interests, and outside interests.

You also know about various educational options such as levels of enrichment and acceleration that are appropriate for gifted and talented children. You know which options, according to the research, fit best with which types of gifted children. This has taken a lot of time and effort on your part, but you have organized the information in order to develop the *Yearly Educational Plan* for your child. It is now time to take the plan you have developed to school and to advocate for your child by requesting and negotiating the changes that will be needed in the ordinary curriculum program options the school offers.

Going to the School

Your first step in asking for the meeting should be to present your plan to the principal. As instructional leader of the school, the principal should be the first person notified. You should meet with the principal very briefly at first to introduce yourself and state your request. Then, let this person have a few days to study the information you have collected via your *Data Collector* and the adaptations you are requesting in your *Yearly Educational Plan* before requesting a larger meeting, such as a face-to-face meeting with a child study team consisting of all of the people you think should be involved in your plan. Depending on whom you have identified to implement the various pieces of your plan, the group meeting may include just the principal and a few teachers, or it could include a school counselor, a gifted resource teacher, and teachers from other grade levels who might have your child for a portion of a day in an acceleration option. Once the meeting date is set, be sure to give advance copies of the information you have collected and the plan itself to each of the persons who will be involved in the meeting.

On the day of the meeting, come prepared with a short summary of your child's gifts, talents, and needs (based on the *Data Collector*) and a short summary of what you are asking from the school. This summary should be no longer than one page double-spaced and should be distributed at the beginning of the meeting. For each point in your summary, you and the others in the meeting can refer to the more detailed information you have submitted previously. Be ready to be flexible and to suggest alternatives to the plan that you have not shared previously. For example, if they say they cannot allow your fourth-grade child to take math with the sixth graders because of scheduling, then be ready to suggest that the sixth-grade math curriculum be brought into your child's classroom to be supervised by your child's fourth-grade teacher, or that your child's fourth-grade math be compacted and that he be provided with appropriate math enrichment activities for the remainder of the year. Keep a list of possible alternatives handy as you and the group systematically consider your plan. By being prepared with alternatives, you may be able to suggest additional ways for the school to meet your child's needs.

Ultimately, you and the group will know just how much the school is prepared and willing to do for your child. Be sure to review in your own mind what parts of the plan are not yet being addressed. Suggest alternative curriculum ideas for these areas that would benefit not only your child but also other bright children. You may recall Mr. and Mrs. Garcia's approach for having their child grouped with others of like-ability once she had been skipped (Chapter 9). Suggest options that are not too costly; for example, a community expert in math might be found to work on a volunteer basis with a group of advanced math students twice a week rather than be a paid tutor for your child.

Once you have negotiated all of the provisions that you brought to the meeting, you will need to go home and review your plan. What parts of it are just not going to get done this year? How will you provide for those parts outside of school time? You will be ready to complete your "at home" plan for the child at this point. The first things you will list in the home plan will probably be under "talent development" and will be the ways you can continue to help your child make progress in specific talent areas. You will want to use some of the ideas presented in Chapter 9 so that you are making "progress" on all nine guideline fronts.

Once the school begins to implement the educational plan for your child, you should ask for another meeting within six to eight weeks to monitor how well the plan is being implemented and how effective it seems to be. You might also request that your child be allowed to briefly attend that meeting to answer any questions the group may have of her. Does she like what she has been doing at school the past few weeks? What changes would she like to have made? What has been the best thing and worst thing about her experiences? Based on the child's responses, the group may wish to make changes in the initial plan.

What if the School Doesn't Cooperate?

Educators may become defensive when they aren't sure themselves what a parent wants for a gifted child or when they aren't sure what to do for such a child. It is hoped that the systematic and rational way in which you approach the school about your child's needs will prevent such defensiveness. But even if persons at the school have decided that you are "pushy," you are the one who has collected the information as carefully and faithfully as you could, and you are only asking for what you believe your child needs in order to be fully educated. Being liked by the school is probably not as important as having your child's true academic needs met, and you may need to remind yourself of that. Even so, try to be as diplomatic and tactful as possible with the school staff. Refrain from critical and inflammatory generalities such as: "That teacher should be fired!" and unrealistic, costly demands such as: "We need a separate daily tutor." Neither criticism nor demands will accomplish change and may instead lead to future resistance by various personnel in the school to consider your requests.

It is important to recognize that any change you can get the school to make is a foot in the door. So be prepared to ask for *one* general thing if your whole plan is not being seriously considered. Ultimately, what is it you want the school system to provide for your child? Are you asking that it be more flexible in what it requires your child to learn? Are you asking the school to differentiate the curriculum and its instructional strategies for management and delivery? Are you asking it to be more flexible in the amount of time it requires your child to remain in school or at a certain grade level?

There is no question that what your child is exposed to on a daily basis—and how often he is exposed to it—is crucial, but you must also bring time into the equation. In 1994, the National Education Commission on Time and Learning published a thought-provoking report that argued that the current school system—so time-bound in its organization (6-hour day, 180-day year, 13 years)—is badly flawed. Among the recommendations of this commission were such things as having world-class standards in academic core areas, experimenting with different variations of time usage in schools, such as block scheduling, flexible days, refocusing the school day on core academic areas, and providing teachers with more preparation and planning time. If just those recommendations were put into place with consideration for gifted children who might be ahead in core academic areas, schools would no doubt develop policies for allowing gifted children to "test out" of the academic areas they have already mastered and to leave the school system when their mastery of the system's graduation standards is complete—regardless of age or grade level. Although some states have a law that mandates how long a student must remain in school, gifted children could start their college programs well before they reached that mandatory age.

Unfortunately, "credit for a child's prior learning" is one part of these far-reaching recommendations that has not been taken into account. In recent years, schools have based their operations more on basic minimum acceptable academic "standards" and achievement test score results for each grade level, and they have experimented with reorganization of school days and the school year. However, thus far, there has been little progress in the concept that children could be released from K-12 school when they have "finished" with what the K-12 system can offer them.

Unfortunately, too many states still award state funds to schools based on counts of the number of students who are sitting in classrooms on any given day. Until school funding can be separated from the concept of the numbers of students who are in classroom seats at each grade, gifted children will probably continue to sit for years in classrooms where little that is new is learned or mastered. Until attitudes about our current lock-step curriculum—where all children of a certain age move ahead at the exact same pace—are changed, our gifted children will find themselves trapped in a slow-motion walk.

An educational plan requested on an individual basis by parents—one child at a time—may be the only method for achieving equity for gifted children. Certainly, special education and legislation policies related to children who are gifted are generally very low on state legislative, local school board, and district policy priority lists.

Is there support for your requests for provisions for gifted children within the legal system? In some cases, yes, but in most cases, not really, and certainly not as much support as is needed. Drs. Frances Karnes and Ronald Marquardt have written three very good books about this issue. The books are titled *Gifted Children and the Law: Mediation, Due Process, and Court Cases* (1991a); *Gifted Children and Legal Issues in Education: Parents' Stories of Hope* (1991b); and *Gifted Children and Legal Issues in Education: An Update* (2000). These books are resources for both parents and educators as they describe cases that have been resolved in the courts.

Assurance of daily challenge, protection against boredom, and adaptation of the curriculum because of a child's gifts or talents have a better chance of being legally protected in states that mandate gifted programming. At present, approximately half of the states have such a mandate. Of the 12 states that mandate individualized education plans for gifted learners, 10 have placed gifted education under special education. For these states, in particular, there are established procedures whereby parents can pursue mediation and due process procedures without having to resort to costly and risky court cases. As Karnes and Marquardt repeat several times throughout their books, going to court should be a last resort in resolving parents' disputes with the schools.

Mediation is an informal process in which parent disputes with schools can be heard and decided. Neither side is expected to use a lawyer, and the dispute is usually decided in a very short time period without having to wait for lengthy court proceedings. The mediator can be a member of a general pool of state mediators or someone from outside of the school district such as an

educator in another school system, an employee of a state department, college of education, or community agency. Both parties—
the school and the family—must agree to the person selected, and
all are expected to come to the mediation meeting with the expectation that the dispute can and will be amicably resolved. Within
the several hours that such a meeting will entail, all issues are discussed, and ultimately some solutions or compromises are
reached between the parties. The mediator then provides all parties with a written document summarizing the resolution.

Due process hearings are a second method for getting
schools to address parental concerns about their child's education.
A due process hearing is led by a hearing officer to allow the family to present its arguments to this "impartial" party. Due process
procedures recognize that the family has a "right" under the 14th
and 15th Constitutional Amendments to legal proceedings regarding their dispute. At the current time, 16 states have made due process procedures possible regarding at least some educational
issues concerning gifted learners. Check with your own state
department of education to learn whether your state has such a
policy in place. The hearing follows much the same procedure as
for mediation, but the outcomes of due process can usually be
"appealed" to the court system.

Taking your case to court should be your last resort. For
those cases about gifted child education that have entered the
court system, the results are mixed—with more losses than
wins for families—and often these cases have dragged on for
years as school systems appeal to higher courts. By the time
some of the legal cases were eventually "settled," the child was
out of the school system or well past the optimum time for the
accommodation to be made. Your best hope for prompt resolution if the school is unwilling to grant any requests is through
mediation and due process hearings.

The Ultimate "Shoulds" for Both Home and School

My experiences with providing educational plans for gifted children and dealing with the schools' responses to these plans form the basis for the "shoulds" listed here. Most of them represent simple, common sense.

The schools probably aren't going to agree to everything you have written in education plan, but neither should you be expected to do all of it. What, as a minimum, should the schools, in all moral and ethical consideration, agree to provide for your child, and what, as a minimum, should you be prepared to do without the school's help?

As stated earlier in this book, an educational plan needs to be a joint agreement between parents and the school, with what is best for the gifted child in heart and mind. Ethically, no school should say to you, "We can't do anything for you here. Try somewhere else." Yet that does happen with increasing frequency. Homeschooling, vouchers, charter schools, and other alternative schooling choices have sprung up for just this reason. But to seek a child's education in these alternative ways allows public schools to abdicate their responsibility and their purpose for existence—which is to provide an education that is commensurate with the abilities and potentials of all of their students, including students who are gifted and academically advanced. As taxpayers, we citizens have agreed to support the schools with tax monies so that *all* students will receive an equitable and appropriate education. Therefore, you and your child have a right to expect appropriate education.

Here are some fundamental "shoulds" for both schools and parents.

"Shoulds" for the Schools

1. Make accommodations so that one and one half to two years' curriculum in most subject areas is accomplished for each year that the academically gifted or talented learner is in the school, using a variety of methods to accomplish this—for example, compacting, grade telescoping, single-subject acceleration, and credit by examination.

2. Arrange for Scholastic Aptitude Tests (SAT) or American College Tests (ACT) to be accessible to gifted students while they are still in middle school. This will open up a wide variety of Talent Search and other national opportunities to students beyond what the school can offer.

3. Provide access to high school classes while the gifted student is still in middle school and to Advanced Placement or International Baccalaureate classes in the first years of high school.

4. Encourage gifted students to participate in post-secondary options (college) courses in their later years of high school. Offer dual credit for these courses if needed.

5. Be open and flexible when additional opportunities cannot be offered by the school, so that the parents of gifted learners can search elsewhere for help and support.

6. Offer on-line tutorial courses via Northwestern University, Johns Hopkins University, Duke University, or Stanford University when the school's coursework cannot be individualized enough for a particular student.

7. Assign one counselor in the school system to "look after" gifted students as they progress from grades seven through 12. It is estimated that the counselor's student load will be as great as all other counselors in the system, but that the nature of the work will be different—there will be more of a focus on academic advising, college counseling, career guidance, special opportunity recommendations for gifted students, etc. In addition, this counselor will have university course as well as other training in the characteristics and needs of gifted learners.

"Shoulds" for the Parents

1. Begin researching college programs early. Start saving money for higher education, and plan to spend a lot on college tuition. High ability does not necessarily lead to scholarships anymore.

2. Inquire about and decide if Early Entrance Programs (EEPs) for college are an answer for your gifted student and your family. If the local schools are not cooperative in providing necessary flexible pacing, EEPs may be your only resort.

3. Develop a bibliography of books for you as a family to read. Use Halsted's *Some of my Best Friends Are Books* as a starting list. Use the *Syntopticon* or *Adult Great Books* programs for reading when the child is older.

4. Arrange for your child to have chances to be with "true peers" on a regular basis or with older children for strategy situations, such as orienteering, chess, games, or simulations.

5. Help your child develop verbal responses to be used in negative situations with age peers. Your child may understand why people, including siblings, act "strangely," but they may need help with the solutions for these problems.

6. Help your child to be involved in service groups such as Scouts or in service projects in your community, religious organization, and school, so that a sense of social responsibility and caring about others will be reinforced.

7. Provide a wide variety of exploratory activities to develop hidden interests, but then allow your child to dig in deeply when an interest is found. Well-roundedness isn't always necessary for maximum personal development.

8. Help your child practice memory skills at home with memory projects, such as memorizing poems, literary passages, lists of information, visual information, and music. Teach mnememic devices to aid memory.

9. Include your child in most educational and recreational decisions that affect him or her, including grade-skips, early college entrance, and participation in a local school gifted "program." If one of these choices does not feel "right" for the child, then select an alternative that does feel comfortable.

Table 10.6. *Yearly Educational Planner*

©2000 by Karen B. Rogers

Child *Tanya* Age *9 yrs 5 mos.* Grade *4* Gender *F*

Date Plan Will Begin _____ School _____

School-Based Essential	Domain	How Often	Who and How Managed	Assessment
Academic Progress				
Grade-skip to 6th grade (middle school)	All academic areas	Once	Middle school principal, school counselor	3 month "grace period," Tanya, counselors, parents, principal, teachers decide if successful
Compact math, social studies, sciences; accelerate replacement curriculum (2 yrs. curriculum per year)	Math, social studies, science	Yearly	GT coordinator, in collaboration with grade 6/7 math, social studies, & science teachers	In-class participation; achievement levels on tests and assignments
Placement in 7th grade Honors English with additional differentiated curriculum	English/ reading	Once	GT coordinator plans instruction, 8th/7th grade teachers oversee assignments	Achievement levels on tests and assignments
Replace 6th grade "Study Hall" with grade 8 foreign language	World languages	Once	Grade 8 language teacher	In-class participation; achievement levels on tests, assignments
Offer formal vocabulary instruction	English/ reading	Yearly	GT coordinator offers as independent study	Achievement levels on tests

Table 10.6. *Yearly Educational Planner*
(continued)

School-Based Essential	Domain	How Often	Who and How Managed	Assessment
Academic Remediation				
Remediate any gaps found in compacted subjects	All academic areas	Yearly	GT coordinator supervises self-directed remediation	Achievement/ mastery of missing content and skills
Offer creative & expository writing exercises	English/ reading	Yearly	Grade 7 Honors English teacher, supervised by GT coordinator	Achievement levels on assignments
Psychological Adjustment				
Keep "mixed-ability" learning activities to a minimum	All academic areas	Yearly	GT coordinator places Tanya in like-ability classes	Informal counseling on esteem, self-efficacy issues
Socialization				
Placement in Jr. Great Books discussion group	Co-curricular	Yearly	Counselor	In-group participation, enjoyment
Involvement in at least one competitive academic team	One academic area of choice	Yearly	Counselor, subject area teacher/ supervisor	In-group participation, enjoyment
Involvement in school-wide service project	Co-curricular	Yearly	GT coordinator, counselor	In-group participation, enjoyment

Table 10.7. *Yearly Educational Planner*

©2000 by Karen B. Rogers

Child *Carson*   Age *5 yrs 2 mos.* Grade *K* Gender *M*

Date Plan Will Begin _____ School _____

School-Based Essential	Domain	How Often	Who and How Managed	Assessment
Academic Progress				
Grade-skip to 2nd grade	All academic areas	Once	School principal, school counselor	3 month "grace period." Carson, counselor, parents, principal, teachers decide if successful
Compact the reading/language arts curriculum year	Reading/ language arts	Yearly	GT coordinator, in collaboration with grade 2 teacher	In-class participation, achievement levels on tests and enriched assignments
Placement in "advanced readers" circle	Reading/ language arts	Yearly	Grade 2 teacher	In-group participation
Placement in accelerated math group	Math	Yearly	Grade 2 teacher	In-group participation, achievement levels on tests, assignments
Pull-out program	Arts, creativity	Yearly	GT coordinator	In-group participation, achievement levels on assignments, performances

Table 10.7. *Yearly Educational Planner*
(continued)

©2000 by Karen B. Rogers

School-Based Essential	Domain	How Often	Who and How Managed	Assessment
Academic Remediation *Supervision of challenge learning center activities to develop persistence, planning, wide-ranging interests* *Remediate any gaps found in compacted reading*				
Psychological Adjustment *Provision of challenge learning center activities for free time*				
Socialization *Pull-out program for arts enrichments and creative development* *Involvement in school-wide service projects*				

Summary

Four school-based essentials must be considered in the development of the education plan, with efforts proportionately placed on academic progress, academic remediation, psychological adjustment, and socialization.

Key Points

- Academic progress should make up approximately 60-65% of the efforts requested in the plan and should reflect a careful match between 1) the information about the child's cognitive functioning, learning preferences, learning strengths, personality, and interests, and 2) the instructional management, delivery, and curriculum adaptations outlined in the plan.

- Remediation should take up no more than 10% of the plan's requested efforts. It is important to include this component, however, so that the school recognizes that the parents are aware that the child is not perfect.

- Requests for experiences or activities that will build on or extend a child's motivation and attitudes toward school and learning or psychological adjustment or that will help enhance the child's self-awareness and self-esteem should comprise approximately 10% of the plan's focus.

- Socialization—requests for how the child can be positively integrated within the school's social climate—should account for the remaining 15-20% of the plan's effort.

References

CHAPTER 1

Bandura, A. (1977). Toward a unifying theory of behavioral change. *Psychological Review, 84,* 181-215.

Cox, J., Daniel, N., & Boston, B. (1985). *Educating able learners: Programs and promising practices.* Austin, TX: University of Texas.

Feldman, D. H. (1980). *Beyond universals in cognitive development.* Norwood, NJ: Ablex.

Gagné, F. (1985). Giftedness and talent: Reexamining the reexamination of definitions. *Gifted Child Quarterly, 29,* 103-112.

Gallagher, J. J. (1965). *Teaching the gifted child.* Boston: Allyn & Bacon.

Gallagher, J. J., & Gallagher, S. (1994). *Teaching the gifted child.* Boston: Allyn & Bacon.

Gross, M. U. M. (1993). *Exceptionally gifted children.* New York: Routledge.

Hansen, J. B., & Feldhusen, J. F. (1994). Comparison of trained and untrained teachers of gifted students. *Gifted Child Quarterly, 38,* 115-121.

Heath, W. J. (1997). *What are the most effective characteristics of teachers of the gifted?* Texas State Report. 30 pp. (ERIC Document Reproduction Service No. ED 411665).

Karnes, F., & Marquardt, R. (2000). *Gifted children and legal issues in gifted education: An update.* Scottsdale, AZ: Gifted Psychology Press (now Great Potential Press).

Schunk, D. H. (1987). Peer models and children's behavioral change. *Equity and Excellence, 23,* 22-30.

Silverman, L. K. (1993). *Counseling the gifted and talented.* Denver: Love.

Tomlinson, C. A., Callahan, C. M., Moon, T. R., Tomchin, E. M., Landrum, M. Imbeau, M., et al. (1995). *Preservice teacher preparation in meeting the needs of gifted and other academically diverse students.* Storrs, CT: National Research Center on the Gifted and Talented.

Webb, J. T. (2001). Mis-diagnosis and dual diagnosis of gifted children: Gifted and LD, ADHD, OCD, Oppositional Defiant Disorder. *Gifted Education Press Quarterly, 15 (1),* 9-13.

CHAPTER 2

Cookson, P., Halberstam, J., Mescavage, S., & Berger, C. (1998). *A parent's guide to standardized tests in school: How to improve your child's chances for success.* New York: Learning Express.

Gagné, F. (1993). Constructs and models pertaining to exceptional human abilities. In K. A. Heller, F. J. Monks, & A. H. Passow (Eds.), *International handbook of research and development of giftedness and talent* (pp. 69-87). Oxford: Pergamon Press.

Marland, S. P. (1972). *Education of the gifted and talented: Report to the Congress of the United States from the U.S. Commissioner of Education.* Washington, DC: U.S. Government Printing Office.

Rogers, K. B. (1986). Do the gifted think and learn differently? A review of recent research and its implications for instruction. *Journal for the Education of the Gifted, 10 (1),* 17-39.

United States Office of Education. (1993). *National excellence: A case for developing America's talent.* Washington, DC: U.S. Government Printing Office.

CHAPTER 3

Renzulli, J. S., & Smith, L. (1977). *Scales for rating behavioral characteristics of superior students.* Mansfield Center, CT: Creative Learning Press.

Renzulli, J. S. (1977). *Interest-a-lyzer.* Mansfield Center, CT: Creative Learning Press.

Renzulli, J. S., & Smith, L. (1975). *Learning styles inventory.* Mansfield Center, CT: Creative Learning Press.

Torrance, E. P. (1966). *Torrance Tests of Creative Thinking.* Bensenville, IL: Scholastic Testing Service.

CHAPTER 4

Hoekman, K., McCormick, J., & Gross, M. U. M. (1998). The optimal context for gifted students: A preliminary exploration of motivational and affective considerations. *Gifted Child Quarterly, 43,* pp. 170-193.

Maker, C. J. (1983). *Curriculum development for the gifted.* Rockville, MD: Aspen Systems.

Renzulli, J., & Smith, L. (1975). *Learning styles inventory.* Mansfield Center, CT: Creative Learning Press.

CHAPTER 5

Bell, T. H. (1981). *A nation at risk: The imperative for educational reform.* Washington, DC: National Commission on Excellence in Education.

Benbow, C. P., & Lubinski, D. (1994). Individual differences amongst the mathematically gifted: Their educational and vocational implications. In N. Colangelo, S. G. Assouline, & D. L. Ambroson (Eds.), *Talent development* (Vol. 2, pp, 83-100). Dayton, OH: Ohio Psychology Press (Now Great Potential Press).

Brody, L., & Stanley, J. C. (1991). Young college students: Assessing factors that contribute to success. In W. T. Southern & E. D. Jones (Eds.). *Academic acceleration of gifted children.* New York: Teachers College Press.

Reilly, J. M. (1992). *Mentorship: The essential guide for schools and business.* Scottsdale, AZ: Ohio Psychology Press (now Great Potential Press).

Reis, S. M., Burns, D. E., & Renzulli, J. S. (1992). *Curriculum compacting: The complete guide to modifying the regular curriculum for high ability students.* Mansfield Center, CT: Creative Learning Press.

Reis, S. M., Westberg, K. L., Kulikowich, J., Caillard, F., Hebert, T. P, & Plucker, J. A. (1993). *Why not let high ability students start school in January? The curriculum compacting study.* (Research Monograph #93106). Storrs, CT: National Research Center on the Gifted and Talented.

Renzulli, J. S., & Smith, L. H. (1978). *The compactor.* Mansfield Center, CT: Creative Learning Press.

Robinson, N. M., Abbott, R. D., Berninger, V. W., Busse, J., & Mukhopadhyay, S. (1997). Developmental changes in mathematically precocious young children: Longitudinal and gender effects. *Gifted Child Quarterly, 41*, 145-158.

Rogers, K. B. (1992). A best-evidence synthesis of the research on acceleration options for gifted learners. In N. Colangelo, S. G. Assouline, & D. L. Ambroson (Eds.), *Talent development: Proceedings from the 1991 Henry B. and Jocelyn Wallace national research symposium on talent development* (pp. 406-409). Unionville, NY: Trillium.

Southern, W. T., & Jones, E. D. (1991). *Academic acceleration of gifted children.* New York: Teachers College Press.

Stanley, J. C. (1996). In the beginning: The study of mathematically precocious youth. In C. P. Benbow & D. Lubinski (Eds.), *Intellectual talent: Psychometric and social issues* (pp. 225-235). Baltimore, MD: The Johns Hopkins University Press.

Winebrenner, S. (1990). *Teaching gifted kids in the regular classroom.* Minneapolis, MN: Free Spirit Press.

CHAPTER 6

Brody, L., & Stanley, J. C. (1991). Young college students: Assessing factors that contribute to success. In W. T. Southern & E. D. Jones (Eds.). *Academic acceleration of gifted children.* New York: Teachers College Press.

Carter, K. R. (1985). Cognitive development of intellectually gifted: A Piagetian perspective. *Roeper Review, 7,* 180-184.

Rogers, K. B. (1992). A best-evidence synthesis of the research on acceleration options for gifted learners. In N. Colangelo, S. G. Assouline, & D. L. Ambroson (Eds.), *Talent development: Proceedings from the 1991 Henry B. and Jocelyn Wallace national research symposium on talent development* (pp, 406-409). Unionville, NY: Trillium.

Southern, W. T., & Jones, E. D. (1991). *Academic acceleration of gifted children.* New York: Teachers College Press.

Veenman, S. (1995). Cognitive and noncognitive effects of multi-grade and multi-age classes: A best-evidence synthesis. *Review of Educational Research, 65,* 319-382.

CHAPTER 7

Aronson, E., & Goode, E. (1980). Training teachers to implement jigsaw learning: A manual for teachers. In S. Sharan, P. Hare, C. D. Webb, & R. Hertz-Lazarowitz (Eds.), *Cooperation in education* (pp. 47-81). Provo, UT: Brigham University Press.

Berge, Z. L. (1990, November). Effects of group size, gender, and ability grouping on learning science process skills using microcomputers. *Journal of Research in Science Teaching, 27,* 923-954.

Carter, G., & Jones, M. G. (1994, October). Relationship between ability-paired interactions and the development of fifth graders' concepts of balance. *Journal of Research in Science Teaching, 31,* 847-856.

Chauvet, M. J., & Blatchford, P. (1993, Summer). Group composition and national curriculum assessment at seven years. *Psychology & Special Educational Needs, 35,* 189-196.

Cox, J., Daniel, N., & Boston, B. (1985). *Educating able learners: Programs and promising practices.* Austin, TX: University of Texas.

Delcourt, M. A., Loyd, B. H., Cornell, D. G., & Goldberg, M. D. (1994). *Evaluation of the effects of programming arrangements on student learning outcomes.* (Research Monograph 94108). Charlottesville, VA: National Research Center on the Gifted & Talented.

Gentry, M., & Owen, S. (1999). An investigation of the effects of total school flexible cluster grouping on identification achievement and classroom practices. *Gifted Child Quarterly, 43,* 224-243.

Goldring, E. B. (1990), Assessing the status of information on classroom organizational frameworks for gifted students. *Journal of Educational Research, 83,* 313-326.

Hacker, R. G., & Rowe, M. J. (1993, March). A study of the effects of an organization change from streamed to mixed-ability classes upon science classroom instruction. *Journal of Research in Science Teaching, 30,* 223-231.

Jones, M. G., & Carter, G. (1994, September). Verbal and nonverbal behavior on ability-grouped dyads. *Journal of Research in Science Teaching, 31,* 603-620.

Kagan, S. L., & Zigler, E. F. (1987). *Early schooling: The national debate.* New Haven, CT: Yale University Press.

Kenny, D., Archimbault, F., & Hallmark, K. (1995). *The effects of group composition on gifted and nongifted elementary students in cooperative learning groups.* (Research-Based Decision Making Series). Storrs, CT: National Research Center on the Gifted and Talented, University of Connecticut.

Kulik, J. A. (1992). *An analysis of the research on ability grouping: Historical and contemporary perspectives.* Storrs, CT: National Research Center on the Gifted and Talented.

Kulik, J. A., & Kulik, C-L.C. (1982). Effects of ability grouping on secondary school students: A meta-analysis of evaluation findings. *American Educational Research Journal, 19,* 415-428.

Kulik, J. A., & Kulik, C-L.C. (1984). Effects of accelerated instruction on students. *Review of Educational Research, 54,* 409-425.

Kulik, J. A., & Kulik, C-L. C. (1987). Effects of ability grouping on student achievement. *Equity and Excellence, 23,* 22-30.

Oakes, J. (1985). *Keeping track: How schools structure inequality.* New Haven, CT: Yale University Press.

Reis, S. M., Westberg, K. L., Kulikowich, J., Caillard, F., Hebert, T. P, & Plucker, J. A. (1993). *Why not let high ability students start school in January? The curriculum compacting study.* (Research Monograph #93106). Storrs, CT: National Research Center on the Gifted and Talented.

Rogers, K. B. (1991). *The relationship of grouping practices to the education of the gifted and talented learner.* (Research-Based Decision Making Series). Storrs, CT: National Research Center on the Gifted and Talented, University of Connecticut.

Rogers, K. B. (1993). Grouping the gifted: Questions and answers. *Roeper Review, 16,* 8-13.

Rogers, K. B. (1998). Using current research to make "good" decisions about grouping. *National Association for Secondary School Principals Bulletin, 82 (595),* 38-46.

Sharan, S., & Hertz-Lazarowitz, R. (1980). A group investigation method of cooperative learning in the classroom. In S. Sharan, P. Hare, C. D. Webb, & R. Hertz-Lazarowitz (Eds.), *Cooperation in education* (pp. 14-46). Provo, UT: Brigham University Press.

Slavin, R. E. (1987). Ability grouping: A best-evidence synthesis. *Review of Educational Research, 57,* 293-336.

Slavin, R. E. (1993). Ability grouping in the middle grades: Achievement effects and alternatives. *Elementary School Journal, 93,* 535-552.

Vaughn, V. L., Feldhusen, J. F., & Asher, J. W. (1991). Meta-analyses and review of research on pull-out programs in gifted education. *Gifted Child Quarterly, 35,* 92-98.

Walberg, H. J. (1984, May). Improving the quality of America's schools. *Educational Leadership,* 19-27.

CHAPTER 8

Barbe, W. B., & Malone, M. M. (1985). Reading and writing. In R. H. Swassing (Ed.), *Teaching gifted children and adolescents* (pp. 276-313). Columbus, OH: Merrill.

Bloom, B. S. (1985). *Developing talent in young people.* New York: Ballantine Books.

Bruner, J. S. (1960). *The process of education.* New York: Vintage.

Callahan, C. M. (1983). Issues in evaluating programs for the gifted. *Gifted Child Quarterly, 27,* 3-7.

Campbell, J. R. (1988). Secrets of award winning programs for gifted in mathematics. *Gifted Child Quarterly, 32,* 362-365.

Clark, G. A., & Zimmerman, E. D. (1994). *Programming opportunities for students gifted and talented in the visual arts*. Storrs, CT: The National Research Center on the Gifted and Talented.

Dunn, R., Dunn, K., & Price, G. E. (1981). Learning styles: Research vs. opinion. *Phi Delta Kappan, 62,* 645-646.

Dunn, R., & Griggs, S. (1985). Teaching and counseling gifted students with their learning style preferences. Two case studies. *Gifted Child Today, 41,* 40-43.

Eberle, R., & Stanish, B. (1985). *CPS for kids*. Carthage, IL: Good Apple.

Feldhusen, J. F., & Reilly, P. (1983). The Purdue Secondary Model for gifted education: A multi-service program. *Journal for the Education of the Gifted, 6,* 230-244.

Freeman, J. (1985). Emotional aspects of giftedness. In J. Freeman (Ed.), *The psychology of gifted children*. New York: Wiley.

Gallagher, J. J., & Gallagher, S. (1994). *Teaching the gifted child*. Boston: Allyn & Bacon.

Gallagher, S. A., Stepien, W. J., Sher, B. T., & Workman, D. (1995). Implementing problem-based learning in science classrooms. *School Science and Mathematics, 95,* 136-146.

Goldberg, M. L., Passow, A. H., Justman, J., & Hage, G. (1966). *The effects of ability grouping*. New York: Bureau of Publications, Teachers College, Columbia University.

Gordon, W. J. (1960). *Synectics*. New York: Harper & Row.

Haensley, P. A., & Roberts, N. M. (1983). The professional productive process and its implications for gifted students. *Gifted Child Quarterly, 27,* 9-12.

Hoekman, K., McCormick, J., & Gross, M.U. M. (1998). The optimal context for gifted students: A preliminary exploration of motivational and affective considerations. *Gifted Child Quarterly, 43,* pp. 170-193.

Johnsen-Harris, M. A. (1983). Surviving the budget crunch from an independent school perspective. *Roeper Review, 6,* 79-81.

Johnson, J. (1999). Jr. Great Books boosts Chicago test scores. HTML:

Karnes, F. A., & Chauvin, J. C. (1998). *Leadership development program.* Scottsdale, AZ: Gifted Psychology Press (now Great Potential Press).

Karnes, F. A., & Riley, T. (1991). Public relations strategies for gifted education. *Gifted Child Today, 14,* 35-37.

Kersh, M. E., & Reisman, F. K. (1985). Mathematics for gifted students. In R. H. Swassing (Ed.), *Teaching gifted children and adolescents.* (pp. 137-180). Columbus, OH: Merrill.

Kingsley, R. F. (1986). "Digging" for understanding and significance: A high school enrichment model. *Roeper Review, 9,* 37-38.

Maker, C. J. (1983). *Curriculum development for the gifted.* Rockville, MD: Aspen Systems.

Olenchak, F. R., & Renzulli, J. S. (1989). The effectiveness of the Schoolwide Enrichment Model on selected aspects of elementary school change. *Gifted Child Quarterly, 33,* 36-46.

Parker, J. P. (1996). NAGC standards for personnel preparation in gifted education: A brief history. *Gifted Child Quarterly, 40,* 158-164.

Paul, R. (1997). *Critical thinking: What every person needs to survive in a rapidly changing world.* Sonoma, CA: Center for Critical Thinking.

Rabinowitz, M. L., & Glaser, R. (1985). Cognitive structure and processes on highly competent performance. In E. D. Horowitz & M. O'Brien (Eds.), *The gifted and talented: Developmental perspectives* (pp. 75-98). Washington, DC: American Psychological Association.

Redfield, D. L., & Rousseau, E. W. (1981). Meta-analysis of experimental research on teacher questioning behavior. *Review of Educational Research, 51,* 237-245.

Renzulli, J. S., Smith, L. H., & Reis, S. M. (1982). Curriculum compacting: An essential strategy for working with gifted students. *The Elementary School Journal, 82,* 185-194.

Rogers, K. B. (1986). Do the gifted think and learn differently? A review of recent research and its implications for instruction. *Journal for the Education of the Gifted, 10 (1),* 17-39.

Rogers, K. B. (1991). *The relationship of grouping practices to the education of the gifted and talented learner.* (Research-Based Decision Making Series). Storrs, CT: National Research Center on the Gifted and Talented, University of Connecticut.

Shore, B. M., Cornell, D. G., Robinson, A., & Ward, V. S. (1991). *Recommended practices in gifted education.* New York: Teachers College Press.

Silverman, L. K. (1993). *Counseling the gifted and talented.* Denver: Love.

Stanley, J. C. (1991). An academic model for educating the mathematically talented. *Gifted Child Quarterly, 35,* 36-42.

Stanley, J. C., & Benbow, C. P. (1983). SMPY's first decade: Ten years of posing problems and solving them. In W. C. George, S. J. Cohn, & J. C. Stanley (Eds.), *Educating the gifted: Acceleration and enrichment* (pp. 172-180). Baltimore, MD: The Johns Hopkins University Press.

Starko, A. J. (1986). *It's about time: Inservice strategies for curriculum compacting*. Mansfield Center, CT: Creative Learning Press.

Starko, A. J. (1996). *Creativity in the classroom: Schools of curious delight* (2nd ed.). Mahwah, NJ: Lawrence Erlbaum Associates.

Start, K. B., (1995). *The relationship of learning pace and ability in concept acquisition*. Paper presented at the Annual Supporting the Emotional Needs of the Gifted (SENG) Conference. San Diego, CA.

Stednitz, U., & Speck, A. (1986). Young children can complete creative, independent projects. *Gifted Child Today, 9,* 19-21.

Sternberg, R. J., & Davidson, J. E. (Eds.). (1986). *Conceptions of giftedness*. Cambridge: Cambridge University Press.

Stewart, E. D. (1981). Learning styles among gifted/talented students: Instructional techniques references. *Exceptional Children, 48,* 134-148.

Szekely, G. (1981). The artist and child—A model program for the artistically gifted. *Gifted Child Quarterly, 25,* 67-72.

Tallent-Runnels, M. K., & Candler-Lotven, A. C. (1995). *Academic competitions for gifted students: A resource book for teachers and parents*. Thousand Oaks, CA: Corwin Press.

Tannenbaum, A. (1983). *Gifted children: Psychological and educational perspectives*. New York: MacMillan.

Torrance, E. P. (1986). Teaching creative and gifted learners. In M. C. Whitrock (Ed.), *Handbook of research on teaching* (3rd ed., pp. 630-647). New York: MacMillan.

Treffinger, D. F. (1986). Fostering effective, independent learning through individualized programming. In J. S. Renzulli (Ed), *Systems and models for developing programs for the gifted and talented* (pp. 429-460). Mansfield Center, CT: Creative Learning Press.

Van Tassel-Baska, J. (1993). *Comprehensive curriculum for gifted learners*. Boston: Allyn & Bacon.

Van Tassel-Baska, J., Avery, L. D., Little, C. A., & Hughes, C. E. (2000). Where the rubber meets the road: An evaluation of the implementation of curriculum innovation: The impact of the William and Mary units on schools. *Roeper Review, 28,* 244-272.

Van Tassel-Baska, J., Bass, G. M., Reis, R. R., Poland, D. L., & Avery, L. D. (1998). A national pilot study of science curriculum effectiveness for high-ability students. *Gifted Child Quarterly, 42,* 200-211.

Ward, V. S. (1980). *Differential education for the gifted.* Ventura, CA: Office of the Ventura County Superintendent of Education for the National/State Leadership Training Institute for the Gifted and Talented.

Webb, J., Meckstroth, E., & Tolan, S. (1982). *Guiding the gifted child.* Dayton, OH: Ohio Psychology Press (Now Great Potential Press).

Whitener, E. M. (1989). A meta-analytic review of the effect of learning on the interaction between prior achievement and instructional support. *Review of Educational Research, 59,* 65-86.

CHAPTER 9

Baskin, B. H. and Harris, K. H. (1980). *Books for the Gifted Child*. New York: Bowker.

Duke University Talent Identification Program (2001). *Educational Opportunity Guide*. Durha, NC, Duke University Talent Identification Program

Elyé, B. J. & Southwick, C. A. (2000). *JumpStart: Ideas to Move Your Mind*. Scottsdale, AZ: Gifted Psychology Press (now Great Potential Press).

Halsted, J. W. (1994). *Some of My Best Friends Are Books*. Dayton, OH: Ohio Psychology Press (now Great Potential Press).

Halsted, J. (2002). *Some of My Best Friends Are Books*, 2nd Ed. Scottsdale, AZ: Great Potential Press.

Lewis, B. A. (1997). *What Do You Stand For?* Minneapolis: Free Spirit Publishing.

Odean, K. (1997). *Great Books for Boys*. New York: Ballantine.

Odean, K. (1997). *Great Books for Girls*. New York: Ballantine.

Rivero, L. (2002). *Creative Homeschooling for Gifted Children: A Resource Guide*. Scottsdale, AZ: Great Potential Press.

Russell, W. F. (1992). *Classics to Read Aloud to Your Children*. New York: Crown.

Russell, W. F. (1992). *More Classics to Read Aloud to Your Children*. New York: Crown.

United States Office of Education (1993). *National excellence: A case for developing America's talent*. Washington, DC: U. S. Government Printing Office.

Westphal, C. (2001). *A family year abroad: How to live outside the borders.* Scottsdale, AZ: Great Potential Press.

CHAPTER 10

Karnes, F. A. & Marquardt, R. (1991a). *Gifted Children and the law: Mediation, due process and court cases.* Dayton: OH: Ohio Psychology Press (now Great Potential Press).

Karnes, F. A. & Marquardt, R. (1991b). *Gifted children and legal issues in education: Parents' stories of hope.* Dayton, OH: Ohio Psychology Press (now Great Potential Press).

Karnes, F. A. & Marquardt, R. (2000). *Gifted children and legal issues: An update.* Scottsdale, AZ: Gifted Psychology Press (now Great Potential Press).

Appendix A

Supplementary Materials

Parent Inventory for Finding Potential (PIP)

©2000 by Karen B. Rogers

Child _____ Age _____ Grade _____ Gender _____ Date _____

Please indicate how often you observe the following behaviors in your child. Check the box that indicates your response.

Behavior or Characteristic	Seldom or Never (1)	Sometimes (2)	Regularly (3)	Almost Always (4)
1. *Reflective*–when asked a complex question or given a new task, tends to take time to think before jumping in				
2. *Connective*–makes connections with what is already known or tries to apply new information to other contexts				
3. *Focused*–stays attentive and alert when new or complex information is being given; long attention span				
4. *Retentive*–remembers information in vast quantities easily				
5. *Enjoys School*–loves attending school and even "plays" school at home				
6. *Enthusiastic*–enters into most activities with eagerness				
7. *Sensitive to Problems*–ready to question or change situations, see inconsistencies, suggest improvements				
8. *Abstract Thinker*–makes generalizations and draws conclusions that summarize complex information easily				

Parent Inventory for Finding Potential (PIP) *(continued)*

Behavior or Characteristic	Seldom or Never (1)	Sometimes (2)	Regularly (3)	Almost Always (4)
9. *Persistent in Own Interests*–tries to follow through on self-initiated work				
10. *Curious*–pursues interests to satisfy own curiosity; wants to know why and how				
11. *Perceptive*–is alert, observant beyond years				
12. *Aesthetically Responsive*–responds to beauty in arts and nature				
13. *Independent Thinker*–follows own ideas, rather than others'				
14. *Sensitive to Others*–easily understands how others feel or think; easily hurt by others' negative actions				
15. *Independence*–uses own set of values to dictate behavior; concerned with free expression of own ideas				
16. *Sensitive to Ideas, Stories*–upset with sad, negative, hurtful events related through some form of communication				
17. *Independent in Action*–plans, organizes activities; evaluates results				
18. *Processing Speed*–learns new information easily; recalls rote information rapidly				

Parent Inventory for Finding Potential (PIP) *(continued)*

Behavior or Characteristic	Seldom or Never (1)	Sometimes (2)	Regularly (3)	Almost Always (4)
19. *Verbal*–learned to speak and read considerably earlier than agemates; uses extensive vocabulary				
20. *Fair*–looks out for welfare of others; compassionate; concerned with justice and fairness				
21. *Sense of Humor*–can laugh at self; enjoys lighter moments, sensitive to hidden meanings, puns				
22. *Self-Accepting*–understands, accepts own feelings, thoughts, and how best to learn; views self realistically				
23. *Intense*–highly motivated and skilled in a specific subject area or domain				
24. *Self-Critical*–mistrusts own ability; lower self-concept than agemates; hard on self in self-evaluation				
25. *Achievement Need*–strong drive to be "the best," be recognized as expert, master domain of knowledge or set of skills				
26. *Persistent in Assigned Tasks*–concerned with completion and follow through when given a task to do				

Parent Inventory for Finding Potential (PIP) *(continued)*

Behavior or Characteristic	Seldom or Never (1)	Sometimes (2)	Regularly (3)	Almost Always (4)
27. *Elaborative*–concerned with detail, complexity; involved with implications of situation				
28. *Dominant*–asserts self with influence in group situations				
29. *Uneven*–is not balanced in skills and abilities; very good in some things but not everything				
30. *Flexible*–approaches ideas from a number of perspectives; is adaptable				
31. *Structurer*–shapes the environment around self so comfortable; negotiates tasks to suit own needs, interests				
32. *Risk-Taker*–takes mental, emotional, and physical risks easily				
33. *Tolerant of Ambiguity*–comfortable in "messy" contexts and with ill-structured tasks which seem impossible to solve				
34. *Confident*–feels can produce at will; positive about own abilities				
35. *Inner Locus of Control*–attributes success and failure to own efforts and ability				
36. *Fluent*–produces large number of ideas easily				

Parent Inventory for Finding Potential (PIP) *(continued)*

Behavior or Characteristic	Seldom or Never (1)	Sometimes (2)	Regularly (3)	Almost Always (4)
37. *Original*–uses original methods; creates unusual, unique products				
38. *Imaginative*–freely responds to ideas, producing mental images, fanciful insights				
39. *Physically Expressive*–enjoys physical activities as means for self-expression				
40. *Energy Level*–has available pep and vigor for carrying on most activities				
41. *Task Analytic*–breaks down tasks into sequential steps through backwards planning				
42. *Global Scanner*–scans complex information quickly to pick out important items				
43. *Perceptual Perspective Taker*–can orient self and figures in space easily				
44. *Popular*–others enjoy and want to be with this person				
45. *Accepting of Others*–relates to others with genuine interest, concern; seeks out others, is warm				
46. *Physically Able*–is coordinated, agile; participates well in organized games				

Parent Inventory for Finding Potential (PIP) *(continued)*

Behavior or Characteristic	Seldom or Never (1)	Sometimes (2)	Regularly (3)	Almost Always (4)
47. *Socially Mature*–able to work with others; can give and take; sensitive to others' wants				
48. *Happy*–cheerful; has satisfied look on face most of the time				
49. *Emotionally Controlled*–expresses and displays emotions appropriately				
50. *Stable*–can cope with normal frustrations of living; adjusts easily to change				
51. *Associative*–finds similarities, differences between cognitive, verbal, and visual pairs easily				

PIP Graph

Instructions

Use the key below to compute the five mean scores for the five scales on the PIP. Plot the scores on the chart below. Scores of 2.67-3.33 indicate the domain to be an area of strength. Mean scores of 3.34-4.00 indicate the domain to be an area of giftedness.

Key

Scale 1:   *Intellectual:* Add scores from items 1-22. Divide by 22 = _____.

Scale 2:   *Academic:* Add scores from items 2, 4-6, 9-10, 13, 15, 17-18, 23-29. Divide by 17 = _____.

Scale 3:   *Creative:* Add scores from items 2, 6-7, 9-10, 12-13, 15-16, 17, 21-22, 27, 29, 30-40. Divide by 24 = _____.

Scale 4:   *Social:* Add scores from items 6-7, 9-11, 14, 16, 17, 20-22, 27-28, 31, 40-51. Divide by 25 = _____.

Scale 5:   *Artistic:* Add scores from items 2-4, 9, 12-13, 16-17, 23-27, 29, 32, 38-39, 51. Divide by 18 = _____.

Intellectual							
Academic							
Creative							
Social							
Artistic							
	1.0	1.5	2.0	2.5	3.0	3.5	4.0

Teacher Inventory of Learning Strengths (TILS)

©2000 by Karen B. Rogers

Child _____ Age ___ Grade ___ Gender ___ Date_____

Please check the box that describes how often you observe the following behaviors in your student.

Behavior or Characteristic	Seldom or Never (1)	Sometimes (2)	Regularly (3)	Almost Always (4)
1. Reflective				
2. Makes connections readily				
3. Concentrates well				
4. Memorizes easily				
5. Enjoys school				
6. Enthusiastic				
7. Sensitive to problems				
8. Abstract thinker				
9. Persistent in own interests				
10. Curious				
11. Perceptive				
12. Aesthetically responsive				
13. Independent thinker				
14. Sensitive to others				
15. Independent				
16. Sensitive to ideas, stories				
17. Independent in action				
18. Quick processing speed				
19. Highly verbal				
20. Concerned about fairness				
21. Sense of humor				
22. Self-accepting				

Teacher Inventory
of Learning Strengths (TILS)

(continued)

Behavior or Characteristic	Seldom or Never (1)	Sometimes (2)	Regularly (3)	Almost Always (4)
23. Intense				
24. Self-critical				
25. Strong need to achieve				
26. Persistent in assigned tasks				
27. Elaborates with details				
28. Self-assertive				
29. Uneven set of abilities				
30. Flexible				
31. Structures, tasks and environment				
32. Takes risks				
33. Tolerant of ambiguity				
34. Confident				
35. Inner locus of control				
36. Fluent				
37. Original				
38. Imaginative				
39. Physically expressive				
40. High energy level				
41. Task analytic				
42. Scans information holistically				
43. Spatial thinker				
44. Popular				
45. Accepting of others				

Teacher Inventory of Learning Strengths (TILS)

(continued)

Behavior or Characteristic	Seldom or Never (1)	Sometimes (2)	Regularly (3)	Almost Always (4)
46. Physically able				
47. Socially mature				
48. Happy				
49. Emotionally controlled				
50. Stable				
51. Sees differences easily				

TILS Graph

Instructions

Use the key below to compute the three mean scores for the three scales: Academic, Personal, and Social. Plot the scores on the chart below. Scores of 2.67-3.33 indicate the domain to be an area of strength. Mean scores of 3.34-4.00 indicate the domain to be an area of giftedness.

Key

Scale 1: *Academic Learning Strengths:* Add scores from items 1-4, 8-9, 13, 15, 17-19, 26-27, 29, 31, 36-37, 41, 43, 51. Divide by 20 = _____.

Scale 2: *Personal Strengths:* Add scores from items 7, 10-12, 16, 23-25, 30, 32-33, 35, 38. Divide by 13 = _____.

Scale 3: *Social Strengths:* Add scores from items 5-6, 14, 20-22, 28, 34, 39-40, 42, 44-50. Divide by 18 = _____.

Academic	
Personal	
Social	
	1.0 1.5 2.0 2.5 3.0 3.5 4.0

Attitudes about School and Learning

©2000 by Karen B. Rogers

Name _____ Age _____ Grade _____ Gender _____ Date _____

To the Student: please check the box that best describes your feelings about the statements below.

Behavior or Characteristic	Always Agree (1)	Usually Agree (2)	Sometimes Agree (3)	Disagree (4)
1. School will help me have a better life.				
2. School is the best place for me to learn.				
3. School excites me. Every day is great.				
4. I look forward to each new school year.				
5. Other students look to me for good ideas.				
6. Teachers think I am one of the best students.				
7. My work at school makes me feel proud.				
8. Teachers count on me for correct answers.				
9. Others tell me my work at school is great.				
10. I am quite satisfied with the grades I get.				
11. I am happy with my schoolwork as it is now.				

Attitudes about School and Learning *(continued)*

Behavior or Characteristic	Always Agree (1)	Usually Agree (2)	Sometimes Agree (3)	Disagree (4)
12. Most of the things we do in school are easy.				
13. My grades depend on hard work and trying.				
14. I like tests because they show me what I know.				
15. If I try, I can get to the top of my class.				
16. I understand what teachers want me to do.				
17. I check my work carefully before handing it in.				
18. I finish my schoolwork quickly and correctly.				
19. I try to improve my school skills.				
20. The harder the work, the more interesting it is.				

Total Score = _____ ÷ 20 = Mean Score of _____

Instructions

Add point allotments for each box checked to obtain the Total Score. Divide the Total Score by 20 to obtain the Mean Score.

A mean score of 2.67-3.33 = Motivated about School. A mean score of 3.34-4.00 = Highly Motivated about School.

Reading/Language Interest and Attitudes

©2000 by Karen B. Rogers

Name _____ Age _____ Grade _____ Gender _____ Date _____

To the student: please check the box that best describes your feelings about the statements below.

Behavior or Characteristic	Very True (1)	True (2)	Sometimes True (3)	Untrue (4)
1. Reading/English is my favorite subject at school.				
2. My reading teachers are usually the best teachers I have in school.				
3. It is important to work hard to be successful in reading.				
4. I am very good in reading.				
5. I plan to study advanced English in high school and college.				
6. Learning new ideas through reading is the most interesting part of class.				
7. Book discussions and reading projects are the most interesting parts of class.				
8. I love to read just about any kind of book.				
9. I try to read whenever I can outside of school time.				
10. Reading/English is easy for me.				
11. I try to do my best work in reading and on reading tasks.				

Reading/Language Interest and Attitudes *(continued)*

Behavior or Characteristic	Very True (1)	True (2)	Sometimes True (3)	Untrue (4)
12. I belong to a book discussion group.				
13. I enjoy visiting my local library regularly.				
14. I would like to do something related to English someday.				
15. I wish I could take more than one reading/English class each day.				
16. I could learn anything about reading/English if I worked hard enough.				
17. I wish most reading classes could be longer.				

Total Score = _____ + 17 = Mean Score of _____

Instructions

Add point allotments for each box checked to obtain the Total Score. Divide the Total Score by 17 to obtain the Mean Score.

A mean score of 2.67-3.33 = Motivated in Reading. A mean score of 3.34-4.00 = Highly Motivated in Reading.

Mathematics Interest and Attitudes

©2000 by Karen B. Rogers

Name _____ Age _____ Grade _____ Gender _____ Date _____

To the student: please check the box that best describes your feelings about the statements below.

Behavior or Characteristic	Very True (1)	True (2)	Sometimes True (3)	Untrue (4)
1. Math is my favorite subject at school.				
2. My math teachers are usually the best teachers I have in school.				
3. It is important to work hard to be successful in math.				
4. I am very good in math.				
5. I plan to study advanced math in high school and college.				
6. Learning new ideas in math is the most interesting part of class.				
7. Solving math story problems is the most interesting part of class.				
8. I love to work on math assignments.				
9. I try to learn more about math outside of school time.				
10. Math is easy for me.				
11. I try to do my best work in math and on math tasks.				

Mathematics Interest and Attitudes *(continued)*

Behavior or Characteristic	Very True (1)	True (2)	Sometimes True (3)	Untrue (4)
12. I work on math problems and puzzlers outside of school.				
13. I enjoy finding out more about math on my own.				
14. I would like to be some sort of mathematician someday.				
15. I wish I could take more than one math class each day.				
16. I could learn anything about math I wanted to if I worked hard enough.				
17. I wish most math classes could be longer.				

Total Score = _____ ÷ 17 = Mean Score of _____

Instructions

Add point allotments for each box checked to obtain the Total Score. Divide the Total Score by 17 to obtain the Mean Score. A mean score of 2.67-3.33 = Motivated in Mathematics. A mean score of 3.34-4.00 = Highly Motivated in Mathematics.

Science Interest and Attitudes

©2000 by Karen B. Rogers

Name _____

Age _____ Grade _____ Gender _____ Date _____

To the student: please check the box that best describes your feelings about the statements below.

Behavior or Characteristic	Very True (1)	True (2)	Sometimes True (3)	Untrue (4)
1. Science is my favorite subject at school.				
2. My science teachers are usually the best teachers I have in school.				
3. It is important to work hard to be successful in science.				
4. I am very good in science.				
5. I plan to study science in high school and college.				
6. Learning new ideas in science is the most interesting part of class.				
7. Doing labs and experiments are the most interesting parts of class.				
8. I love to read about science.				
9. I try to learn more about science outside of school time.				
10. Science is easy for me.				
11. I try to do my best work in science and on science tasks.				

Science Interest and Attitudes *(continued)*

Behavior or Characteristic	Very True (1)	True (2)	Sometimes True (3)	Untrue (4)
12. I watch science programs on television outside of school.				
13. I enjoy visiting science museums and exhibits.				
14. I would like to be some sort of scientist someday.				
15. I wish I could take more than one science class each day.				
16. I could learn anything about science I wanted to if I worked hard enough.				
17. I wish most science periods could be longer.				

Total Score = _____ ÷ 17 = Mean Score of _____

Instructions

Add point allotments for each box checked to obtain the Total Score. Divide the Total Score by 17 to obtain the Mean Score.

A mean score of 2.67-3.33 = Motivated in Science. A mean score of 3.34-4.00 = Highly Motivated in Science.

Social Studies Interest and Attitudes

©2000 by Karen B. Rogers

Name _____ Age _____ Grade _____ Gender _____ Date _____

To the student: please check the box that best describes your feelings about the statements below.

Behavior or Characteristic	Very True (1)	True (2)	Sometimes True (3)	Untrue (4)
1. Social studies is my favorite subject at school.				
2. My social studies teachers are usually the best teachers I have in school.				
3. It is important to work hard to be successful in social studies.				
4. I am very good in social studies.				
5. I plan to study advanced social sciences courses in high school and college.				
6. Learning new ideas in social studies is the most interesting part of class.				
7. Learning about the past and present is the most interesting part of class.				
8. I love to learn about geography and read about different cultures.				
9. I try to learn more about social studies outside of school time.				
10. Social studies is easy for me.				
11. I try to do my best work in social studies.				

Social Studies Interest and Attitudes *(continued)*

Behavior or Characteristic	Very True (1)	True (2)	Sometimes True (3)	Untrue (4)
12. I watch history shows and programs about cultures on television outside of school.				
13. I enjoy visiting museums and exhibits.				
14. I would like to work in a social studies-related field someday.				
15. I wish I could take more than one social studies class each day.				
16. I could learn anything about social studies if I worked hard enough.				
17. I wish most social studies periods could be longer.				

Total Score = _____ ÷ 17 = Mean Score of _____

Instructions

Add point allotments for each box checked to obtain the Total Score. Divide the Total Score by 17 to obtain the Mean Score.

A mean score of 2.67-3.33 = Motivated in Social Studies. A mean score of 3.34-4.00 = Highly Motivated in Social Studies.

Interest and Attitudes about Arts Learning

©2000 by Karen B. Rogers

Name _____ Age _____ Grade _____ Gender _____ Date _____

To the student: please check the box that best describes your feelings about the statements below.

Behavior or Characteristic	Very True (1)	True (2)	Sometimes True (3)	Untrue (4)
1. Art, music, and drama are my favorite subjects at school.				
2. My arts teachers are usually the best teachers I have in school.				
3. It is important to work hard to be successful in the arts.				
4. I am very good in the arts.				
5. I plan to study the arts in high school and college.				
6. Learning new skills in the arts is the most interesting part of class.				
7. Making things in art or performing in music and drama are the most interesting parts of class.				
8. I love to learn about the arts.				
9. I try to learn more about music, art, or drama outside of school.				
10. Arts learning is easy for me.				
11. I try to do my best work in the arts and on arts-related tasks.				

Interest and Attitudes about Arts Learning *(continued)*

Behavior or Characteristic	Very True (1)	True (2)	Sometimes True (3)	Untrue (4)
12. I watch music, art, and theater programs on television outside of school.				
13. I enjoy attending performances and art exhibits.				
14. I would like to be an artist, actor, or musician someday.				
15. I wish I could take more than one arts class each day.				
16. I could learn anything about the arts I wanted to if I worked hard enough.				
17. I wish most arts periods could be longer.				

Total Score = _____ ÷ 17 = Mean Score of _____

Instructions

Add point allotments for each box checked to obtain the Total Score. Divide the Total Score by 17 to obtain the Mean Score.

A mean score of 2.67-3.33 = Motivated in Arts Learning. A mean score of 3.34-4.00 = Highly Motivated in Arts Learning.

How Do You Like to Learn?

©2000 by Karen B. Rogers

Name _____ Age _____ Grade _____ Gender _____ Date _____

To the student: please check the box that best describes your feelings about the statements below.

Way of Learning	Really Dislike (1)	Dislike (2)	Neutral (3)	Like (4)	Really Like (5)
1. Someone explaining to me what I am supposed to do					
2. Discussing things with others so we can understand them					
3. Studying with a friend to master difficult material					
4. Giving answers out loud when the teacher asks questions					
5. Being asked to make connections between what I am learning now and earlier					
6. Making something that applies what I have learned					
7. Going to the library on my own to look up information on a topic of my choice					
8. Being given some materials or a task to learn on my own time					
9. Having a contest in class to see who has learned the most					
10. Teaching something to someone else in my class					

How Do You Like to Learn? *(continued)*

Way of Learning	Really Dislike (1)	Dislike (2)	Neutral (3)	Like (4)	Really Like (5)
11. Having to learn new materials very quickly so that I must stay alert					
12. Discussing class materials with a group of students in my class					
13. Finishing assignments where I find out right away if I am right					
14. Acting out a situation or event I have learned about					
15. Teacher explaining a concept or idea to the class					
16. Working on practice problems to be sure I have understood what I was learning					
17. Working on a task where the questions are ordered from easiest to most difficult					
18. Sharing my own ideas with others in the class					
19. Helping another student get ready for a test					
20. Learning new facts, ideas, and concepts every day at school					
21. Putting the finishing touches on a project or idea					
22. Being allowed to work for a long period on something that interests me					

How Do You Like to Learn? *(continued)*

Way of Learning	Really Dislike (1)	Dislike (2)	Neutral (3)	Like (4)	Really Like (5)
23. Learning how to do something by role playing					
24. Other students presenting to class on topics they researched					
25. Reading a book to learn about a new topic					
26. Working on assignments that ask me questions on work I was assigned to study					
27. Becoming an expert on a topic so I can teach it to someone else					
28. Working through applications of what I have learned on my own					
29. Working to finish learning about a topic with other students					
30. Going off on my own to study a subject I like					
31. Having a competition to see if my team can answer more questions than other teams					
32. Discussing an issue on which several students disagree					
33. Being given time to review and practice for a test					
34. Listening to the teacher lecture on a topic					

How Do You Like to Learn? *(continued)*

Way of Learning	Really Dislike (1)	Dislike (2)	Neutral (3)	Like (4)	Really Like (5)
35. Finding out the big idea behind what I am learning					
36. Learning how to solve a problem from another student in my class					
37. Teacher calling on students to recite information such as math facts or states and capitals					
38. Planning a project I will work on myself					
39. Taking a course by myself by correspondence or on-line					
40. Working on a project with other students who have the same interests or abilities					
41. Teacher asking questions about materials that were assigned					
42. Being able to skip parts of a subject when I already know them					
43. Listening to a guest speaker					
44. Having a classmate teach me something s/he is good at					
45. Playing a game using flashcards to practice what I have already learned					
46. Teacher leading a discussion on a new topic					

How Do You Like to Learn? *(continued)*

Way of Learning	Really Dislike (1)	Dislike (2)	Neutral (3)	Like (4)	Really Like (5)
47. Working with others on a project with little help from the teacher					
48. Working by myself to learn something new					
49. Being allowed to move through new material as quickly as I can learn it					
50. Learning a concept by playing a game					
51. Reviewing regularly what I have learned before					
52. Preparing on my own to make a class presentation					
53. Hearing other students talk about ideas presented in class					
54. Taking notes while the teacher talks					

How Do You Like to Learn? Graph

Instructions

Use the points allotted to each box and total each scale's item scores. Divide each total score by the number shown below to obtain an average scale score. Plot each average scale score on the graph below. An average scale score of 3.67-4.33 indicates the activity is a *preference*, while a mean score of 4.34-5.00 indicates the activity is a *strong preference*.

Key

Challenge Tasks: Items 5, 11, 20, 35, 42, 49. Divide by 6 = ____.

Lecture: Items 1, 15, 24, 34, 43, 54. Divide by 6 = ____.

Discussion: Items 2, 12, 18, 27, 29, 31, 32, 36, 40, 44, 46, 53. Divide by 12 = ____.

Peer Learning: Items 3, 10, 19, 27, 36, 44, 46, 47, 53. Divide by 9 = ____.

Drill and Recitation: Items 4, 26, 33, 37, 41, 51. Divide by 6 = ____.

Projects: Items 6, 21, 29, 38, 40, 47. Divide by 6 = ____.

Independent Study: Items 7, 22, 25, 30, 48, 52. Divide by 6 = ____.

Self-Instruction: Items 8, 13, 16, 17, 28, 39. Divide by 6 = ____.

Games, Competition: Items 9, 14, 23, 31, 45, 50. Divide by 6 = ____.

Group Learning: Items 2, 3, 4, 9, 10, 12, 18, 19, 24, 27, 29, 31, 32, 36, 40, 44, 46, 47, 53. Divide by 19 = ____.

Individual Learning: Items 1, 5, 6, 7, 8, 11, 22, 25, 26, 28, 30, 35, 38, 39, 42, 48, 49, 52, 54. Divide by 19 = ____.

New Learning: Items 1, 3, 5, 7, 8, 11, 13, 15, 17, 18, 20, 22, 23, 24, 25, 27, 28, 30, 34, 35, 36, 38, 39, 40, 42, 43 44, 46, 47, 48, 49, 50 52, 54. Divide by 34 = ____.

Old Learning: Items 2, 4, 6, 9, 10, 12, 14, 16, 19, 26, 29, 31, 33, 37, 41, 45, 51, 53. Divide by 18 = ____.

	1.0	1.5	2.0	2.5	3.0	3.5	4.0
Challenge Tasks							
Lecture							
Discussion							
Peer Learning							
Drill and Recitation							
Projects							
Independent Study							
Self-Instruction							
Games, Competition							
Group Learning							
Individual Learning							
New Learning							
Old Learning							

Rogers' Interest Inventory

©2000 by Karen B. Rogers

Name _____ Age ___ Grade ___ Gender ___ Date_____

Directions: Please answer the following questions about your interests.

1. Your school has decided it wants to raise money for new equipment for the playground. You and your two best friends have been asked to brainstorm a list of possible fund-raisers. You have quite a long list now and must decide which three to recommend to the school principal. Mark your first choice activity with a 1, second choice with a 2, and third choice with a 3. Pick ones that you think would be FUN to do.

    _____ Sell candy door-to-door

    _____ Put on a school play and charge for tickets

    _____ Offer a class on using computers to parents in the school

    _____ Arrange a class team basketball tournament and charge for tickets

    _____ Make children's toys and sell them

    _____ Put on a fund-raising telethon

    _____ Charge admission for viewing science fair exhibits at the school

    _____ Create a literary magazine of students' creative writing and sell it

    _____ Visit local businesses and solicit donations

    _____ Host a math or chess competition and charge admission

2. It's summer vacation and you will now have lots of time to read. What kind(s) of books will you read (fiction, mysteries, fantasy, adventure, joke, science, history, biography, reference books, etc.) ?

    _____

    What are the titles of some books you have already read but want to read again?

    _____

    What are the titles of some books you have never read, but really want to read?

    _____

3. Put a check next to those book titles below that sound interesting enough for you to read.

_____ *The Stinky Cheese Man and Other Fairly Stupid Tales*

_____ *The Illyrian Adventure*

_____ *Carry On, Mr. Bowditch*

_____ *Cam Jansen and the Mystery of the Haunted House*

_____ *Anne Frank: Diary of a Young Girl*

_____ *The Wizard of Earthsea*

_____ *Freckle Juice*

_____ *The Way Things Work*

_____ *The Man Who Lived Alone*

_____ *The Dog That Stole Football Plays*

_____ *The Hobbit*

_____ *Anne of Green Gables*

_____ *My Father's Dragon*

_____ *Prince Caspian*

_____ *A Time to Fly Free*

_____ *Honest Abe*

_____ *A Slowly Tilting Planet*

_____ *The Lemming Condition*

_____ *The Science Book of Electricity*

_____ *Phoebe, the Spy*

_____ *A Heart to the Hawks*

_____ *Grizzly Riddles*

_____ *The Girl Who Could Fly*

_____ *A Good Courage*

_____ *The Great American Elephant Chase*

_____ *Number the Stars*

_____ *The Sword and the Circle*

_____ *The View from Saturday*

_____ *The Mystery of the Missing Bagpipes*

_____ *Across Five Aprils*

_____ *Owls in the Family*

_____ *The Mozart Season*

_____ *Marco Polo*

_____ *My Teacher is an Alien*

_____ *The Midwife's Apprentice*

_____ *The Stone Book*

4. Your parents have promised that you can invite any famous person you want to come stay at your house for two weeks. Who will you invite?

First Choice   _____

Second Choice   _____

Third Choice   _____

5. A time machine has been invented that would allow you to travel back in time and visit anyone you wish. Who will you choose to visit?

First Choice   _____

Second Choice   _____

Third Choice   _____

6. How do you like to spend your spare time? Playing certain games? Building things? Collecting things? Learning about things? List the things you like to do, with your favorite activity listed FIRST.

Things I Like to Do   # of Years Doing It

_____   _____

_____   _____

_____   _____

_____   _____

_____   _____

7. What are some other things you would like to do if you had more time and money?

_____

_____

8. *Part I.* Your teacher has asked you to help plan a class field trip. You must select THREE things for the class to do. What three things do YOU think would be the most fun or most interesting? Mark your first, second, and third choices by placing a 1, 2, and 3 in the space below.

Part II. Pretend your class is going to take a trip to a large city. After visiting the zoo, the historical sites, and going to a sports event, each student can choose one place where he or she can spend an entire afternoon. Mark your first, second, and third choices by placing A, B, and C in the space below.

____ Historical site   ____ Local business

____ Aquarium   ____ Magazine publisher

____ Radio station   ____ Zoo

____ Backstage tour of Children's   ____ Nursing home
     Theater and play
                                        ____ Planetarium
____ State government building
                                        ____ Sculpture garden
____ Archaeology dig site
                                        ____ Movie studio
____ Sports event
                                        ____ A plant nursery
____ Orchestra concert
                                        ____ Federal Reserve bank
____ Courthouse

9. Your school is having a "Career Day" and you get to choose to spend three separate days with three different people in different careers to see what their jobs are like. Which careers will you choose to find out about?

First Choice _____

Second Choice _____

Third Choice _____

10. You have been hired by a Magazine to be in charge of a monthly special feature, such as ones listed below. Mark your first, second, and third choices with 1, 2, and 3.

____ Historical site	____ Humor
____ Fashion	____ History
____ Education	____ Computers
____ Architecture	____ Arts and Crafts
____ The Latest Books	____ Famous Celebrities
____ Consumer Advice	____ Nature
____ Foreign Cultures	____ Home Decorating
____ Politics	____ Business
____ Animals	____ Music
____ Puzzles and Games	____ Religion
____ Photography	____ Sports and Health

11. Which of these activities have you done at home or at school? Which would you like to do or do more of? Check the appropriate boxes.

	Done at School	Done at Home	Would Like to Do
Wrote a newspaper article or editorial			
Fixed something that was broken, like a toy or tool			
Did an experiment on an animal or plant			
Photographed an unusual object, person, or place			
Kept records of bird or animal behaviors			
Built weather equipment for studying the weather			

	Done at School	Done at Home	Would Like to Do
Printed your own magazine or book			
Collected stamps or coins from foreign countries			
Studied art books to learn about a particular artist			
Set up a neighborhood business, such as a lemonade stand			
Was a member of a neighborhood club			
Performed with a music, dance, or theater group			
Took lessons to learn how to draw, paint, or sculpt			
Put on a show (comedy, theater, music, puppet)			
Drew/wrote your own cartoon feature			
Helped raise money by selling something door-to-door			
Wrote a letter to an adult expressing your opinions about something			
Built or used a telescope to study the stars or planets			
Learned to play an instrument by yourself			
Learned to weave or carve or build models			
Entered a contest or competition (essay, chess, math, music, etc.)			
Designed something you wanted to make or build			
Wrote a song, story, or play on your own			
Memorized a famous speech or poem			
Designed your own board or computer game			

	Done at School	Done at Home	Would Like to Do
Kept a journal or diary for at least three months			
Planted and tended your own garden			
Helped on a neighborhood or community project or event			
Started a butterfly or flower collection			
Raised a pet to enter in a contest			
Made a video, complete with narration and music			
Created your own secret language			
Tried to learn a foreign language on your own			
Read a magazine you regularly subscribe to			
Created a scavenger hunt for others to follow			
Designed an exercise plan for yourself			
Made complicated objects out of Legos® or building blocks/shapes			
Was in a club for playing chess or other games of strategy			
Made up mazes or puzzlers for others to do			
Set up a school to teach younger kids how to do something			
Planned a trip for your family to take			
Drew or copied maps of the world			
Tracked how well a stock was doing in the newspapers for several weeks			
Sat in on the rehearsal of a play or concert			
Visited a local museum			
"Cleared" a library shelf at the local library (read every book on the shelf)			

12. What would you like to learn more about in school? Check each topic for each school subject below that sounds interesting to you.

Topic	Sounds Interesting!
MATHEMATICS–harder materials at an older grade level	
MATHEMATICS–puzzlers, game theory	
MATHEMATICS–word problems	
MATHEMATICS–famous mathematicians and their ideas	
READING–independent reading from a given list of books	
READING–book discussion club	
READING–author study (read everything an author has written)	
READING–biographies of famous people	
READING–the classics (the best books ever written)	
SCIENCE–experiments to do on your own	
SCIENCE–genetics	
SCIENCE–aerodynamics	
SCIENCE–paleontology	
SCIENCE–geology	
SCIENCE–anatomy (human or animal)	
SCIENCE–insects	
SCIENCE–famous scientists and their ideas	
SCIENCE–botany	
SOCIAL STUDIES–history	
SOCIAL STUDIES–psychology	
SOCIAL STUDIES–economics	
SOCIAL STUDIES–geography	
SOCIAL STUDIES–futuristics	
SOCIAL STUDIES–historical fiction	
LANGUAGE ARTS–foreign language	

Topic	Sounds Interesting!
LANGUAGE ARTS–writing stories or plays	
LANGUAGE ARTS–writing poetry	
LANGUAGE ARTS–vocabulary	
LANGUAGE ARTS–speech and debate	
LANGUAGE ARTS–theater performance	
TECHNOLOGY–computer programming	
TECHNOLOGY–website creation	
TECHNOLOGY–creating or playing computer games, simulations	
TECHNOLOGY–designing computer graphics, illustrations	
TECHNOLOGY–Internet research	

I read on my own about _____ hours a week.

I watch television about _____ hours a week.

What else would you like to do? _____

What else? _____

What else? _____

My favorite activity AT SCHOOL is _____

My favorite activity AT HOME is _____

My favorite television shows are _____

_____

The *Data Collector*

©2000 by Karen B. Rogers

Child _____ Age _____ Gender _____ Date _____

Cognitive Functioning	Learning Strengths	Learning Preferences	Interests
Objective Measures	Parent Input Intellectual	Reading	In School Reading
	Academic	Math	Language Arts
	Creative	Science	Mathematics
	Social	Social Studies	Science
	Arts	Arts	Technology
	Teacher Input	Challenge	Social Studies
Subjective Measures	Academic	Group Learning	Arts
	Personal	Individual Learning	School Attitude
	Social	New Learning	Outside of School Building/Crafts
	Achievement	Old Learning	
		Lecture	Business
		Discussion	Collections
		Peer Learning	Fine Arts/Design
		Drill and Recitation	Games, Competitions
			History

The *Data Collector* (continued)

Cognitive Functioning	Learning Strengths	Learning Preferences	Interests
		Projects	Humor
		Independent Study	Law/Gov't./ Religion
		Self-Instruction	Nature
		Games, Competitions	Performing Arts
			Reading
			Research
			Science
			Sci Fi/Fantasy
			Service/Charity
			Sports
			Technology
			Writing
Comments	Comments	Comments	Comments

Yearly Educational Planner

©2000 by Karen B. Rogers

Child _____ Age _____ Gender _____ Date _____

Date Plan Will Begin _____ School _____

School-Based Essential	Domain	How Often	Who and How Managed	Assessment
Academic Progress				
Academic Remediation				
Psychological Adjustment				
Socialization				

Appendix B

Sources of Materials

Creative Learning Press
P.O. Box 320
Mansfield Center, CT 06250
(888) 518-8004

**Critical Thinking
Books & Software**
P.O. Box 448
Pacific Grove, CA 93950
(800) 458-4849

Duke University
Talent Identification Program
1121 West Main Street
Suite 100
Durham, NC 27701
(919) 683/1400

Free Spirit Publishing
217 Fifth Avenue North
Suite 200
Minneapolis, MN 55401
(800) 735-7323

Great Potential Press
(formerly Gifted
Psychology Press)
P.O. Box 5057
Scottsdale, AZ 85261
(877) 954-4200

Nathan Levy Associates
P.O. Box 1199
Hightstown, NJ
(609) 514-0800

Prufrock Press
P.O. Box 8813
Waco, TX 76714
(800) 998-2208

Royal Fireworks Press
(formerly Trillium Press)
P.O. Box 209
Monroe, NY 10950
(914) 783-2999

Index

About the Author

Karen B. Rogers, Ph.D., is Professor of Gifted Studies in the Curriculum and Instruction Department at the University of St. Thomas in Minneapolis, Minnesota. She received her Ph.D. in Curriculum and Instructional Systems from the University of Minnesota and also holds Master's degrees in Special Education of the Gifted and in Psychological Foundations of the Gifted.

Dr. Rogers has been an elementary classroom teacher and a coordinator of programs for gifted and talented students. She was the curriculum author and creator of the widely heralded OMNIBUS enrichment program for gifted children, a program that is still being used in 23 states. She is the author of over 80 articles, 10 book chapters, and was co-developer of a one-week televisions series on the nature of giftedness, called "One-Step Ahead," which is housed in the PBS Network Library in Nebraska.

Dr. Rogers has served on the editorial boards of the *Journal of Secondary Gifted Education*, *Roeper Review*, *Journal for the Education of the Gifted*, *Gifted Education International*, and *Gifted Child Quarterly*, and she is a regular reviewer for the *American Educational Research Journal*. In 1992, she was designated "Early Scholar" by the National Association for Gifted Children for her "contributions to the research of the field." She is a past-president of The Association for the Gifted of the Council for Exceptional Children.

She has been an invited lecturer at several universities in the United States and Australia and is a frequent keynote speaker for state, national, and international conferences on gifted and talented children. Her technical paper on ability grouping and educational alternatives for gifted children, which she wrote for the National Research Center on Gifted and Talented, has been read by over 500,000 people worldwide. During the past 30 years, Dr. Rogers has consulted with numerous families and school systems to help them match the educational program to the child. As an educator, and as a parent and a grandparent, she understands the need for educational flexibility in order to provide high-quality learning experiences for gifted learners.